SEPARATE AND UNEQUAL

Separate and Unequal

Black Americans and the US Federal Government

DESMOND KING

CLARENDON PRESS · OXFORD

Oxford University Press, Great Clarendon Street, Oxford OX2 6DP
Oxford New York
Athens Auckland Bangkok Bogota Bombay
Buenos Aires Calcutta Cape Town Dar es Salaam
Delhi Florence Hong Kong Istanbul Karachi
Kuala Lumpur Madras Madrid Melbourne
Mexico City Nairobi Paris Singapore
Taipei Tokyo Toronto
and associated companies in
Berlin Ibadan

Oxford is a trade mark of Oxford University Press

Published in the United States by
Oxford University Press Inc., New York

First published 1995
First issued as paperback 1997

British Library Cataloguing in Publication Data
Data available

Library of Congress Cataloging in Publication Data
King, Desmond S.
Separate and unequal : Black Americans and the US federal government / Desmond King.
Includes bibliographical references and index.
1. Afro-Americans in the civil service. 2. Afro-Americans—Segregation. 3. United States—Armed Forces—Afro-Americans. 4. United States—Race relations. I. Title.
JK723.A34K56 1995 331.6'396073—dc20 95–5865

ISBN 0–19–828016–5
ISBN 0–19–829249–X (Pbk.)

Printed in Great Britain
on acid-free paper by
Bookcraft (Bath) Ltd.,
Midsomer Norton, Avon

To the Memory of
Kieran Hickey 1936–1993

Acknowledgements

I AM immensely grateful to the following institutions for providing grants without which the research for this study could not have been undertaken: the British Academy; the Mellon Fund at the University of Oxford; and St John's College, Oxford. I wish to thank the many archivists and librarians in those American and British archives and libraries listed at the end of the book for their assistance in locating material for this study. I should like also to thank the staff at Rhodes House Library, Oxford, for their courteous and professional assistance in locating material.

Eric Foner and an anonymous reader read the manuscript for Oxford University Press. They provided encouraging and valuable responses. I am especially grateful to Eric Foner for his detailed observations and unfailingly constructive comments. At Oxford University Press, Tim Barton and his staff have been impressively professional and supportive in overseeing the production of the book.

I am grateful to the following colleagues and friends in the United States and Britain for taking the time to discuss, comment upon, or read material for this project in various drafts (and none of whom can of course be held responsible for misjudgements or errors which remain): Nigel Bowles, Michael Burleigh, Carolyn Cowey, Jonah Edelman, David Goldey, Ira Katznelson, Daniel Kryder, Ross McKibbin, Byron Shafer, Robert Singh, Alan Ware, Margaret Weir, Gavin Williams, and Stewart Wood. In addition to reading portions of the manuscript, Carolyn Cowey has provided invaluable moral support during its drafting.

The book is dedicated to the late Kieran Hickey. Kieran, a professional film-maker and historian, was an old and deeply lamented friend. I learned of Kieran's tragically premature death while in Washington working on this project, after a day spent researching in the National Archives and about to visit the cinema. My appreciation of, and engagement in, both activities owe much to Kieran's friendship and the dedication is a small token of that gratitude.

Preface

THIS book was prompted by my earlier project on Federal welfare and training programmes in the United States. While researching for that book I became aware of the disparities in the opportunities available to White citizens in the US Federal government compared to those offered to comparably qualified Black Americans. Black Americans were, for example, effectively excluded from federally funded apprenticeship programmes, and few Black Americans achieved senior positions in the Federal civil service before the 1960s. Not only were Black employees in the Federal civil service likely to have been relegated to lower positions and to have been disadvantaged by recruitment procedures and consignment to segregated units, but for many of their fellow citizens outside public employment, the US government constituted a powerful institution upholding arrangements privileging Whites and discriminating against Blacks. In the eight decades before 1964, the Federal government used its power and authority to support segregated race relations. Historically, the segregation of Black American citizens in the Federal bureaucracy is a major but neglected aspect of the US Federal government, with implications for both the position of these citizens in the United States and the character of the state.

In Chapter 1, post-Reconstruction race relations are discussed, segregation is defined, and the legal and political factors permitting its dissemination outlined. The major themes advanced in the study are specified: first, segregated race relations were inherently unequal in their treatment of Black Americans both in the Federal government and through Federal programmes in society. Second, the Federal government played a role in sustaining and fostering segregated race relations to an extent little acknowledged by scholars. Third, the universality of segregated race relations in the Federal government is often overlooked by a disproportionate emphasis upon their presence in the South. Chapter 2 then analyses the difficulties facing Black Americans attempting to join the civil service and the inadequacy of the US Civil Service Commission's monitoring of both recruitment and promotion. In Chapter 3, I present an occupational profile of the almost universally lowly positions attained by Black employees in government, and use hearings from the FEPC (and its successor bodies) to examine how discrimination flourished within the 'separate but equal' framework. By examining Federal government departments and programmes, it is possible to establish how far more fully national was the accommodation with segregation. Chapter 4 examines segregation in the military and resistance to its abolition. Chapter 5 analyses segregation in Federal prisons, institutions which reproduced segregationist pressures, even in those penitentiaries located in parts of the country outside the South. In Chapter 6, I examine how the intervention of the American Federal government in society reproduced the inequalities associated with segregation, taking as examples Federal housing programmes and employment exchange services. Both Federal mortgage assistance programmes and public housing dwellings mirrored the segregationist order in which they were installed, consolidating, not threatening, residential separation by race. The USES's field offices were, notoriously, segregated in the facilities provided for Black American and White job-seekers, and in the staff hired to administer them. In the concluding chapter, I report the transformation in the position of Black Americans in the Federal government since the civil rights legislation of the 1960s. Black employees now occupy a different occupational profile in Federal agencies.

The United States has a remarkable capacity, demonstrated by its history, to absorb and transcend social and political problems. In part, this ability reflects the principles and values bequeathed Americans by the Founding Fathers in the Constitution of 1787. Although this document has been exploited by proponents of segregation and discrimination, it has also provided a set of entrenched rights to which Black Americans have turned, and subsequently successfully mobilized, to advance their interests and to establish their equality. Citizens of other countries can rightly look with envy to these entrenched rights afforded American citizens. This study demonstrates also how Americans are prepared to consider their history critically and are willing to provide uncensored access to the documents mandatory for such appraisals.

The archival material, reported in the ensuing chapters, provides diverse and rich sources with which to study Black American employees' role in, and relationship to, the Federal government. It includes the papers of Racial Relations Advisers in Federal departments, the records and annual reports of government departments such as the Federal and Public Housing Authorities and the US Bureau of Prisons; the records of the US Civil Service Commission; President Franklin Roosevelt's FEPC, the FEB, and its successor bodies—the President's Committee on Government Employment Policy (1955–61) and the President's Committee on Equal Opportunity Policy (1961–4); the proceedings of President Truman's investigatory committees on civil rights, the Armed Services, and government contracts; and the studies of interest groups working in behalf of Black Americans, such as the NAACP and the NUL.[1] This sort of material imposes two limits on the study: first, I do not attempt a comprehensive survey of Black American employment in, and experience of, all Federal government agencies but concentrate on a selected sample. Second, the scope of the study is affected by the fact that much of the archival material relates to the years between 1933 and the late 1950s, a period of enormous historical significance for the relationship between Black Americans and the US polity.

To as great an extent as possible the empirical material marshalled in the ensuing chapters is that expressed directly by Black Americans, groups working on their behalf, and Federal officials in government departments rather than secondary summaries of their views. This strategy is intended to restore voices long displaced from the historical record.

D.K.

St John's College, Oxford
January 1995

Contents

List of Figures xii
List of Abbreviations xiii

PART I: THE HISTORICAL CONTEXT

1. The Politics of Segregation in Post-Reconstruction America 3

PART II: SEGREGATION IN THE US FEDERAL GOVERNMENT

2. Joining the Government: 'Because I Dared to be Black' 39
3. Working in a Federal Agency: Social Ostracism and Discrimination 72

PART III: THE FEDERAL GOVERNMENT AND SEGREGATION BEYOND WASHINGTON

4. 'A Great Shadow over our "Civil Rights"': Fighting for the Government 111
5. Serving Time with the Government: Federal Penitentiaries 142
6. The Federal Government in a Segregated Society: Public Employment Exchanges and Housing Programmes 172

PART IV: THE LEGACIES OF SEGREGATED RACE RELATIONS

7. Conclusion 205

Appendix 1. The Politics of Segregation in the United States 211
Appendix 2. Segregation in Government 220
Appendix 3. Statistical Profile of Black American Employees in the Federal Government 227
Appendix 4. Strikes settled by the FEPC 1943–1944 243
Appendix 5. Major Civil Rights Laws 1957–1991 244
Notes to Chapters 245
Bibliography 315
Index 331

List of Figures

1.1. Shall the Negro Rule? 22
3.1. Segregation in Government Service 73

Abbreviations

AAA	Agricultural Adjustment Act
ADC	Aid to Dependent Children
AFDC	Aid to Families with Dependent Children
AFL	American Federation of Labor
ATS	Auxiliary Territorial Service
BES	Bureau of Employment Security
CAF	Clerical–Administrative–Fiscal
CGCC	Committee on Government Contract Compliance
CIO	Congress of Industrial Organization
CPC	Crafts, Protective, Custodial
DDEL	Dwight D. Eisenhower Presidential Library, Abilene, Kan.
EEOC	Equal Employment Opportunity Commission
EO	Executive Order
FDRL	Franklin D. Roosevelt Presidential Library, Hyde Park, NY
FEB	Fair Employment Board
FEPC	Fair Employment Practice Committee
FERA	Federal Emergency Relief Administration
FHA	Federal Housing Association
GAO	General Accounting Office
HEW	Health, Education and Welfare Dept.
HHFA	Housing and Home Finance Agency
HOLC	Home Owners' Loan Corporation
HSTL	Harry S. Truman Presidential Library, Independence, Mo.
ICESA	Interstate Conference of Employment Security Agencies
LBJL	Lyndon B. Johnson Presidential Library, Austin, Tex.
LC	Library of Congress, Manuscript Division
MOA	Mass-Observation Archives, University of Sussex, England
NA	National Archives and Record Administration, Washington
NAACP	National Association for the Advancement of Colored People
ND	Northern Democrat
NIPL	National Independent Political League
NRA	National Recovery Administration
NUL	National Urban League
OPA	Office of Price Administration
PL	Public Law
PRO	Public Record Office, Kew, England
PWA	Public Works Administration
RG	Record Group nos., National Archives
SD	Southern Democrat
SES	State Employment Service
TVA	Tennessee Valley Authority

USBP	US Bureau of Prisons
USES	United States Employment Service
VA	Veterans' Association
WHCF	White House Central File
WMC	War Manpower Commission
WPA	Works Progress Administration

PART I

The Historical Context

1

The Politics of Segregation in Post-Reconstruction America

SOON after Woodrow Wilson entered the White House in 1913, the Acting Secretary of the Treasury, J. S. Williams, prepared a memorandum about the department's Bureau of Engraving and Printing, reporting his 'pleasure of going through the Bureau last evening between 7 and 8'. He noted an arrangement, however, in the 'sizing department' disturbing to his sensibilities: 'young white women and colored women were working together side by side and opposite each other. At one end of the machine would be a young white girl and opposite a colored girl.' Williams reprimanded the Bureau's Director for tolerating such proximity of the races: 'I feel sure that this must go against the grain of the white women. Is there any reason why the white women should not have only white women opposite them on the machines? And is there any reason why the white women and colored women should not be to some extent segregated?'[1]

These Black American workers, in common with many others in Federal agencies, were duly segregated as Southern (Jim Crow) rules of race relations[2] were imposed in Washington,[3] legally sanctioning segregation of Black Americans from Whites in all areas of public life such as housing, transportation, education, prisons, hospitals,[4] and even, indeed, in cemeteries. Publicly funded services were provided on a segregated basis and Federal government agencies segregated their employees on the basis of race. Between the enactment of 'separate but equal' statutes in the 1890s and the constitutional decisions overturning them in the 1950s,[5] Black Americans' experience of the US Federal government was defined by social and legal segregation. Three decades after Woodrow Wilson's presidency, President Harry Truman's investigative committee on civil rights reported the thoroughness with which segregation had penetrated Washington:[6] 'For Negro Americans, Washington is not just the nation's capital. It is the point at which all public transportation into the South becomes "Jim Crow".' Stepping outside the major railway terminal, Union Station, a Black American left 'democratic practices behind. With very few exceptions, he is refused service at downtown restaurants, he may not attend a downtown movie or play, and he has to go into the poorer section of the city to find a night's lodging.'[7] Public services were provided not just separately but at inferior (often dangerously bad) standards in Black American neighbourhoods.[8] The experience of segregation was not limited to the South or to Washington; it was, rather, far more widespread, manifest in many midwestern and eastern cities. Conspicuously absent from Edward Hopper's quintessential urban paintings, Black American citizens were an invisible group to Whites in the United States.

Segregation's origins lay in the collapse of Reconstruction (1865–76) and its aftermath, when segregation of Black Americans by Whites developed in the Southern states and extended into Northern states and cities (in some instances, restoring *ante bellum* practices), and into the District of Columbia. From 1896 these practices enjoyed Federal judicial approval under the guise of 'separate but equal'. With the election of Woodrow Wilson in 1912, many Federal government departments[9] were segregated, giving this administration (1913–21) a special significance for the relationship between Black Americans and the Federal government (see Table A1.1). The preceding thirty years had not been free of segregation in government departments but, as Chapter 2 demonstrates, Black applicants were assessed equally with Whites. After 1913 Black American employees in Federal agencies were disproportionately concentrated in custodial, menial, and junior clerical positions and were frequently passed over for appointment at all.[10] Other parts of the Federal government were also segregated, such as Federal penitentiaries and the US Armed Services.[11]

This Federal support of segregated race relations shaped Black Americans' relations with the government. As the Black leader A. Philip Randolph pointed out in 1943, Black Americans occupied 'a position different from that of any other section of the population of this country'. Black Americans found themselves compelled to struggle against the state: 'The Negroes are in the position of having to fight their own Government . . . because the Government today is the primary factor, the major factor, in this country in propagating discrimination against Negroes. It is perpetuating and freezing an inferior status of second-class citizenship for Negroes in America.'[12] In the decades before the Civil Rights Act of 1964, the Federal government used its power to impose a pattern of segregated race relations among its employees and, through its programmes (such as housing and employment services), upon the whole of American society well beyond the Mason–Dixon line. This pattern structured the relationship between ordinary Black Americans and the US Federal government—whether as employees in government agencies, inmates or officers in Federal prisons, inductees in the Armed Services, consumers of federally guaranteed mortgages, job-seekers in USES offices, or visitors to National Parks in which the facilities were segregated (or, often, non-existent for Black Americans[13]). In all these instances, racial segregation did not imply just separation but also profound racial inequality. Despite possessing equal qualifications, Black employees in the Federal government were systematically assigned to low positions, often in segregated conditions. Under the judicial cloak of 'separate but equal', discrimination thrived.

Rooted in the elemental fissure of American politics, the North–South sectional divide,[14] Southern-type segregation was more integral and universal to the US Federal government and to Federal programmes[15] than commonly recognized.[16] Thus, in his magisterial account of Reconstruction, Eric Foner argues that Reconstruction and the settlement of 1877 ensured the 'South's racial system remained regional rather than national'.[17] But this view neglects the introduction and maintenance of segregated race relations in the Federal government itself, and the effects upon public policy. For Black Americans, the US Federal government was a defender of the constitutionally and legally sanctioned practice of segregation and its consequences.[18] The government to which they turned to articulate and defend their civil rights was itself flawed—a broken spear rather than a magic one healing all wounds.[19] As the NAACP observed in a letter to Woodrow Wilson in 1913, Black Americans misguidedly believed that 'living [in Washington] under the shadow of the National Government itself they were safe from the persecution and discrimination which follow them elsewhere because of their dark skin'.[20] In fact, the 'National Government' was a pillar of segregated race relations. A correspondent of the NAACP in 1924 drew one obvious inference of segregation in Federal agencies: 'while . . . segregation exists in the departments in Washington, the United States sets an example which justifies the Ku Klux Klan and every other effort to keep the colored people down.'[21] Segregated race relations imposed second-class status upon Black American employees. It was not until the outbreak of the Second World War that this consequence was acknowledged within the government. One wartime confidential report, titled 'Negroes in a Democracy at War', conceded the harm of Black Americans' exclusion from government: 'in the fact that the Government itself fails to employ Negroes in jobs for which they are qualified lies a pretext which private industry utilizes for its persistent discrimination against the colored race.'[22]

Segregation was obviously an arrangement favoured by many White Americans and consistent with post-Reconstruction racial attitudes in the United States.[23] These racist views were grotesquely conveyed in a letter from the Southern novelist Thomas Dixon, upon the occasion of President Woodrow Wilson's nomination of a Black American to a post in the Treasury: 'I am heartsick over the announcement that you have appointed a Negro to boss white girls as Register of the Treasury.' The promotion of Black American employees to positions of authority sent shivers down Dixon's spine: 'The establishment of Negro men over white employees of the Treasury Department has in the minds of many thoughtful men and women long been a serious offense against the cleanliness of our social life.'[24] Dixon's last sentence illustrates how most proponents of segregation saw it, at the very least, as a method for ensuring inequality of the races and marginalizing Black Americans from mainstream White society.[25] Racist attitudes and beliefs were rooted in American society and politics. They reflected the sectional division between the North and the South manifest during the first seven decades of this century.[26] Prior to the end of segregation, the United States was subnationally a divided polity. Two political systems, mirroring two societies, the one democratic and the other oligarchic, existed side by side.[27] This sectionalism defined almost every other aspect of the political system, including presidential elections, congressional politics, and the powers and limits of the Federal government.[28]

The regional differences between the North and South had to be accommodated nationally in the post-Reconstruction century. In practice, the price of the South's integration was acceptance by the North of Southern race relations, especially though not exclusively in the South.[29] Under the Federal principle of states' rights, each state's racial policy was considered its own business. However, Federal politics tolerated and reproduced this Southern-originating pattern: from the 1880s national politics were progressively imbued with segregationist views, whose origin lay in *ante bellum* attitudes and arrangements, augmented by fresh prejudices propagated in the post-Reconstruction years.[30] C. Vann Woodward stresses how segregated Northern society was at the outbreak of the Civil War (1861–5), and how this segregation translated into doctrines of White supremacy to which Republicans were compelled to align themselves for electoral reasons after the 1860s.[31] State laws in the North often denied Black Americans the suffrage and outlawed interracial marriage. In Woodward's judgement, a consequence of these racial attitudes was that the 'major parties vied with each other in their professions of devotion to the dogma of white supremacy. Republicans were especially sensitive on the point because of their antislavery associations.'[32] Republicans happily accommodated both antislavery and anti-Black views, committing themselves for example to excluding Black American workers from competition with Whites.[33] Republican Senators Lyman Trumbull of Illinois and Henry Wilson of Massachusetts warmed to such views, the latter ridiculing 'any belief "in the mental or the intellectual equality of the African race with this proud and domineering white race of ours"'.[34]

The interests of Black Americans were marginalized by the major political parties after Reconstruction. Since the Democrats were identified powerfully as a party of White Southern interest, this distancing was unremarkable. However, the Republicans began also increasingly to accept the Jim Crow practices spreading throughout the South, and to absorb commonplace criticisms of Black American politicians' inadequacies in the Reconstructed Southern states. Since Republicans were overwhelmingly the dominant party after 1877 (Table A1.1), this shift in their position toward Black Americans was significant. This position was not inconsistent with the party's *ante bellum* views. Woodward concludes that at the end of the Civil War, 'on the issue of Negro equality the party remained divided, hesitant, and unsure of its purpose'. As a result, the 'historic commitment to equality it eventually made was lacking in clarity, ambivalent in purpose, and capable of numerous interpretations'.[35] This ambivalence was not clarified by the persistence in the North of racist attitudes and, in some cases, segregated practices. Reconstruction was increasingly judged a failure, as Eric Foner notes, amongst Northern Republicans: 'the Liberal critique of Reconstruction had by now sunk deep roots among mainstream Republicans. As one wrote privately, "the truth is, the negroes are ignorant, many of them not more than half civilized . . . [and] no match for the whites . . . Our Southern system is wrong." '[36]

The *fin de siècle* did not halt the fading of Black Americans' interests from the national agenda in either the North or the South. V. O. Key, Jr. notes the progressive Theodore Roosevelt's (1901–9) role in prodding the Republicans toward a more rigid position about race relations, shifting 'Republican policies in the same direction that the Democrats had been moving, only not so far'.[37] Theodore Roosevelt's decision as president, taken in 1907, summarily to discharge dishonourably 170 Black American men from the (all-Black) Twenty-fifth Infantry, despite a lack of evidence about their culpability (on a charge of shooting and riot), revealed a further weakening in his commitment to equality (the men were given honourable discharges retrospectively in 1971).[38] By the first decade of this century, Republicans weakly defended the right of Black Americans to vote (a commitment given up by Theodore Roosevelt in 1912 when he was the Progressive party's presidential nominee). Frederickson traces this change in the Progressive Theodore Roosevelt: 'earlier in his Presidency he had talked and acted as if he had some concern with maintaining the rights of Negroes to citizenship and political participation, but by 1905 he had obviously decided that the best approach was one which relied on the paternalisitic mercies of the "better class" of Southern whites.'[39] Democratic control of the presidency was rare between 1877 and 1932, and the Republicans also dominated Congress in the fifteen years before 1913 (see Table A1.2). Thus the neglect of Black Americans' interests by Republicans was significant, and indeed Theodore Roosevelt 'reduced the number of Negro officeholders'.[40] By the 1920s and the Harding–Coolidge presidencies, Republicans had no electoral or political interest in addressing Black American voters, whose vote they were accustomed to receiving as the party of Lincoln.[41]

Unsurprisingly, racial doctrines informed debate in the United States' national political forum, Congress. Self-consciously racist statements were not uncommon and seldom challenged in the post-Reconstruction decades, a pattern observable until the New Deal (1933–8). Nor were the views expressed solely those of Southern Americans, but were common with attitudes held in varying degrees of intensity throughout the United States.[42] In 1923 the Georgian Congressman William Lankford waxed lyrical about segregation: 'The so-called "Jim Crow" law which makes whites and negroes ride in separate coaches on trains, use separate seats in street cars, and use separate waiting rooms at the stations is a most excellent law for both races.' Lankford found race relations in the North far less convivial: 'a white family is, while travelling, all the while face to face with the impudence, the insults, and the offensive conduct of the northern negro, who takes special delight in being offensive to the white race with whom he feels equal and to whom he feels superior.' He also alleged support for such views outside the South: 'You can not tell me the white people of the North all do not want to associate with negroes. The same feeling we have in the South is here and is growing rapidly.'[43] In 1928 Congressman Malcolm Tarver from Georgia objected to Congress's appropriation of funds to Howard University because its president allegedly advocated interracial marriage.[44] In the same year South Carolinian Senator Cole L. Blease expressed Southern beliefs in uncomplicated terms: 'in the South we believe that white supremacy is a part of the Christian religion, that the white people are superior to negroes, and we never expect under any conditions or circumstances to permit social equality in that section of the country.'[45]

Congressional and presidential support for segregation converged with attitudes in American society. The hostility of White Southerners to Black Americans is familiar. In the North-east and Midwest, blue-collar White workers, often acting through their unions, prevented Black workers being hired or trained in defence industries during the Second World War and, more generally, excluded them from apprenticeships.[46] The AFL excluded Black American workers from its locals, thereby limiting their capacity to acquire skilled employment.[47] During the Second World War, the local offices of the US Office of Education reported unions colluding with employers, especially in the Southern states though also in the North-east and Midwest, to exclude Black workers. The admission of Black workers often provoked strikes, while Black workers also struck against their conditions of employment (see Table A4.1). The latency and generality of racist attitudes was apparent during the Second World War when racial tension intensified, both in Southern towns with training camps and in Northern cities with defence production industries, and in the Armed Forces.[48] Training camps in the South were centres of constant racial tension and violence. Housing residence throughout the old North-eastern and Midwestern cities segregated Black Americans into prescribed areas, and when the Federal government attempted to provide funds for housing available for purchase by Black families in other areas, this initiative was fiercely and on occasions violently resisted by local authorities and White citizens.[49]

Segregated race relations had deep and poignant roots in American society and politics. Crucially, post-Reconstruction Federal politics tolerated and reproduced aspects of these relations nationally. Instead of thwarting such patterns, the Federal government participated in their maintenance and diffusion. This is the book's first theme, explored through detailed examination of Federal government departments and programmes.

SEGREGATION AS INEQUALITY: 'A PEOPLE SET APART, ALMOST AS LEPERS'

Segregation was an arrangement whereby Black Americans, as a minority, were systematically treated in a separate, but constitutionally sanctioned, way. As the NAACP observed, they were treated 'almost as lepers'.[50] Its introduction coincided with widely accepted doctrines of natural racial hierarchies in which Whites were assumed superior to other, particularly Black, races.[51] Such cultural attitudes prevailed in the District of Columbia, the United State's political and administrative centre, and were soaked up and sedulously aped by Northerners living in Washington.[52] The election of a Democratic administration and Congress in 1912 gave a fuller opportunity to the articulation and implementation of these views. Segregation occurred in Federal government departments before 1913[53] but it was limited, received little White House consideration, depended largely on individual administrators, and did not prevent some Black Americans gaining promotion. Furthermore, the Civil Service Commission emphasized meritocracy in making appointments in the three decades after 1883 (see Chapter 2). This changed in 1913.

That inequality was the ineluctable result of segregated race relations is the book's second theme. In the Federal government, this inequality was manifest in several ways: first, the unequal treatment of Black Americans compared with Whites, which thereby conferred second-class citizenship upon them; second, such relations were frequently justified as being beneficial to Black Americans themselves, and their support for them was commonly invoked; and third, in Federal government departments segregation was often disguised as a rational reorganization, the outcome of which happened to isolate Black American employees from their White peers and to consign them to the worst jobs. These characteristics were exemplified during the Wilson presidency.

1. Segregation meant inequality of treatment for Black Americans. Despite a pretext of racial equality, segregation acquired its own logic—as intended by many of its architects—which resulted in intense inequality. In practice, 'separate but equal' proved to be spurious. This outcome was obvious to Black American activists unsuccessfully protesting the Wilson

administration's acceptance of segregation in the Federal civil service. Addressing President Wilson in November 1914 at a meeting in the White House, the Black leader William Monroe Trotter explained that differentiation of the sort permitted by segregation apodictically precluded 'equality of citizenship . . . for races, especially when applied to but one of the many racial elements in the government employ'. Despite all protests to the contrary, physical segregation implied inferiority: 'for such placement of employees means a charge by the government of physical indecency or infection, or of being a lower order of beings, or a subjection to the prejudices of other citizens, which constitutes inferiority of status.'[54] Demarcation of one race—Black Americans—under segregation could never ensure that group's equality. In August 1913 Moorfield Storey wrote from the NAACP to Woodrow Wilson accusing his administration of establishing 'two classes among its civilian employees. It has set the colored people apart as if mere contact with them were contamination.' The inequality of segregation was evident immediately: 'To them is held out only the prospect of mere subordinate routine service without the stimulus of advancement to high office by merit.'[55] The same points were communicated to members of Wilson's Cabinet. The NAACP wrote to the Secretary of Agriculture, explaining percipiently that 'segregation means discrimination against the negro employees and consequently less favorable conditions of work than those which have been enjoyed in the past and which will be continued to be enjoyed by white employees in the future'.[56]

In Federal government agencies, inequality was common after 1913. Black American employees were disproportionately concentrated in the lower- and middle-rank positions, rarely achieving senior promoted positions (see Chapter 3).[57] As a consequence, White employees were dominant in the senior and professional Federal positions. The Director of the Treasury's Bureau of Engraving and Printing hastened to replace a Black supervisor with a White one in the Wetting Division, profusely thanking the complainant 'for bringing this matter to my attention'. He reported that 'upon investigation, I find that the chief of the wetting division under the rule of seniority had permitted Louis H. Nutt, a negro, to be in charge of the work . . . I wish to state that I have this day placed Irving P. Tade, a white man, in charge of the work in question, and I am sure there will be no further cause for complaint on this account.'[58] It would have been impossible for a Black American to initiate a comparable complaint about White employees. In ensuing years such modifications to personnel appointments were made unnecessary by the rarity of Black employees' promotion.

Speaking in 1948, the Director of the US Bureau of Prisons aptly captured the inherent problem of 'separate but equal' when he used the terms segregation and discrimination synonymously: 'segregation or discrimination—call it what you like—must be minimized.'[59] This identity of the two conditions alarmed the NAACP in the long decades during which it campaigned for desegregation. As Thurgood Marshall, the NAACP Special Counsel (and later Supreme Court Associate Justice), explained, attempts to 'draw a line between a policy of "discrimination" and a policy of "segregation"' were intrinsically flawed, because 'segregation is in itself discrimination. The moment you tell one citizen that he cannot do what another citizen can do, simply because of his race, you are maintaining a policy of discrimination.' Marshall added that a 'large part of the injustices against Negro Americans has resulted from efforts to draw this hazy line'.[60]

It was Black employees who were required systematically to demonstrate the inequities and inadequacies of the segregated codes and the discrimination arising from them. Conversely, it was invariably the complaints of White employees about the intermingling of employees of different races which provided the pretext for segregation. Thus the Secretary of the Treasury was informed about a violation of segregation codes requiring action in 1913: 'three colored employes persisted in using tables assigned to white girls after a committee of white girls from the Printers' Assistants' Labor Union had made objections to them occupying the same tables and it was necessary to give them positive instructions on the subject.'[61] In the US Armed Services, where segregation existed until the 1950s, a prejudiced view of Black recruits prevailed among White officers, precluding equality of opportunity and treatment. The presence of such attitudes was highlighted by one member of President Harry Truman's Committee on Equality of Treatment and Opportunity in the Armed Services (1949). Lester Granger, Executive Secretary of the NUL, commented that the Army held a tenebrously homogeneous conception of Black recruits—'a composite Negro soldier'. Addressing the Secretary of the Army, he continued: 'You constantly speak of the intelligence, of mental characteristics, and performance characteristics of the Negro soldier. Now, there is no such assumption of a composite soldier with other racial and special groups in the Army.'[62] Granger's remark illustrates how segregation by race was associated with the assumption of inferiority in the minds of the dominant, White, race. Whether the source of this attitude was intrinsic to the military or implanted from society, it none the less defined the often degrading experience of Black American recruits until the 1950s.

Thus, the US Federal government's own organization provided a licence with which Black employees were harmed by segregation. The distinct character of segregation has been documented in many aspects of American politics but not as it operated in the Federal government or in federally funded programmes.[63] Black American citizens and activists fully appreciated and opposed it. For instance, the Black activist William Trotter wrote to President Woodrow Wilson in 1913 that 'the separate eating tables' permitted at the Treasury 'means [either] a declaration of foulness, indecency, disease, rudeness or essential inferiority, *by the government itself*, or a decree that these citizens barred from the general tables shall be subjects of the race prejudice of all the others'. Such arrangements amounted to '*inequality of citizenship*'. What is most disturbing about these arrangements is that they were undertaken by the Federal government itself, thereby aligning it with a pernicious pattern of race relations. Trotter went on to explain why, despite claims to the contrary, segregation could never ensure equality since it implied that 'the segregated are considered unclean, diseased or indecent as to their persons, or inferior beings of a lower order, or that other employees have a class prejudice which is to be catered to, or indulged'. The Federal government colluded in creating inequality of citizenship: 'No citizen who is barred because of the prejudice of another citizen can be his equal in citizenship. By subjecting the former to the latter's prejudice, the Government denies equality.'[64] Writing in support of the NAACP's opposition to segregation, the editor of the *Congregationalist and Christian World* noted that the condoning of segregated race relations within the government provided a litmus test for segregationists in society.[65] This implication proved entirely valid.[66] The Federal government was supporting the inequality inherent in segregated race relations. What the Federal government tolerated in its own organization was both imitative of and imitated by society, a point stressed by the NAACP: 'discrimination by the Federal Government will be a precedent for similar discrimination everywhere.'[67] Similar points were made by Trotter, an indefatigable opponent of segregation, about segregation in Federal agencies: 'if separate toilets are provided for Latin, Teutonic . . . Slavic, Semitic and Celtic Americans, then and then only would African Americans be assigned to separation without insult and indignity.'[68]

Partly to illustrate how Black American employees found themselves consigned to the least skilled and attractive positions, Tables A2.3 and A2.4 provide a detailed profile of employment in the US Department of Agriculture in 1914. The former disaggregates the Department into its constituent bureaux; the latter provides totals. It is striking how the majority of Black American employees are concentrated in the unskilled positions and how few are in senior posts. However, compared with later years the number of Black vets and meat inspectors is high.

2. In both civil society and government agencies, segregation was often justified and promoted as beneficial to Black Americans. Woodrow Wilson himself argued this. He assured the NAACP that he believed 'segregation to be in the interest of the colored people, as exempting them from friction and criticism in the departments, and I want to add that a number of colored men with whom we have consulted have agreed with us in this judgment'.[69] Writing separately to the editor of the *Congregationalist and Christian World*, who subsequently published an editorial highly critical of segregation in the civil service, Wilson gave the policy fulsome support:

I would say that I do approve of the segregation that is being attempted in several of the departments. I have not always approved of the way in which the thing was being done . . . but I think if you were here on the ground you would see, as I seem to see, that it is distinctly to the advantage of the colored people themselves that they should be organized, so far as possible and convenient, in distinct bureaux where they will center their work. Some of the most thoughtful colored men I have conversed with have themselves approved of this policy. I certainly would not myself have approved of it if I had not thought it to their advantage and likely to remove any of the difficulties which have surrounded the appointment and advancement of colored men and women.[70]

Writing to Oswald Villard of the NAACP, Wilson repeated his justification: 'it is true that the segregation of the colored employees in the several departments has begun upon the initiative and the suggestion of several of the heads of departments, but as much in the interest of the negroes as for any other reason, with the approval of some of the most influential negroes I know.' He rejected claims that segregation damaged Black Americans' interests: 'It is as far as possible from being a movement *against* the negroes. I sincerely believe it to be in their interest.' That Villard did not share his enthusiasm clearly puzzled the former president of Princeton: 'And what distresses me about your letter is to find that you look at it in so different a light.'[71] Wilson's view conformed with prevailing racial attitudes. In further correspondence with William Monroe Trotter, Wilson again fell back on the claim that his policies would advance Black employees' interests: 'in my view the best way to help the Negro in America is to help him with his independence.' For some reason, independence required segregation: 'my colleagues in the departments . . . were seeking, not to put the Negro employees at a disadvantage, but they were seeking to make arrangements which would prevent any kind of friction between the white employees and the Negro employees.'[72]

Proponents of segregation during Woodrow Wilson's first presidency invariably claimed the support of Black Americans. At the Treasury Department, the Director of the Bureau of Engraving and Printing cited such cooperation: 'colored employes have expressed themselves as believing that arrangements of this kind, including separate toilet facilities, were very satisfactory and proper, and it would seem that the claim of discrimination is made only by colored persons who do not desire to associate with members of their own race.'[73] Such a view must have been very consoling to Treasury Secretary William McAdoo[74] (a native of Georgia) and indeed to President Wilson. The same employees even colluded in separate dining arrangements: 'a number of colored assistants preferred to keep together at lunch-time and eat their luncheons in the dressing rooms instead of at the tables in the lunch-room and to accommodate these girls, stools and tables were *provided in an enclosed portion of the dressing room very near the lunch-room* and this arrangement has proven very acceptable and satisfactory to those that take advantage of it.'[75] In another memorandum, the logic of separating Black employees deserted the Bureau's Director and he resorted to the undemanding standard of stereotype: 'in the lunchroom used by the printers' assistants, many of whom are colored, and where there are six tables, two of the tables were assigned especially for the use of the colored girls for the reason that it is believed that it would be better for them to associate together when eating their luncheons.'[76]

Similar patterns of inequality persisted throughout the 1920s and 1930s. Marshalling a commonplace view, the Secretary of the Treasury in 1928, Andrew Mellon, justified segregation in terms of career opportunities for Black American employees, despite the inequality of such arrangements. Mellon argued that the creation of a 'colored section' in the Register's office 'afforded the Department the opportunity to appoint a colored chief and assistant chief of section'. When the Treasury moved building, the Secretary concluded that it was 'the logical, and indeed the only course' to place this section separately 'in one of the rooms that were available'. While the White and Black employees could have been located together physically, this option seemed unappealing to the Treasury Secretary: 'It would be possible at the present time, of course, to combine the two sections, though this is of doubtful wisdom even from an administrative standpoint.' No specification of this 'administrative standpoint' was offered. The clinching point concerned promotion: 'the inevitable result of the amalgamation would be to do away with the two supervisory positions now held by colored employees.'[77] Evidently the Secretary could not contemplate the promotion of Black American employees if they were in the same group as Whites. In 1942 the Director of the Bureau of Prisons also grasped at tenuously articulated 'administrative reasons' to justify segregation, in this case of prisoners in Federal penitentiaries: 'for administrative reasons we usually house the Negroes separately, and consequently they usually eat in separate sections of the mess hall.'[78]

3. The very notion of 'segregation' proved nebulous, since its proponents often refused to see it as such. Thus during Woodrow Wilson's first administration, Treasury Secretary William McAdoo declined to accept that a directive he issued amounted to segregation, informing the NAACP that 'there is no "segregation issue" in the Treasury Department. It has always been a mischievous exaggeration.' However, McAdoo then described practices—'to remove causes of complaint and irritation where white women have been forced unnecessarily to sit at desks with colored men'—which to most observers would be adjudged segregation: 'In dealing with such cases negroes have been put at separate desks in the same room with whites, and there has been no discrimination against them in the matter of light, heat, air, furniture or treatment.'[79] He does not reveal who made the complaints about integration, though we may assume that they arose from White employees.

Thirteen months later, McAdoo remained embattled in correspondence defending racial practices under his authorization. He wrote to the editor of the *Congregationalist and Christian World* that the 'charge' of segregation is '*untrue* as to the Treasury Department except to this extent: *separate toilets* have been assigned to whites and blacks in the Treasury building and in the office of the Auditor of the Interior Department.' He then sought to reassure his correspondent on issues secondary to the crucial question of segregation: 'The toilets assigned to the blacks are just as good as those assigned to the whites. There is no discrimination in quality. I do not know that this can properly be called segregation.' If this arrangement was not segregation it is difficult to imagine what apportionment would have qualified as such. Incautiously, McAdoo advanced a convoluted justification for this separation of ablutions facilities, which serves only to illustrate the inherent inequality of 'separate but equal' racial distinctions and the disproportionate advantaging of Whites in such schemes: 'I am not going to argue the justification of the separate toilet orders, beyond saying that it is difficult to disregard certain feelings and sentiments of white people in a matter of this sort.' McAdoo's defence exposes the unequal power relations between Black Americans and White employees, if only in crude numerical calculations: 'The whites constitute the great majority of the employees and are entitled to just consideration, especially when such consideration does not involve the deprivation of the negro of any essential and inherent right—any more, for instance, than the provision of separate toilets for the higher officials of the department would be a denial of the rights of the ordinary employees.'[80] In fact this counter-example is quite distinct since it locates rights in hierarchy. 'Separate but equal' was supposed to guarantee equality across the same categories, and was therefore not comparable to McAdoo's example.

The failure to acknowledge that separate treatment of Black American employees constituted segregation persisted. In 1928 the Republican Secretary of the Treasury, Andrew Mellon, maintained that any segregation observed arose from factors other than race: 'in the Register's Office the colored and white employees are working together in the same room. In the Treasurer's Office there is no grouping of employees by reason of color although it *happens* that the separation of certain colored men and white women employees in separate rooms has resulted in placing the five colored employees in a separate room, but it will be obvious to you that this separation on the basis of sex is more pleasant for both groups and this was the reason for the separation.'[81] In further correspondence, the NAACP tried to explain to Mellon why such demarcation was objectionable: 'many whites cannot understand why Negroes object to segregation in their work, and regard such matters as complaints about separate locker rooms and segregated parts of lunchrooms as trivial. Not only are fundamental principles involved in segregation ... [But] it is obvious that a worker whom a caste prescription segregates has very little opportunity for advancement, and a segregated locker room loses its insignificance when it becomes a symbol of the belief that the Negro is unfit to associate with his fellow workers of the other race.'[82]

Practice varied across government departments. Four White officials from the Department of the Interior taking lunch at the US Government Printing Office found themselves abruptly and unceremoniously ejected from a table in the cafeteria: 'scarcely had we seated ourselves . . . when a *white* woman employee . . . hurried up and notified us that we were in the section of the cafeteria reserved for colored people.' Upon enquiring whether the 'colored people objected to our sitting' in the section, 'she insisted that we move in any case'.[83] The same writer accepted that Black Americans were 'subjected to discrimination and segregation for a long time' but objected to official collaboration: 'a sharp distinction ought to be drawn between segregation practiced by private individuals and segregation on a racial basis practiced by the Federal Government or by any of its agencies.'[84] In response, the Public Printer disclaimed responsibility since the Department did not operate the cafeteria (it was the responsibility of an elected board of employees), predictably cited the consent of Black American employees in the segregated arrangements and bad-temperedly regretted the comments and interference of an uninvited 'outsider'.[85] At Agriculture, the Under Secretary, Paul Appleby, apologized profusely to a representative from the Associated Negro Press refused service in the Department's cafeteria and pleaded astonishment at the refusal since there was 'no restriction' on dining facilities: 'Negroes are welcome in the main cafeterias at all times.' However, he added a caveat which to outsiders might have seemed closer to segregated race relations than the Under Secretary was willing to appreciate: upon request of a 'group of colored employees', the Board of Directors of the Department Welfare Association 'established a special cafeteria for Negro employees, but this does not prevent employees or visitors of any race from using the other lunch rooms'.[86] Experience suggested the hollowness of this latter guarantee.

In sum, it is a fundamental feature of the US government before the 1960s that its own internal organization was segregated. The entrenchment of segregated race relations in the Federal government could not but define in part the character of the American polity, and ensure unequal treatment for Black American employees.[87] Segregation constituted a standard against which society could measure and applaud itself. As the NAACP rightly argued, it operationalized the assumption of racial inferiority: 'Those segregated are regarded as a people set apart, almost as lepers. Instead of allaying race prejudice, as some of the advocates of segregation would have us believe, by recognition, it has simply emphasized it.' Significantly, 'government approval in some cases has aroused it where it did not exist'.[88] William Trotter was even firmer about the consequences: 'it creates in the minds of others that there is something the matter with us—that we are not their equals, that we are not their brothers, that we are so different that we cannot work at a desk beside them, that we cannot eat at a table beside them, that we cannot go into the dressing-room where they go, that we cannot use a locker beside them, that we cannot even go into a public toilet with them.'[89] The consequences and significance of this arrangement outlived President Woodrow Wilson and his articulation of human rights in the League of Nations.[90]

If the NAACP and other observers had no doubts about the consequences of segregation in the government for the relationship between Black Americans and the US state, then these have been disregarded by most historians of the American Federal government[91] and by students of US politics and government. They rarely pay heed to that institution's treatment of Black Americans[92] or to the effects of Federal programmes in American society for Black Americans.[93] Even the scholarly and fastidious V. O. Key, Jr. ignores this characteristic in his discussion of the reform and development of the Federal bureaucracy.[94] The system of classification designed to control entry into the civil service and to weaken patronage itself became a tool with which to manipulate and limit the entry of Black Americans.[95] Examination of these processes does not simply enhance understanding of the Federal bureaucracy: it augments understanding of how segregated race relations functioned throughout American politics and society in the half-century before the Civil Rights Act of 1964.

LAW, POLITICS, AND SEGREGATION 1896–1954

The initiation and maintenance of segregation reflected several forces in American society including: judicial authority, racial attitudes, partisan interests, and congressional support. The Supreme Court's acceptance of the 'separate but equal' doctrine as a justification of racial segregation in 1896 gave this arrangement constitutional authority. In Congress, unabashed segregationists often found themselves sufficiently powerful and united to foster segregation and to thwart opponents of segregated race relations. The principle of seniority in congressional committee assignment, combined with the Democratic party's hold on the South, were bulwarks against change.[96] In this section, I analyse these legal, political, and partisan sources of support for segregated race relations. The attitudes and values supporting segregated race relations were articulated and vouchsafed in the United States's judicial and political institutions—the Supreme Court, Congress, and presidency—from the 1890s until the early 1960s. Segregation informed partisan interests and political loyalties throughout this period and was mostly supported by them.

Plessy v. Ferguson and the Legality of Segregation

The practice of segregation relied greatly upon the sanction proffered for fifty-eight years by the Supreme Court. In 1896 the Court delivered what proved to be a seminal majority judgement (from which Justice John Harlan dissented) in *Plessy* v. *Ferguson*, a test case of the Jim Crow laws.[97] The Justices' decision enabled public facilities, such as schools, accommodation, transportation, parks, swimming pools, restaurants, cemeteries, hospitals, asylums, and prisons to be organized on a 'separate but equal' basis, a precept quickly and widely implemented.[98]

Plessy v. *Ferguson* was decided by a 7 to 1 vote.[99] The case came from Louisiana where the state Supreme Court had upheld an 1890 Louisiana statute requiring state railroads to provide 'equal but separate accommodations for the white and colored races'. The state law forbade passengers to use carriages other than those reserved for their race. Plessy was a passenger who, because he was one-eighth Black, was required to travel in the coloured passengers' carriage. After his arrest for refusing to leave a White passengers' carriage, Plessy pursued his case, arguing the statute's violation of the Thirteenth and Fourteenth Amendments to the Constitution. The former amendment outlawed slavery; the plaintiff also appealed to the 'equal protection of the laws' clause of the latter. Both grounds were rejected by the Supreme Court. The Thirteenth Amendment was taken to prohibit only the reintroduction of slavery, whilst the 'separate but equal' clause, despite introducing a new form of racial distinction, was not equated with this intention. Regarding the Fourteenth Amendment, the Supreme Court's majority opinion held that separation of the races did not mean inferiority for one race; such a construction required one race to interpret the law in such a manner (which, of course, is what occurred).[100] The single dissent to this case, penned by Justice John Marshall Harlan, argued that the Thirteenth Amendment should be more broadly construed than as a bar on slavery. Harlan also maintained that the Constitution drew no distinction in terms of colour: the 'Constitution is color-blind, and neither knows nor tolerates classes among citizens'.[101]

This regime was first weakened by the Supreme Court itself in decisions taken in the late 1930s. In 1938 the Court found against a statute in Missouri which excluded a Black American from the state university.[102] In a 1950 judgement the Court held, unanimously, that the state of Texas was failing to provide a law school education of equal quality for a prospective Black student, Herman Sweatt, thus violating the 1938 *Gaines* decision.[103] In a companion case, the Court declared unconstitutional, again unanimously, the University of Oklahoma's practice of providing a separate classroom, library, and dining-table for a Black student.[104] The Court was also vigorous in prohibiting segregation on interstate transportation systems, such as its ruling in *Morgan* v. *Virginia*.[105] In 1944 the Court held in *Smith* v. *Allwright*[106] that all-White primaries were unconstitutional but the fundamental judicial attack upon segregation came ten years later in the justly famous Brown case.[107] The momentous *Brown* v. *Board of Education in Topeka, Kansas* decision finally ended the 'separate but equal' *Plessy* doctrine, finding that such arrangements in public school education facilities fostered inequality, and violated the equal protection clause of the Fourteenth Amendment.[108] It vindicated opponents of segregated race relations.

Neither *Brown* nor its predecessors dissipated segregated race relations in United States government or society.[109] The termination of segregation required extensive political and legal struggles and actions at both the federal and state levels—not least the passage of the Civil Rights Act in 1964 and the Voting Rights Act in 1965.[110] The year 1954 did, however, mark unequivocally the end of constitutional and legal legitimacy for this system, and provided a legal framework with which opponents of racial inequalities could pursue equality. It precipitated President Eisenhower's reluctant deployment of Federal authority to desegregate schools in 1957. In this sense, it closes one era of Black Americans' experience of the US Federal government.

The *Plessy* doctrine of 'separate but equal' influenced aspects of state–society relations where the Supreme Court had made no specific ruling, which gave the judicial precedent added significance. For instance, it was regularly alluded to in the notorious area of housing where segregation in public accommodation and private home ownership—especially in the Mid-west and North-east—was almost complete.[111] Although never explicitly applied to housing, proponents of segregation invoked the *Plessy* doctrine. An internal US Federal Housing Authority memorandum, prepared in 1950, observed that 'though many persons appear to assume its applicability, the Supreme Court of the United States has never applied the "separate but equal" doctrine to the provisions of housing accommodations'. In fact the Court had issued rulings with anti-segregation implications: in *Buchanan* v. *Warley*, decided in 1917,[112] the Court ruled that Black Americans had the right to occupy housing in any part of a city and disallowed the municipal practice of 'racial zoning', dividing residence into White and Black sections.[113] In practice, *contra* this ruling, until 1948 residential segregation was accentuated by including restrictive covenants (specifying that a property could not be sold subsequently to a Black American buyer) in property ownership.[114] Such covenants were outlawed by the Supreme Court in 1948,[115] but those existing prior to the ruling limited Black buyers' choices and the Court ruling in 1917 outlawing racial zoning had actually encouraged a greater use of covenants.

The *Brown* decision galvanized many senior Federal officials. The ruling was the main issue discussed by wardens of Federal penitentiaries at their annual meeting in December of 1954,[116] and at the FHA detailed memoranda were prepared assessing the significance of the Supreme Court's decision.[117] Interest groups working in behalf of Black Americans were quick to exploit its potential. In October 1954, the NUL sent a telegram to President Eisenhower requesting a reform to Federal housing loan programmes which would extend the Court's ruling to housing. The NUL maintained that 'in guaranteeing mortgage loans for housing which is not open to Negro occupancy, the Federal Housing Administration is violating the broad principle of non-discrimination which the Supreme Court has recently reaffirmed in public education'. It maintained that 'the Federal government has the . . . right and power and duty to require non-discrimination in FHA mortgage insurance'.[118]

In sum, the Court's support, and then rejection, of segregation was hugely important to the character of Federal government and programmes.

Congress and Race

In national politics, the twenty years from 1896 to 1916 marked a transition in the universality of segregated race relations. *Plessy* sanctified 'separate but equal' demarcations. Progressivism, the influential political movement, incorporated a conception of race relations compatible with the segregation of the racially inferior Black Americans. Racial inferiority was assumed by Woodrow Wilson and his ascendance to the White House in 1913, together with Democratic control of the Congress, politically empowered this assumption. Indeed, this partisan shift must be seen as the fundamental factor behind the diffusion of segregated race relations within the Federal government and the Federal government's role of defender of segregation. As one Republican senator, John Norks, remarked, dissociating himself from the new race relations, 'we are under Southern Democratic rule in this country and they are only following out their own convictions on that subject'. Furthermore, Democratic dominance of Congress ensured that Federal government officers would receive no reprimand for segregating: 'the head of any Department may make these orders and it is not likely that Congress will do anything to prevent their being carried out so long as Congress is controlled by the Democratic party; and the Democratic party in Congress is in control of both Houses.'[119]

From the first Wilson presidency, Congress became a staunch defender of segregated race relations, practices less salient though far from eroded during the Republican party's dominance in the 1920s. The Federal government's endorsement of segregation outlasted the Wilson administration. Indeed, it determined the relationship between Black Americans and the Federal government for the ensuing fifty years.

The Democrats' electoral success in 1912 was followed by the introduction of numerous bills into the House of Representatives proposing to segregate Black employees from Whites in the Federal civil service (see Table A1.3).[120] Bill HR 13772 (introduced in 1914) proposed to segregate Black employees from Whites in the Federal government while HR 17541 proposed to make it unlawful for Black recruits to obtain either commissioned or non-commissioned positions in the Army or Navy.[121] HR 5968, introduced in 1913, proposed to 'effect certain reforms in the civil service by segregating clerks and employees of the white race from those of African blood or descent'.[122] The data in Table A1.3 makes clear that the upsurge in bills to segregate employees in the civil service by race with the election of Woodrow Wilson and Democratic majorities in Congress was no coincidence. Although these bills failed, their introduction and discussion in the Congress indicates the atmosphere fuelling race relations and encouraging the marginalization of Black Americans. In 1916 hearings were held before the House Committee on the District of Columbia (chaired by Ben Johnson from Kentucky) to discuss a set of bills proposing to outlaw 'intermarriage of whites and negroes' and to require 'separate accommodations in street cars'.[123] By the 1920s few politicians dissented publicly from the desirability of segregation and opponents lacked the political power effectively to prevent its diffusion.

In Congress, Republicans distanced themselves from the concerns of Black American voters but infrequently engaged in racist or segregationist policy. The migration of tens of thousands of Southern Black Americans to northeastern and midwestern cities had stimulated massive racism and conflict and Republicans did not wish to alienate White supporters. A more robust approach to segregation was embraced by many Democrats.[124] Southern Democratic Senators such as Hoke Smith of Georgia, Benjamin R. Tillman of South Carolina, and notoriously James K. Vardaman of Mississippi were eagerly flexing the new power granted them in the Sixty-First Congress (1913–14). All three were active in the Democratic Fair Play Association formed in 1913 to advance Southern Democratic interests in Washington. Woodrow Wilson was an honorary member. Fig. 1.1 reproduces a flyer circulated in 1913 advertising a meeting of the Association.[125] Speaking in the Senate in July 1913 to oppose a motion appropriating funds to Black Americans to celebrate fifty years of freedom, Senator Vardaman assured his colleagues that 'really the white man has done more for the negro than the negro has done for himself. As a matter of fact, there is no race of people on earth who have received as much help from others as the negroes of the South have received from the white people of the South.' He did append one caveat to this benevolence: 'the white people have assisted them in every possible way, except to make citizens or voters of them, and, of course, that ought not to be done and, indeed, will never be done.'[126]

A representative from Louisiana, James B. Aswell, was equally emphatic about the racially inferior position of Black Americans. Explaining that he

SHALL THE NEGRO RULE?

All other questions are minimized under the shadow of social equality and preference for Negroes in the employ of the government of the United States.

SENATOR JAMES K. VARDAMAN

And other prominent speakers will address the people at a public meeting to be held under the auspices of the National Democratic Fair Play Association which stands for segregation of the races in government employment, and "reorganization of the civil service" as declared in the National Democratic platform of 1912. At this meeting the policy of appointing Negroes to government positions will be fully and freely discussed.

AT OLD MASONIC TEMPLE
COR. 9th AND F STS. N.W.
WASHINGTON, D. C.

WEDNESDAY NIGHT, AUGUST 6, 1913

ADMIT BEARER AT 8 O'CLOCK

FIG. 1.1. 'Shall the Negro Rule?'
Source: National Committee on Segregation in the Nation's Capital, *Segregation in Washington* (Chicago: National Committee on Segregation in the Nation's Capital, 1948), 61.

was from the South 'where the negro is contented and happy', Aswell condemned a speech by NAACP official Villard for leading Black Americans 'astray': '[Villard] . . . seems to be shedding crocodile tears because some negro clerks in one of the departments are seated behind white clerks, many of whom are white women . . . He thinks that to segregate the races in the Government service is a stupid political policy.'[127] For Aswell, affirming a widely held opinion, the necessity for segregation was both compelling and self-evident: 'would Mr Villard or any other white man suggest a negro being President of the United States, in the President's Cabinet, on the Supreme Bench, or a Member of the House or the Senate? The average negro himself would not suggest such an absurd proposition. Would Mr Villard or any other good white man be willing for his sister or daughter to marry a negro?' His conclusion was self-evident: 'Thus by the logic of facts the negro's position in society and in the Republic is circumscribed, graded, limited . . . For negroes and whites to occupy the same worktables, the same bathrooms, and use the same towels is the beginning of social equality which the majority of the people of this country will never permit. The Government has no right to break down established social standards.'[128] Such attitudes, far from those of a minority, illustrate why the whole 'separate but equal' fabric could never be a safeguard for equality but instead institutionalized inequality.[129] Aswell lauded the Democrats for their 'brilliant record' of segregation and concluded that 'for every negro vote a party loses by segregation it will gain ten white votes'.[130] Before entering Congress, Aswell served as state superintendent of public education, a role in which he no doubt exercised his magnanimous attitude to the 'child race'.[131]

In the years following Woodrow Wilson's presidency, Democratic members of Congress were quick to criticize desegregation in Federal departments. Thus the abolition of segregation in the Census Bureau of the Department of Commerce in 1928 by the then secretary Herbert Hoover,[132] was immediately criticized by Senators Cole L. Blease of South Carolina, Hubert D. Stephens of Mississippi, and Thomas J. Heflin of Alabama in Congress. Blease inserted critical articles in the *Congressional Record* and launched a blistering attack on Hoover and his presidential ambitions. In graceless and racist language, Blease assured his colleagues that Hoover would never 'break the solid South by putting "chocolate drops" in the same water-closet with young white girls'.[133] Senator Stephens asserted that 'there has been no demand for this change except that coming from negro politicians outside the service'.[134] Senator Thomas J. Heflin from Alabama concurred with Blease's attack on desegregation: 'what right has he [Hoover] to disturb the splendid segregation arrangements established in the Commerce Department by the Democratic Party, under which the negroes were working and getting along well in one section and the whites were working in another and pleased with the situation?'[135] A week later, Senator Cole Blease re-entered the fray, charging Hoover's supporters with weakening segregation in the Interior and Treasury departments: Hoover had devised a 'systematic plan to humiliate white girls from whatever part of this Nation they may happen to come by placing some of them in the same category with negro employees not only in the offices but in closets in the various departments'.[136]

The renewed electoral strength of the Democrats in Congress from 1932 (according them dominance of congressional committees) was reflected in the close monitoring of race relations in the Federal government (Tables A1.1 and A1.2). In the half-century before 1964 Congress either rejected or diluted any inroads to the system of segregation and deflected criticism of the inequality and discrimination it generated. Even when Democrats failed to control the House or Senate, an alliance of conservative Republicans and Southern Democrats ensured Congress's resistance to desegregation. As V. O. Key Jr observed, during the Truman administration the 'House Rules Committee . . . was often at odds with the House leadership and with the President. It obstructed legislation desired by the majority party and facilitated legislation desired by right-wing Democrats and Republicans.' In the 1951 competition to select a Democratic majority leader in the Senate, the moderate Joseph O'Mahoney of Wyoming lost to the conservative E. W. McFarland of Arizona, who had opposed Truman's Fair Deal and civil rights programmes.[137] On those occasions when legislative proposals to establish civil rights were introduced in the Senate, the practice of filibustering, virtually of unlimited scope, ensured defeat. Without support from Southern Congressmen, civil rights legislation could not succeed. These congressional characteristics circumscribed the opportunities for an executive, such as President Truman, intent upon advancing civil rights and ending segregation. In 1946 the Republicans won control of both the House and Senate: naturally their priority was opposing the executive and paving the way for a republican presidential victory (though 1948 disappointed on this second count and the Democrats reclaimed their congressional majorities). These Republican victories not only limited the influence of Northern liberals in the Congress, but made Truman all the more dependent upon Southern Democratic support. In the event, the President was unable to avoid a breach in the Democratic party in 1948, though this did not preclude his re-election.[138]

From the 1930s, as New Deal programmes expanded Federal government responsibilities, congressional defence of segregated race relations was accomplished by several tactics:

1. Congress made strategic use of the 'power of the purse' during appropriations decisions to ensure that administrators in the Federal civil service who were tempted to challenge segregated race relations desisted. Southern Democrats were prepared to respond quickly and irascibly to liberal initiatives in the Federal bureaucracy, as the Director of the USES discovered in 1938. Congressman John J. Cochran (a Democrat from Missouri) complained about the activities of the USES's Negro Affairs Advisor, Lawrence Oxley, in Kansas and Missouri. Alluding to talks given by Oxley, Cochran declared: 'I do not want Government Employees going around making speeches that cause our Administration trouble.' Since Cochran was chairman of the House Committee on Expenditures in Executive Departments his influence over appropriations was not trivial. He continued: 'I am not going to sit idly by and see appropriations used for purposes other than that which are specified by the Administration, [or to fund] speeches that result in the Administration being criticised.'[139]

2. Segregationists in Congress successfully subverted or circumscribed initiatives to use Federal powers of investigation to expose discrimination and inequalities perpetrated within the 'separate but equal' order. In 1946 Congress terminated appropriations for the FEPC, an agency established by President Roosevelt to monitor hiring procedures in defence-related industries and in the Federal government. The circumstances of the Second World War[140] compelled President Roosevelt to advance antidiscrimination hiring policies especially among employers holding lucrative government contracts (see Chapter 3).[141]

Roosevelt created the FEPC in response to Black workers' pressure, organized by A. Philip Randolph who threatened a mass march on Washington.[142] The proposed march was abandoned after a meeting between Randolph and President Roosevelt at which the latter agreed to desegregate defence industries. On 25 June 1941 the President issued Executive Order 8802 'Reaffirming Policy of Full Participation in the Defense Program by All Persons Regardless of Race, Creed, Color, or National Origin', and creating the FEPC. It investigated cases of employment discrimination in war industries, government contracts, government employment, and unions.[143] The shortage of labour in war industries[144] made employers more pragmatic about hiring minority workers: 'as the needs in industry became more acute, resistance to the use of minority group workers diminished accordingly.'[145] The number of Black Americans working in government rose from approximately 40,000 in 1938 to over 300,000 during the war.[146]

Despite the demands of liberals and Black interest groups, Southern Democratic senators used the filibuster truculently to stop bills introduced in 1945 and 1946 to establish a permanent committee on fair employment practice (see Table A1.4). Deploying Federal power to investigate discrimination and inequality of treatment was a profoundly divisive issue for the Democrats, provoking the so-called Dixiecrat revolt at the party's 1948 convention when, at the instigation of liberals led by the Mayor of Minneapolis, Hubert Humphrey, the platform included a commitment to fair employment practice.[147] Truman stuck courageously to this promise, though legislation to create a permanent investigative committee failed during his presidency (Table A1.4).

Individual members of Congress also kept a watchful and circumspect eye on the activities of Federal departments, alert to activities weakening segregated race relations. On arriving in the Department of Agriculture in 1945, Secretary Clinton P. Anderson received a letter from Congressman Dan R. McGehee (Democrat from Mississippi), chairman of the Committee on Claims, objecting to a proposed bulletin from the Department analysing class and race in the South. McGehee warned Anderson to watch out for the 'many long haired, cracked brained, Un-American birds . . . in the Department of Agriculture'.[148]

3. For segregationists, decentralization of federal programmes was always preferable to centralized ones because it minimized interference with local racial practices.[149] This preference is illustrated by another congressional decision in 1946 to return the USES to state control (it was federally administered during the war);[150] the USES was created in 1933 to provide a national system of employment offices to assist job-seekers to find work. The conflict over the USES's return to the states after the war demonstrates the political strength of Southern Democrats in Congress, supported by Southern democratic state governments,[151] and aided by the weakness of opponents such as organized labour[152] and the NAACP. Proponents of federalization attempted a write-in campaign to 'keep USES Federalized', urging newspaper readers and others to write to President Truman. They implored the President to resist pressures to return the USES to the states.[153]

Defederalizing the USES was of fundamental importance to Southern Democrats, who wanted to restore the pre-war status quo—states' rights and segregation—as quickly as possible; accordingly, they co-ordinated to limit Federal intervention in the states.[154] On the key congressional committees (Ways and Means in the House, Labor and Education and Finance in the Senate, and appropriations committees), there was strong support from senior members for state control, a preference disproportionately reflecting Southern members' interests. It also received strong support from Representative Everett M. Dirksen (a conservative Republican from Illinois)—illustrating the Southern Democratic–conservative Republican axis operative after 1946 (though the two groups had different motives).[155] The Senate was less committed to defederalization but House supporters of the USES succeeded in attaching an amendment to a bill which did not face a conference committee.[156]

The Southern pressure to defederalize[157] prevailed.[158] Returning the USES to the states was supported by almost all Republicans in the House and 74 of 100 Southern Democrats; of 108 non-Southern Democrats 95 voted against.[159]

4. Congress was energetic and vigilant in ensuring that the District of Columbia remained a paragon of segregated race relations and legislated accordingly.[160] This is highly significant because the Federal government and Congress ran the District, and race relations within it were a powerful manifestation of the government's approach and role in maintaining segregation. Each chamber had its own committee responsible for the District of Columbia, dominated by Southerners between 1913 and 1920 and after 1932 (see Table A1.2). Administrators in government departments were able repeatedly to avoid responsibility for segregation in certain facilities, such as cafeterias, by pleading that they were organized by the District.

The congressional record in the District was profoundly segregationist: 'Congress has not enacted special legislation protecting civil rights in the

District. In one or two areas it has enacted legislation which assumes or provides for segregation.'[161] In 1923 Congressman William Lankford of Georgia beseeched his colleagues to enact stringent segregation laws for the District, based on Southern practices: 'The South is right about the race question . . . I truly believe in the supremacy of the white race.' In his view Washington was insufficiently segregated: 'I have pleaded and still plead for equal but separate accommodations for the races as being best for both.'[162] Segregation remained thirty years later. In response to criticisms about segregation in the District's parks, the Chairman of the National Capital Park and Planning Commission wrote in 1948 that 'the dual system of schools and of public recreation is not the result of recent attempts to bring about or enforce segregation but has existed by authority of Congress for 85 years.' It was maintained by annual congressional funding decisions: 'This dual system is recognized annually in the appropriation of funds by the Congress.'[163] The District of Columbia had segregated *de facto* from the 1890s and early 1900s, providing a model for Federal officials mindful to imitate such arrangements.

In sum, from the second decade of the twentieth century Congress was a powerful promoter, and then protector, of segregated race relations. This role was practised most visibly from the first Wilson administration and, once assumed, members of Congress proved wedded to it, despite Republican presidents in the 1920s and 1950s. From the 1930s the dominance of Southern Democrats in Congress, either through their control of committees or in alliance with conservative Republicans, guaranteed that Federal policy accommodated segregated race relations, rarely challenging them. These priorities ensured the scrupulous monitoring of segregation within the Federal government.

Presidential Politics and Race

In the United States, national political power is shared by Congress and the President. Since Woodrow Wilson's presidency (1913–21), incumbents of this office, especially Democrats, have played major roles, at different times, in establishing, accepting, disturbing, and undermining segregated race relations. Woodrow Wilson, Franklin D. Roosevelt (1933–45), Harry S. Truman (1945–53), and Lyndon B. Johnson (1963–9), for profound party political and personal reasons, have been unavoidably linked to race relations policy. Because the Democratic Party's electoral strength depended in part upon Southern voters (below the congressional level, Southern states were in effect single-party systems before the 1970s),[164] aspiring candidates had little choice but, implicitly at least, to endorse or to tolerate segregated race relations. The electoral support propelling Roosevelt into the White Office in

1933, and the mainstay of Democratic support until the end of Johnson's presidency, relied upon a parlous coalition of White voters and Black voters, whose social interests were the obverse of each other.

With the exception of Dwight Eisenhower (1953–61), Republican presidents in the five decades after Woodrow Wilson were less directly affected by race relations, able to pay lip-service to the need for civil rights and to blame Democrats for their absence. Neither Warren Harding (1921–3) nor the fiercely conservative Calvin Coolidge (1923–9) actively encouraged segregation but both failed to respond to requests from Black interest groups to desegregate, and disregarded the surge of Ku Klux Klan organizing and baneful violence in the 1920s. The increase in White racism accompanied the large-scale migration of Southern Blacks—close to a million in the whole decade[165]—to the North. Republicans hoped to retain the traditional loyalties of the Black American electorate but were unwilling to appeal to them directly for fear of alienating White Northern voters. This migration fostered both racist attitudes and sharper residential segregation. With the brief exception of Herbert Hoover (1929–33)—perhaps anticipating the electoral sea change of 1932—who attempted to appeal more directly to Black voters in 1928 by desegregating one section of the Commerce Department, Republicans looked as askance upon Black voters as did Democrats in the 1920s. Eisenhower's reluctant deployment of federal troops in 1957 to desegregate schools in Little Rock, Arkansas, proved the first step in the movement which culminated with Lyndon Johnson's Civil Rights Act of 1964, but it was not a step which Eisenhower took enthusiastically.

Some of these points can usefully be illustrated by a brief review of selected presidencies.

Woodrow Wilson and Segregation in the Federal Government

Woodrow Wilson, formerly governor of New Jersey, was elected to the White House in 1912 and the Democrats also won majorities in both houses of the Congress (though the Senate remained indirectly elected until 1913). As already explained, this resurgence of Democratic support was shamefully accompanied, not only by a failure to replace Black American Republican executive appointees with Black American Democrats, but by the introduction of segregation in Federal government departments in Washington. Some segregation had existed in the Federal government before 1913, but Wilson's election marked a sharper accent upon the segregationist propensity in Washington: '*never before has there been an Administration that dared to cater to this feeling, except in surreptitious ways.* There has always been in the Departments in Washington, a *wish* to do it, but not the *courage*.'[166] His presidency broke with the policies of his republican progressive predecessors, Theodore Roosevelt (1901–9) and William Howard Taft (1909–13).[167]

The new accent was rooted in party political interests, including his rewarding of racist Southerner supporters by appointment to Cabinet positions, and his desire to entrench the Democratic Party in the Federal state, in the knowledge that his electoral success of 1912 owed everything to a split in the Republicans rather than to the extent of his own support. Democratic party success also had much to do with this new rigour. Democratic party strength grew in the Congress to 291 Representatives and 51 Senators, compared with 228 and 41 under the previous Republican administration.

Segregated race relations were never the subject of a formal executive order or congressional act but they were encouraged during these years[168] (see the data reported in Table A2.3). In July 1913 the Auditor of the Treasury Department issued an order, on the authority of newly appointed Secretary William McAdoo (a Southerner), designating separate toilets for White and Black employees. The Assistant Secretary, Williams, wrote to his Chief Clerk on 12 July 1913: 'I think it would be best for this Department if you should make arrangements by which white and colored employees of this Department shall use different toilet rooms. Please arrange accordingly.'[169] Whether this instruction constituted a formal directive or order was much disputed.[170] The measure was imitated by several departments. Writing to the Secretary of the Treasury, the Bureau's Director denied a new policy: 'It has been usual in this Bureau for a great many years to provide the colored employes with separate lockers and dressing rooms and they have used the lunch-room in common with the white employes except that there have been tables provided which the colored employes usually occupied. There has been very little difficulty with regard to this question until recently.'[171] As already explained, Woodrow Wilson himself supported segregation on the grounds that it was in the best interests of Black American employees.

The development of segregated race relations in Federal departments was the subject of a series of reports by the NAACP. Its first study, issued in October 1913,[172] revealed that the practice initiated in the Treasury Department was rapidly emulated in other departments, such as the Post Office,[173] though some (such as Agriculture) had resisted the trend.[174] In the Bureau of Engraving and Printing, the study's author, May Nerney, learned that 'colored clerks are segregated in work by being placed at separate tables and in separate sections of rooms whenever possible. White guides told the investigator that it was to be the future policy of the Bureau to segregate all its colored employees.' Furthermore, 'colored girls no longer use the lunch rooms which for nine years they have been using in common with white girls'. A similar eviction from dining-rooms befell Black American workers in the Post Office Department: 'no lunch room is provided for the colored employees in the Post Office Department. The white employees have a very attractive room.' The reason offered for this disparity was imaginative: 'The guide advanced as a convincing argument in explanation of this condition that as no restaurants in Washington were open to colored people, the government could not be expected to furnish one.'[175] That the Federal government might act differently and set standards appropriate to equality of citizenship eluded these officials.

Segregation in the government outlasted Wilson's administration, as the NAACP meticulously recorded.[176] In 1927 thirty-six Black employees in the Department of the Interior wrote to the Secretary, Hubert Work, protesting a reorganization in the Pension Bureau which happened to result in segregation: 'This division which has been created for colored employees exclusively, all white clerks having been removed, is known as the "Files Division" and the allocation in it are among the lowest in the office.'[177] Moorfield Storey called on President Coolidge to 'carry out' his expressions of support for Black Americans, a request disregarded.[178] The NAACP protested to President Coolidge about segregation—'a situation in the Government Departments in Washington which is deeply stirring the sentiment of colored citizens throughout the United States'. The letter continued: 'colored people feel that under your administration they have a right to expect that such practices, expressive of the Jim Crow spirit and a relic of slavery days, will receive the rebuke which they deserve.'[179] However, the Republican administrations of the 1920s were uninterested in addressing these issues and the Party was by now closer to the Democratic party's position on segregation. The NAACP's 1928 survey of segregation was based on visits to each department in Washington and interviews with both departmental heads and clerks; it found a pattern of segregation.[180] (Table A2.2 summarizes some of the main findings.) Table A3.1 gives an aggregate summary of the number of Black employees in US Federal government in 1923 and in 1928. These data provide a profile of the distribution of Black employees across departments. The statistics for 1928 left the Assistant Secretary, Walter White, deeply dejected about both the appointment of Black applicants to positions in the Federal government and their lack of promotion.[181] In other departments and bureaux studied by the NAACP researchers, it was on occasion impossible to obtain reliable information about segregation. Some departments, such as State, avoided overt segregation by hiring Black employees for custodial positions only.[182] The Director of Public Buildings excused segregation in the restaurants and cafeterias in the executive buildings on the grounds that they were 'not Government institution(s) . . . but are operated under concession agreements of one kind of another'. The Director noted: 'in making such agreements this office . . . insists upon the same food and the same service and prices being made available to colored people as to white people. I do not believe there is any discrimination, nor any segregation which is in any way distressing or humiliating.'[183] A similar explanation was offered by the GAO, the Navy, and the Interior.[184]

Thus the segregated race relations disseminated in the Federal government during Woodrow Wilson's presidency (and helped immeasurably by the requirement from 1914 that candidates for the civil service supply a photograph) survived the incumbencies of his Republican successors, and from the 1930s were unquestioningly deemed the norm in government departments (see Chapters 2 and 3). From that decade, such relations were transferred more generally into American society under the impetus of Roosevelt's New Deal programmes.

Franklin D. Roosevelt, the New Deal, and the Second World War

The election of Roosevelt in 1932 heralded the New Deal expansion of Federal government (see Chapter 3), in which Black Americans hoped to participate. This aspiration was unfulfilled. Black Americans did not benefit proportionately from New Deal programmes, as the NAACP complained to Eleanor Roosevelt: 'there is hardly a phase of the New Deal program which has not brought some hardship and disillusionment to colored people.'[185] The *Pittsburgh Courier* expressed the general Black American sentiment in 1939: 'for the Negro the New Deal has been the Old Deal in new clothes . . . Worse, it has helped spread jim crowism over the country where it had not before existed.'[186] In the view of the FEPC, 'the rank and file Negro Federal worker achieved little during the pre-war New Deal administration. In 1938 Negroes were 8.4 per cent of all Government employees in Washington. Ninety per cent of these were custodial, 9.5 per cent were in the Clerical-Administrative-Fiscal or Clerical-Mechanical category, and .5 per cent were Subprofessional.'[187] Public works programmes had obvious implications for segregated race relations since they required a significant expansion in the Federal government employment and its field administration. This expansion, and the accompanying growth of civil service positions, was viewed suspiciously by Southern Democrats, alert to any erosion of segregated race relations.[188] Thus the tensions inherent in the North–South cleavage were exacerbated with the election of Franklin Roosevelt,[189] and the diverse groups forming his electoral support required a careful balancing which rarely promoted the interests of Black Americans. Furthermore, the Federal government's intervention in new activities—principally underwriting mortgage finance and establishing employment exchanges (see Chapter 6)—was marked by adherence to segregated race relations, shaping the relationship between Black Americans and the Federal government in new areas beyond Washington.

These trends were intensified by the USA's entry into the Second World War, when the huge expansion of defence industries and growth of government agencies presented employment opportunities in the public sector on an unprecedented scale. Black Americans were determined not to be excluded from them as they had largely been from the New Deal expansion.

The wartime increase in opportunities for Black Americans was not welcomed by those Whites already employed. In the Bureau of Engraving and Printing, White workers staged a boycott of the cafeteria, 'because Negroes are not so rigidly segregated in the diningroom'.[190] The situation was explained by an employee: 'the dominant group of people resent the fact that its fellow Americans, the colored people, who pay the same price for the food, became tired of walking the entire length of the cafeteria to segregated sections, but felt free to eat a little nearer to the steam tables.' 'Dominant group' is synonymous with White, the group which also controlled skilled positions: 'another thing the colored people notice at this government building, is the total absence of colored printers among the multitude of printers of the dominant group.'[191] Where segregation did not exist—usually because no Black Americans were employed before 1941—it had to be imposed to ensure that expansion did not overturn segregated race relations. The Machine Records Branch of the War Department, employing forty-eight persons in three consecutive shifts each lasting twenty-four hours, was suddenly segregated in March 1943.[192] The Geological Survey unit in the Department of Interior designated segregated lavatory facilities for its employees in April 1943 at its Clarendon Virginia branch: 'it appears that for a considerable time, when there were only four women employed in the unit—two Negro and two white, there was no segregation in the use of toilets. But with the recent addition of fifteen colored women to the staff, separate facilities were ordered.'[193] At the TVA housing, educational and recreation facilities were segregated to conform with 'established laws and customs in the area'.[194] In 1942 the Norfolk Navy Yard employed eight hundred women of whom eight were Black, and the White majority insisted on segregation as the manager informed the FEPC: the Management 'showed skepticism as to the feasibility of working white and colored women together . . . It was pointed out that the eight colored women now employed were removed from contact with white women after it appeared the whites resented their presence.'[195] In August 1944 6,000 employees of the Philadelphia Transportation Company began a strike in response to the Company's hiring and training of eight Black workers for operators' jobs, an initiative under its non-discrimination policy.[196] The strike developed into a riot in the city.

The lure of fighting inequality, injustice, and racism abroad in the Second World War soon faded for Black recruits and Black workers familiar with the injustices and inequalities perpetrated and maintained by the domestic Jim Crow system.[197] A. Philip Randolph, leader of organized Black workers, was keen to exploit the inconsistency between the USA's domestic treatment of Black Americans and its self-proclaimed international role as defender of human rights. His pressure forced Franklin Roosevelt to establish the FEPC, despite hostility in Congress whose members ensured that the Committee was of temporary status and terminated in 1946. Southern Democrats prevented the inclusion of a commitment to a permanent FEPC in the party's platform at the 1944 national convention and, in Key's assessment, 'some southern delegates appeared to regard this matter as the most important issue before the convention'.[198] Southern Democratic alarm rehearses the centrality of race to the Democratic party and highlights the complex mixture of interests constraining party leaders. President Roosevelt won the support of Northern Black voters and this influenced his policy: 'the ever increasing number of Negroes in the North had begun to shift into the Democratic party . . . They had begun to vote their self-interest and not their gratitude to Abraham Lincoln.'[199] Roosevelt's electoral support included also Southern White Democrats whose social interests were, however, entirely antithetical to those of Black voters.

Harry Truman and the End of War

The end of the Second World War posed a severe test for segregation and for its legal and political support. The end of the First World War coincided with extensive race riots in the USA and many feared a recurrence after 1945. Throughout the war period, racial tension was palpable, frequently riotous, both in Southern towns with training camps and in Northern cities with defence production industries.[200] In a memorandum prepared as early as August 1943, one White House staffer warned that Black Americans' expansion into industrial employment challenged the 'limited participation in community life by minority members' presupposed by segregation. Furthermore, as 'employment and wage levels begin to approach prevailing levels for whites, Negro participation in community life increases to the point where segregation as a pattern is threatened'.[201]

The pressures thus facing President Harry Truman signalled a new intensity in racial conflict as supporters of Jim Crow attempted to ensure that segregated race relations were restored. Black Americans—whether government employees, members of the Armed Services, or citizens—were loath to permit their re-establishment. Furthermore, Northern indifference to segregated race relations in the United States, especially in the South, had declined, and the savage experiences of discrimination and racism endured by many Northern Blacks during the war years ensured their mobilization against segregation after 1946 (see Chapter 4).[202] American race practices increasingly received negative publicity from other countries, including allies of the United States. They were a blemish acknowledged by Dean Acheson, the Acting Secretary of State, a year before Truman's civil rights report. Acheson observed that Americans abroad found themselves being 'reminded over and over by some foreign newspapers and spokesmen that our treatment of various minorities leaves much to be desired'. And he conceded that such commentators were able 'all too frequently to point with accuracy to some form of discrimination because of race', about which it was 'next to impossible to formulate a satisfactory answer'.[203] The American ambassador to Denmark confessed in 1952 that 'as an American', he was 'deeply and painfully conscious of the existence of such undemocratic practices as segregation and all forms of discrimination' deployed against Black Americans.[204]

A White House memorandum toward the close of the war warned of post-war employment problems: the 'prospect of decreasing employment and the return of troops raises the same danger signals that preceded the riots of 1919. The Federal government should assume some responsibility and be ready to act.'[205] Many Black Americans who had obtained work in the government had been restricted deliberately to temporary positions, checked in their efforts to win permanent status (see Chapter 3). President Truman anticipated the likely restoration of pre-war segregation and prejudice within the Federal government. He issued a circular to all heads of government departments, agencies, and independent establishments urging them to ensure no discrimination occurred as the number of personnel was reduced.[206] He directed all departmental heads to undertake 'careful analysis of your personnel policies, procedures and practices in order that you can assure me that they are in accord with national law and policy'.[207] Unfortunately these 'procedures and practices' were part of a state itself premissed upon segregation.[208] Truman's concerns about discrimination in civil service departments were vindicated. At the Department of Labor, Black Americans seeking to fill an opening in the Bureau of Labor Statistics were rebuffed for reasons of race. According to an affidavit signed by the chairman of United Public Workers of America Local 10, Blacks faced discrimination in the Bureau of Labor Statistics: the hiring officer 'stated that he deliberately had discriminated against Negroes by intentionally refraining from appointing any Negro to the professional staff of the Prices and Cost of Living Section'.[209] In the same department's Women's Bureau, the promotion of a Black woman to a supervisory position resulted in crude notes to Black employees reflecting a 'deeply hostile attitude toward Negroes'.[210] Truman's circulars were worthy and important documents but modifying the fundamental relationship between Black Americans and the Federal government, solidified over forty years, required more elaborate mechanisms.

Truman's contribution to this process was the creation of investigative committees examining the position of Black Americans in society and in government. The genesis for this approach lay, appropriately enough, in an individual Black American's horrific experience in 1946, brought to Truman's attention by the NAACP. Writing to the Attorney-General Tom Clark, Truman recorded a visit from the Association: 'they told me about an incident which happened in South Carolina where a Negro Sergeant, who had been discharged from the Army just three hours, was taken off the bus and not only seriously beaten but his eyes deliberately put out, and the Mayor of the town had bragged about committing this outrage.'[211] Such incidents were commonplace in 1946, as returning Black American veterans were attacked by Whites reasserting the segregationist order. The investigative committee strategy is suggested in Truman's final paragraph: 'I think it is going to take something more than the handling of each individual case after it happens—it is going to require the inauguration of some sort of policy to prevent such happenings.'[212] Truman's committees provided reports excoriating American race relations, dispelling any lingering doubts about the benefits of such exclusionary arrangements.

In beginning the process of desegregation, President Truman demonstrated different motives and calculations to those of his Democratic predecessors, but again they were linked to the Democratic Party: the conflict within the party between Southerners and Northerners over civil rights, sufficiently severe to provoke a split at the 1948 convention;[213] the recognition of the continuing electoral importance of Black voters in the North; the demands of the United States' post-Second World War role as defender of human rights and democracy; and the chips to the 'separate but equal' doctrine by the Supreme Court in the fourteen years before the 1954 *Brown* decision. The reports of his investigative committees on civil rights, the Armed Services, and government contract compliance, and his gradual alignment of the Democrats with civil rights, began the process for legislation. This process was continued modestly by Presidents Eisenhower and Kennedy, but decisively and effectively by President Lyndon Johnson, himself a Southerner, whose formidable political adroitness and personal imaginative commitment to equal rights resulted in the USA's most significant legislation for Black American citizens, the Civil Rights Act of 1964.

PART II

Segregation in the US Federal Government

2

Joining the Government: 'Because I Dared to be Black'

HISTORICALLY, all Western democracies have had to devise mechanisms to regulate entry into their national civil services, to classify positions hierarchically within the bureaucracy, and to determine the conditions for promotion. Britain rationalized entry into its civil service from the 1870s through the imposition of competitive examinations.[1] Comparable reforms were implemented in Canada, Prussia, and France.[2] The dominant principle informing all these national reforms was the establishment of merit criteria for civil service employment, determined principally by performance in competitive examination. The obverse of merit—appointment by patronage—was the principal object of reform.

In the United States, these tasks were more problematic than in other countries because a powerful system of patronage and political-party spoils was entrenched (especially in the decades after the Civil War) prior to rationalization of the civil service. Political-party patronage and competing sectional interests set the framework within which the US Federal government developed. The so-called 'spoils system' was endemic to the American polity. The dispensation of spoils was jealously guarded as a right of electoral victors. Before reform in 1883, one scholar notes, the 'civil service gave the politician his strength. Not only did it provide a payroll for his staff of hacks and ward heelers; it was also the primary source of that important commodity with which elections are won—money. Local, state and federal politicians might assess a civil servant yearly from 2 to 7 per cent of his annual salary.'[3]

In this chapter, I briefly review the reform of the Federal civil service from a patronage- to a merit-based system and then explain how the entrance mechanism deployed by the US Civil Service Commission—the 'rule of three'—discriminated against Black American applicants. The Civil Service Commission proved an inadequate monitor of civil service recruitment, thereby contributing to a legacy of unequal opportunity for Black Americans in the Federal government. The Commission's ineffectualness rested on several factors including: a biased appointment procedure; a weakening of the Commission's impartiality after 1913; and indifferent congressional oversight until the 1960s, by which time the Commission's role in accommodating

TABLE 2.1. *Major civil service legislation in the USA*

Year	Measure	Content
1883	Pendleton Act	Established Civil Service Commission and competitive examinations for entry
1912	Lloyd–LaFollette Act	Granted Federal government employees the right to organize and to petition Congress.
1923	Personnel Classification Act	Set out positions—classes, grades, and services—in the civil service
1940	Ramspeck Act	Extended meritocratic criteria to over 80% of civil service
1978	Civil Service Reform Act	Replaced Civil Service Commission with Office of Personnel Management

segregation was too secure easily to dislodge. Within Congress, the maintenance of segregation and limiting of Black recruitment were the supreme political concerns of the Southern Democrats, who enjoyed committee dominance from the 1930s (see Table A1.2), and whom President Roosevelt could not afford to alienate on this question for fear of the political consequences. The Commission became a bastion of this sectional interest instead of an independent arbiter of equality of employment. The civil service became a key institution through which the US Federal government asserted and maintained segregated race relations.

FROM PENDLETON TO NEW DEAL 1883–1932

Table 2.1 lists the major reforms of the US civil service. The first important reform occurred in 1883 with the passage of the Pendleton Act[4] imposing competitive entry examination requirements for a proportion of recruits to Federal agencies, thereby establishing a meritocratic system.

Coming six years after the collapse of Reconstruction, the Pendleton Act signalled the emergence of an élite, urban-based movement driving reform in public life and government—at the national, state, and municipal levels—culminating in the era now known as Progressivism (1897–1914). Invariably sanguine about the prospects for rational reform and management, Progressives believed the disagreeable effects of the party-political and the spoils system could be ended, and this influenced their proposals for legislation. Merit and rationality were to replace preferment and tradition as the founding principles of government. If these changes benefited Black Americans also, this was to be welcomed, but such an effect would have seemed improbable to many

Progressives. Furthermore, acquiring the skills and resources—principally formal education—privileged by meritocracy was beyond the reach of not only many White Americans, but the vast majority of Black Americans (though some institutions such as Howard University and Fisk University permitted a trickle of Black American graduates to enter public life).

The Civil Service Reform (Pendleton) Bill, HR 6962, was reported back to the House of Representatives floor in December 1882 from the Committee on Reform in the Civil Service.[5] The Senate bill, S 133, was read on the floor after committee consideration on 4 January 1883.[6] Senator George Pendleton, from Ohio, was the principal architect of the reform. The bill regulated entry to the civil service and established the Civil Service Commission. Speaking in the Senate during consideration of the bill, Pendleton laid a series of charges, congruent with those later articulated by Progressives, against the extant civil service: 'the civil service is inefficient; it is expensive; it is extravagant; it is in many cases and in some senses corrupt.' Furthermore, the Service was a party-political machine: it 'has welded the whole body of its employees into a great political machine; it has converted them into an army of officers and men, veterans in political warfare, disciplined and trained, whose salaries, whose time, whose exertions at least twice within a very short period in the history of our country have robbed the people of the fair results of Presidential elections'.[7] Pendleton provided a detailed example from the Treasury department: 'there are 3,400 employees, and . . . of this number the employment of less than 1,600 is authorized by law and appropriations made for their payment, and . . . more than 1,700 are put on or off the rolls of the Department at the will and pleasure of the Secretary of the Treasury, and are paid not out of appropriations made for that purpose but out of various funds and balances of appropriations lapsed in the Treasury . . . which are not by law appropriated to the payment of these employees.' On learning of this system Pendleton remarked, 'I was amazed.'[8]

During its hearings for the reform, the Committee on Civil Service Reform received several testimonies demonstrating how many government departments employed unneeded workers, enjoying the fruits of political patronage but utterly useless to their departments.[9] Underpinning this system were the payments made by clerks: 'a systematic pressure has been brought upon the clerks in the Departments of Government . . . to extort from them a portion of the salary that is paid to them.' All sides conspired in the fiction that this contribution was voluntary: 'the President himself scouts [the contribution] as being voluntary, and [clerks] are led to believe and fairly led to believe that they have bought and paid for the offices which they hold and that the good faith of those who take from them a portion of the salary is pledged to their retention to their positions.' The entire edifice was corrupt and corrupting: 'this whole system demoralizes everybody . . . It demoralizes the clerks who are appointed. That is inevitable. It demoralizes those

TABLE 2.2. *Growth of merit-based civil service in the USA*

Year	No. of positions		%age subject to examination
	subject to examination	in the executive civil service	
1883	13,780	131,208	10.5
1888	29,650	159,356	18.6
1893	45,821	180,000	25.4
1899	94,893	208,000	45.6
1903	154,093	301,000	51.2
1909	222,278	370,000	60.1
1913	292,460	435,000	67.2
1918	592,961	917,760	64.6
1924	415,593	554,986	74.8
1930	462,083	608,915	75.0

Source: Derived from L. D. White, *Trends in Public Administration* (New York: McGraw Hill, 1933), 249.

who make the appointment. That is also inevitable. And it demoralizes Senators and Representatives who by the exercise of their power as Senators and Representatives exert pressure upon the appointing power.'[10]

Pendleton advocated his bill as a necessary and urgent corrective to corruption, based on the 'simple and single idea that the offices of the Government are trusts for the people'.[11] He recorded the deeply partisan principle of appointment then in existence,[12] citing his own observations on arriving in Washington: 'I saw offices distributed to incompetent and unworthy men as a reward for the lowest of dirty partisan work.'[13] Pendleton believed that the spoils system 'must be killed or it will kill the Republic'.[14] Principally enjoyed by the Republican party in the years before Pendleton's speech he was conscious that members of his party, the Democrats, looked forward to exercising similar graft, an ambition of which he was contemptuous: 'I believe that the adoption of this policy as our party creed will hasten the day of the victory of our party and its adoption as a law will under any administration fill many offices with Democrats.'[15]

The Pendleton Act was designed in large part to address and control the tension arising from the competing claims of patronage and meritocratic appointments. It established the US Civil Service Commission to regulate the meritocratic principles and to monitor political influences within the civil service.[16] (Table 2.2 charts the growth of meritocratic placements in ensuing decades.)

The Pendleton Act reforms were imposed upon a highly politicized civil service, intimately linked to presidential politics. This politicization did not evaporate after its enactment. At the core of the US civil service created between the 1880s and 1920s persisted a conflict between the old party-political patronage system and the new meritocracy system. This tension was manifest both in the mechanisms formulated to assure the dominance of meritocratic principles and in the efforts to counter discrimination. Thus the 'rule of three' (discussed below), designed to be a neutral and impartial mechanism for regulating entry, proved an inadequate defence against discrimination by appointing officers (who from 1914 had photographs to consult). This contradiction was not dissolved by a Congress, many of whose members relied upon securing administrative appointments as patronage in their own districts and states, appointments to the postal service being a prime example. Since the Pendleton Act's entry examination requirements were applied at first principally to appointments to lower-level clerical and field positions, important aspects of the patronage system were weakened though not ended. Ultimately, patronage appointments were removed entirely from these lower levels, a change assisted by Theodore Roosevelt's presidency, and consolidated in the political appointments to senior administrative and policy-making offices made by presidents. (Roosevelt was a former commissioner of the US Civil Service Commission and used his tenure to improve the Commission's role in monitoring abuses of the appointment process.)[17] Patronage appointments did grow in the 1930s, in parallel with the expansion of government and under the Roosevelt administration's tutelage, but the passage of the Ramspect Act in 1940 imposed further limits on this process.

The Civil Service Commission 1883–1913

There is amongst historians a consensus that the Commission performed its regulatory tasks competently until 1913.[18] Between Pendleton and the Woodrow Wilson presidency, the Commission succeeded in limiting patronage and in propagating impartial standards of recruitment. Skowronek concludes that the Civil Service Commission enhanced the efficiency of the Federal government in the 1880s and 1890s.[19] With the Pendleton Act just over 10 per cent of civil service positions were placed under the merit system. By March 1885 15,573 positions were classified; under President Cleveland (1885–9) the figure rose to 27,330 by March 1889; and under President Harrison (1889–93) the number reached 42,928 in March 1893.[20] At the beginning of the twentieth century, in the executive civil service over 110,000 positions were still within the patronage sphere.[21] To the chagrin of reformers, Congress retained the power to exempt both 'specific employees or whole classes of employees from merit procedures'.[22] Patronage appointments dominated civil service positions outside Washington—field positions

—where the power of local party leaders had necessarily to be respected by presidents in Washington. The higher echelons of the Federal civil service were also patronage positions. These omissions reflected party-political interests. Therefore, the merit system had the greatest applicability to lower- and middle-ranking clerical and administrative positions in government departments in Washington. In such a context the Civil Service Commission was incapable of constituting 'more than a symbol of a new American state. Party power and patronage politics remained the central preoccupation of governmental elites and preempted the development of a merit *system* for civil administration. The commission took selected officers *out* of politics. It ruled a huge, dormant zone—a neutralized, nonpartisan space in the American party state.'[23]

In its own annual reports the US Civil Service Commission frequently alluded to party-political influences upon appointments: 'partisan feeling and bias often show themselves in the service in the discriminations in favor of the adherents of one party and against those of another, not only in the matter of dismissals, but also in connection with promotions and reductions.' In the same year, 1893, the report noted: 'The most common form of this discrimination in connection with dismissals is to dismiss employees of one political faith for offenses which are allowed to pass unnoticed or with slight reprimand when committed by employees of the opposite political faith. This form has been of more frequent occurrence in the recently classified Post Office than elsewhere.'[24] Indeed, the Pendleton Act did not enable the Commission to end abuse in the preciously important, for patronage, postal service: initially many post offices were exempted from its inspection (only those with fifty or more employees were covered). Congress ardently defended its control of local appointments to the Post Office in the decades after the passage of the 1883 Act.[25]

In 1901 President Theodore Roosevelt gave the Comptroller of the Treasury authority to withhold the salary of any civil servant occupying a merit position but inappropriately appointed; and in 1902 he rigorously defined neutrality for merit-appointed civil servants as prohibiting any political activity while in office and gave the Civil Service Commission responsibility for enforcing this requirement.[26]

These directives undoubtedly strengthened the executive and civil service neutrality at the expense of congressional patronage powers. Certainly for those positions falling within the classified and merit-based system, patronage was weakened. Stephen Skowronek concludes that Theodore Roosevelt's initiatives succeeded in 'driving a wedge between national administration and local politics', and thereby 'altered the position of civil administration and civil administrators within the federal government'.[27] This Progressive thrust was continued by Roosevelt's Republican successor, William Taft. Neither president depoliticized the Federal government, and neither would have welcomed such a diminution in patronage, but they did facilitate professionalization at the middle and lower levels of the service. On the eve of Woodrow Wilson's election, the Civil Service Commission pointed with pride to the growth of classified, merit-based, and competitively filled positions in the Federal service: 'on June 30, 1912, there were approximately 395,460 officers and employees of the executive civil service. Of these, 236,061 held positions subject to competitive examination under the civil-service rules, an increase of 4,648 during the year, and about 6,500 were unclassified laborers subject to tests of physical fitness under the labor regulations.'[28]

The Civil Service Commission repeatedly urged the President and Congress to devise regulations clearly and precisely defining 'political activity', disallowed for unclassified employees. The minutes of the Commission are vitiated with the problem of 'political activity' amongst government employees, with significant numbers removed from the Service. This problem is notably salient in the minutes after 1913. The Commissioners often express their dissent from Executive Orders and decisions taken by the President to appoint candidates or to reappoint individuals dismissed for 'political activity'. The post-1913 dominance of patronage is well conveyed in correspondence from Wilson's secretary Joseph Tumulty and his US Postmaster General Albert Burleson, the former of whom kept a detailed 'black book' of all patronage appointments.[29] In its Thirty-First Annual Report in 1915, the Commission stated that 'the time has now come when uniform and definite restrictions should be placed upon the political activity of unclassified officers and that a civil service rule to this effect should be promulgated'.[30] This was a last gasp, however, unrealized in subsequent decades. This failure was particularly significant for Black Americans.

Black Americans and the Post-Pendleton Commission: From Facilitator to Obstacle

The meritocratic principles influencing the Pendleton Act and imbuing Progressivism augured well for those relatively few Black Americans sufficiently qualified to seek employment in the public service. Indeed, the Commission argued that the introduction and enforcement of competitive merit-based entry advantaged Black Americans. Although Black employees were appointed after the Civil War, by the time of the passage of the Pendleton Act there were only 620 Black civil servants in the Federal government.[31]

The Commission's 1891 report included a section on 'Benefit to the Colored Race', in which the Commission announced, astonishingly, the 'elimination not only of the questions of politics and religion but the question of race' in appointments in Southern States. It continued: 'a fair proportion of the men appointed from these States has been colored', who were 'in many cases graduates of the colleges or higher institutions of learning established for their race'. These graduates were differentiated from the Black Americans dominant in post-Reconstruction politics: 'they rarely belonged to the class of colored politicians which has hitherto been apt to monopolize such appointments as colored men received at all. On the contrary they were for the most part well educated, self-respecting, intelligent young men and women who having graduated from their colored schools and colleges found but few avenues open for the employment of their talents.' The Commission praised the opportunities presented by moving to a meritocratic system of recruitment: 'it is impossible to overestimate the boon to these colored men and women of being given the chance to enter the Government service on their own merits in fair competition with white and colored alike.' Unsurprisingly, patronage had failed Black American graduates: 'it is noticeable that a much larger proportion of colored people receive appointments under the civil service law than under the old patronage system. The civil-service law has been the means of materially enlarging the fields of pursuits open to those members of the colored race who have contrived to get a good education and to fit themselves for the higher walks of life.'[32]

These observations are remarkable in several respects. They give no hint of the segregation and inequality which were to infiltrate and dominate the civil service from 1913, and thereby eradicate the very virtues of competitive entry celebrated by the report's authors. While patronizing in tone, the report makes no suggestion that Black American employees should be assigned to special tasks or segregated physically. On the contrary, invoking the meritocratic principles and ideology shaping civil service reform in most Western democracies and integral to Progressivism, it is clearly envisaged that Black American employees will benefit from these opportunities in the same way as White workers. Furthermore, the evident racist consequences of the spoils systems and party-political appointments is fully appreciated. The statement does include a barbed reference to Black Reconstruction politicians, implicitly assuming categories of suitable Black American recruits and reflecting the general perception, noted in Chapter 1, of their incompetence and corruption. And an item in the Commission's 1894 report about discrimination in the Bureau of Engraving and Printing was a portent of subsequent segregationist practices.[33] But otherwise, the comments give no hint of the role Federal government departments would assume in promoting segregated race relations. It is instructive that the Commission promoted the civil service as a career for Black Americans discriminated against in the private labour-market.

In 1893 the US Civil Service Commission's annual report included an initial inventory of Black employees in the Federal service (numbering 2,393), listed in Table A2.1. The item was accompanied by an optimistic assessment of the number of Black American employees in the civil service, the total salary bill for whom was $1,370,623.98. In contrast to the dominant post-1913 trends, Black employees were not confined to custodial and junior clerical positions.

In a harbinger of later developments a group of Black American women complained to the Commission in 1894 about their treatment in the Bureau of Engraving and Printing within the Treasury,[34] charging that they were removed from office because of their race. The secretary of the Civil Service Commission investigated, singling out the appointment of a new chief of the Bureau as coincident with the dismissals. There was a sudden upsurge in the number of Black women dismissed, none of whom received an explanation for their removal. Fewer Black women were selected from those certified as eligible: 'in the year ended June 30, 1894, 45 women were passed over upon certification without selection, of whom at least 10 are known to be colored. In the period from June 30, 1894 to December 1 1894, 18 women were passed over upon certification without selection, of whom at least 10 are known to be colored.'[35] The Commission contrasted unfavourably the regime of the new chief, Mr Johnson, with that of his predecessor, Mr Meredith, in respect of both appointments and dismissals (the partisan affiliation of neither was reported). The Commission wrote to the Secretary of the Treasury alleging discrimination in the Bureau of Engraving and Printing. Naturally, the Bureau's chief rejected the charge and explained the pattern by reference to the failings of the individuals dismissed; he also charged that the efficiency standard of those appointed and subsequently dismissed was unsatisfactory. Adopting a resigned tone—'there was nothing further that the Commission could do in the matter'—the Commission none the less concluded its annual report with the following acidic remarks about the Bureau: 'it did not believe that the line of cleavage between efficiency and inefficiency could by a mere coincidence so closely follow the color line, not to speak of the passing over of colored women in making selections from the certifications of eligibles.'[36] Commenting on this case, Commissioner Theodore Roosevelt confided to a friend that the Commission could do nothing except publicize 'the facts'.[37]

This incident was an omen of future treatment of Black Americans in the Federal government. The Commission's favourable record was significantly weakened in general during the First World War and in particular for Black Americans. The combination of the Woodrow Wilson presidency and wartime pressures resulted in a commission in the 1920s denuded of its impartiality and lacking autonomy to exercise its policing powers effectively, as Black Americans were later to discover to their cost. At the conclusion of the First World War, Congress resisted applying the merit system widely, reverting to the traditional patronage procedures. Opposition to this and similar reversals was voiced by the National Civil Service Reform League but it received little support in Congress.[38] Party-political interests informed the approach of presidents to the Federal government: as Skowronek shrewdly observes, 'the advantages of a merit system were trapped within boundaries set by party interests'.[39]

Black American activists' fears were stirred over a different aspect of Black employment in the Federal government in May 1914, when the US Civil Service Commission made photographs mandatory on all application forms.[40] Coming just over a year after Woodrow Wilson entered the White House, this requirement—superseded only in 1940 with the requirement that a fingerprint be provided—became a galvanic grievance to Black Americans for several decades, and an obvious instrument of discrimination in the appointment of applicants, since it abrogated the principle of merit.[41] It is not insignificant that its introduction coincided with the return of Democratic power in Washington.

For item 12 of the Commission's meeting of 27 May in 1914, the minute records that as a 'means of identification and preventing impersonation', applicants for civil service examinations would be required to 'furnish to the examiner on the day of the examination photographs of themselves taken within two years'. However, significantly, the same minute noted a second reason for the new measure: photographs were required also for the 'purpose of enabling appointing officers to form some opinion in regard to eligibles certified'.[42] This clause could obviously constitute a basis for abuse, though undoubtedly the problem of impersonation was a real one.

The NAACP complained to President Wilson in 1915 that the Commission had conceded that photographs were used for several purposes: 'in correspondence with our attorney, officers of the United States Civil Service Commission have admitted that these photographs are not to be used solely for purposes of identification to prevent impersonation at examination but, it is acknowledged, they are also to be available to the appointing officer to assist him in making his choice from among the candidates certified by the Commission as successful.'[43] The shift to photographs strengthened Black American groups' criticisms of the Democratic administration and although it is unknown 'whether or not this change was directed solely at Negro applicants for public office',[44] given the political context and the existing concerns about segregation its association to the latter policy can hardly have escaped the Commission. The measure easily complemented the policy of segregation under way in departments such as the Post Office and Treasury. Writing ten years later, the President of Howard University described the damage caused by requiring a photograph from applicants and contrasted it with the Progressive era. Commissioner Theodore Roosevelt had 'insisted that every applicant should have a square deal, and especially that there should be no discrimination on account of race or color'. As a consequence, 'many competent colored men and women entered the Service in those days, and have served the government with satisfaction. But at the present time the applicant is required to submit a photograph, and is left at the mercy of the head of the bureau to which he is certified.' He rejected the need for such a requirement: 'The only practical purpose served is to exclude the applicant whose face shows pigmentation. The option of the head of the bureau to select from several submitted names works to the same end where he has foreknowledge of the race identity of the contestants.'[45]

The same writer engaged in public debate with the President of the Civil Service Commission about the use of photographs.[46] He urged the substitution of photographs with fingerprints. The 1928 survey of segregation in government departments by the NAACP reported that some 'Department Heads frankly admitted that the photograph required by the Civil Service Commission is of value in eliminating Negro eligibles after certification by the Civil Service Commission',[47] powerful evidence of the Federal government's role in segregating by race within the Civil Service; it suggests the discretion provided by the phrase to enable 'appointing officers to form some opinion in regard to eligibles certified' in the 1914 minute adopting photographs.

The percentage of Black employees fell from 6 in 1910 to 4.9 in 1918.[48] Writing in 1958, Van Riper argues that 'the period from 1913 to 1921 deserves to be considered the most critical period in the recent history of Negro federal civil employment. Historically, the Negroes have received their greatest inducement to enter the public service under Republican administrations.'[49] Van Riper's second sentence gives insufficient emphasis to the barriers erected to Black American entry of the Federal government during the first years of the Wilson presidency, and is probably slightly buoyant about the preceding years.[50] These obstacles remained significant throughout the Republican presidencies of the 1920s. The Wilson administration's tolerance and encouragement of segregation in the Federal government was left untouched by the succeeding Republican presidencies.[51]

The photograph requirement was dropped in 1940 (see the section 'Abolishing the Photograph Requirement', below), though the Civil Service Commission continued to defend its use and opposed its deletion. A bill to remove the photograph requirement, introduced in the Seventy-sixth Congress and subsequently integrated into the 1940 Ramspeck Act,[52] was criticized by the Commission. Its president rehearsed the problem of impersonation as the principal grounds for its retention: 'prior to the adoption of this means of identification the Commission was troubled with more or less frequent attempts to perpetrate fraud upon the Government through impersonation.'[53] As a consequence of the requirement, he concluded, impersonation had become 'practically an impossibility'.[54] He then argued that a fingerprint was less feasible and more costly than a photograph, and favoured the latter because of its durability 'throughout the entire process' of application, from taking the examination to appointment.[55] President Mitchell did not, however, address the possible abuses arising from the role of the photograph, a principal concern of the reformers led by Congressman Ramspeck.

In sum, the Pendleton Act and later measures institutionalized the principle of merit appointment, to which process the passage of the Personnel Classification Act in 1923 provided a significant impetus by specifying a set of classes and services in the service, and hierarchical grades within them.[56] Its remit was confined to offices in Washington; field offices were exempted. The Act established the Personnel Classification Board which initially formulated criteria for the designation of all civil service positions, and then designed efficiency ratings by which a civil servant's work could be evaluated (and assessed for promotion).[57] Although the classification system applied to only about two-thirds of civil service positions, its significance for Black American employees was considerable, since its scope affected lower-level and low-grade positions. It was in these latter that Black American employees in the Federal civil service found themselves disproportionately concentrated. Since merit-appointed civil servants rarely rose to the senior, patronage-dominated, administrative positions, the importance of the 1923 Act is self-evident.[58]

None of these institutional arrangements or organizational principles prevented discrimination against Black job-seekers in the making or precluding of appointments,[59] once segregation commenced during the Wilson administration. What this legislation did do was significantly to weaken the patronage principle for appointment to lower- and middle-level positions in the Federal civil service. By the end of the 1920s nearly 80 per cent of Federal employees were hired through merit.[60] Reporting at the end of 1933, the fiftieth anniversary of the Pendleton Act, the Commission boasted that 'fewer than 14,000 positions were made competitive in 1883. Today, more than 450,000 positions, or approximately 80 per cent of all those in the Federal executive civil service, are filled through open competitive examinations. No President since 1883 has failed to extend the scope of the civil service law.'[61]

The Civil Service Commission had also established itself as the principal authority for monitoring employment conditions in the Federal government. Although the Commission ameliorated appointment and promotion practices it paid little regard to the unjust consequences of the system of segregation present throughout the government departments. Extension of the merit system and codification of positions occurred within a framework, which *de facto* assumed segregation of Black employees from White employees. Few of the standard histories of the civil service attend to this fundamental characteristic. The extent of this discrimination became much more public during the 1930s and 1940s under the combined bureaucratic expansion engendered by the New Deal and war mobilization. As noted in Chapter 1, Black Americans were ill-placed to benefit from the New Deal expansion of government. The new Democratic president was unrivalled in assiduity to the needs of local party officials. Consequently, he supported the removal of many civil service positions from merit requirements proposed by Congress. Van Riper summarizes the results: 'by the end of 1934 Congress had exempted from merit system regulations the personnel of almost sixty new agencies, totalling approximately 100,000 offices, and had placed only five agencies under the jurisdiction of the Civil Service Commission.'[62] It is unfortunate that Van Riper did not attempt to consult or use records about Black American employment to establish the dimensions of this trend. A report by the Senate Civil Service Committee, issued in 1957, was caustic about the Roosevelt period, noting that in the 1930s, although 'an expanding Government' provided 'enough jobs to meet a great portion of the demands for patronage', nevertheless, the 'Democratic administration [i.e. Congress] removed several groups of positions that previous administrations had put under the career system. In the years following 1936 major portions of the new staff were blanketed into civil service status, sometimes through non-competitive examinations, sometimes without any examination at all.'[63] Furthermore, by the 1930s the Commission was no longer considered an instrument capable of preventing discrimination in appointments.

THE CIVIL SERVICE COMMISSION AND THE 'RULE OF THREE'

Before Black Americans suffered the discrimination and prejudice common in the post-First World War Federal civil service, they had to join it, a problematic task. Non-discrimination in Federal government employment was notionally maintained through regulations based on the Civil Service Act of 1883 which provided for open competitive examinations, the Classification Act of 1923, and various Executive Orders.[64] In the view of many critics, the rules of appointment were significantly biased against Black Americans seeking to join.

Central to the Commission's hiring system was the 'rule of three'. A hiring officer selected a candidate from a list of three certified eligibles supplied by the Commission; the eligibles had successfully completed competitive examinations. Speaking in 1947, the Commission's President emphasized the anonymity of this system, especially regarding race: 'in certifying these eligibles there is, of course, no means of identifying the eligibles as to their race or religion and the appointing officer, therefore, when he receives a certificate is also unaware of the race or religion of these eligibles.' He continued: 'the appointing officer is required by law to select one of the three highest available eligibles from among those certified to him by the Commission with the sole reference to merit and fitness.' If the appointing officers failed to apppoint one of the three highest available eligibles, and selected a candidate lower on the list of eligibles, he was required to 'furnish the Commission with his objections to the eligibles he wishes to pass over'. These objections were then 'carefully scrutinized by the Commission before approving the appointment, and if the objections do not warrant such action, the appointment of any eligible not one of the three highest available is disapproved'.[65] From the minutes of the US Civil Service Commissioners' meetings, it is evident that, on occasions, these objections were rejected, though often patronage and political influence disabled the Commissioners' preference.[66]

Having being considered, but not appointed, on three occasions a certified candidate no longer remained on the list of three eligibles. In congressional hearings in 1943,[67] the then Commissioner, Arthur Flemming, traced the origin of the 'rule of three' principle to a judgement rendered by the Attorney General in 1871: 'Congress cannot restrict the choice of the head of a department to the point where he would have no choice, but it is not unconstitutional for an examining board to furnish a certain number of names obtained by the test from which the head of a department shall make selection.' This ruling provided the basis for the appointment system: 'that opinion of the Attorney General has come down through the years; has never been challenged and has constituted the legal basis for what in normal times we refer to as the "rule of three".'[68]

This apparently neutral system was vigorously criticized by Black Americans. Principally, they maintained that appointing officers were able too easily to bypass candidates despite their inclusion on the list of three and that such a strategy discriminated against Black American applicants. The NAACP's District of Columbia branch passed a resolution in 1919 deploring the 'gross discrimination' of the Civil Service Commission, manifest in the failure to 'appoint Colored applicants who have passed the Civil Service tests, in some cases having been many times certified by the Civil Service Comission, in others where the applicants have received written notice that they had been accepted or appointed, but have been refused employment on account of race or color'.[69] President Roosevelt's FEPC reached a similar conclusion in 1945: 'the "rule of three" states that the appointing officer shall make selection for the first vacancy from the group of the three highest eligibles willing to accept appointment. For the second vacancy, selection must be made from the group consisting of the two remaining eligibles considered for the first vacancy and the next highest available eligible.' This procedure was to be followed 'in filling additional vacancies until each eligible willing to accept appointment has been considered in connection with three actual appointments'. Crucially, the 'appointing officer need not consider further any eligible whom he has previously considered for three separate vacancies'. The implication of this clause was fundamental: 'this rule permits the rejection of any nonpreference eligible regardless of his earned rating and makes possible the complete exclusion of Negroes from appointments except in those cases where all in the group of three highest eligibles are colored.'[70] An example in the Post Office pursued by the NAACP illustrates the biases of this system. Mr Chauncey Borras attempted to join the Post Office in Florida, as he explains: 'in April 1936 I took the examination for mail carrier at the Pensacola post office. On August 1, I received my rating of 95.8 and was informed that I was number 2 on the register. Several days later friends of mine in the post office told me I was number 1 on the register.' Puzzled at his non-appointment, Borras investigated: 'so I went to see the local Civil Service secretary and he told me that through an error of the Commission an eligible from the clerk register had been placed on the mail carrier register ahead of me but that this error had been soon corrected and my name was really first as it should have been from the beginning.' However, the correction of this 'error' did not result in Borras's appointment. In a letter from the Fifth US Civil Service District at Atlanta, he was informed that 'seven (7) probational and one (1) temporary appointments have been made from the register established at Pensacola, July 31, 1936'. Predictably, 'all of these appointees are white. The Commission also informed me that my name was still number 1 on the register. As to my prospects it appears that as long as the present Postmaster is in office my name will remain number 1 until the register is exhausted.'[71]

The NAACP wrote on Borras's behalf to the Postmaster General of the USA charging 'flagrant discrimination'.[72] The response was unhelpful: 'because the postmaster is held responsible for the proper conduct of the service, the selection of personnel is left to his discretion. The Department has never taken the attitude to direct or influence the postmaster's selections from the eligible register. All appointments, however, must be made in accordance with Civil Service rules and regulations.' Defending the discretion of local appointing offices was a common theme for the Commission. The Postmaster General then marshalled the 'rule of three' mechanism: 'the records of the Department indicate that all of the postmaster's recommendations for appointment were in accordance with Civil Service rules. It might be explained that when an appointment is to be made, the postmaster is permitted, under Civil Service rules, to make his selection from not more than the three highest names certified on the register for each appointment to be made.'[73] This case illustrates how appointing officers could hide behind the 'rule of three' mechanism to defend the systematic non-appointment of Black American candidates. The NAACP's counsel did not let the matter rest. Accusing the Postmaster General of 'cavalierly dismissing' Borras's case, he suggested the universality of the observed bias throughout the United States: 'this is not an isolated case of discrimination against Negro eligibles by southern postmasters. Over the past two years we have been filing with you sufficient cases from other cities to indicate an established policy on the part of southern postmasters to reduce or eliminate Negroes from the service and to make appointments of Negroes only where the same cannot be avoided.'[74] He continued: 'the Department in Washington cannot escape responsibility . . . The Department selects the postmasters; the postmasters are its agents and the thousands of Negro voters hold the Post Office Department responsible. I must confess that the callousness and indifference of your letter dismissing a complaint that eligible Number 1 on the list had been passed over eight times in making appointments were a great shock to me.'[75]

The protest produced little satisfaction from the Post Office Department. The rule of three was again cited and the charge of bias disingenuously dismissed: 'you invite attention to the fact that the eligible who was No. 1 on the register, and who is a colored man, was passed over many times. In this connection it should be explained that it is not uncommon for white men who are applicants and who are within reach for selection to be passed over and others with lower ratings selected.'[76] Evidence of the latter problem does not feature, however, in the FEPC hearings or reports and none was offered by the Commission.

Other cases of discrimination appear frequently in the archival records. The FEPC entered into lengthy correspondence with the Department of Labor about the repeated failure of its Chicago office to appoint a Mr George Nesbitt to a position—despite his listing as 'candidate #1 on a certificate of names issued by the Civil Service Commission'—without rectification.[77] In Washington, a Mr James Cunningham sought the NAACP's assistance in securing appointment as a customs inspector. Having successfully completed the Civil Service examination for the position, Cunningham watched helplessly as a series of White men were appointed to the position over him.[78] The NAACP enlisted the support of Senator William Calder, whose influence succeeded eventually in getting Cunningham his desired position.

The US Civil Service Commission remained the sole organization responsible for monitoring recruitment under the rule of three. Ominously, it opposed a measure, considered for inclusion in the 1940 Ramspeck Act, to reform the system by requiring the appointing officer to select the candidate at the top of the list of eligibles rather than choosing from the top three.[79] The Commission was questioned about this rule and its abuse by the House Civil Service Committee in 1943. A Democratic Congressman from New York asked the Commissioner, Arthur Flemming, whether there had been 'any cases in which the Commission has told an appointing officer that his reasons for not taking any man on that list were not sufficient, and he had to take them'.[80] Upon Flemming's reply that 'I am very sure that in a good many instances that has happened', the Congressman observed:

> I am very much concerned with the practice of certain departments in discriminating between certain employees for many reasons: religion, race or even political opinion, and I do not know, frankly, what the solution of that problem is, whether

you can get to it, whether the Civil Service Commission can determine whether the reason was sufficient. In no case would the appointing officer give his exact reasons for not appointing them.

FLEMMING: That is correct, sir. An appointing officer might advance a reason that was not his real reason, and of course it is the job of the Civil Service Commission to try to get down underneath the situation and determine what is the real reason.

KLEIN: You know of the existence of that problem, of course?

FLEMMING: Yes, sir. And what we have to do is to determine what the situation really is.[81]

Flemming's responses give a dispiriting account of the Commission's capacity to excise injustice in the appointment process.

The Commission itself was not immune to charges of discrimination, as the experience of Henry Alston demonstrates. Attempting to join the Civil Service in Fort Worth, Texas, he was informed 'both by the girl and the man in charge that the only blanks available to me were for laborer at the quartermaster's depot', not the advertised skilled trades. He noted: 'I have passed civil service examinations as senior clerk, junior clerk and housing manager supervisor but can't even get to first base. In college I majored in Mathematics and since graduation I have followed teaching and mechanics but am denied a chance to try for the assembly lines because I dared to be black.'[82] Alston fell foul of the 'rule of three' appointment principle, as did many other Black applicants.[83] The Commission wrote to him in January 1941, in a letter of Kafkaesque logic:

Your name appeared on the Hospital Attendant register established for Fort Worth, Texas under date of March 24, 1939, rating 80.80 preference. The records show that your name was three times considered but not selected by the Medical officer in Charge, U.S. Public Health Service Hospital, Fort Worth, Texas. Under the regulations, Appointing Officers are not required to indicate reasons for passing over the name of an eligible in the exercise of the choice of selection permitted under the rules, that is, from among the three highest eligibles certified and our files, therefore, are without information as to reasons for your failure of selection. An eligible brought within reach of consideration in connection with three vacancies actually filled need not be further considered for appointment except at the option of the Appointing Officer. In this connection, your attention is invited to Paragraph 6 of Form 2424, copy enclosed. Your eligibility on the register referred to expired with the establishment of a new register of eligibles for Hospital Attendant-Guard at Fort Worth under date of December 23, 1940. Your name appears No. 25 on this register, from which no selections have been made.[84]

That Black applicants certified as eligibles were concentrated disproportionately on civil service registers prior to the establishment of new registers was a further strategy, in the view of the NAACP, to discriminate against them. In a statement prepared in 1940, the NAACP called for an investigation of this practice since 'it is known that a number of Negro stenographers with ratings in the upper 80's and lower 90's are still being certified to agencies on current registers now reduced so low that a new examination has been announced in order to create a new register'. Consequently, these 'Negro stenographers with high ratings' failed to secure 'appointments although the register from which they are being certified is in an unusually active status because of the increased Federal activities incident to the defense program'. The NAACP explained why this instance assumed significance: 'the certification processes make eligibles available to requisitioning officers in groups of not less than three; therefore, if Negro eligibles are not selected, at some point approaching the withdrawal of a given register, these eligibles must tend to attain a position which would effect their concentration in these certificate groups.' On the creation of a new register, 'it is possible that the displaced register carries a disproportionately high number of Negro eligibles'.[85]

Discrimination could occur through abuse of either the power of selection or the power of appointment. The former rested primarily with the Civil Service Commission; but 'this is not exclusively the fact since the final selection from among two or three persons rests with the appointing officer', whom the Commission was extremely reluctant to reprimand.[86] The wartime and post-war procedures differed: 'under wartime regulations . . . the power of selection and the power of appointment are apt to be vested in the same person. Under peacetime conditions and with fully competitive Civil Service, there is still room for discrimination by the appointing officer.'[87]

The organizations successively established from 1941 in the executive to monitor discrimination in employment were each concerned in turn with the weakness of the US Civil Service Commission and with the operation of the rule of three. At a meeting in January 1942 of the President's FEPC, there was a long discussion about removing certain classifications such as stenographers, clerks, and typists from the system of the rule of three. One Committee member, Earl Dickerson, 'was of the opinion that the Committee should not admit the soundness of the "rule of three" with respect to any classification'. This proposal was rejected. The Committee resolved to send a letter to the Civil Service Commission to 'recommend that the Civil Service Commission act as a placement pool for all classification'.[88] An FEPC analysis of the hiring practices of Federal agencies showed that the power of the appointing officers was enhanced by wartime conditions: 'the discretion permitted appointing officers is greater than ever, making it extremely difficult to detect discriminatory actions. The President's Committee has had to rely, then, on the vigorous prosecution of proved cases of discrimination and the sincerity and determination of department heads in seeing that the Order is carried out.'[89] One FEPC member considered this criterion deeply problematic, entrenching the barriers faced by Black Americans such as Henry Alston. Complaints of discrimination were numerous as the cases from the FEPC's regional offices reveal. The complaints were overwhelmingly from

Black Americans. However, because of wartime pressures, proving discrimination was 'well-nigh impossible . . . On one plausible pretext or another, the Negro eligible is passed over in favor of a "more qualified" applicant. When an eligible is passed over once, that proves nothing. But when an eligible is passed over ten, fifteen or even twenty times, discrimination becomes perfectly apparent, although it remains impossible to pin it on any one of the ten, fifteen or twenty establishments involved.' In New York, the FEPC's enquiries resulted in a dispiriting 'chain-letter-writing process [in which we] learn little and waste vast amounts of our and other officials' time'.[90]

The FEB, established in 1948, shared the FEPC's concern about the rule of three. At their meeting in May 1951, a long discussion was held about the best means of exposing the discriminatory consequences of the system. One suggestion was to require a written explanation for why a candidate had been passed over three times. Other changes were suggested to establish, in particular, that 'agencies are refusing to appoint eligibles because of three prior considerations even though there is such a shortage of qualified applicants for the particular job that specialized recruitment has been undertaken'.[91] The Board was both tentative about addressing the problem and apprehensive about winning support. In a memorandum circulated to all government departments in 1949, the Board reported its results of a charge of discrimination against an agency's hiring practices from the list of eligibles supplied by the Civil Service Commission. In this case, all White eligibles had been hired compared with only 40 per cent of Black eligibles. From its investigations, the Board judged the system largely successful: 'in all cases the requirement of the Civil Service Regulations that each eligible must be considered for three separate vacancies was met.' Examining the applicants' records carefully, the Board 'found that substantial reasons for non-selection were present in certain cases, and at least plausible reasons for all others with one exception'.[92] In this single exception a Black eligible 'was passed over on a third consideration and a white eligible lower on the register was appointed'. The Board observed that 'the record of experience of the eligible appointed in his stead was not superior to that of the appellant and the appellant had substantially more education. Furthermore, the appointing officer selected six other eligibles lower on the certificate, one with a rating of but 70.6 with 10-point preference, all six of whom were white.' It ended: 'the record showed no adequate justification for non-selection on the basis of merit and fitness.'[93] Significantly, the Fair Employment Board lacked the powers necessary to enforce this finding.

Abolishing the Photograph Requirement

The NAACP, together with other groups, lobbied vigorously for the abolition of photographs on civil service application forms, and for their replacement with fingerprints. After considerable lobbying, this measure was adopted in 1940. Senator James Mead led the campaign against photographs. He received a letter from the US Civil Service Commission in November 1940 in which the Commission's President reported its decision: 'photographs have been required by the Commission solely for the purposes of preventing impersonation and fraud in examinations, and the Commission is convinced that such impersonations and frauds can best be detected by the use of fingerprints . . . The Commission will take steps immediately to abolish the use of photographs in connection with civil service examinations.'[94] Photographs were replaced with fingerprints and all references to race were eliminated from the application forms.[95]

Although the Ramspeck Act of 1940 extended merit positions within the civil service, it did little to assist the position or promotion prospects of Black employees. The Roosevelt administration offered few incentives for such modification. Van Riper addresses this omission rather blandly: 'a completely competitive and nonpolitical federal or state civil service in which a Negro might reach a place of power and prominence could not be considered . . . [T]he Negro and states' rights must be considered as basic to [the Act].'[96] His analysis reveals again the Federal government's unwillingness to disturb the system of segregated race relations. The Chairman of the Senate Appropriations Committee, Senator Kenneth McKellar of Tennessee, was a supporter of non-merit appointment criteria.

Addressing Truman's Committee on Civil Rights in 1947, the President of the Civil Service Commission noted that application forms included no reference to race or religion, examinations were sat under a number, not the candidate's name, and appointing officers purportedly had no information regarding race when selecting successful candidates.[97] President Mitchell's assurances about the absence of discrimination in the civil service were bland, based on a mechanical recitation of rules and regulations under which appointments were made. He was certain that 'sufficient policy and procedural safeguards regarding nondiscrimination are in effect . . . for regular civil service appointments made from the Commission's registers.'[98] As Chapter 3 documents, discrimination within the Civil Service Commission itself was not uncommon.

While the US Civil Service Commission never conceded the problem of discrimination in appointment to Federal departments, those employed at lower levels sometimes did. In 1942 Charles Rossell of the Civil Service Department in New York acknowledged to an NAACP official that there was a problem: 'although out of approximately 13,000 persons who have been hired during the last year, about 3,000 of them are Negroes, there are civil service offices that discriminate against Negroes and there are some who even refuse to hire individuals.'[99] Rossell was himself criticized by the FEPC for failing to improve his own standards, reinforcing the Civil Service

Commission's uniformity with the remainder of the Federal government. In a submission to the FEPC, the NAACP observed: 'when it comes to hiring its own employees, the Civil Service Commission is on all-fours with the agencies most loudly complained against.' According to the NAACP, Rossell 'had a couple of Negroes working as Junior Examiners or in some such minor professional capacity . . . and a sprinkling of Negro girls working as clerks, stenographers typists etc. Out of almost 100 recruiting officers, not one was a Negro.' The reason for this oversight was not cogent: 'Mr Rossell stoutly insisted that it would be entirely impracticable to put on any Negro recruiting officers and when I pressed him on this he shifted ground and insisted that not a Negro could be found in all New York who possessed the necessary qualifications. This is the kind of talk one is accustomed to hear from discriminatory employers, rather than from an administrator of the Federal Government's merit system.' The pattern was institutionalized in New York, however: 'Civil service has a huge force of investigators . . . not one of these is Negro. This pretty plainly shows that the Civil Service Commission's house is not in order in this respect.'[100] Also in 1942, the FEPC received criticisms from the Urban League in Kansas City (Missouri) about the failure of the Commission and other Federal agencies to hire Black workers. The FEPC's field representative was informed that 'Federal agencies are still in the forefront of discriminatory employment based on race and color, rather than merit; [and] that the employment practices of the Government handicap the efforts to improve the situation in private industry'.[101] The report attached detailed complaints from Blacks denied employment in the Department of Agriculture and OPA: in the former case, a Black woman applying for an advertised vacancy as junior clerk-typist learned on appearing for interview that an accountant was required![102] Black Americans were also denied places on training programmes.

THE CIVIL SERVICE COMMISSION AND ITS CRITICS

The Civil Service Commission was frequently criticized by organizations acting in behalf of Black Americans. Many of these critics made submissions to the FEPC and appeared before President Truman's Committee on Civil Rights.

The NAACP became a staunch critic of the Commission. This organization had consistently called for compliance mechanisms to complement Roosevelt's 1941 executive order against discrimination in hiring. In response to Roosevelt's letter to the heads of agencies in 1941 prohibiting discrimination, the NAACP requested 'the setting up of specific machinery in the Civil Service Commission to implement your request of all departments and agencies of the Federal government to abandon forthwith any discrimination on account of race, creed, color or national origin'. In particular, it sought 'placement of a qualified Negro either as a member of the Civil Service Commission or with sufficient authority to devise procedures and to carry out such procedures which would insure as speedy abolition as is humanly possible of such discrimination'.[103] In common with the FEPC, advocates of equality of opportunity wanted compliance procedures to be in place. These requests fell on deaf ears.

In a letter to President Truman, NAACP Secretary Walter White expressed his organization's concern about 'instances of discrimination against colored persons seeking employment or transfers in government agencies'. By this time, confidence in the Civil Service Commission was low: 'we have carefully considered the possibility of preventive action by the Civil Service Commission and have reached the conclusion that it will not be effective in checking discriminatory hiring practices on the part of personnel officers and other government officials.'[104] An instance of White's concerns was supplied some years earlier in an affidavit by Luella Thompson. Summoned to a meeting about a vacancy by the District Manager of Tennessee, Thompson reports: 'I was received very graciously, but was informed that there was no place in the set-up for colored workers, and [he] was quite surprised when he found that I was colored.'[105] The affidavit was included in a letter to the BES in Washington disputing that bureau director's claim that qualified Black Americans were unavailable to work in the Black section of the Tennessee employment service.

The NAACP asked President Truman to create an agency to investigate 'complaints of discrimination and take effective steps to remedy such discrimination when it is found'.[106] The body would operate until Congress established a permanent FEPC. This request was subverted by the Executive Secretary of Committee on Civil Rights, Robert Carr. Carr considered White's request unlikely to succeed on the grounds that 'it is quite clear that the Committee's final report will cover the problem which is concerning Mr White'.[107] In fact, the problem persisted, and Congress failed to establish a permanent FEPC.

A delegation of Black workers and White workers in the District of Columbia complained to the US Civil Service Commission in 1940 both about the lack of equal treatment of Black Americans in the Federal government and about the failure to refer Black job-seekers to defence-industry employment. On both counts, Black Americans were in a parlous position. Apart from a 'small fraction' of employees, 'all negro workers under the Civil Service in federal agencies located in the District are in the category of custodial workers—and they remain in this category even though they qualify for promotion in rank'. Those Black Americans seeking higher positions were ignored: 'at the same time Negro clerical and professional workers on the Civil Service list remain unplaced, and some 3,000 Negro clerical and professional workers in the active files of the D.C. Employment Center remain without jobs.' Resentment was based upon blatantly racist practices: 'in requesting applicants for 300 Civil Service jobs as coders and classifiers in connection with the National Defense program, the D.C. Employment Center recently made its appeal to "white qualified workers".'[108]

Criticisms of the US Civil Service Commission's regulation of discrimination did not diminish in the post-war years. In 1951 the FEB (located in the Commission) wrote to the BES seeking clarification about the complaint that 'Federal agencies in the City of Baltimore have submitted job orders to the Maryland state office of the USES which are in effect discriminatory, inasmuch as they specify the race of the applicants to be referred'.[109] This was not an isolated incident.

The National Committee on Segregation in the Nation's Capital, a lobby group, was reluctant for the Civil Service Commission to assume responsibility for non-discrimination in Federal employment. The Committee held a dim view of the Commission: 'I've talked to several people at the Commission. It is inconceivable to me that, if that outfit were given a general directive to do something substantial about nondiscrimination and left to its own devices, it would come up with any effective controls.'[110] The same speaker argued that no one at the Commission appreciated the scale of discrimination. The Commission adamantly maintained that discrimination was exaggerated: most of the Commission staff 'argue that about all that ought to be done or can be done is to provide the sort of formal procedures for appeals which they now have for veterans. In my opinion, formal appeal procedures above the agency level are about on a par with anti-lynching legislation: they prevent only the crudest and most obvious forms of oppression.'[111] In common with the NAACP, Bradbury urged the creation of an agency with sole responsibility for investigating complaints of discrimination within government employment. Bradbury concluded that it 'would be tragic if the President's Committee didn't recommend some kind of independent set-up to deal with discrimination in government employment'.[112] President Truman's Committee on Civil Rights established a subcommittee[113] on fair employment practices. It recommended establishing a permanent commission to monitor employment practices not only in the private sector but also in Federal agencies. The subcommittee advocated the creation 'within the Civil Service Commission and the personnel departments of the various agencies, on-the-job training programs and such machinery as is necessary for hearing and acting on discriminatory practices in hiring, promoting and transferring of federal employees'.[114] It was many years before such mechanisms were formalized.

Malcolm Ross, who headed the wartime FEPC, doubted the Civil Service Commission's capacity to implement non-discrimination.[115] He argued that in the absence of a government agency with enforcement powers it was virtually impossible to get either trade-unionists or employers to accept Black workers: 'with the Government out of the picture you only have two sides of that triangle, and unless there is an extraordinary interest of either the union or the employer the thing won't work out.' Without government support, no improvement could be expected: 'the recalcitrant, if allowed to remain recalcitrant, with nobody finally slapping him down, can ruin the whole underpinnings of quiet, persuasive work. Certainly we have had enough administrative experience in this country to know that.'[116] Representing public-sector workers affiliated with the CIO, Thomas Richardson[117] began his testimony to the Committee on Civil Rights with a searing condemnation of the Civil Service Commission: 'job discrimination by Government against minority groups, particularly Negroes, has reached serious and alarming levels. The subtlety with which this discrimination is being practiced does not reduce in the least its widespread effectiveness and makes it all the more sinister.' He belittled the Commission's role in preventing such discrimination: 'the inclinations of the Civil Service Commission . . . to deny the existence of racial discrimination permits those prejudiced persons who conduct such practices to work with additional freedom . . . Bitterness and disillusionment on the part of Negroes concerning Government's protestations that every citizen has a right to a Government job according to his ability is growing.'[118] These complaints applied to both Southern and Northern states.

Richardson argued that the right of Black Americans to government employment before the war was academic: it was difficult to join and promotion was rare. The recruitment hurdle was bolstered by the Civil Service Commission, whose 'regulations and procedures were so constructed as to make it possible for prejudiced hiring officers to give full vent to their desire to keep Negroes out of Government jobs'.[119] He alluded to the 'rule of three'. In 1938, of Black Americans working in government, only 10 per cent were not in custodial positions: 'the well-known fact that large numbers of Negro college graduates had taken and passed Civil Service examinations or clerical and professional jobs in the '30's and the significant number of Negroes with college training in the custodial force indicates that it was not a lack of qualifications which kept these people in jobs below their abilities.'[120] Black workers easily discharged clerical and professional positions in government during the war. This implied that their failure to win appointment in 'the Government service before on such a scale was the unprincipled and prejudiced discrimination against them as a minority group'.[121] According to Richardson, many of the temporary War Agencies adopted liberal recruitment policies compared with the permanent Commission, a view shared by other observers. This approach facilitated an expansion of Black employment. The termination of these agencies harmed Black Americans' opportunity to gain government employment: 'when the Negro clerical or professional worker, laid off from a War Agency, attempted to secure employment in an old-line Agency, he began to run into the subtle but effective Negro discrimination which had been a characteristic of Government hiring during the war.'[122] Richardson reported that his union, the United Public Workers, had raised numerous instances of discrimination in post-war government-hiring in the North and South but to no avail: 'instead, we have seen on the part of the Civil Service Commission and various Government officials a concerted effort to excuse the actions of prejudiced hiring personnel and a general unwillingness to apply firmly the President's policy against discrimination.'[123] If discrimination against Black Americans was this entrenched, then the effort to end segregation and establish equality of treatment and opportunity would have to be a powerful one based in national agencies holding enforcement powers and sanctions. Federal government departments were evidently upholding segregated race relations and the associated inequalities of treatment instead of eradicating them.

Richardson provided 'conclusive' evidence of discrimination in ten government agencies after 1945, including the Wage Stabilization Board and the Bureau of Internal Revenue. He recounted one incident—'an illegal and most shameful expression of racial prejudice'—from the Bureau of Internal Revenue: 'over 50 white employees engaged in a work stoppage because a Negro was placed in their section. The Agency has so far failed to create the kind of atmosphere which would eliminate this sort of friction. By atmosphere, I mean the complete abolition of segregated sections, segregated payrolls, and segregated lunchrooms.' The Bureau ignored presidential directives: 'the Agency has demonstrated no insistence whatsoever that President Truman's policy on this question must be observed by *all* government workers.'[124] There was a disproportionately high number of Black workers in the Bronx division of the Internal Revenue, reflecting, according to Richardson, the unpopularity of this location. Post-war hiring of Black workers in the Bronx office was often limited to six-month contracts, at the end of which period they were fired instead of promoted to the next grade for which they were eligible. Richardson cited other instances of discrimination in the Interior, Agriculture, and Labor departments and the Federal Trade Commission.

The Department of Labor included one of the most striking aspects of segregation in the United States: the maintenance of segregated facilities in the USES, the agency charged with helping job-seekers to find work (and the subject of Chapter 6). Through the USES the Federal government upheld a segregated labour-market. Segregated USES offices in the District of Columbia assumed added significance in 1945,[125] since it 'helped to restrict Negro opportunity during the period when a number of old-line Agencies were bringing staff up to normal strength after having been restricted by wartime manpower shortage'.[126] Accusations of discrimination against Black Americans attempting to obtain employment in the USES itself were common. A letter in May 1937 to the USES's Adviser on Negro Affairs from a man in

Birmingham, Alabama, is representative. Of several 'young Negro men of this city' sitting the examinations for interviewers in the National Re-employment Department, 'three of us have survived through the final examination and are now on the eligible list for employment as Junior Interviewers'. However, inclusion on the eligible list did not result in appointment: 'we wonder why we have not been able to secure any employment here as there are no Negro interviewers to work with our group which constitutes 40 per cent of the population.'[127] Segregated facilities did not extend to staff in USES offices, since White employees commonly worked in the sections for Black American job-seekers. During the Second World War the USES was taken out of the control of the states and placed under the War Manpower Commission. The NAACP, amongst others, opposed returning the USES to the states, arguing that its local offices practised discrimination, failing consistently to place Black job-seekers in skilled positions regardless of their qualifications.[128] Such protests failed, as the Southern Democrats in Congress were determined to defederalize the USES, and succeeded.

In sum, the US Civil Service Commission operated a recruitment mechanism, the rule of three, which resulted in discrimination. It bolstered instead of deflected segregated race relations in the Federal government. Segregation persisted because of its compatibility with Jim Crow laws and attitudes in American society, practices which were supported by well-placed members of Congress. Reform initiatives were all conceived of in terms of segregation. Even within the allegedly 'separate but equal' framework, the opportunities for Black Americans were limited: appointment to positions other than the custodial and clerical levels were rare, and promotion was improbable because of hostility to Black employees supervising Whites in any capacity. Such practices were embedded in the Commission's structures and rules of appointment.

The Commission, of course, attempted to address some of the criticisms, notably abolishing the photograph requirement for applicants and formulating procedures for those employees charging discrimination.[129] Rule 1, section 2 of the 1883 Pendleton Act forbade discrimination on grounds of politics or religion, as the Commission regularly observed, though the use of photographs from 1914 undermined this regulation; with this requirement, 'it soon came to pass that Negroes were seldom called for an interview for the higher clerical positions, since an appointing officer with a choice of three persons open to him usually overlooked the Negro's papers certified by the Commission'.[130] The 1883 Rule was amended in 1940 to include discrimination on grounds of race also. The Ramspeck Act (1940) explicitly forbade discrimination in the classified services on grounds of race, creed, or colour in respect of: 'the fixing of compensation schedules; allocations of positions to grades and the fixing of rates of compensation by department heads, including review and revision; increase in compensation; efficiency ratings; transfer or promotion of employees; ascertainment of facts as to duties and responsibilities of positions; review of allocations, changes of allocations affecting pay or incumbency; and restoration of wage rates and adjustment of such'.[131] In November 1943 the Commission reached an agreement with the FEPC about monitoring discrimination, agreeing 'formally that the Commission will submit to FEPC copies of all complaints which allege such discrimination. Reports of action taken in these cases by the Civil Service Commission also are submitted to the Committee. If a report is not satisfactory to the Committee's Regional Director, the case is docketed in the regional office, with the Civil Service Commission given as a source of the complaint, and thereafter is processed according to regular FEPC procedure.'[132] A year later the FEPC established that the Commission had the power to remove eligibles appointed after 100 days in those cases where discrimination was demonstrated.[133]

The relationship between the FEPC and the Commission was never a smooth one, however. The former wanted the Commission strenuously to enforce non-discrimination practices, and thereby to supplement the Committee's work. The Commission, unremarkably, was reluctant to play such a role, and 'loath to invade the autonomy of personnel officers in the several agencies at a time when best practice and war necessity indicated that personnel administration in Government agencies should be released from centralized restrictions'.[134] The Commission was also very cautious about how far its jurisdiction extended in the assessment of discrimination, especially regarding work conditions or assignments where administrative discretion was judged superior. The FEPC, of course, did have jurisdiction in these matters, but even its members often found it more difficult to tackle discrimination in government than in the private sector (see Chapter 3).

CONGRESSIONAL OVERSIGHT

The interest registered above of Congressman Klein in the workings of the Civil Service Commission was unusual for a member of Congress. Throughout the period 1913–65 the civil service ranked low amongst congressional members' interests. According to a study in the mid-1950s, in both Houses, membership of the civil service committee was the second least sought-after slot.[135] As a consequence two patterns occurred: first, most members served briefly on the civil service committees using their seniority speedily to join more prestigious ones; and second, those members who remained acquired seniority quickly. The former trend had obvious implications for the capacity of the committees to exercise consistent and well-informed oversight of the civil service and of the Civil Service Commission.

The incentive for long-serving committee members to delve deeply was delimited by their commitment to patronage, as Harris observed in 1964: 'in the past both committees have included among their members many patronage-minded congressmen who were unsympathetic to the merit system.'[136] These propensities were reinforced in the decades before 1964 by the committees' dual responsibility for the postal service. Long-serving members were more commonly from rural constituencies in the South and Midwest in whose jurisdictions postal service employees were the main Federal category. Few members representing metropolitan districts in which Federal civil service positions were concentrated served on the committees in either chamber.

These trends resulted in civil service committees little interested in improving the standards of the service but rather keenly committed to maintaining the *status quo* and to controlling Federal government employees' behaviour. This was not uniformly the case—with Robert Ramspeck's incumbency of the chair of the House civil service a conspicuous exception—but it was not uncommon. Furthermore, the House and Senate committees had limited responsibility for personnel policy in the civil service since it was enacted in individual departments or investigated by other committees. Significantly, officers in the executive exercised greater control over personnel administration than did the two civil service committees.

These patterns did not, however, diminish the legislation regulating personnel policy, a trend criticized by the Civil Service Commission whose members favoured administrative rules and regulations.[137] In 1956 the House civil service committee issued a special report about the Civil Service Commission, stressing its independence of the executive, but also its need fully to inform and co-operate with the congressional committees.[138] Efforts to legislate to appoint civil service commissioners for fixed terms, rather than at the pleasure of the president, were pursued. Attempts to enact this reform continued fitfully until 1960 but were abortive.

THE POST-WAR LEGACY OF UNEQUAL ACCESS

After the Second World War, discriminatory and segregated hiring patterns reappeared in the public sector. Roosevelt's FEPC was maintained initially during the post-war transition period but then, against its wishes and those of President Truman, terminated by Congress. Appearing before Truman's investigative Committee on Civil Rights, former FEPC chairman Malcolm Ross discussed how his Committee's data revealed, as many had predicted, that 'Negroes after the war, in the change-over period, lost their skilled and semi-skilled jobs and the wages that went with them vastly more in proportion than the white workers did . . . They were in skilled positions and doing perfectly acceptable work, but they had to step down afterward for no other reason than their race.'[139] The fact that Black Americans were concentrated in temporary positions eased their dismissal after 1946.[140] One analyst in the War Manpower Commission accurately anticipated the resurgence of discrimination: 'the return to civilian life of many soldiers identified with racial and other minorities is going to create a problem of some magnitude.' Such veterans restored segregation and prejudice: 'to assume that these men will be able to take their rightful places in employment, under the pattern which may exist generally at the moment, is the height of wishful thinking. Prejudices are just as old as the people and the land. The unusual times will have passed, and we may expect some return or attempt to return to time-worn customs and traditions in employment practices.'[141]

The NUL submitted a programme for action to Truman's Committee on Civil Rights. It discussed housing and education discrimination in addition to employment. The paper cited many cases of discrimination by labour unions. Its authors observed that 'through constitutional or ritualistic provision or by tacit consent of the union membership, Negroes are often excluded from training and employment opportunities which are easily available to other workers'.[142] In its study, the NUL identified a number of agencies which had 'indicated that they would have clerical positions for white workers but not for Negroes'. These were: the Bureau of Statistics of the Department of Labor; the General Accounting Office; the Bureau of Standards of the Department of Commerce; the Patent Office; the Federal Security Agency; the Public Health Service; the Bureau of Internal Revenue in the Treasury Department; the Public Buildings Department of the Federal Works Agency; and the International Bank.[143] The employment opportunities of many Blacks were systematically limited, even when they qualified through the US Civil Service Commission procedures.

In an independent study of Federal government employment, commissioned for President Truman's Committee on Civil Rights, Stewart and Murtha reported that while discrimination was 'expressly prohibited . . . it does exist'.[144] The two writers concluded, bleakly, that Black employees in government 'face the loss of gains which they made during the war years'. Departments of the Federal government which were willing to accept Black employees temporarily would seize the first opportunity to sack them: 'agencies which had never employed Negroes were forced by 1943 to accept them because of the manpower shortage. More progressive agencies employed them in high administrative positions. The available Negro manpower was in many respects superior to the available white, indicating the extent to which discrimination had operated in the past.'[145] The authors recommended strengthening the Civil Service Commission's role in excising discrimination, a recommendation ignored for two more decades. The Commission's attention to recruitment issues was limited.[146] Chapter 3 explains how confining

Black Americans recruited during wartime to temporary positions was a deliberate strategy.

Two years after the abolition of the FEPC, the FEB was created (in 1948) in the Civil Service Commission to monitor discrimination and hiring practices in the Federal government. In 1955 the FEB was terminated and replaced with a new President's Committee on Government Employment Policy which existed until 1961. Both organizations continued to find poor employment prospects for Black Americans in the Federal government, particularly at middle and senior levels. The President's Committee conducted surveys in 1956 and 1960 confirming these dismal trends.

At the start of the Kennedy presidency, the President's Committee on Government Employment Policy was invited by the US Civil Service Commission to review the position of Black American employees in government. Its executive secretary was sanguine. Alluding to the Committee's surveys, he concluded that the 'picture . . . is one of momentum—of more Negroes moving into the service and of more moving up into higher grades. In short, the past five years have not been just a matter of Negroes holding the gains they made in the 1940s; on the contrary, they have continued to make new gains.'[147] This view differed markedly from earlier trends. The report's author was not insensitive to continuing complaints from Black Americans, and acknowledged the continuing barriers to Black Americans' employment. He characterized the Committee's approach as 'much more that of persuasion and education rather than that of a police force interested in compliance'. He recognized the limits of this approach in the eyes of some critics: 'and it is precisely with this that our critics now take issue. In the future they want the emphasis on compliance.'[148] The same views had faced the FEPC and the FEB. The implications of such criticisms were not trivial: 'there are some areas in which the emphasis can be put on compliance—as in the adjudication of complaints when the Committee is convinced discrimination has been a factor . . . But this is not what our critics are really interested in. They are talking about compliance in the absence of complaints, and this is where the problem becomes extremely difficult.'[149] This approach of 'persuasion and education' rather than issuing enforceable directives typified the Federal government's engagement with discrimination from 1941 until the mid-1960s. I return to it in Chapter 7.

CONCLUSION: 'THE PAST IS THE PAST'

The legacy of Black Americans' biased treatment under civil service rules was considerable. The New Orleans branch of the NAACP complained in 1961 that Black American candidates for the civil service continued to confront bias against their appointment. It cited the 'evasive and discriminatory methods used by appointing officers in this area in the past to by-pass or exclude Negro eligibles' as the main reason 'why Negroes at all levels are not as interested as they might be in federal employment'. For a Black American gaining certification, the 'chances of being appointed is either limited or non-existent'.[150] Examples cited included the Customs Service, the US Engineers, the VA Hospital, the Internal Revenue Service, and the Social Security Administration—in each case the New Orleans branches had few Black appointees, most were recently hired, and almost all were in menial positions. The Post Office Department's record was the most disgraceful, according to the correspondent. Before 1942 'at no time in the history of the New Orleans Post Office were there more than 38 Negro post office clerks and substitutes, while there were many Negro letter carriers'. The rule of three prevented Black American employment: 'for at least 13 years, all high-ranking Negro eligibles were arbitrarily bypassed. A presentation of facts and figures to the Post Office Department in Washington DC in August 1941 resulted in an investigation which subsequently opened the door of opportunity for Negroes to become clerks.' Since the rule operated systematically and intentionally, the characterization 'arbitrarily' is misplaced. Continuing complaints led to another Senate subcommittee investigation in 1948: 'the report revealed flagrant violations of the appointment procedures which were detrimental to the interests of Negro eligibles.' The complaints extended to promotion also: 'no Negro had ever been promoted to a supervisory position here until 1952 after a complaint had been filed with the Fair Employment Practices Committee of the US Civil Service.'[151]

The legacy of these biases in recruitment was that few qualified Black Americans considered joining the US Civil Service, or indeed were able to join. One regional director of the Commission bemoaned the absence of Black candidates for executive positions. Writing to the NAACP in New Orleans, the director observed: 'from over 10,000 competitors in our Federal Service Entrance Examination in this Region last year we obtained only sixteen Negro eligibles who indicated interest in Federal employment in the Eighth Civil Service Region.'[152] He particularly sought graduates of Black American colleges. However, since 'this Region' had been consistently hostile to Black job-seekers, the Director might have proposed an obvious explanation for the observed pattern. He noted that of the 10,000 competitors, 3,185 were listed as eligibles of whom 604 were hired; of the 16 Black candidates 6 were hired. This director plainly wanted a new approach to the hiring of Black Americans, and reported his efforts to recruit graduates of Black colleges. He desired a new beginning, reflecting the ambitions of the new Democratic administration, and cited new anti-discrimination mechanisms to assist applicants: 'what is past is past. If you feel now or in the future that any Federal agency is deliberately evading the equal opportunity policy the facts should be discussed with the Fair Employment Policy Officer of the agency concerned. If satisfaction is not obtained, the matter may be presented to the President's Committee on Equal Opportunity.'[153] These monitoring instruments were still too weak, however.

Director Lyons's sentiments caught the sense of mission energizing the civil service in the 1960s when equality of employment was finally realized. This accomplishment required substantial federal legislation and enforcement. It should not have surprised him that eroding the effects of both the segregation justified by 'separate but equal' and the 'rule of three' selection mechanism on Black Americans' perceptions could not occur speedily.[154] The Federal government had maintained segregated race relations instead of guaranteeing equality of treatment. Nationally, the US Civil Service Commission and Federal government were widely criticized by Black interest groups in the 1960s for failing to effect equal employment opportunities. Criticisms by the NAACP and others of discrimination on the part of Civil Service Commission examiners in the regions continued, and the inequities of the 'rule of three' system persisted.[155] In 1965 President Johnson issued an executive order[156] directing the Civil Service Commission to ensure that discrimination charges in the Federal service were addressed effectively and swiftly. As a consequence, the Commission formulated a five-point plan of action. This plan introduced 'new administrative approaches to the problem', expanded and emphasized training, 'increased involvement of Federal officials in community activities affecting the employment of minority groups', and inaugurated a 'thorough review of the entire system in order that any artificial barriers to employment and promotion might be removed'.[157] Employment statistics about minority employees in the Federal service were collated. Also in 1965, the US Civil Service Commission committed itself to equal employment opportunity, as the chairman explained in a long letter to the NAACP, and cited statistics on minority employment in support of this priority.[158]

Born of congressional parents as an agency ineluctably structured between the competing demands of party patronage and meritocratic efficiency, the US Civil Service Commission successfully paved an impartial role for itself in the decades before 1913, sufficiently confident to boast about the benign effects of the Pendleton Act for Black Americans. It lobbied for more positions to be placed in classified, merit-based grades beyond the reach of patronage. From the election of Woodrow Wilson in 1913, the party political interests informing presidential and congressional interest in the Federal government assumed a Democratic guise, hostile to Black Americans. These political interests exercised their power to consolidate Democratic Party electoral support and to institutionalize segregated race relations in the Federal government. The consequences for Black Americans were multiple: entry into the Federal government was more difficult; promotion within the Service occurred on a derisory scale; and the Commission itself, charged with ensuring non-discrimination, became tainted with these sectional interests. In 1978, under the Civil Service Reform Act, President Carter abolished the US Civil Service Commission and transferred its responsibilities to the newly created Office of Personnel Management whose senior officials were presidential appointees. This Office has applied itself energetically to the monitoring of equal employment opportunity and treatment in both recruitment and promotion in the government.

3

Working in a Federal Agency: Social Ostracism and Discrimination

IN 1937 the Department of Commerce requested a 'colored messenger' for its statistical department. It hired a Black worker who held not only a bachelor's degree but also a law degree from Howard University. The messenger was engaged in moving large ledger volumes between rooms, as he explained to a hearing of the FEPC:

> my duties were . . . I came in the mornings and dusted off the desk of the Chief of the division; I usually went down and got the mail, and I opened that and put it on the desk of the secretary of the Chief of the division; and for the rest of the time I ran such errands as were assigned me. There were some heavy, bound books, tabulated books, which I got when the various clerks would request them as a result of visitors coming from other agencies to examine the imports and exports; and a part of the time I used in binding the books; and occasionally I would go to the supply room to get supplies. I think that constitutes the sum of the duties.[1]

The messenger, Leslie Perry, complained about his failure to be promoted[2] or to be assigned additional responsibilities after five years performing the same menial functions, below even those of his technical civil service grade, under-clerk CAF-1. If you were Black and worked for the Federal government prior to the 1960s this meant more than likely that you held a menial job.

This chapter explains how segregated race relations, tolerated by the Federal government, facilitated discrimination and inequality of treatment for Black Americans in Federal departments and agencies. It focuses particularly on the two decades after Franklin Roosevelt's election in 1932, including the effect of wartime mobilization. These outcomes are graphically conveyed in Fig. 3.1, taken from a study of segregation in Washington in 1948. The precept of 'separate but equal' proved empty for Black Americans working in the Federal government. This outcome was driven by party-political and sectional interests: once ensconced in Congress, Southern Democrats had no interest in improving the position of Black employees in the government. Segregated race relations, and the associated discrimination in government departments, were supported by, and indeed urged upon, Federal agencies by congressional overseers who could cite constitutional-legal authority and

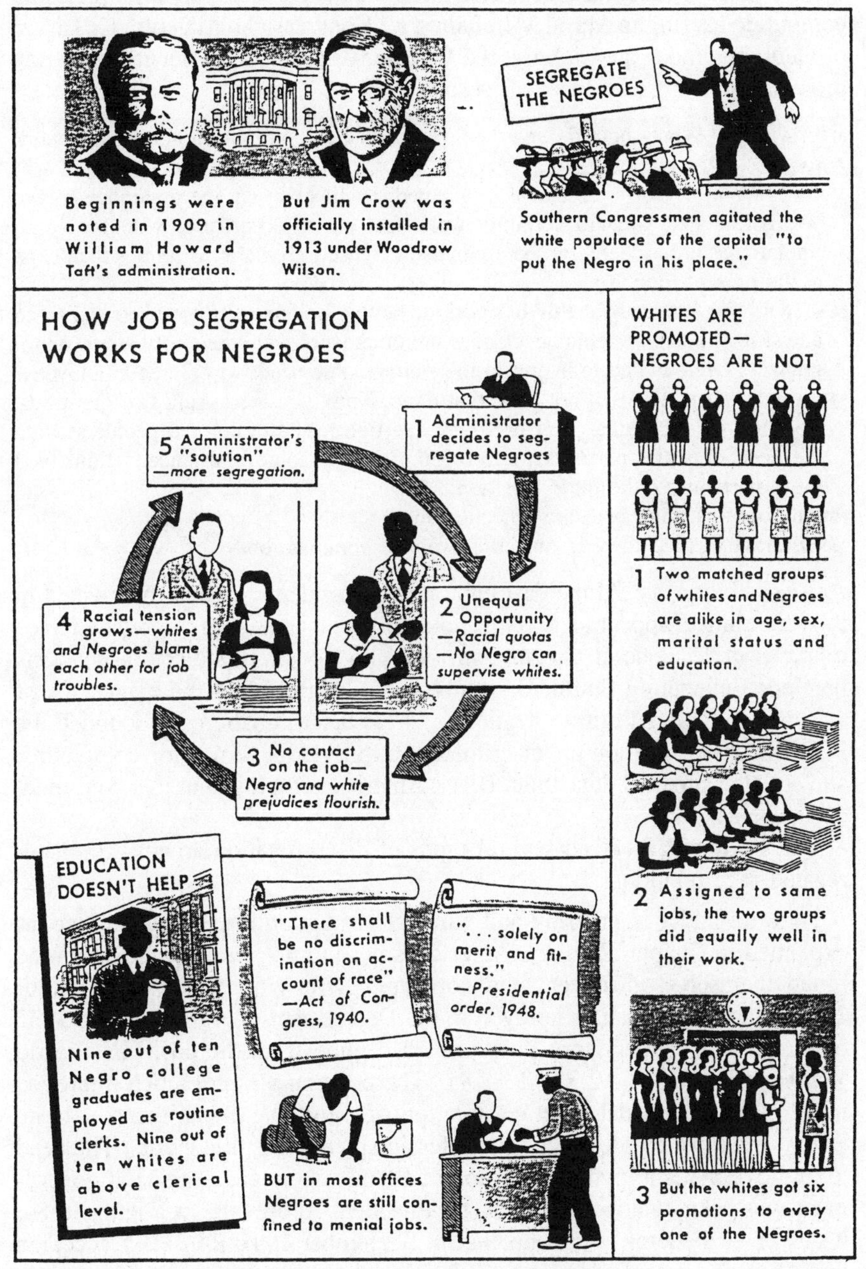

FIG. 3.1. Segregation in Government Service

Source: National Committee on Segregation in the Nation's Capital, *Segregation in Washington* (Chicago: National Committee on Segregation in the Nation's Capital, 1948), 72.

exercise sanctions through their control of appropriations. An example of these pressures comes from the following exchange before an appropriations committee hearing in May 1941 chaired by Congressman Malcolm C. Tarver of Georgia. Under questioning, the Director of the Federal Security Agency promised to segregate local offices:

MR TARVER: What about mixing them [white and colored] all up in the same work room?

MR ALTMEYER: So far as that is concerned, I will give you the assurance I gave you before that we will certainly work that out in accordance with the space limitations so that there will be no greater offense to social sensibilities than exist at the present time.

MR TARVER: What about this business of having colored stenographers called to attend to the stenographic needs of white employees and conversely white stenographers being called to attend to the stenographic needs of colored employees?

MR ALTMEYER: We will not have that done. Now, you are asking two questions. I do not think there has ever been any question raised of colored people serving the need of white person[s] or furnishing stenographic assistance. I think you mean particularly the other situation.

MR TARVER: I think both are objectionable.

MR ALTMEYER: If there is objection we will eliminate both.[3]

Any possibility that Altmeyer might act independently is overtly crushed in this committee appearance. This political context shaped segregated race relations in the Federal government. Franklin Roosevelt's electoral interests precluded alienating Southern members of Congress, but the exigencies of wartime did compel him to begin to address discrimination. He founded the FEPC in 1941[4] to monitor discrimination, provide a forum for complaints, and collate statistical data about Black American employment in government departments.

Black Americans faced several types of discrimination arising from segregated race relations:

First, difficulty in entering and winning promotion in the civil service, as explained in Chapter 2. Black Americans wishing to join or to be promoted found themselves disadvantaged compared with Whites. For instance, of 1,100 Black Americans employed in the Department of Agriculture in 1932 only two held 'supervisory positions', a decline from the post-First World War era (see Tables A2.3 and A2.4).[5] The position was not much improved in 1939, by which date the Washington office of the Department had one Black American employee in the professional and scientific grade.[6] The need to improve the employment position of Black Americans in Federal government was acknowledged publicly by President Roosevelt. In a letter to the heads of all Federal establishments in September 1941 Roosevelt accepted that 'there is in the Federal establishment a lack of uniformity and possibly some lack of sympathetic attitude toward the problems of minority groups, particularly those relating to the employment and assignment of Negroes in the Federal Civil Service'. This prejudice had been vigorously denied by Federal government officers during the three previous decades.[7] To address this prejudice, he directed all Federal government departments and independent establishments to 'make a thorough examination of their personnel policies and practices to the end that they may be able to assure me that in the Federal Service the doors of employment are open to all loyal and qualified workers regardless of creed, race or national origin'.[8] The FEPC was made responsible for tackling and eliminating discriminatory practices in 'all agencies of the Federal government'.[9] This brief was made explicit under Executive Order 9346 issued in May 1943. It instructed employers, including Federal government agencies and labour organizations, 'to eliminate discrimination in regard to hire, tenure, terms or conditions of employment, or union membership because of race, creed, color or national origin'.[10] Wartime demands made these inequalities all the more glaring, as the FEPC recognized: 'very early in its official life the Committee came to the conclusion that its chances of success in securing cooperation from private employers would be lessened if the government's own employment practices were open to serious criticism.'[11] This motive informed President Roosevelt's letter to all agency heads. The Committee claimed success for these initiatives, except in field offices (see the section 'Black Americans in Field Offices' below).[12] The FEPC also pressed its recommendations upon the US Civil Service Commission, though with unsatisfactory results, to modify the hiring process.

Second, discrimination of the sort Leslie Perry experienced at the Department of Commerce, what the FEPC termed 'discrimination by job level: that is, condemning an individual because of race or creed or national origin to a low level of occupation, low in the sense of being below his guaranteed, obvious abilities and skills, and training'.[13] Leslie Perry, a messenger at level CAF-1 in the Department of Commerce, complained about the low level of competence which his position required, after five years in the Department.[14]

Third, FEPC statistics about Black American employment quickly exposed significant differences between hiring in Federal government offices in Washington and the field offices of the same agencies outside Washington. While the numbers of Black American employees in the former improved during the war and after, the figures for field offices remained unimpressive, suggesting deep bias.

Fourth, the assignment of Black employees, because of their race and prejudice towards it, to temporary instead of permanent positions;[15] and failure to move them from temporary to permanent positions as vacancies arose. Temporary appointments were permissible under the Civil Service Commission's War Service Regulations, authorized by Executive Order 9063 and issued on 16 March 1942. Under one of the regulations all appointments

TABLE 3.1. *Agencies created by the executive to monitor and enforce non-discrimination*

Agency	Years	President
FEPC	1941–6	F. Roosevelt
FEB	1948–55	H. Truman
President's Committee on Government Employment Policy	1955–61	D. Eisenhower
President's EEOC	1961–4	J. Kennedy
US Commission on Civil Rights	1965–	L. Johnson

were temporary and could be 'terminated at any time, in the discretion of the Commission, regardless of whether the war has been declared ended'. Those appointed under this Executive Order lacked permanent status in the 'grades and classifications to which they are appointed'; and for those entering the Civil Serice as new workers there was no 'permanent Civil Service status at all'.[16] Confinement to temporary positions disqualified the incumbent from sitting civil service examinations to seek permanent appointments.

Fifth, discrimination resulting from 'token employment'. This referred to those government departments which tried to satisfy Roosevelt's 1941 executive order to employ Black Americans by 'giving to a few Negroes . . . employment in . . . a government department, and by such token attempting to give the impression of whole-hearted conformity to the Executive Order and to the principle itself'.[17]

Sixth, Black Americans faced discrimination if they wished to participate in federally funded apprenticeship programmes or to be hired on projects funded with government contracts. Government contracts and training programmes, administered beyond Washington, both replicated the segregated race relations tolerated in Federal government departments.

Each of these dimensions is examined in this chapter.

Executive Investigation of Discrimination

Our knowledge of the extent of these biases derives not from official government statistics but from departmental records and principally from a series of committees established by the executive, beginning in 1941, to monitor the employment of Black Americans, to provide a forum for charges of discrimination and bias to be articulated, and to encourage the hiring of Black Americans (see Table 3.1). The US Civil Service Commission did not collect statistics about the employment of Black Americans,[18] and data before 1941 was haphazardly collated by individual researchers and departmental racial advisers;[19] some departments claimed to have no information about the topic.[20] The most important of these committees was the FEPC established by President Franklin Roosevelt to monitor and enforce equality of employment opportunities and conditions for Black Americans.[21] Its establishment was prompted particularly by the expansion of defence-related industries, employment in which was sought by Black Americans. More immediately, the threat of a mass demonstration in Washington by organized Black workers in June 1941, under the banner of the March on Washington Movement led by A. Philip Randolph,[22] encouraged Roosevelt to issue the executive order creating the Committee.[23] Since Black workers were needed in defence industries, the President was not in a position to disregard their protest. Wartime was a powerful exogenous shock to segregated race relations in the US Federal government. The Committee was the first step toward a non-discrimination policy and a redefinition of the Federal government's traditional role: from being a practitioner of segregation it became its critic.

However, the FEPC was under constant congressional pressures. Judged a success by many,[24] the FEPC was a controversial and threatening organization for Southern Democrats and politicians. For instance, Georgian Senator Russell became a formidable and unremitting opponent of the FEPC.[25] Southerners successfully opposed efforts to establish a permanent FEPC after the war (see Table A1.4).[26] It never lost its temporary status and Congress happily terminated the Committee once the war ended. Bills to establish a permanent FEPC were introduced in January 1944 in the House and Senate, favourably reported from committees in August and November. The same process was repeated in 1945 but eventually defeated through adroit manœuvring by Southerners on the House Rules and Appropriations committees. Efforts to get the bill passed as part of the War Agencies Appropriations Bill in July 1945 also floundered.[27] FEPC policy was consistently scrutinized by Congress and Committee members found themselves required to defend their actions and decisions to Congress. In 1944 the FEPC Chairman wrote to the Chairman of the House Appropriations Committee dissociating the FEPC from alleged 'quota systems' in respect of Black employment: 'its affirmative action is limited to the receipt, examination and processing of specific complaints that available workers have been denied employment solely on the ground of race, creed, color or national origin.'[28] V. O. Key, Jr. maintained that opposition to the inclusion of a commitment to a permament FEPC on the Democratic Party's platform was the most important issue at the party's 1944 national convention.[29]

Executive Order 8802, founding the FEPC, was issued on 25 June 1941. It imposed a duty upon all employers and trades unions to 'provide for the full and equitable participation of all workers in defense industries, without discrimination because of race, creed, color, or national origin'. A second Executive Order (number 9346 issued on 27 May 1943) enlarged the

Committee's staff and strengthened the original directive to employers, including government departments, instructing them 'to eliminate discrimination in regard to hire, tenure, terms or conditions of employment, or union membership because of race, creed, color or national origin'. This Executive Order also required contracting agencies of the Government to include a non-discrimination provision in all their subcontracts (Executive Order 8802 had made this a provision for full contracts only). The Committee's power derived directly from those possessed by the President under the Constitution, and its functions were 'performed by the Committee . . . for and in the name of the President'. This authority derived from constitutional power vested in the President, as administrative head of the executive branch of the government and as commander-in-chief. President Roosevelt used the former authority to empower the Committee 'to investigate discrimination on the part of Government agencies, Government-sponsored training programs and private industries involved in the performance of Government contracts'.[30]

The Committee had jurisdiction over war industries, government contracts, government employment, and trade unions.[31] The Committee held hearings in Los Angeles (October 1941), Chicago (January 1942), New York (February 1942), and Birmingham, Alabama (June 1942), to encourage contractors to use Black workers.[32] It did not hold public hearings on Federal government employment, no doubt because such a tactic would have been too damaging of the Federal government's efforts to monitor private employers.[33] It was empowered to investigate complaints against companies submitting discriminatory vacancy requests to the USES and, throughout its existence, monitored corporations, often issuing sharp letters to them, and trade unions.[34] Malcolm Ross was the longest-serving and most influential chairman.[35]

The efforts of President Roosevelt to encourage employers to hire minority workers benefited from the effects of labour shortage: 'as the needs in industry became more acute, resistance to the use of minority group workers diminished accordingly.'[36] The number of Black Americans working in government rose by several hundred thousand during the war.[37] The FEPC reached agreements with trade unions, particularly CIO affiliates, requiring them to admit Blacks to training programmes and other facilities, and agreeing procedures for investigating discrimination charges.[38] Enforcing these agreements was, of course, often problematic.

The FEPC's existence was resented by private employers, especially in defence industries, and the dominant Southern Democratic coalition in Congress viewed it as a dangerous threat to the Jim Crow *status quo*. The FEPC also faced hostility in any investigation of discrimination within the Federal government, whose agencies reproduced, for the most part, racist attitudes and discriminatory practices consistent with those found in society. For these reasons, much of the FEPC's work was couched in pragmatic language, a tactic imitated by its successor organizations too. Rather than speaking of the outrage constituted by discrimination and segregation, it was more politic to stress wasted labour resources during a national emergency: 'from the purely practical approach of manpower utilization, discrimination in employment is, in the present crisis of manpower shortage, of paramount importance. Those who question or oppose plans to increase our army and navy as recommended by our military authorities might more profitably direct their energies to the elimination of impediments which now bar the full use of available manpower and womanpower.'[39] In 1943 the War Manpower Commission estimated that over 200,000 Black Americans were unemployed, a statistic the FEPC used to bolster its theme of waste: 'all criteria indicate that there is substantial and continuing waste of available manpower and skills resulting from discrimination in violation of declared national policy. If for no other reason than the practical necessity arising out of manpower shortages, there is need for vigorous, prompt and effective action in eliminating irrelevant considerations other than qualification and capacity in utilizing our labor supply.'[40] That this minority might also be disaffected with American political institutions did not escape the FEPC. The Committee urged strengthening the 'faith of one-quarter of our population in the fundamental justice of our democratic institutions'[41]—a difficult task given the role those 'democratic institutions' played in limiting Black Americans' equality of citizenship (see Chapter 4). The Committee contended that such discrimination was anathema to the United States: 'even the briefest study of our national history will make clear the reasons why Know-Nothing and Ku Klux Klan movements flourished only briefly; why the concept of permanent "minority groups" is alien to our . . . constitutional doctrine.'[42] The Committee spoke boldly about the improvement of Black Americans' status: 'such practices . . . do violence to our basic constitutional concepts which envisage only one class of citizens with equal rights.' Citing the Supreme Court's early attack on 'separate but equal' claims—'in decisions in recent years, the Supreme Court has made it increasingly clear that our constitutional doctrine must prevail against any prejudice of race, creed or national origin'—the Committee argued that inequality in employment was no longer tolerable: 'a similar clarification is becoming evident in the political and economic scene. This underlying fact is basic to any consideration of the problem of racial or religious discrimination at any particular time.'[43] These strong sentiments did not do justice, however, to the rebarbative and baneful barriers often confronting Black Americans seeking employment in the Federal government or defence industries.

Two years after the FEPC was denied permanent status, the Fair Employment Board was established under the jurisdiction of the US Civil Service Commission to undertake similar monitoring of discrimination and inequality (see Table 3.1). In 1955 President Eisenhower abolished the FEB and created, by Executive Order 10590,[44] the President's Committee on Government Employment Policy. This committee was charged with assisting government departments and agencies to implement equal opportunity for all Federal civil servants and those wishing to join the bureaucracy. In 1961 this committee was terminated[45] and its responsibilities again transferred, on this occasion to the new president's EEOC. The importance of the executive to these initiatives is self-evident; the unenthusiastic attitude of many members of Congress toward them can be easily inferred. In 1965 Executive Order 11246 terminated this last committee and transferred its responsibilities to the Department of Labor.[46]

BLACK AMERICANS IN THE FEDERAL GOVERNMENT UNDER SEGREGATED RACE RELATIONS: A SKEWED DISTRIBUTION

Until the middle of the twentieth century Black Americans were employed in relatively few numbers by the Federal government. In 1930, of a total Federal government payroll of 608,915, 54,684 were Black Americans (Table A3.2).[47]

The FEPC began monitoring non-discrimination within government service[48] by requesting in April 1942 that heads of all eighty-three government departments and independent establishments furnish a progress report, 'indicating steps taken to open opportunities for employment to Negroes and a statement of the number of Negroes employed'.[49] Six months later fourteen departments, including Justice and Labor, had failed to reply and several who had promised reports never delivered them. From the data supplied it was apparent that of a total of 171,103 personnel 9.1 per cent were Black, of whom only 2.3 per cent were in positions other than junior or custodial ones, and of whom significant numbers were in temporary positions: 'sixty-two per cent of the Negro employees . . . were in custodial classifications—an extremely disproportionate ratio.'[50] The FEPC's surveys produced one common finding: those Black Americans who did work in government agencies were located overwhelmingly in low-grade custodial and clerical positions. This was complemented by the dominant trend amongst professional and clerical positions in all Federal departments about whom the FEPC could obtain information (Table A3.3): the striking concentration of Black employees across agencies in the clerical positions and relative exclusion from professional grades. Not only was the 'number of Negro workers in the Government . . . very small', but 'Negroes have been confined, for the most part, to custodial positions. Those in clerical capacities have been very few and the number in administrative or technical positions almost negligible.'[51] For example, at the Treasury Department, where Black American employees constituted 22.9 per cent of the workforce, only one [Black] employee was in the professional layer.

The FEPC's 1943 study provided data about Black American government employees in thirty-eight agencies. These agencies employed 141,103 people, of whom 9 per cent were Black. In December 1943 the FEPC prepared a confidential report about Black employment in forty-four Federal agencies. Of 1,957,858 employees covered by the survey, Black Americans constituted 12.5 per cent or 246,109.[52] This was a limited sample since total Federal employment in 1943 was 3,223,375 civilians. The FEPC received no returns from War and Navy field establishments or from the following embarrassingly long list of agencies, employing in total 389,235 workers: the Executive Office of the President: the White House Office, and the Bureau of the Budget; War Establishments: Alien Property Custodian, Smaller War Plants Corporation, War Production Board, War Relocation Authority, War Shipping Administration, Office of Censorship, Office of Economic Warfare, Office of Strategic Services; Executive Departments: Agriculture and Labor Departments; Independent Establishments: American Battle Monuments Commission, Board of Investigation and Research, Export-Import Bank, Federal Deposit Insurance Corporation, Federal Power Commission, Federal Trade Commission, Maritime Commission, National Capital Park and Planning Commission, National Mediation Board, Panama Canal, Panama Railroad Company, and the Tariff Commission.[53] These omissions are striking and suggest the disregard in which the FEPC was held by many (White) administrators in the US Federal state. The gaps limited the data available for monitoring Black employment. Categorizing the returns they did receive across three types of agencies—War Establishments, Executive Departments, and Independent Establishments—the FEPC concluded that 'the proportion of Negro personnel to total personnel in the Independent and War Establishments is almost twice that in the Executive Departments'.[54] Crucially, it was these latter which were the core of the civilian Federal government, making this trend a disturbing one. It suggested the marginalization of Black Americans from the centre of the Federal government.

The FEPC's final report, issued in January 1945, was based on returns from fifty-seven government agencies and departments with 2,295,614 employees. Only the Agriculture, Labor, and Justice departments failed to return employment data by race. A bias toward Black employment in field offices was salient: 'Negroes were 273,971 or nearly 12 per cent (11.9) of all Federal employees reported in the study. In departmental service they were 41,566 or 19.2 per cent of the total and in field service they numbered 232,415 or 11.2 per cent of the total.' The difference between Black American and White employees was sharp: 'whereas 9.4 per cent of all Federal employees were in departmental service with the remaining 91.6 per cent in the field, 15.2 per cent of Negro Federal employees were in departmental service with 84.8 per cent in field service.'[55] Black employees remained overwhelmingly excluded from professional positions and concentrated in low-level grades: 'comparisons between the classification patterns of total and Negro workers show that the latter lagged far behind all workers in the Professional and CAF categories.' This skewness was a general pattern: 'in neither departmental, field or total Negro employment did Negro Professionals account for as much as one per cent of all Negro workers.' The professionals category accounted for 8.9 per cent of employees in departmental service, and 5.0 per cent in the field.[56]

The report's authors searched out positive news where they could find it, a considerable challenge: 'although Negroes have scored impressive occupational gains in Government service, they still show more concentration in the CPC category than other workers.'[57] This pattern was especially pronounced in Federal executive departments, a significant trend since these offered the most permanent employment. Thus, 'while Negroes were nearly 12 per cent of all Federal workers, they were only 7.0 per cent of all classified Federal workers but were 17.2 per cent of unclassified personnel. Thus Negroes have made their greatest numerical gains in that part of Federal service which will be most drastically curtailed after the war.'[58] The final sentence was prescient about post-war Black employment. Reported gains in Black American employment were very much a function of the exigencies of wartime. Wartime mobilization galvanized the Federal government and Executive Order 9063, issued on 16 March 1942, allowed an expansion of the civil service without conferring permanent status on those appointed. Black Americans were disproportionately concentrated in this temporary category. The FEPC assumed that at the end of the war, 'it can be expected that many Negro Federal workers without permanent Civil Service status will either lose Government employment entirely or be retained at lower grades or in different classifications'. The high numbers of Black American employees in temporary positions exaggerated their presence in the Federal government departments: 'because permanent Civil Service status was conferred prior to March 16, 1942 when relatively small numbers of Negroes were employed in Federal service, the proportion of Negroes who have such status is much smaller than that of other Federal workers.' However, temporary status for Black Americans was not entirely a new experience: 'the percentage of Negroes in the total number of permanent Civil Service employees is smaller than the percentage of Negroes in total employment prior to March 1942 since even at that time many Negro employees were given temporary appointments (often being reappointed every six months) rather than permanent Civil Service status.'[59] The report's authors correctly recognized that those holding permanent civil service status would be well placed (indeed in a 'preferred position') for the posts made available at the end of the war. This conclusion had obvious implications for Black Americans: 'since fewer Negro workers have permanent Civil Service status than other Government workers, they will be at a definite disadvantage in the transition period. The hiring done by

Government agencies in that period will doubtless affect the total postwar picture of the employment of Negroes in the Federal Government.'[60] This expectation proved accurate and the fear about Black employment well founded.

Reflecting on their findings, the FEPC report's authors were reluctant to infer discrimination. Accepting that the trends documented above 'show some discrimination against the Negro', the analysts noted that 'they also reflect comparative educational levels. The qualifications of the individual applicant are the object criteria for the determination of bias. In the final analysis discrimination is particular and concrete, not general and abstract.'[61] The particularity and concreteness of discrimination, however, seemed to affect Black Americans more than other Americans. Reviewing the factors likely to affect post-war employment for Black Americans in government, the authors included bizarrely the 'extent to which Negroes have entrenched themselves in the higher classifications in the permanent agencies'.[62] Their own data suggested that any inference of Black employees' entrenchment was misplaced and premature. Of more importance, as the authors appreciated implicitly, was the re-establishment of pre-war entrance requirements for Black job-seekers, including the perennial 'rule of three'.[63]

These disadvantages persisted. A survey by the President's Committee on Government Employment Policy[64] of Black employment in the Federal government in 1956, focusing upon the offices of Federal departments in five cities—Washington DC, Chicago, Los Angeles, St Louis, and Mobile[65]—produced results depressingly familiar to the earlier surveys. The study examined Black employment in three groups of positions in the Federal civil service: first, the eighteen General Schedule grades (white-collar workers rising in seniority from Grade 1 to 18) specified under the Classification Act of 1949; second, hourly paid workers in the Wage Board positions (blue-collar workers), also covered by the 1949 Act; and third, 'Other' positions excluded from coverage by the Classification Act, many in the Post Office. Together these positions accounted for 349,856 employees in the five cities, of whom 23.4 per cent were Black employees. However, these latter remained disproportionately concentrated in the 'Other' category of positions, as the authors of the study recognized though they attempted to present this finding positively: 'since 68.9 per cent of all Negro employees are in Classification Act or "Other" positions, it is to be noted that the majority of Negro employees are not in the laboring or custodial positions which are a part of the Wage Board group. The high percentage of Negroes in "Other" positions is largely a reflection of the field service of the Post Office Department, in which many Negroes are employed as carriers and clerks.' The General Schedule data also revealed disappointment for Black Americans: 'a very large percentage of Negro employees are in positions classified below Grade 5 . . . this holds true to a greater extent in the field offices outside of

Washington; here the percentage below Grade 5 is ninety or above in all four cities.'[66] The Committee was cautious in deducing the causes of these patterns: 'the fact that Negroes have come into the white-collar types of positions in great numbers largely during and since World War II may play a part; the great majority of these workers came in at the lower grades.' Before the war Black Americans failed to achieve any foothold: 'the lack in some localities of educational opportunities for the Negro group may mean that fewer Negroes than whites have been qualified for technical, professional, and higher administrative jobs. Finally, the factor of discrimination in making it more difficult for Negroes than for whites to move into top jobs certainly cannot be discounted.'[67] Since Black employees were frequently unable during the war period to move beyond low-grade positions or to shift from temporary to permanent openings the first factor is a poor explanation. The Committee claimed that their findings regarding the number of Black employees in the General Schedule marked a significant improvement in aggregate terms but accepted that distributionally the results were less heartening: 'Negroes are performing many of the clerical types of jobs and few of the top scientific, professional, and administrative jobs.' Curiously, in considering this skewed pattern, the Committee judged it 'difficult to assign any relative weight to the factor of discrimination'.[68] The tabular presentation of the data in this Committee's report is extremely difficult to read because they are comparing so many issues across sixty-two agencies (see Tables A3.3, A3.4, and A3.6).

BLACK AMERICANS IN FIELD OFFICES

The FEPC documented a significant difference, in many government departments, between the number of Black Americans employed in Washington and those in field offices. For instance, the OPA's record was reasonable in Washington but much less so in field administration (see Table A3.5). Of 345 Black Americans employed in Washington in July 1943, 85 per cent were employed 'above custodial classification (3.2 per cent professional—82 per cent CAF)'. However, in the OPA's field offices, 'Negroes represented only 1.1 per cent or 558 of a personnel of 51,897'; a mere eight persons were in professional positions.[69] In the Armed Service Forces' field establishments 19,789 Whites held professional positions; there were 128 Black Americans employed in comparable capacities.[70]

The contrast between executive and field offices was significant for numerical reasons, since 'only about 10 per cent of all federal employees are in the departmental service. The other 90 per cent are in field offices and establishments.'[71] In March 1943 Elmer Henderson prepared, for the FEPC, an assessment of the extent to which the position of Black employment in

Federal agencies had improved over the previous year. According to Henderson, success should be assessed by 'the number of Negroes who have actually gained employment with the Government and the spread of occupations in which they are engaged. To determine this, the President's Committee requested all government agencies to submit progress reports on the employment of Negroes at periodic intervals.'[72] Henderson reported some improvement in departmental offices in Washington in the early 1940s. The position in field services was unimpressive: 'only 5 per cent of the field employees of the reporting agencies were Negroes. This, of course, considerably outweighs the 17 per cent in the departmental service and tends to reduce the percentage of Negro employees to total employees in the government to well below 10 per cent.' Black American employees in field agencies were also unpromoted: 'thirty-eight per cent of the Negro employees in the field were found to be in CAF and professional classifications.'[73] In both departmental and field offices, the skewness of Black employment was undeniable, though Henderson did not emphasize it: 'the increase in the range of occupations in which Negroes are employed in the departmental service has been caused for the most part by the appointment of women into service as clerks, typists, and stenographers. Only a few Negroes anywhere in the governmental service hold positions of administrative or executive responsibility.' In certain parts of the United States, Henderson suggested, simply contemplating the employment of Black Americans in middle or senior ranking positions was unthinkable: 'in some regions of the country, there is a tendency not to employ Negroes in positions where they will come in contact with persons of other races.'[74]

The FEPC's 1943 report noted how common it was for the Washington office of an agency to employ Black Americans but for the same agency's field branches to do so to a much more limited degree—if at all. The OEM employed 1,727 (19 per cent) Black Americans in their Washington office (though 71 per cent were in junior CAF positions) but a mere 7 per cent of their field personnel were Black: 'the National Youth Administration employed 1,125 Negroes of whom 49 were employed in professional capacities. In field establishments, only two of the OEM agencies, namely the National War Labor Board and the Office of Civilian Defense, utilized the majority of their Negro personnel in clerical, administrative or fiscal capacities.'[75]

In executive departments in Washington in July 1943, Black employees constituted 16 per cent of total departmental employment of whom 36.6 per cent were CAF, 29.1 per cent CPC, and 0.3 per cent professional: 'only 3.1 per cent or 3,807 of total field personnel were Negroes. This is a small proportion of a total field employment of 120,862. Excluding the field report for the Post Office Department, those in CPC were approximately a fourth of the total Negro personnel.'[76] 'CPC' denoted low-level crafts, protective and custodial positions. Table A3.3 provides a summary for six departments, three of which—the Treasury, Post Office, and Commerce—had employed Black Americans before the 1930s. The US Civil Service Commission was more impressive. It employed 450 Blacks, 15.5 per cent of 2,900 employees. Of these, '82.2 per cent were classifed CAF. In field offices, Negroes were still less than 2 per cent of total field personnel. However, 60 were in clerical positions leaving only seven in custodial jobs.'[77] The disproportionate concentration of Black American employees in custodial and menial positions was reproduced in many agencies. For instance, at the Federal Works Agency, 'Negroes constituted 47.4 per cent of total departmental personnel, but 97.5 per cent of them were in custodial jobs. In the agency's field offices, Negroes were 19.6 per cent of the total field personnel. Here again, more than three fourths were in custodial jobs.' At the Railroad Retirement Board, 'Negroes made up less than 2 per cent of departmental personnel' with none in the field offices. At the VA, Black American employees constituted 10 per cent of total departmental personnel, of whom '71.4 per cent were in clerical jobs. In the field, Negroes were 10.2 per cent of total field personnel and 2,417 or 72.7 per cent were in the sub-professional classification.' At the TVA, Black Americans constituted 12.9 per cent of total personnel, but 'the majority were in unskilled occupations'.[78] These unimpressive percentages did not prevent the report's authors finding an upbeat note on which to conclude: 'an outstanding fact which should be noted is that in departmental service, an increasing number of Negroes are being employed in clerical and administrative positions, while in field service the majority are still in the custodial classifications.' It concludes that 'discriminatory employment practices are more prevalent in the field rather than in departmental services'.[79] This was an understatement.

Further claims about improvements in Black American employment in Federal government agencies were published in 1943. Again, however, these latter were much more pronounced in departmental than field offices and even in the departments improvement referred to temporary positions principally. For instance: 'in July 1942, the Justice Department employed only 165 Negroes in the Headquarters office; 123 or three fourths of these were in crafts, protective, or custodial jobs. As in the State Department, Negroes are confined, for the most part, to custodial positions.' The pattern in Justice Department field offices was unimpressive: 'out of a total field personnel of 24,114 persons, only 444 or 1.8 per cent were Negroes. Almost three-fourths, 71 per cent were unclassified workers.'[80] Comparable trends were recorded for other departments. Remarkably, the report's author ended positively—'in general, the July 1943 reports seem to indicate an increase in the utilization of Negro personnel and in the range of occupations in which they are employed'—rounded off with a patronizing pronouncement: 'further, it would appear that Negroes have the capacity to hold positions entailing responsibility and to work cooperatively with other racial groups.'[81] Such attitudes suggest how deeply embedded opinions compatible with segregated race relations were in the Federal government. It is also a striking vindication of the fears expressed by Black activists during the Woodrow Wilson administration in 1913 that segregation, far from providing an opportunity for advancement, would ineluctably result in inequality for Black employees. Outside Washington, especially though certainly not exclusively in the South, local representatives of Federal agencies were unlikely voluntarily to hire Black employees.

BLACK AMERICANS AND WARTIME AGENCIES

Wartime agencies were generally praised by Black American interest groups for having better employment records than more established departments. A study of segregation in Washington, issued in 1948, commented that war agencies 'were new, with no office tradition against Negroes. They were set up in a period of labor shortage, and needed all the qualified help they could get. And the nature of the war itself created a sentiment against master-race doctrines.'[82] (Black recruits in the Armed Services might well have dissented from this last opinion, as Chapter 4 reports.) The OPA, under Chester Bowles's control, is representative of such wartime agencies. It was responsible for price control, rent control, and rationing work. Prompted by the FEPC, the OPA endeavoured to improve its employment practices, coordinated by its racial relations adviser (appointed in July 1943). Its achievements were modest, and the differential between the national office in Washington and field offices did not diminish. In November 1945 Bowles issued a circular about Black employment, ebullient in tone: 'we all have some reason for pride in the attached analysis of a report on Negro employment in the National Office as of March 31, 1945.'[83] This pride rested on modest advances, with Black employees increasing in aggregate number but concentrated disproportionately in the least attractive positions. Revealingly, no evidence about employment in the field offices was offered. Good reason for this silence is contained in a confidential memorandum prepared by the OPA in January 1946, marked 'not to be released'; it tabulated data about field offices. The memorandum divided the OPA's 1,885 local price and rationing boards into eight regions. Of the total number of boards, only 89 had Black members[84] (see Table A3.5).[85] The position had not improved by March 1946.[86]

The OPA put considerable effort into improving the position of Black Americans served by their boards. In a memorandum in 1944, titled 'OPA and the Negro', the Racial Relations Adviser identified two major reasons for the low numbers of Black American employees: '1) the limited experience Negro people have had in actively participating in and carrying responsibility for programs of general welfare—due to a policy of omission or exclusion practiced unconsciously or otherwise by so many agencies and institutions in American life; 2) the limited experience and skill most white staff and volunteer members have had in working with Negro groups and individuals.' The second problem rested frequently on existing attitudes.[87] These points were equally applicable to other Federal agencies' relations with Black Americans.

Wartime gains for Blacks in the Federal government proved parlous once conflict ceased and Whites sought both to reassert the Jim Crow *status quo* and to reclaim their former positions. In a report prepared for President Truman in August 1945, the FEPC outlined pending problems. Some elementary statistics conveyed the scale of the problem in Federal departments: 'only 30 per cent of all Negro workers in the Federal Government are in classified Civil Service jobs. These form only seven per cent of all persons in classified work. Moreover, of the Negro workers in classified Civil Service jobs, 57.7 per cent were employed in temporary war agencies.'[88] Similar trends were evident in industrial employment.[89] Bills were introduced to Congress during 1944 and 1945 to give priority to veterans in civil service positions after the war, but these failed to benefit Black American veterans.[90]

WORKING IN GOVERNMENT: THE TEMPORARY APPOINTMENT STRATEGY

The FEPC received many complaints about the Civil Service Commission's inadequate monitoring of appointment to Federal departments.[91] These complaints came from almost all Federal government agencies (see Chapter 6). Demarcating the FEPC's jurisdiction over Federal agencies was not unproblematic.[92] Chairman Malcolm Ross believed it had jurisdiction and acted as if this were the case. He cited paragraphs 4 and 5 of Executive Order 9346 (27 May 1943) which authorized the Committee to 'make recommendations to the various federal departments and agencies and to the President which it deems necessary and proper to make effective the provisions of this Order . . . receive and investigate complaints of discrimination forbidden by this Order . . . [and] conduct hearings, make findings of fact, and take appropriate steps to obtain elimination of such discrimination'.[93]

For obvious political reasons, the FEPC was reluctant to pursue issues of discrimination within the Federal government, and loath to make any hearings about such complaints public: 'we have not, and at present do not intend to have hearings in public on governmental agencies, attempting rather to keep the matter in the family for the time being.'[94] That the FEPC recognized there was significant discrimination in the Federal government there can be little doubt. In November 1942 one FEPC member observed that the

Committee's responsibility for the Federal government 'gets us into the hair of our colleagues in the Federal service who, on the whole, pay no more mind to developing a *positive and deliberate* nondiscriminatory policy than do private employers'. The same writer continued: 'it is only realistic to admit that past patterns . . . are discriminatory. These patterns [will] persist . . . unless we recognize them for what they are and make a strong, concerted effort to alter them.'[95] Getting into the metaphorical hair of colleagues was difficult. None the less, the frequency of complaints about employment in the Federal government made such ruffling of feathers imperative.

In 1942 four employees complained that the Personnel Classification Division, located in the US Civil Service Commission, discriminated against them because of their race. An FEPC hearing, chaired by Mr E. Trimble, was held in December 1942 to investigate the claims. He summarized the charges of discrimination: 'first, that colored clerks were given only temporary appointments, while white clerks were given indefinite appointments. Secondly, that the Negro clerks were required to work at night, while the white clerks were permitted to work during the day.'[96] These charges were presented by one of the four complainants, Miss Fox. She began: 'the original members of the night force arrived between the 20th and 23rd April of this past year, and the force was mixed.' Of this group, permanent employment was restricted to Whites: 'indefinite appointments were given to the white employees—not all at one time—gradually—and it was supposed to be on the basis of their efficiency. None of the Negro employees were given these appointments, and we feel that our efficiency was as good as the others. All of us have the same amount of service in the division.' Despite the fact that all the clerks, Black and White, completed the Junior Clerk exam and received equally good grades, the White employees were placed 'on an eligible register', an advantage denied Miss Fox and her colleagues, denying her candidacy for a permanent appointment. The White employees were also shifted from night-work: 'during this period of time, these people that received indefinite appointments—except one—were shifted to the day force . . . All these original white workers that came on the night force with the exception of one, were transferred to the day force, and the girl that remained came in a month or two after we did, and she is at present our supervisor.'[97] Thus, not only were the Black clerks refused transfer and permanent appointment but a White woman appointed after these temporaries were hired was promoted above them. Miss Fox said the Black clerks sought the right to work on the day force. However, their 'main interest is to achieve an indefinite appointment, and we feel since we have been in the division as long as the other workers, and our work is—our efficiency is acceptable—that we should be considered for it as well as anyone else'.[98]

Defence of these practices was spiritedly undertaken by Joseph Spilman,

Associate Chief, Personnel Classification Division.[99] Under Spilman's supervision was Mrs Ellen Manchester, the main supervisor of the clerks. Spilman claimed at the hearing that the positions were misadvertised: the request had 'specifically stated that this work was to be night work' but this had been omitted. Consequently, those recruited had been under the misapprehension that the positions were 'to be day work . . . I immediately called a meeting . . . and I explained the situation to them. Well now, at that time, Miss Settle and Miss Miller, two of the complainants, indicated they had no objections to working nights.'[100] Spilman also explained away the clerks' temporary status: 'as time went on, and as this work became more formalized, why we found we would need these folks beyond June 30, so we put in for an extension, and then subsequently requested another extension.' Some of the new clerks were given permanent appointments, as Spilman conceded:

> Now, as these indefinite vacancies occurred, it is true folks have been switched from the temporary role over to the indefinite role.
>
> MISS LANDES: How many?
>
> MR SPILMAN: Seven. In each of those cases—in the opinion of the supervisors—they have been by reason of their general efficiency the logical people to be selected.
>
> MR TRIMBLE: They are all white?
>
> MR SPILMAN: Yes.[101]

Regarding supervision, Spilman then explained magnanimously that 'as a matter of fact, at the time we received your letter, we were seriously considering, if we extended this force, whether or not one of the girls should be placed in the job as supervisor over them.'[102] Miss Fox was invited to question Spilman.

> MISS FOX: You said that they were the logical people to fill these definite ratings. I am afraid I'm not quite clear about that.
>
> MR SPILMAN: Based on the reports of the supervisors—logical only from the standpoint that the supervisors indicated that in their opinion, these people were the people who should be placed in those jobs.
>
> MISS FOX: Why recourse to a supervisor's opinion when the working reports are handed with the work of everybody?
>
> MR SPILMAN: The monthly work reports which are handed in under normal circumstances could not be construed as the production record because we have never been able to figure out, to determine, what the average unit of work should be.[103]

Miss Fox turned to the issue of supervision.

> MISS FOX: Is it in accordance with commission policy to appoint someone as acting supervisor less experienced than the people that she is supervising? Also, if Mrs Creecy is so efficient as to rating an indefinite job, why is it necessary to have someone with the day force to alternate weekly in charge? I mean to say that most of them don't do anything.

MR SPILMAN: That involves a question of administration as to your relative efficiency and the relative efficiency of Mrs Creecy. The only way that I could get at it would be from hearing your side of it, and hearing the side of the chief of the section, and the assistant chief of the section. I have no other way of getting at that unless there is some evidence presented to me, which would indicate that the decision made by the supervisor is wrong.

MISS FOX: It feels rather strange to be supervised by some one that you helped to instruct.

MR SPILMAN: That again involves a question as to whether or not some one who came in a month or so after you, has made as good or better progress than you? That is what it amounts to, doesn't it?

MISS FOX: That is the way it is presented it amounts to, but I don't believe Mrs Creecy has made as good progress.[104]

One of the FEPC members asked Miss Fox when she and her colleagues came to believe they were being discriminated against:

MISS FOX: We realized we were being discriminated against long before we brought the matter up to anybody.

MR BARRON: Can you say how?

MISS FOX: In the first place, the other employees were always taught advance work before we were, although we all came in about the same time. We would file cards for a couple of weeks, and they would go on to something else. We realized then that it was a racial matter, because all of us were college students or college graduates, and two of us have Master Degrees. I believe we asked Mr Spilman on several occasions about indefinite jobs. I think it was clearly understood that the question we were raising was because of our race—did we have—was there going to be any objections to our receiving indefinite positions.[105]

Chairman Trimble questioned Spilman about the difficulties of raising charges of discrimination and the personal costs of doing so.

THE CHAIRMAN: If one of these supervisors did discriminate against the colored employees there in choosing someone to be supervisor or to recommend for indefinite appointment, you would not have had any way of verifying the fact, would you?

MR SPILMAN: No, not unless one of them came to me.

THE CHAIRMAN: If the appointing official said, 'No, it wasn't because of race that I didn't choose one of these girls, but I choose this white girl because I think relatively she is more efficient,' you would have no way of knowing whether she was telling the truth or not?

MR SPILMAN: That is right.

THE CHAIRMAN: And if they appeal to you and you decide against them, they have run the risk of incurring the ill will of their immediate supervisor.

MR SPILMAN: As a matter of fact, not only do they have the right under our procedure of appealing to me, but over and above me to the Chief of the Division, and over and above the Chief of the Division.

THE CHAIRMAN: I wasn't questioning the right—I was questioning the wisdom.[106]

The Chairman also pursued the issue of movement from temporary to permanent positions:

I have the same difficulty Mrs Bowser [one of the complainants] has. It was indicated here that there was a sufficient shortage of workers—that the supervisor here wanted to keep a girl who had ability and knew the work. Now, Mrs Bowser asked if she could have any hope of being given one of these indefinite appointments, some of which had gone to members of this group, and she was presuming I suppose, that her own work was satisfactory, but she was told no, there was no chance. Now, in view of the fact that some had been given indefinite appointments out of this group, I don't quite see why Mrs Manchester needs to confine her statement to this particular job that Mrs Bowser was filling. I can see that Mrs Manchester might have meant that the position you are in now will be made indefinite, but I don't see how in view of the fact that people had been given indefinite appointments in permanent service—I don't see why she needed to make her statement quite so narrow.[107]

The Committee questioned Spilman about the reluctance of members of his Division to give information about other positions within the civil service to the Black clerks when requested. Clarence Mitchell, the FEPC's Senior Employment Specialist, remarked:

The Civil Service as we read in the newspapers, are the ones who are constantly stressing the importance of upgrading employees who are already within government agencies, and in order to have a correctly functioning up-grading system, it would seem that there ought to be at least some degree of awareness on the part of persons who were in supervisory positions on the possibility of individuals who perform their duties correctly, going up the steps to better paying jobs.

MR SPILMAN: That is right.

MR MITCHELL: It doesn't seem unreasonable to me that a supervisor would say, 'Now of course, I don't see any possibility in this particular job you are doing become an indefinite one, but as you know, we are having persons leave the service quite frequently, and it is quite possible—if you do your work well—you may be moving into one of those.'

MR SPILMAN: Yes.

MR MITCHELL: I think it would be unfair to take advantage of a technicality and assume because the individual didn't make it quite clear that she was talking about a job other than that she was performing, that you wouldn't intimate there was a possibility of going somewhere else. Do you agree with that?

MR SPILMAN: I think that is generally true, looking at it from the overall standpoint.[108]

One of the complainants recollected her effort to shift from night to day work for the Committee, indirectly delineating the inequality inherent to segregated race relations:

MISS SETTLE: . . . I expressed my most earnest desire to work on the day shift, and I gave her my reason why I desired to work then, and she said, 'Well, we just can't have you working on days,' and I said, 'Why?' I wanted to know a good reason why since other people were being gradually shifted to day work, and she said, 'It wouldn't be to the welfare of other workers to work on days,' and I asked her just what she meant, although I knew at the time no colored employees were working on the day shift. I asked if that was what she meant, and she said, 'Certainly, I don't think they would continue working if you were shifted to days permanently.' Of course, I have been shifted to day work—two Saturdays since I've been there, and when I was shifted there, working those Saturdays which was a half day, I of course experienced what you call social ostracism. Then on November 14, I again asked Mrs Manchester whether or not I could be permanently assigned to day work—that is permanently as long as I was going to be there, and she said she would ask Mr Spilman or consult with someone else. At that time I got a call, and she said the call was related to me and said I could not work on the day shift.[109]

Spilman attempted to defend his actions, blaming both the complainant and bureaucratic procedures over which he had no control: 'I didn't understand that was Miss Settle's understanding at the time.' He did accept that Miss Settle had discussed 'this question of going from night to days a little while ago—she said last of September or first of October, and I said, "I would look into that and see what we could do about it."' The problem was one of 'making space'. He continued: 'now, Miss Settle also says we have some additional space. Of course, it is true—we have some additional space on that floor, but that additional space is for new trainees who are to be appointed very shortly from elsewhere in the Commission.' Miss Fox helpfully intervened at this point:

MISS FOX: Well, there are three empty desks in the file section, and I'm quite sure that trainees—there is plenty of space in the back of the room for them.

MR SPILMAN: You may know as a matter of fact, those desks haven't been assigned to anybody?

MRS MANCHESTER: How would you be in a position to know that?

MISS FOX: I worked on the day force for a half day about two weeks ago. The desk that Mrs Bowser used and the desk Miss Settle did use has never been occupied by anyone in the daytime.[110]

Spilman was questioned about the race of those transferred from night to day shifts, reminding the Committee that 'originally as I said, we had all these folks under a misunderstanding, due to the fact that Personnel had recruited them for day duty'. He then explained the individual transfers: 'now, it wasn't possible to put Mrs Corbin on day work at that time, but we did later on. In fact, we didn't put her on until a couple of months afterwards. Miss Seay of the original seven who have been made indefinite is still on night work, and Mrs Dorwin was changed from night work to day, and Mrs Corbin was changed from night to day. The others were always on night work.' The race of these individuals was identified: 'Miss Landes [FEPC]: Is Mrs Dorwin the only Negro? Mr Spilman: Mrs Dorwin is white. Miss Landes: Are there any Negroes? Mr Spilman: No.'[111] According to

Miss Fox, of those White clerks transferred from night to day shifts, many were asked whether they wanted such a move: 'some of the white employees that used to work on the night shift and are at present working on the day shift were asked if they wanted to work on the day shift. They didn't request it themselves, whereas other requests had been put in for day work.'[112]

Clarence Mitchell exposed one of the ways in which those holding temporary positions faced additional difficulty in securing a permanent position.

MR MITCHELL: Mr Spilman, will you clear up one or two points? You mention a space which has been set aside for trainees. Where do these people come from?

MR SPILMAN: Those people take a competitive promotion examination and are selected on the basis of the mark they make in their examination, their efficiency, their over-all educational background, there are about five or six different factors that we consider including their ability to get along with people, whether or not they possess tact and poise—in other words—those are the jobs for people who are in training for investigators or specification writers.

MR MITCHELL: Would these people be eligible to take those examinations?

MR SPILMAN: No, they wouldn't be up until the time that they are given an indefinite position. If they receive an indefinite position anywhere in the Commission, regardless of whether it is in the division or any place else, or any other division of the Commission, then they would be eligible to take the examination.

MR MITCHELL: Do you know whether any of the white persons who have been transferred from the night force to this day force working on an indefinite basis have since been given examinations for these trainee jobs and are now working in that capacity?

MR SPILMAN: Not to my knowledge.

MRS BOWSER: There was one—Mrs Dorwin took it.

MR SPILMAN: I could add to that record—Miss Fox took that examination, and Miss Fox passed that examination, but because of the fact that she was temporary, why of course, they couldn't put her on the list.

MR MITCHELL: Then what it amounts to is that not only if an individual is working on that temporary basis, as long as she is held in that temporary basis, has not only the inconvenience of working at night, but it precludes her being promoted to positions that may be higher or more desirable?

MR SPILMAN: That is true.[113]

I have examined this FEPC hearing in detail because the issues raised by the four Black women clerks are central to, and powerfully illustrative of, the experience of Black Americans in the Federal goverment before the 1960s. Similar complaints are repeated in other hearings and confronted the FEPC's various successor organizations. It is instructive that the case concerned employees in a division of the US Civil Service Commission, the agency charged with monitoring discrimination in government departments. The structuring of rules and narrow interpretation of opportunities for Blacks are both revealed in the exchanges. While personal relations between the Black clerks and their white supervisors were not hostile, the latter evidently acted in ways which not only discriminated against the former but ensured the persistence of practices and arrangements which restricted the possibilities for Black workers. Miss Fox also notes that she quickly suffered 'social ostracism' when she worked on the day shift. They deliberately promoted White women over Black women employees, and limited the opportunity for Black women to achieve permanent employment status. The FEPC was unequivocal about the unacceptability of policy and behaviour toward these Black women, finding that 'discrimination was exercised against these complainants because of their race, on the part of their immediate supervisors'.[114] The Board made several recommendations including: '1. In view of Mr Spilman's testimony that the complainants are capable and even superior to workers now being recruited, measures should be taken immediately to offer them indefinite appointments, consonant with their qualifications, in the Personnel Classification Division, where vacancies may exist.' To compensate for past behaviour, a further recommendation deemed that 'these complainants shall have the first opportunity to fill any vacancy in the Personnel Classification Division for which they are qualified'. Consistent with Miss Fox's 'indefinite appointment', and with civil service procedure, her name was to 'be placed on the eligible trainee register, in keeping with the grade received by her in the competitive examination'. Miss Settle was to be offered an 'indefinite appointment . . . in conformity with her qualifications, to any existing vacancy in the Personnel Classification Division'.[115] The Civil Service Commission prevaricated. It contested the recommendation concerning Miss Fox, maintaining that the findings were 'not in accordance with the facts and hereby categorically denies that Miss Fox was the object of discrimination on the basis of her race'. The Commission found itself 'unable to understand the position of the Staff Board of Review in this regard. Miss Fox was tendered a temporary appointment on April 23, 1942, which she accepted.' Because of this temporary status, she was precluded from sitting public examinations: 'she, like all other temporary employees of the Commission, was, at the time of the announcement of the promotion examination, specifically barred from competing in that examination, not on the basis of her race or any other irrelevant factor, but solely on the basis of the fact that she was a temporary employee and as such was not, under the Civil Service Rules and Regulations, eligible for promotion.' The Commission defended the restriction to temporary status: 'this ineligibility of temporary employees for promotion is not a disability peculiar to that particular promotion examination. Temporary employees are not now and never have been eligible for promotion from one grade to another higher grade.'[116] Miss Fox successfully completed the examination but the Commission still declined to promote her, on the grounds she was a temporary employee and ineligible for promotion. The FEPC disputed this decision, pointing out that 'by virtue of the discrimination practiced against her, she was a temporary appointee when she should have been made an indefinite appointee, and thereby she was denied opportunity for promotion'.[117] The Committee insisted, delicately but resolutely, that this injustice be remedied.

BLACK AMERICANS, GOVERNMENT CONTRACTS, AND APPRENTICESHIPS

Outside Washington, the problem of discrimination within the segregation framework was apparent in both government contract compliance and federally monitored industrial apprenticeships. Federally funded projects were supposed to offer equality of employment. Entrenched racist attitudes supporting segregation and discrimination were unearthed by President Truman's CGCC,[118] and presented in its report 'Equal Economic Opportunity', completed in January 1953. The Committee found the 'non-discrimination provision almost forgotten, dead and buried under thousands of words of standard legal and technical language in Government procurement contracts'.[119] Many contractors considered 'the provision as just another contractual clause of relatively minor importance'[120] and disregarded it. Contracting officers in almost all agencies lacked sufficient power or resources with which to enforce the non-discriminatory requirement and 'in many cases even the will has been absent to make efforts to require contractors to meet their obligations under the clause'.[121] The Federal government began administering and monitoring apprenticeship programmes with the enactment of the Fitzgerald Act in 1937,[122] which created a Federal committee on apprentice training appointed by the Secretary of Labor.[123] Although enacted during the Great Depression, the Act's remit was focused (in common with much New Deal legislation) on the period after recession: 'there is a constant need for some Federal Agency to bring employers and employees together in the formulation of national programs of apprenticeship and to attempt to adjust the supply of skilled workers to the demands of industry.'[124]

The CGCC studied training, apprenticeship, and employment service activities of the government seeking the relevant agencies' view. The results were not encouraging. Thus the BES, which administered state employment service offices, believed that 'if state employment services were to refuse to accept discriminatory orders after educational efforts have failed, many employers and workers now served would be inclined to use other recruitment sources. The Bureau thus would lose its opportunity to influence employers to change employment practices where they are discriminatory.'[125] The Bureau of Apprenticeship 'held that its function is merely to bring labor and management together to develop apprenticeship programs . . . [and] . . . the Federal Committee on Apprenticeship (a statutory advisory committee representing labor and management) turned down a request by the Committee to take an affirmative position urging that the labor-management constituents in the apprenticeship program accept group members in *all* apprenticeship programs.'[126] The Maritime Administration pursued a non-discriminatory training programme but had 'no permanent machinery to enforce it'.[127] The CGCC's report concluded thus: 'the testimony of officials of the six agencies convinced the Committee that both legislative and administrative remedies are needed to implement the national policy of non-discrimination in their training, education and employment programs.' Such an initiative required government policy: 'the Committee so far has had only a small measure of success in its attempts to persuade these key agencies to establish the principle of equal employment opportunity as one of the basic operating criteria of their programs.'[128] In discussing discrimination, the President's Committee stressed the harm to the labour force, which they judged 'the greatest of our nation's resources'; revealingly, this latter was the 'premise on which the Committee . . . based all its studies'.[129] It continued: 'Negroes bear the brunt of discriminatory practices, especially in employment . . . set apart from other Americans by color and frequently segregated by law and custom, they are travelling the longest road to equality of economic opportunity . . . To see bias in stark boldness, one need only read the "help wanted" section of almost any daily newspaper and note the advertisements signifying "white only".'[130] It provided copious evidence to substantiate these claims: Black workers were the first to be laid off; when excluded on grounds of qualification, this decision frequently 'stems from the restrictions barring minorities from the opportunity to participate in training and educational facilities';[131] and the economic position of Black Americans lagged far behind that of Whites: 'with few exceptions, Negroes are paid less, are less protected from inroads on their health, and accordingly have a shorter life span than do whites.'[132]

Following the publication of its report, the Committee worked with Federal government agencies to agree upon and insert non-discrimination clauses in their contracts.[133] The senior official in each department or agency was required to ensure appropriate contract compliance in their organization, and to issue guidelines specifying requirements and mechanisms for their enforcement. As an official at the Department of Justice noted, inadequate enforcement suggested the need for such explicit arrangements: 'there is probably enough past experience to demonstrate that it is not enough simply to say that the responsibility for enforcement of the contract anti-discrimination clause is in the head of each agency.' Consequently, a 'concrete program of action for the key contracting agencies' was required.[134] The same writer concluded that 'there is no question that the present contract clause is a dead letter',[135] and urged a fuller role for the Justice Department. This fuller role was assumed, to great effect, after 1964.[136]

Throughout the crisis of the Second World War, the training of Black Americans in both apprenticeships and defence industry was commonly

TABLE 3.2. *Black American participation in defence training programmes*

State	Negro population (%)	Negro trainees (%)
Miss.	49.5	3.30
SC	43.0	4.20
L.	36.0	4.00
Ala.	34.8	3.40
G.	34.7	5.30
F.	27.0	0.17

Source: NA RG 228, FEPC Records, Legal Division, Box 329, Folder Verbatim Transcripts 13 Apr. 1942: Text of letter from FEPC included in Hearing of the President's FEPC on Discrimination in Defense Training, 13 Apr. 1942, p. 7.

criticized for discrimination. Writing to the Commissioner of Education in 1942, the FEPC noted that 'the matter of discrimination in war industry training programs is acute. Into the Committee there pour complaints, particularly from Negroes and Jews, that Federal funds are being expended on defense training in direct violation of Executive Order 8802.' This Executive Order required non-discrimination in the administration of vocational and training programmes. Such complaints were not limited to the South: 'there is a good deal of evidence that the violation is widespread.' The effects were unsurprising: 'available and qualified persons are being denied training opportunities supported by Federal funds solely because of their race or color.'[137] Table 3.2 shows the statistics the FEPC hearings received about Black American participation in defence training programmes. In the view of one witness from the US Office of Education, without a strong Federal role inequities in training funds would remain. This assessment was applied most vigorously to the Southern states: 'I say that the Negro cannot get fair treatment from Federal funds unless the Federal Government insists upon it. The Negro cannot expect fair treatment in funds if the Federal Government simply passes them out to given states and allows the state to administer them.' Instead, direct intervention was required: 'if the Federal Government wants to administer equitably the money, it will have to see to it by sanctions and penalties that its money is distributed equitably.'[138] The Chief of the Minority Groups Service of the US Office of Education, Dr Will Alexander, described despairingly his efforts to incorporate Black workers into defence industry training in Mobile, Alabama, when it was expanding rapidly in 1941: 'I went out to the shipyards and saw cars by the thousands around there of workers with tags from all parts of the country, from Ohio, and as far away as Minnesota, of white labor that had been brought in and at that time, Mobile was asking for something like 5,000 new houses to house these workers that were coming in from all over the country to build ships.' Predictably, Black American workers were scarce on the ground: 'there were no Negroes working in that shipyard, and there were estimated by the Employment Service to be at least 3,000 Negro workers that were available in that community that were already housed.' Building new housing was more plainly expensive than hiring local labour: 'those houses were costing around $4,000 a house. So, we had every possible argument for the use of these Negroes in this shipbuilding enterprise.' This logic was unpersuasive to local officials: 'when we went to the Labor Supply Committee looking all these facts in the act, insisting that we go ahead with the steps that would enable us to utilize this Negro labor which was training, we met an adamant opposition on the part of the vocational educational people, the state people in Alabama.' The same officials objected to the proposal that Blacks be hired: 'after much discussion, the Representative of the Office of Education, Mr Plowden, finally demanded to know who was stirring all this up, and I very modestly informed him that it was the Commander-in-Chief of the Army and Navy and the President of the United States. Mr Plowden's reply was that they were not going to do this, and if they were required to do training of Negroes, they were not going to do any training at all.'[139] Alexander supplied a further instance from Florida, where the Director of Vocational Education declared: '"We don't need to take this thing [training of Blacks] too seriously. There is a lot of talk about this and so on, but we really don't need to do it", reflecting the same kind of an attitude that we have found almost universally on the part of the people who administered vocational education in the South.'[140]

In testimony to the FEPC Robert Weaver, Chief of the Negro Employment and Training Branch of the War Production Board, regretted the absence of procedures and mechanisms to ensure that Black Americans were included in defence training programmes newly established. The FEPC's field representative, John Beecher, confirmed these problems: in Alabama 'only 205 Negroes [were] enrolled in national defense training courses in the entire state'. Local administrators took procrastination to new heights: in Mobile, 'the courses haven't been started and if one were to check into it, I think one will find that a pretty deliberate process of slowing down and of sitting in requisition and of just arranging for two or three steps in the process for leaving out another one, that all that is going on'.[141] In Beecher's view, in the South a situation existed 'where there is a great need, especially in the shipbuilding industry, for additional workmen and where there is a large local labor supply which is not being used in spite of that need'.[142] Robert Weaver complained about the inadequacies of the training offices in facilitating Black employment: 'under the present system, it is assumed the training authorities know, for example, that there is a certain aircraft plant which is going to require men . . . they assume that all of those men are going to be white unless the employer specifically says, "I can use a few Negroes here in the foundry" . . . It is assumed that they will be white. They don't have to write discriminatory specifications.'[143] This point was underlined by FEPC investigations in Alabama, Tennessee, and Georgia, in which states employers in the war industries used the excuse of untrained Black workers as a reason for not hiring them: employers 'when approached about hiring Negroes in skilled or even semi-skilled occupations, could and did . . . point out in many instances that qualified Negro workers were unavailable because of the lack of the necessary pre-employment training'.[144] The Federal government's failure to ensure that Federal funds for training were open to all citizens provided a pretext for private employers to reject 'untrained' Black workers.

A hearing of the FEPC in April 1942 included a lengthy discussion of the appropriate Federal responses to discriminatory job orders and the torpid progress of local and state authorities in addressing the training needs of Black job-seekers. The Commissioner of the US Office of Education, whose local branches had responsibility for training, defended his office and espoused his opposition to discrimination. Some of the FEPC members were unhappy with the progress of the Commissioner's Office: 'You see, Mr Studebaker, Executive Order 8802 is nothing more or less than a pious wish unless we have cooperation of Governmental departments that can cooperate, if they will.' The same Committee member, John Brophy, observed: 'we are pushing this as hard as we can, but we have got to have the cooperation of Governmental departments. We can't wink at discrimination being practiced or accepted as a matter of course and get away with much pressure on private employers.'[145]

Brophy was making a point which had exercised the Committee for some time. Its remit included government employment as well as private-sector employers, and the persistence of discrimination by agencies nominally and formally part of the US Federal government damaged the Committee's credibility. As Brophy explained: 'I think it is perfectly despicable on the part of private employers to indulge in discrimination against minorities, but I think it is positively vile when Governmental bodies wink at discrimination, or don't apply themselves because discrimination has become a vested interest or a vested situation in certain sections.'[146] An example of such practices was the four complainants in the Civil Service Commission discussed above, indicative of the embeddedness of discrimination within the framework system of segregation to which Federal agencies adhered. Another example was the actions of officials in training programmes. The FEPC's hearings in Alabama, Tennessee, and Georgia included the finding that 'the state officials in charge of defense training . . . have because of their race denied and are denying Negroes opportunities for adequate, equitable and necessary defense training financed by Federal funds'. Furthermore, the FEPC argued that legislation enacted in October 1940 accorded the US Office of Education 'ample power to prevent discrimination against persons because of race, in the administration and execution of defense training programs in the several states, but that the Office of Education has failed to use such power effectively'.[147] The Committee's indictment of the Office of Education did not end at this point. It found that the US Office of Education failed to comply with Executive Order 8802 and, as a consequence, 'that (a) it has acquiesced in and permitted the denial of adequate and equitable training for Negroes in Alabama, Georgia and Tennessee; (b) it has failed to require the officials in those states to provide in their training programs necessary and equitable facilities and opportunities for the training of Negroes, and (c) it has neglected to issue sufficient instructions and directions prohibiting discrimination by reason of race or color'. The Committee also accused the Office of Education of failing, as instructed, to 'inspect the various defense training programs then in operation as the result of plans approved by the Office of Education' to ascertain whether the programmes were in fact administered to ensure equal training opportunity to persons without regard to race, creed, colour or national origins, and of failing to submit a report based on such an inspection.[148] Evidently the winking at discrimination which so alarmed the FEPC persisted in the Office of Education. The Office was also accused of failing to issue instructions to all state officials administering defence training programmes about ending discrimination and of failing to eliminate discrimination in those federally funded programmes it administered. This latter oversight had actually exacerbated discrimination for Black job-seekers: 'because of the shortage of machinery and equipment for training purposes, this failure of the Office of Education to act has aided and abetted the increased discrimination against Negroes in defense training opportunities, particularly in areas where state laws require separate schools.'[149] The Committee issued three directives to the US Office of Education. First, that it 'cease and desist from approving defense training plans which do not contain adequate provisions against discrimination'. Second, that the Office re-examine the programmes in the three states studied and withhold funds for defence training there until discrimination against black workers was eliminated. Third, that the Office inspect the plants to ensure discrimination did not resurface.[150]

Discrimination was widespread in apprenticeship programmes, as a study prepared by the NAACP in 1960 documented. Entitled 'Negro Wage Earners and Apprenticeship', the study's author calculated that at existing levels of enrolment it would 'take Negroes 138 years, or until the Year 2094 to secure equal participation in skilled craft training and employment'.[151] There was, of course, a powerful historical legacy of exclusion from apprenticeships experienced by Black workers (a phenomenon closely related to the dominance of craft unions in the American Federation of Labor),[152] first challenged only during the Second World War: 'although slow in emerging, a discernible trend towards equal opportunity in skilled-craft positions became evident as the war progressed.'[153] The FEPC's work helped improve the position of Black workers. These advances should not be overstated: in 1940 Black workers constituted 4.4 per cent of skilled workers and foremen in the USA compared with 15.9 per cent for Whites; and in 1950 the figures were respectively 7.6 per cent and 19.3 per cent.[154] The NAACP linked these patterns in skilled work to apprenticeship opportunities: 'underlying the absence of Negroes in significant numbers from skilled-craft employment is their almost total exclusion from apprenticeship training programs.' Put in stark language: 'Negroes do not become apprentices.'[155] Black workers constituted a mere 1.69 per cent of the total number of apprentices in 1950.[156] According to the NAACP, the practices of craft trade unions continued to act as a substantial obstacle to equal opportunity: 'no significant advances have been made by Negroes into those craft unions which have historically excluded non-whites.' This conclusion applied with a 'special force' to the apprenticeship programmes controlled by the same unions.[157] This latter conclusion acquired increased significance from the responsibility delegated to unions to administer federal apprenticeship programmes, as the NAACP recognized: 'Negroes are also denied apprenticeships by unions substantially controlling apprenticeship programs because the granting of skilled-training opportunities to non-whites entails intra-union political considerations and ramifications.' Apprenticeship places were too lucrative to waste on Black Americans: 'apprenticeships are prizes which are eagerly sought by members for their offsprings or friends', and were used as patronage, thereby perpetuating exclusion: 'Negroes—because of past discriminatory practices—are not usually constituents. Hence, and from the very limited viewpoint of most local unions, nothing can be gained, but much might be lost, by accepting Negroes into apprenticeship training.'[158]

Such inequities by unions were supposed to be regulated and overturned by Federal and state bureaux of apprenticeships. Plainly, these bodies were failing in their responsibilities: 'public apprenticeship agencies have not exercised any of their considerable powers to insure that apprenticeship programs are open to all youth regardless of race, creed, color or national origin.' The problem was not even acknowledged by the regulatory authorities: 'public funds are being extensively used, directly or indirectly, to support apprenticeship programs from which one racial group is largely excluded, in direct violation, of course, of the Fourteenth Amendment.'[159] The NAACP chastised also state agencies responsible for fair employment practices for ignoring apprenticeships.

The NAACP naturally enough urged significant changes in apprenticeship programmes and in the role of public agencies regulating their practices.

Regrettably few of these suggestions were implemented and, throughout the 1960s, criticisms of discrimination in apprenticeship schemes continued.[160]

THE PERSISTENCE OF DISCRIMINATION 1946–1964

In November 1950 the FEB wrote to each Federal agency requesting information about its fair employment practices. Under Executive Order 9980, each department and agency was required to appoint a fair employment officer and to promulgate procedures for remedying charges of discrimination. Most departments established such measures.[161] The FEB directed each department to issue instructions to employees about fair employment policy; and they quizzed each department annually about its policy.[162] These letters mostly produced standard and unctuous replies from government agencies stating their compliance with fair employment practices. Departmental fair employment officers often stalled in establishing whether non-White employees were progressing in their agencies, pleading lack of appropriate data. For instance, according to the officer at the Department of Interior (writing a month after the deadline for the requested information), this task was too large: 'I have been unable to devise a reporting form which would result in meaningful statistics without making it so voluminous as to prohibit its use.'[163] The same department could report in 1952 the persistence of segregation in its working conditions: 'if Negroes . . . are assigned to segregated work units it is an exigency of the service.' This latter phrase apparently meant that 'the practice would exist only because the work being done requires that members of the staff conducting it be set apart whether they be white or Negro or mixed'.[164] Of course, the staff set apart did not have to be composed of one race! This tortured explanation mystifies rather than clarifies the reason for segregation.

The FEB had great difficulty in getting Federal agencies to supply requested information on time (and in some cases, at all) and not to obfuscate their responses.[165] Its members were often sceptical about the claims received from agencies. In a letter in November 1951, the Fair Employment Officer in the Post Office Department assured the Board that, 'while no specific surveys have been taken, employment and/or promotion is based entirely on merit and fitness as an established policy. Negroes and members of other minority groups have been regularly integrated into the work force in accordance with the long established employment policy of the Department.' The Officer added: 'the Department does not have segregated work units.'[166] Alongside each of these statements someone at the Fair Employment Board has penned a large question mark provoked, presumably, by disbelief. Congressional hearings and task forces were established in the 1960s to examine discrimination in the postal service.

On a more positive note, a representative from the Fair Employment Board informed a congressional hearing in 1952 that a third of the Federal government agencies had either promoted Black Americans to supervisory positions, which included supervised racially mixed groups, or appointed Black Americans to professional and executive positions for the first time.[167]

Although the FEB was located within the Civil Service Commission, its members recognized the Commission's ambivalent role in combating discrimination against Black employees and job-seekers. The 'rule of three' system remained a source of concern.[168] President Truman's adviser on minority affairs, Philleo Nash, was reluctant for the Board openly to criticize the Commissioners, a preference communicated to the FEB: 'Mr Nash expressed the opinion to the Chairman that the Board was "on the right track." . . . The Chairman advised Mr Nash that the Board was planning to "lay it on the line" with the Commission thru its report to the President . . . Mr Nash requested the Board not to precipitate a crisis.'[169] The White House suggested a weaker view.

The FEB conducted further surveys in 1951 and 1954 of Federal agencies to determine the numbers of Black employees, the presence or absence of segregated work arrangements, the procedures for ensuring fair employment practice, and the occupational distribution of Black workers. Once again, departments equivocated in responding to these requests.[170] Succeeding the FEB, President Eisenhower's Committee on Government Employment Policy conducted surveys of the percentage and hierarchical distribution of Black employees in the Federal government, the results of which are used in Table 3.3. Cases of discrimination were referred to the Committee if the agency within which they arose was unable to satisfy the complainant.[171] Table 3.3 gives a selected example of the sort of complaints received by the Committee and its decisions. These data have two major findings: first, the comparative rarity of a finding of discrimination, and second, the overwhelming importance of race as the grounds for filing a complaint. By January 1961 the President's Committee had received almost 1,700 complaints.[172] The Committee conducted detailed analyses of those complaints referred to it after the agency concerned had failed to take sufficient measures to satisfy the complainant. For example, the Committee found in favour of Mr Cecil E. Golder's complaint against the Department of the Navy in October 1958 that his failure to be promoted at the Naval Avionics Facility, Indianapolis, arose from his race.[173] The Committee ordered that Golder receive promotion forthwith. As the selective data in Table 3.3 reports, the Navy was commonly the object of complaint by Black Americans.

One Black pressure group, the Southern Regional Council, judged the President's Committee to be less effective than it ought to have been in monitoring and assessing discrimination. The Committee had a 'hopelessly small staff'. The mechanisms for complaining were inadequate because they

TABLE 3.3. *President's Committee on Government Employment Policy: Selected example of complaints 25 August 1954–30 August 1957*[a]

Dept.	No. of complaints
Navy	27
Interior	2
VA	4
Commerce	1
Army	20
Labor	1
Air Force	10
Post Office	18
Government Services Administration	4
Treasury	2
HEW	4
FHA	2
TVA	1
Civil Service Commission	2
Government Printing Office	1
TOTAL	99

Note: Of the 99 complaints, 92 were based on grounds of race, and 7 on religion. In 14 cases the Committee found that there had been discrimination, and in 83 not.

[a] Some of the cases were pending at the time of the Committee's establishment.

Source: NA RG 220, President's Committee on Government Employment Policy 1955–61, Appeals Files, Box 35.

relied too much on the offending agency: 'the procedures outlined by Executive Order 10590 require the filing of complaints by individuals and the investigation of these by the accused agency itself. The Committee has seen its primary task to be long-range education rather than immediate compliance.'[174] The Committee held regular meetings of government department employment officers to familiarize them with non-discrimination policy.[175] The Southern Regional Council recommended shifting the Committee's focus to a 'continuing review of agency practices' rather than the processing of complaints.[176] The Council also sought a general review of government hiring, believing that many agencies failed to enforce non-discrimination: 'there should be overall review of federal employment practices, without waiting for complaints and with the aim of immediate compliance with the policy of non-discrimination. Agencies whose functions are critically related to civil rights have a pressing need for Negro staff.'[177]

In 1961 President Kennedy established the President's EEOC, chaired by then Vice President Lyndon Johnson. The EEOC reported in November

TABLE 3.4. *Complaints received by the President's EEOC 1961–1963*

Dept.	Total no. of employees	Negro employment		Complaints received	
		No.	% of total	No.	% of total
Post Office	577,639	86,981	15.1	369	18.4
Army	345,851	42,838	12.4	317	15.8
Navy	312,798	42,880	13.7	343	17.1
Air Force	276,373	21,316	7.7	282	14.1
VA	150,847	35,281	23.4	164	8.2
Agriculture	92,104	2,890	3.1	29	1.5
Treasury	79,691	9,627	12.1	127	6.3
HEW	70,489	13,882	19.7	62	3.1
Interior	55,093	1,933	3.5	14	0.7
Fed. Aviation Agency	39,795	1,031	2.6	13	0.7
Commerce	29,383	3,440	11.7	81	4.0
Defense	23,712	4,951	20.9	15	0.7
All others	206,218	26,303	12.8	189	9.4

Source: EEOC, *Report to the President* (Washington: GPO, 1963), 106.

1963. Alluding to complaints about discrimination in the Federal government, the Committee reported that such grievances were concentrated in a selected group of larger agencies: 'four-fifths of the complaints received by the Committee, and about the same fraction of the total Government employees, are in seven departments and agencies—Post Office Department, Departments of the Army, Navy, and Air Force, Veterans Administration, Department of Agriculture, and Treasury Department' (see Table 3.4).[178] Complaints to the EEOC did not follow any obvious geographic pattern. Thus in its first two years, 'about one-fourth of [complaints] have come from the two civil service regions comprising most of the South, i.e., the Atlanta and Dallas Regions, 23.2 per cent. The New York, Philadelphia and Boston Regions, which include most of the populous Middle Atlantic and New England States, account for 24.3 per cent of all complaints received.' Elsewhere, 'metropolitan Washington, D.C. has accounted for 18.8 per cent, the Far West, 13.6 per cent (San Francisco and Seattle Regions); and the Midwest 13.5 per cent (Chicago Region)'.[179] Of the 2,005 complaints received by the President's EEOC, the vast majority arose from a grievance about race: 1,840 (91.8 per cent) compared with 83 and 82 complaints charging discrimination on grounds of creed and national origin respectively.[180] This distribution was not dissimilar to that recorded in Table 3.3, above, for the earlier President's Committee on Government Employment Policy. However, the dismissal rate was slightly lower: one-half of the complaints were dismissed but corrective action was taken in 36.1 per cent of the cases, 423 in number. The remainder were dismissed or withdrawn.

Segregation in Federal departments began to be tackled resolutely in the 1960s, though instances of its persistence remained. In 1961 Black employees in the Government Printing Office maintained that 'there are certain areas of the Printing Office where there is little hope of a Negro employee ever advancing to a higher level of work',[181] and in April 1964 a group of Black workers in the GAO complained about segregation.[182] The passage of the Civil Rights Act in 1964, however, marked a serious commitment against discrimination and segregation, and implemented mechanisms in the Federal government departments to achieve their eradication.

CONCLUSION

Working in the Federal civil service did not constitute participation in a Goffman-like total institution.[183] None the less, it was and remains an organization which functions according to its own formal and informal codes, and in the decades before the 1960s these stipulated *de facto* a subordinate position for Black American employees, both in terms of the occupations they held and in relationship to White employees. These features are conveyed clearly in the hearings held by the FEPC and the various surveys conducted of employment patterns in Federal agencies. Even the distribution of Black employees remained skewed (see Tables A3.8 and A3.9).

By 1965 the White House was able to claim an improved profile for Black Americans in the civil service. The chairman of the US Civil Service Commission announced (in November 1965) that Black Americans had gained footholds in the middle and upper grades of the Federal government compared with the beginning of the decade (Tables A3.9–A3.15). Since the 1960s employment in the civil service has increased in importance for Black Americans, and their distribution across levels is less skewed than it has been historically. Public employment is now a more significant source of work for this group than it is for White Americans. This development suggests the scale of discrimination within the Federal government before the 1960s: Black employees have evidently had no difficulty in satisfactorily discharging senior positions, once promoted to them.

Segregated race relations clearly had profound effects upon the working experience of Black employees in Federal government. None of the positive gains anticipated by President Woodrow Wilson in 1913 was achieved. Not only were such workers delimited physically to accord to the principle of segregation but, despite the alleged impartiality of 'separate but equal', their occupational distribution cogently demonstrates that separation meant inequality. Black American workers infrequently advanced beyond the lower grade or the more unattractive clerical and custodial bureaucratic positions. Attempts to break from this pattern exposed how segregation was a thin disguise for discrimination: the failure of the four Black women workers in the Personnel Classification Board either to attain permanent status or to move from night to day shifts (modifications proffered to their White colleagues) illustrates this problem.

Until the 1960s and President Johnson's successful enactment of civil rights legislation, congressional committee members, predominantly Southern Democrats, provided a powerful check on desegregation and racial equality within government agencies. They were more powerful and well organized in defending their sectional interests than the non-discrimination directives and fair employment agencies created by Presidents Roosevelt, Truman, Eisenhower, and Kennedy designed to ameliorate the position of Black employees in the US Federal government.

PART III

The Federal Government and Segregation beyond Washington

4

'A Great Shadow over our "Civil Rights"': Fighting for the Government

IN February 1940 a Black American, Bernard Randolph, wrote to the NAACP about his failure to join the Army. He was 'told point-blank that there's no place for Negroes' in the Armed Forces. In Randolph's view, a 'great shadow is being cast over our "civil rights" by what we have been schooled to revere as our flag. It is a shadow that must be brightened if complete equality in the name of democracy is ever to evolve in our midst.'[1] The NAACP's reply assured Randolph that his rejection was far from exceptional:

> We have been pressing this matter of fair treatment of Negro citizens in the armed services of the country for many years. We have found that in all our dealings with the government, the War Department is the toughest nut to crack. It is . . . staffed almost from top to bottom with southerners. These men have succeeded in stamping their ideas into the department so that their prejudices have become the pattern for the treatment of Negroes.[2]

When Woodrow Wilson was elected president in 1912, several bills were introduced into the Congress proposing to exclude Black recruits entirely from the Armed Services and to prevent them from receiving commissions. Southern Democrats did not confine their racial agenda to segregation in the Federal civil service but monitored segregated race relations in the military, and limited the promotion prospects of Black recruits.

Segregated race relations were a characteristic of the US Armed Forces from the founding of the USA and the War of Independence. They were thus deeply ingrained. General George Washington decided not to use Black Americans in the Army during the War of Independence, issuing an order to that effect on 12 November 1775. This order was based upon a recommendation of a committee in the Continental Congress.[3] The policy was quickly reversed, however, as the British encouraged Black Americans to rise up against the colonists.[4] In the Civil War (1861–5), Black Americans were accepted in the Army but only in segregated all-Black units.[5] The end of that war saw 178,985 Black American recruits in the Union Army. Six all-Black units were established in the post-Civil War peacetime army, though, as Reddick notes, this was for pragmatic rather than segregationist reasons.[6]

By the Second World War, segregation of Black American recruits was standard policy and systematically enforced. Bitterness at the limited opportunities provided to Black Americans in the Great War diminished the willingness of Black American activists to encourage enlisting in 1941, as they did readily in the earlier conflict.[7] And indeed, even in 1917 the NAACP noted the irony of the United States defending freedom abroad given the 'one difficulty that silently or articulately must give every American pause'. This difficulty was the death of 'democratic government . . . in a third of the land', and the harbouring of 'caste'.[8] In 1941 war was accompanied, from Black Americans, not with appeals to join ranks with White Americans but by an 'intensification of Negro demands for equality in all phases of the national effort'.[9]

One legacy of these experiences was an understandable scepticism amongst some Black Americans about the United States' self-proclaimed role as a defender of civil rights and democracy abroad at a time when such privileges were denied to many citizens at home. Discrimination in the war industries intensified this ambivalence, as a survey in 1942 documented: 'Negroes in the United States have only partially identified their own interests with those of the nation. They are a special segment within a society dominated by white symbols and values.' As a consequence of this subservient and unequal citizenship, Black Americans had applied their 'energies . . . to winning for their own race a greater measure of freedom and opportunity'.[10] The same report found that Black Americans were loyal to the United States, in fact 'deeply devoted to American ideals', but conscious of how little these ideals were 'realized in relation to themselves'.[11] The conflict was perceived as a 'white man's war. This is a feeling fostered in part by the impediments to Negro participation and in part by doubts as to the benefits which victory may confer upon the colored race.'[12] This attitude resulted in covert support for the Japanese, also excluded from the White world. Because of 'resentment against the white population', many Black respondents harboured a 'desire to see the whites humiliated, to see white supremacy toppled by a people with darker skins. The military successes won in the Far East by the Japanese have given to many Negroes a measure of satisfaction.' Crude wartime jingoism intensified their support: 'they are disposed to identify themselves as brothers of the colored Asiatics who are assailing the white man's civilization—a disposition which has been stimulated by contemporary references to the Japanese as "little yellow men" or by other aspersions on their color.'[13] Anticipated consequences of a German victory were far more pessimistic amongst the same group; however, significantly, the researcher found a 'substantial number of Negroes so embittered by the treatment accorded them in this country as to feel that Nazi intolerance could be no worse'.[14]

These concerns were articulated by Black American leaders, notably A.

Philip Randolph, and groups such as the NAACP and the 'Double-V Campaign' (victory for democracy at home as well as abroad). The former dimension was paramount: 'to many Negroes, the achievement of democracy at home takes precedence over the conflict abroad and is a condition of their contribution to the national effort.' The commitment to this priority was unwavering: 'some of them declare that they would rather die, if necessary, fighting for democratic rights in this country than in foreign fields.'[15] That leading allies such as Britain had their own colonial records did not escape Black Americans either.

This set of accumulated grievances and concerns were in many instances baldly exacerbated by recruitment drives for the US Armed Services or for employment in war industries since, in both cases, Black Americans encountered prejudice and discrimination instead of opportunity and equal treatment.[16] The same 1942 survey interviewed Whites in addition to Black Americans, finding better-educated members of the former supportive of amelioration in the political rights of Blacks, but this did not extend to the less well off: 'the poor whites . . . are not conspicuously anxious to help Negroes get better jobs or wages.'[17]

This attitude was consistent with historical prejudices and with the racism of most organized labour movements. A comment later in the same report revealed some appreciation of the problem: 'the fact that slightly more than three-fifths of the poor whites expect the treatment of Negroes to be unchanged may perhaps be interpreted as an indication that they are indifferent to the conditions under which Negroes live or unprepared to make any concessions to them.'[18] Such views provided the political context within which many White Americans endeavoured energetically and violently to reassert the Jim Crow *status quo* after 1945.

THE SECOND WORLD WAR AND SEGREGATION

As this survey suggests, the Second World War posed awkward questions about segregation. It exposed not only the peculiarity of fighting for democracy abroad when it did not exist fully in the United States but also the profound inequalities facing Black American recruits in the Armed Services. As one report, prepared in 1942, noted of the latter issue: 'Negro attitudes toward the armed forces are colored by a long-standing resentment against their policies of segregation and exclusion; the war, the operations of the Selective Service Law and the treatment accorded Negroes recently brought into the Army and Navy merely sharpened these feelings and produced a keener awareness of them.'[19] At the centre of Black American resentment toward both branches of the Armed Forces was their internal segregation: 'there is a strong feeling among them [Black Americans] that no distinction ought to be made among men wearing Uncle Sam's uniform.'[20] A dramatic manifestation of Black Americans' disaffection was the finding that in response to the question whether defeating the Japanese and Germans was more important than making democracy work better at home, 90 per cent of White respondents identified the former compared with only 50.5 per cent of Black Americans. Thirty-eight per cent of Black Americans thought the second aim more important compared with 5 per cent of whites.[21]

By the end of the war, three million Black Americans had registered to serve in the Armed Services, of whom 695,264 were inducted and nearly half a million served overseas. The experience generated pressure for changes after the war: 'most of these servicemen had written home about their military experiences, sowing the seeds for widespread Negro dissatisfaction with the Defense Department.'[22] In his autobiography, the journalist Carl Rowan recalls returning to Norfolk, Virginia, for demobilization and the frustration of searching for a job: 'I had looked around at Norfolk, still relentlessly Jim Crow, and at black families, still carrying the scars of the Great Depression, still mired in unemployment, and I realized that I was angry. "We fought for nothing," I told myself again and again.' These feelings were not helped by a rapid encounter with racism: '"Where you goin', boy?" the bus driver asked me, sending my blood vessels bulging . . . I got off the bus to stretch my legs at a rest stop . . . and was infuriated by the signs: WHITE WAITING ROOM/COLORED WAITING ROOM. And on the toilet doors: WHITE LADIES/ COLORED WOMEN.'[23] During 1942 and 1943 George Nesbitt supplied the District of Columbia Branch of the NAACP with regular memoranda from Fort Stewart in Georgia about the position of Black recruits there.[24] In his own words, Nesbitt declared, 'I write not for your information but for the sake of posterity.'[25] (After the war Nesbitt became a racial relations adviser in the FHA.) He described the arrival of recruits in Georgia: 'we met Jim Crow when we disboarded at Atlanta Georgia for exercise. The lavatories were labelled "white" and "colored", thus assuring proper organisation and classification of the excretary.'[26] The Black recruits were informed curtly by a Southern White lieutenant: 'you men may come from sections of the country where you can be independent. But you'll have to learn to salute us.'[27] From early 1943 Nesbitt predicted an outbreak of serious violence in the Camp because of racial tension, as indeed occurred.

Many Americans, including President Truman, appreciated the hollowness of US pretensions to promote democracy in the new global community while tolerating the suppression of civil rights domestically. As A. Philip Randolph told Truman in 1947: 'Negroes do not want to shoulder a gun to fight for democracy abroad unless full democracy is obtained at home.'[28] The White House characterized Randolph as 'a nasty guy'.[29]

Despite the bitter experience of Black recruits during the war and the efforts of Randolph, the political impediments to desegregating the Armed

Forces were overwhelming. Franklin Roosevelt's dependence upon electoral support from White Southern voters had ensured that he adroitly downplayed and sidestepped the issue of racial practices, though he did have to create the FEPC. During Truman's presidency the increasing electoral power of Black American Democratic voters encouraged him to challenge the party's traditional opposition to civil rights. Truman faced comparable obstacles in Congress to those limiting Roosevelt's antidiscrimination initiatives. In 1946 the congressional elections produced results indicative of a national rightward shift. Partly to attract the electoral support of Northern Black voters, Truman issued executive initiatives tackling segregation. Because of the hostility of White Southerners in the party, this strategy was costly. The Democrats divided at their 1948 national convention over the inclusion of civil rights reforms in the party platform (in response to the report issued by President Truman's Committee on Civil Rights).[30] Such an agenda was anathema to Southern Democrats in the Party and, through the Southern Governors' Conference, they mobilized against it.[31] Southern delegates were pledged to walk out if civil rights were retained on the platform. At the convention the delegates from Mississippi and half of those from Alabama left, the remaining Southern states voting to nominate Georgian Senator Richard B. Russell, but Truman obtained a plurality. This so-called Dixiecrat revolt did not prevent Truman's nomination nor his electoral victory in the presidential contest, but it did demonstrate powerfully the continuing salience of race to the party and the capacity of this issue to divide its supporters. However, Truman, genuinely moved by the post-war racist attacks on demobilized Black American recruits and no doubt conscious of the party's shifting electoral needs, was unequivocal in addressing the civil rights of Black Americans.

For many Southerners, re-establishing the old Jim Crow rules after 1945 was a priority. The pre-war barriers to equal Black American labour-market and public-sector participation were restored. Congress refused to create a permanent fair employment practice committee and some members attempted to taint the wartime FEPC as communist-influenced. President Truman understood well the politics of this defeat, recalling in 1947 that 'no sooner were we finished with the war than racial and religious intolerance began to appear and threaten the very things we had just fought for . . . [Consequently] I created this Committee [on Civil Rights] with a feeling of urgency.'[32] In this national political setting, Truman set about prodding change by establishing committees of inquiry and exercising the powers he held as chief executive.

Meeting with the Committee on the Armed Services,[33] attended by the Secretaries of Defense, the Army, the Navy, and the Air Force on 12 January 1949, President Truman alluded to the potential application of executive action to improve civil rights for Blacks. The meeting lasted ten minutes. Truman explained his intention thus:

Well, gentlemen, I issued an Executive Order, last spring on the better treatment—not 'fair' treatment, but 'equal' *treatment in the Government Service for everybody*, regardless of his race or creed or color, and if it's slowly and gradually taking hold. And I have asked you gentlemen to serve on this Commission in an effort *to expedite the thing in the Government Service* so that you can actually carry out the spirit, as well as the letter, of the order . . . *Of course, as Commander in Chief, I can issue orders to the Armed Services*, and, if there is some legal approach in all the rest of the branches of the Government, we might as well make a complete program out of it while we are at it. That's what I have in mind all the way down the line.[34]

To Secure These Rights, issued by President Truman's Committee on Civil Rights in 1947, provided an important background to the investigation of segregation in the Armed Services. The report's recommendation that segregation in the United States be ended was seized upon by A. Philip Randolph. Rallying his Committee against Jim Crow in Military Service and Training,[35] Randolph threatened to organize a mass civil disobedience campaign, demanding immediate desegregation in the Services.[36] This threat exposed the persistence of segregation and the limited promotion prospects of Black Americans in the military. When the Senate Armed Services Committee considered a bill to introduce selective service for all young American men, Randolph pushed his offensive: 'I would like to make it clear to this committee and through you to Congress and the American people that passage now of a Jim Crow draft may only result in mass civil disobedience.'[37] Randolph's appearance outraged conservative committee members, such as Richard B. Russell of Georgia, wedded to segregated race relations. Although Randolph's movement lacked the resources and organization to deliver the threatened protest it focused attention on segregation in the military. The cause of segregation was not bolstered by General Eisenhower's comment to the same Senate committee that 'there is race prejudice in this country . . . When you pass a law to get somebody to like someone, you have trouble.'[38] Eisenhower's remarks provoked a letter of protest from the NUL to the Secretary of Defense.[39] Predictably, amendments to the bill introduced by Adam Powell and Jacob Javits to desegregate the military were defeated. The bill passed Congress and was signed by President Truman with no change to segregation.[40]

SEGREGATION AND THE ARMED SERVICES

In the Armed Services both prior to, and during, the Second World War, Black American recruits were segregated by units and initially excluded entirely from certain branches of the Service, such as the Marines. At the beginning of the United States's participation in the war, all Black recruits in the Navy were in the stewards' branch and 'no other Navy jobs were open to Negroes'.[41] Life in the Armed Services was completely segregated. Mirroring arrangements in Federal government departments, throughout the Armed Services, Black recruits served disproportionately not in combat but in support positions such as building roads, loading and unloading war materials, and transportation. Senior military personnel were convinced that Black recruits were inferior soldiers and restricted their access to combat. This belief was pervasive and entrenched amongst White officers. It held sway with the commanding officers who had grown up in a segregated society and who had absorbed and reproduced the associated beliefs of Black Americans' inferiority. In discussion with enlisted men, officers were instructed to avoid political issues, of which integration was considered a prime example. As Stillman notes: 'the fear of introducing a social reform and of alienating Southern conservatives arose at the mere suggestion of integration. And in the years before the Brown Decision, integration was a pretty startling suggestion even to the average white American.'[42] The Pentagon appointed civil rights' counsellors (William Hastie for the Army Air Corps, Truman Gibson for the War Department, and Lester Granger for the Navy Department), but they had limited success in persuading the Armed Services to break down segregation. One Black soldier, Benjamin O. Davis Sr., was promoted a brigadier-general during the war but his position was confined to that of racial adviser to other generals.

A report in 1947 identified four problems confronting Black recruits while serving in the Armed Services: (1) limited recruitment and poor promotion prospects; (2) what the report's authors termed a 'backlog of prejudice against them among white officers and men'; (3) the official policy of segregation in the Service; and (4) the 'tension between Negro soldiers and white civilians', especially but not exclusively in 'Southern communities and in others where public transportation and recreation facilities were inadequate'.[43] The first three impediments mirrored those facing Black American employees in civilian government positions. The segregated facilities, a hallmark of Southern society, were harsh and unfamiliar to many conscripts from the North (though prejudice and discrimination were hardly novel). Black Americans used to exercising their liberties as citizens suddenly and violently found themselves the object of White southerners' anger and abuse in public places.

Black soldiers constituted about 10 per cent of the US Armed Services. Their educational level was notably higher than that of Black recruits during the First World War. One in every four had had some high school training; whereas 95 per cent of Black soldiers had only grade school education in 1916–18, during the Second World War the figure was 57 per cent. 'The natural consequence' of these developments, in the report's inimitable language, 'was a more prevalent intense feeling on the part of Negroes that they were entitled to continuing improvements in their assignments in the forces'.[44]

The assignment of White officers to Black units magnified these grievances and the incidences of violence against such officers was high; naturally, military police, responsible for enforcing Jim Crow segregation rules upon Black Recruits unused to Southern codes, were White. Conflict was endemic. Consequently, 'after a bitter summer of violence [in 1942], the war department officially acknowledged the existence of a serious morale problem among Negro troops and urged all white officers to treat blacks with the utmost care and diplomacy'.[45] A confidential report prepared in 1942 emphasized the level of disaffection amongst Black Americans arising from both their treatment in the Armed Forces and continuing discrimination in the United States. An accompanying survey found over two-fifths of the Black respondents prioritizing the achievement of democracy in the United States over defeating Germany and Japan: 'right now do you think it is more important to concentrate on beating Germany and Japan or to make democracy work better here at home?' In response, 'nearly two-fifths of the New York Negroes felt that primary emphasis should be placed on the first half of the their two-edged sword—democracy at home, as well as abroad'.[46] The report's authors speculated that the 12 per cent failing to answer this question were perhaps 'reluctant to voice an opinion out of keeping with the prevailing white pattern of thought'.[47] These findings came from New York, where the misery of segregation and discrimination were in some respects less salient, though far from absent, than in other parts of the United States.

A report[48] recommending integration of the Armed Services prepared before the US entry into the war was rejected by the Secretary of War, who judged such a policy inappropriate at that time. John McCloy, Assistant Secretary of War and responsible for minorities, explained to the Fahy Committee that the wartime policy toward Black recruits became one of establishing combat units composed of minorities, 'to show that minority troops could make good combat soldiers, because there was a very definitely prevalent opinion that . . . the quality of Negro troops was not up to standard in combat'.[49] He explained also how pressures to integrate combat units in the line were resisted: 'I remember the Secretary [of War Stimson] spent a lot of time giving thought to that [integration].' The analysis was not favourable: 'we came to the conclusion that, at least during the period of war, that it would be unwise to do that.' Grim scenarios were predicted: 'there were all sorts of terrible prophecies of what they might become, but we didn't want to take the risk of a shake in morale that might be involved.'[50]

Unremarkably, the President Committee's report focused upon the efficient utilization of Black soldiers in the wartime Armed Services rather than upon the urgency of establishing equality. This task would require: the selection and training of 'sufficient Negro Officer Candidates for training in the established Officer Candidate Schools'; the assignment of junior Black officers to small detached units and to the performance of morale functions; and 'Negro flying and non-flying personnel for Air Corps combat forces must be directed through channels other than the Tuskegee bottleneck in order to make timely use of a substantial pool of needed man-power'.[51] There was only limited movement toward widening the opportunities for a small number of Black recruits;[52] for the vast majority, Armed Services experience was one of segregation, the worst service jobs, and, often violent, racism. The first two patterns mirrored those of Black American employees in the US Federal government who were disproportionately concentrated in menial positions and discriminated against within the segregation framework. Thus, the Army Air Force refused to train more than one all-Black fighter unit during the war (at the Tuskegee Institute in Alabama where all training was undertaken by White officers and eating facilities were segregated).[53] Even agreeing to this one unit caused much anguish. It was established after lobbying and complaints by Black American groups. Revealingly, the Air Force did not anticipate this one unit being ready for combat until 1944, a fact which prompted the following observations in a memorandum from the Acting Civilian Aide to the Secretary of War: 'the assumption of the Army Air Forces seems to be that Negroes can not be developed into Army pilots. If this were not so, then there would be some consideration of a continuing training program.'[54] In fact, pressure from the NAACP and other interest groups forced the Armed Services to train some Black recruits in White training units. At these units, unsuccessful Black candidates were differently treated from Whites, according to the NAACP. White candidates flunking out were 'in most cases immediately transferred to another branch of the Air Forces, but Negroes who fail are sent home and presumably inducted by the draft board for general military service'.[55] Gibson concluded in his March 1943 memorandum that 'there are no plans existing for using Negroes in any other branch than the single engine fighter type of organization'. Thus the opportunity for Black American recruits to succeed was circumscribed: 'even if Negroes prove themselves the war would have long since ended before any plans could be developed for any effective utilization.' He added, caustically, that 'even Great Britain has found it possible to use Negroes in all types of aircraft'.[56] In January 1943 William Hastie, civil rights counsel to the Army Air Corps, resigned because of the Army's procrastination in training Black flyers.[57] His well-publicized resignation contributed to the formation of the 99th Fighter Squadron. Hastie continued to campaign against segregation in the military.[58]

The system of segregation and concentration of Blacks in lower positions remained unreformed during the war. That the opportunities for Black American recruits in the Army Air Force were restricted to a single fighter unit is also significant, demonstrating an indifferent official commitment. Under-Secretary of War Robert Patterson tried, rather lamely, to explain this indifference: 'because of the technical and other features present in flying, it was decided to proceed toward the formation of more complicated units after having gained experience with the simpler units.'[59] In simpler language, Black Americans were considered too stupid to become pilots. In the same letter, Patterson admitted that 'no Negroes qualified to be service pilots have yet been used by the Air Forces. To date there have been very few applicants for this duty, but their number will increase as individuals who are now attending school become qualified. The use of qualified Negro service pilots is now under study.'[60] Patterson's tone was conciliatory—'the War Department will exert every effort to safeguard the interests of white and Negro personnel alike'[61]—but the practice in the Armed Services was discriminatory within the impoverished pretence of 'separate but equal' treatment.

In 1942 the Navy was forced to abandon segregation,[62] and to permit Black American recruitment beyond the stewards' branch. However, at the war's end, Black recruits in the Navy were still disproportionately concentrated in lower ranking positions and they had only marginal representation amongst officer positions.

The Second World War undoubtedly wrought some changes in the Armed Services but segregation remained at its conclusion. A sense of how segregation rigidly structured military values is suggested by an icy discussion of the racial categorization of new recruits conducted in front of Truman's investigative committee:[63]

MR GRANGER: There's a question I'd like to ask. Puerto Ricans, of course, are of varying shades, and many of them if born on the mainland would be considered White; others would be considered Negro; and the rest would be half way in between. Now coming to this Country, they have a language bond which makes them regarded not as White or Colored but as Puerto Ricans. Suppose two Puerto Ricans presented themselves for service, one being markedly fair and the other being, say, in the dividing line . . . Would the Army have any scheme for deciding which Puerto Ricans are White and which Puerto Ricans are colored?

COLONEL MCFADYEN: So far as the Army is concerned—

MR GRANGER: They are American citizens.

COLONEL MCFADYEN: Yes.

MR GRANGER: So a Puerto Rican of my complexion, if he were to present himself, would he go along with his fellow Puerto Ricans, or would he be cast out into outer darkness . . . Would he be treated as a Negro, or an American citizen? I mean would the segregative process be applied to a Puerto Rican because of his color? This isn't a facetious question. I am trying to find the Army psychology on the subject.

COLONEL MCFADYEN: Let me tackle that question from this angle. I am going back to the year 1946. In Puerto Rico there were two National Guard units composed of Puerto Ricans and the 65th Infantry, a regular US outfit that had been permanently stationed in Puerto Rico. At that time we had in the Organized Reserve units that were classed as Negroes.

MR GRANGER: But the Spanish speaking Puerto Rican born person, was he in the Negro unit?

COLONEL MCFADYEN: Not unless the local authorities had said that he was a Negro. The only ones that I recall that came from the Virgin Islands were from the surrounding islands.

MR GRANGER: Then, as I can make out, there is no real policy on Negroes of foreign background if they present themselves for service in this Country?

MAJOR GENERAL BROOKS: I wouldn't want that to be answered that way.[64]

These exchanges illustrate how embedded assumptions and attitudes, congruous with segregation, were amongst White Army officers. Recall that this discussion occurred in 1949, four years after the cessation of hostilities. The attitudes expressed before the President's Committee had developed historically and had come to be accepted as normal,[65] both within segregated institutions and in significant parts of society. The testimony received by the Fahy Committee demonstrates how this 'normality' dictated the construction of institutional arrangements. Genetics reveals the commonality of humanity, not its diversity.[66] Specification by race requires political and cultural intervention to define the bases of distinction and to justify them.

Racial Conflict in the Military

The contradictions of segregation within the US Armed Services did not remain abstract. They were often violent. The strain of maintaining segregated units was manifest throughout the war with racial conflict a constant problem. As Assistant Secretary of War John J. McCloy, responsible for minorities during the war, concluded: 'there was a period there in my term of office when I had the feeling that I was in front of a series of three separated steam jets that were escaping and I had two hands to cover them—I would get one problem covered and another one would be popping up.'[67] There were riots and arguments as the personnel needs of the war forced an expansion of the number of Black Americans enlisted and strained the Armed Services defence of segregation. In testimony before the Fahy Committee, he outlined some of the problems arising as the 'size of the Army increased and we had the problem of distributing and training them [minorities] throughout the country'.[68] The concentration of training camps in the South provoked clashes with local residents: 'the brawls were occurring between white soldiers and Negro soldiers, between Negroes and the citizens of local communities.' Enforcing Jim Crow in transportation was a singular problem: 'there were discriminatory practices which the Army set out to break and that caused a lot of local difficulties, and we had to install our own transportation systems, and we were constantly agog in those communities with these problems.' McCloy thought conditions could have deteriorated further:

'I marvel, as a matter of fact, that [in] some of these cases where there was a large accumulation of troops and the feeling was very tense that we escaped some ugly difficulties.'[69]

Racial disturbances reported at Army bases and Navy ports were caused by the prejudiced treatment of Black recruits by White officers, the resentment amongst Black soldiers about their limited opportunities, conflicts between White and Black recruits, and conflicts in local communities.[70] Following a riot at Guam, forty-five Black soldiers were court martialled and gaoled.[71] Walter White ardently protested this decision. He berated the Navy for its failure to curb the abuses preceding and provoking the incident: 'for a period of many weeks these and other Negro servicemen on the island of Guam were subjected to verbal and physical assault with virtually no action by the island authorities to protect these men from being attacked.' He singled out the four Navy base companies quartered in tents on the 'Agat-Sumay Road running from the Island Command of Guam to the Navy supply depots and other Naval installations'. White maintained that the 'white officers in command of these Negro troops were among the most inefficient it has ever been my experience to encounter'. The officers displayed callous 'indifference to the attacks upon their men and sought to hush up attacks upon them instead of insisting upon punishment of the attackers. There were repeated instances of Negro Navy personnel being physically assaulted in the town of Agana.'[72] These incidents show how the 'legitimacy' underpinning segregation rested on coercion and sanctions. The Roosevelt administration reacted principally by suppressing, to as great an extent as possible, news about riots and conflicts: the risk of alienating Southern Democratic Party support powerfully weighed upon the President, as did the likely impact on the morale of Black Americans resident in the United States.

Encountering rigid segregation in the South was a shock for many Black recruits from Northern states, familiar with racism but unused to the impunity with which White racists and vigilantes could behave. The confidential survey in 1942 unearthed this concern: 'another important grievance against the Army was that Negro troops are not protected from abuses by civilians, particularly in the South, and by white MPs in the Army.'[73] Transportation, rigidly segregated in the South, was a consistent focus of conflict.[74] The NAACP complained in 1943 that the Army failed to make any 'effort toward a solution of the dangerously alarming practice of spreading segregation in areas where it had never existed before—or, at least, had not been the accepted custom or legal practice'.[75] One recruit recalled a fateful visit he and a colleague made from their base to a small town. As he was about to leave a store the owner stopped him and forced him to hide under the building's porch. From this secluded vantage point he observed the grizzly sight of his colleague being dragged up and down the main street, tied to the back of a truck, until he died.[76] One recruit from New York described his experiences in the South at Fort Bragg: 'prejudice dominates and dictates nearly every phase of southern existence . . . Much of that hatred and bias is intensely expressed where [the] colored soldier is concerned.'[77] Segregation in public transportation was a new experience for northern recruits and its enforcement aroused conflict for the war's duration.[78] The NAACP had some success in desegregating bus journeys between the War Department Building and Washington but not further South. The Secretary of War asked the NAACP not to publicize this success![79]

Dismissing Black American recruits as inefficient in the discharge of their responsibilities was a common tactic to limit their promotion prospects. NAACP Assistant Secretary Wilkins wrote about the removal of Black personnel in the induction centre at Fort Benning, Georgia, and their replacement with Whites: 'the removal of the Negro personnel is being requested now on the ground that they have demonstrated inefficiency in handling the work of the induction center.' As Wilkins noted, tactics similar to those deployed in the Federal government agencies harmed Blacks: 'if this report is true, the excuse given is the same old one of the War Department on Negroes and the trick goes back to World War I.' There was a deliberate strategy to maintain the image of Black American inferiority: 'the pattern is to assign Negroes to a task either for which they have not been trained or to give them an impossible job to do and then to say they are not efficient and to mark them in the records as failing in that particular assignment. Then, the 10,000 magazine articles, stores and books that will be written on this war will tell the next two generations of Americans that Negroes do not have the ability, etc., etc.'[80] Such an approach mirrored that found in the Federal government.

Segregation in the Navy

Between 1918 and June 1942 the Navy accepted Black recruits only to the Steward Branch, an arrangement which excised the need for formal segregation in the rest of the Service. Representing the Navy, Captain Stickney explained to the Fahy Committee that this category consisted of 'the minority races'. He elaborated: 'two-thirds of them are Negroes, and the other one third is made up of other normally considered minority races of Filipinos and Chamorros. I think we do have some Japanese, Korean, and Puerto Ricans, but whether or not there are some in there, or not, we don't know. We haven't kept an accurate record on minorities.'[81] After 1942 Black Americans remained concentrated in stewardship positions. A conference between the NAACP and the Secretary of Defense, Forrestal, in 1948 reported little improvement in this pattern. It was conceded that a 'stigma attaches in the minds of most Negroes to types of employment in which Negroes may be categorized as "servants", whether in uniform or out'. It was a particular grievance of Blacks in the Navy that being a steward required wearing a uniform, as if a servant. The conferees were informed that although 'the Stewards' Branch is open to personnel of all races', in fact 'only Negroes, Filipinos, and, in a few rare cases, Guamanians are actually to be found in this branch'. The conferees recommended that employment in the steward service should 'be rotated among enlisted men in general in the same way as cooks and helpers' assignments in the food service for enlisted personnel'.[82]

Instead of recognizing the inferior status imposed upon Black recruits, segregation could be justified as a mechanism advancing Black recruits' interests under the prevailing norms. This was precisely the grounds on which Woodrow Wilson enthusiastically endorsed the introduction of segregation into Federal departments in 1913. Thus, according to Captain Stickney, the Steward Branch advantaged Black recruits by affording an 'opportunity for many [of them] who would otherwise not be qualified to make a career in the Navy'. He cited tests to support his view: 'I say that because a study was completed by our Research Division of the general intelligence and aptitude scores attained by a sample of the stewards.'[83] The designation of Black recruits to the Steward Branch meant that aboard ship, the Navy 'never had what is normally considered segregation. Individuals are assigned to their duties and in so doing they fall in various divisions in the ship's organization.'[84] *De jure* segregation was unnecessary since it existed *de facto*. After 1942 segregated training took place in the Navy but efforts to man ships on racial lines were dropped: 'it was soon revealed that this was not utilizing the individual to the best of his qualifications.'[85] Training was subsequently undertaken on a non-segregated basis.

A Black American physician, Dr Harold Franklin, was rebuffed in his efforts to join the Navy to serve in a medical capacity. A graduate of Howard University, Franklin was allowed to proceed from his physical examination to written, practical, and oral tests, although the latter could not be taken without first satisfying the former. Receiving no response from the Navy about his application, he contacted Washington in September 1941. He was informed by Lieutenant-Commander Allison at the Brooklyn Naval 'that there must be some mistake as my oral and practical and written examinations were "quite good"'. Commander Maher, Chairman of the Examining Board, stated that 'he could not understand it as I was found physically fit and that the board had recommended my appointment. He added that I was "fine Navy material."' From Rear Admiral Ross T. McIntyre, Surgeon General of the Navy and private physician to the President, Franklin received an answer dated 15 September 1941 which gave no reason for 'my alleged disqualifying features'. Submitting to further physical examination, Franklin concluded that 'my rejection was based not on fact but prejudice'.[86] After writing to Eleanor Roosevelt, Franklin received a reply from the Secretary of the Navy, giving a bizarre reason for his rejection, based on 'a review in the Bureau of Medicine and Surgery of your examination conducted at the Naval Hospital, Brooklyn, New York on August 11, 1941'. This review disclosed that 'on the left side of your dental arch you lack a minimum of two directly opposed molars. The Manual of the Medical Department of the Navy which has the approval of the President and has the force of law, requires the rejection of any candidate who fails to meet the minimum requirement in this respect.'[87] Reflecting on his rejection, Franklin noted sardonically that 'it is quite ironic in view of the state of our country that a qualified physician is denied the right to serve his country in his field unless very intimate hand to hand fighting is anticipated'.[88] The NAACP pursued the matter by preparing and circulating a pamphlet on the Franklin case.[89]

Marine Corps

Prior to April 1942 no Black Americans were eligible to join the Marine Corps. When membership was permitted, a quota system operated. Black recruits came through the Selective Service and not voluntary enlistment.[90] Truman's Committee was informed that of 8,200 officers in the Marine Corps (75,000 enlisted strength) in 1949, one was Black.[91] Even chairman Fahy[92] was startled by this figure:

MR FAHY: How do you justify only one Negro in the Marines on the basis of any program that you say you have of nondiscrimination—one Marine officer?
CAPTAIN STICKNEY: There were none until very recently in the Marine Corps.
MR FAHY: The progress you talk about, then, is from zero to one?
CAPTAIN STICKNEY: Well, they had none, and there are four in the Reserves.
MR FAHY: Four and one.
CAPTAIN STICKNEY: And until the war there was none in the Marine Corps enlisted.
MR FAHY: Doesn't that indicate to you the policy of exclusion of Negroes?
CAPTAIN STICKNEY: Not at all.[93]

Captain Stickney's responses demonstrate how deep-seated segregated race relations were in the Navy, certainly until the war, institutionally based and bolstered by the prevailing values. According to a survey in 1942, this view of the Navy was widely shared amongst Black Americans who believed it to be the branch of the Armed Services least open to them: 'nearly one-half of the Negroes interviewed said that they considered the Army unfair to members of their race. A full two-thirds of this sample held the same view respecting the Navy.'[94]

The difficulties for Black Americans seeking to join or remain in the Marine Corps were documented in detail in a letter to the NUL by Gilbert Johnson in 1947. Aside from addressing his own circumstances, Johnson explained how measures to limit Black recruits operated. In his view, the reformed Corps was still able to discriminate against Black recruits, having 'utterly failed' to plan for 'this phase of the Negro participation in the post war Marine Corps':

Our classification statistics show that the General Classification and Mechanical Aptitude scores made by more than seventy-five per cent of the men who were enlisted during the period 14 June 1946 to 20 January 1947 are far too low to be considered as reflecting the mental qualification of the cross section of Negro youth. It is clear that the Marine Corps Recruiting Offices picked up just anything and threw [them] at us. Some of the men could not even talk, two men had never talked plain in their lives. Others were epileptic, neurotic and afflicted with any number of mental and physical defects, which made them unsuitable material for the Marine Corps. Out of 1,400 that were enlisted, more than two hundred were discharged within four to six weeks by reason of unsuitability for Marine Corps service, and perhaps two or three hundred more should have been discharged as they were neuro-psychiatric suspect at one time or the other, during the course of their recruit training. At office hours daily the Commanding Officer's office is literally swamped at times with these same persons coming up for punishment for having committed some infraction of military discipline. If the Recruiting Offices had made a more careful selection of Negro personnel for the post war Marine Corps this situation would not be a common occurrence.[95]

Such mischievous recruitment and selection procedures were a ploy to limit the number of Black recruits.

The Gillem Board

In the Armed Services, particularly the Army, the persistence of segregationist values trammelled efforts such as those of the Gillem Board to reform recruitment and promotion prospects. The Board was set up on 4 October 1945, headed by Lieutenant General Alvan C. Gillem, 13th Army Corps Commander, with three other Army generals. It was charged to study War Department policies toward Black recruits during both world wars and to recommend reforms. The Gillem Board report's eighteen recommendations were based on four principles. First, the utilitarian motive to 'develop the full capabilities small or great, of every man allotted to it'. Second, given that Black Americans were increasingly well educated, to ensure that 'a broader base of selectivity [was] available'. Third, facilitating Black Americans to 'fulfill their responsibilities as citizens in national defense'. And, finally, 'the experiences of white and Negro troops during the war indicated that modifications of policy are desirable'.[96] These eighteen recommendations included: ensuring that Black soldiers constituted about 10 per cent of the Armed Services; broadening the peacetime experience and training of Black units; replacing White officers with Black officers in Black units; and stationing Black units in communities where attitudes were least hostile to them.

The NAACP criticized Gillem's recommendations for its most pronounced and significant silence: it did not question the appropriateness of segregation. All the Board's proposals assumed the system's inveteracy: 'this report presents the most documented and clearest set of facts to prove the need for ending discrimination in the armed forces that has ever been made.' Yet the report did not make the logical proposal: 'its failure, however, lies in the lack of any concrete plan on the part of the Board to correct "Jim Crow" units in the Army.' Despite highlighting the 'excellent record of Negroes during the war just concluded', documenting the 'ascending trends of Negro participation in the armed forces, in industry, in government, and in education', the report still concluded that 'we . . . need separate Negro units in the Army'. This assumption vitiated the report whose authors 'assumed from the outset that there would still be separate Negro units when they finished their report'. However, the NAACP, rejecting 'this a priori judgement on the part of the Gillem Board', concluded that the report's 'findings are nonetheless significant and mark a step forward'.[97]

The Army did not believe it was responsible for what it dismissively termed 'social reform'. This position informed the Gillem Board directives. William Hastie concluded that the 'Gillem Committee is interested only in the use of Negro personnel in the Army and, therefore, could very properly say that matters involving the relations between the races in the south is beyond the scope of the authority of the Committee'.[98] The Gillem Board report assumed the viscidity of segregated race relations. Its recommendations were structured within this framework.

Walter White quickly regretted his support, expressed to the Board, for reform within the framework of segregation. He wrote to the General: 'coming back on the train I reached the conclusion that I should withdraw my suggestion that the program of integration be done piecemeal by the establishment of a volunteer division. I am convinced that the most effective way to do the job is to do it completely and simultaneously.'[99] A conference between White and the Secretary of Defense in 1948 produced an equally bleak response from the Army to that given Gillem. Asked about establishing 'demonstration projects' as a trial for integration, Secretary Royall declared that '"after careful study and consideration with those who know a great deal about the military", he had concluded that at this time such demonstration projects should not be attempted'. Furthermore, the Secretary 'dismissed as "political" any inferred connection between the Army's racial policies and the standing of this nation as a democratic example before the attention of the world'.[100] The NAACP expressed their dissatisfaction with Army practice, observing how other branches had ameliorated conditions for Black Americans: 'in its insistence upon racial segregation because of "military expediency", and in its contention that "experience" argued in favor of separation of the races, the Army assumes a position which is at variance with the experience of other branches of the defense services, and which has never been justified even by the Army's own experience.' It chastised the Army for never experimenting 'on any broad scale with the integration of Negro enlisted personnel in mixed company groups. The insistence, therefore, expresses an *attitude* rather than *acquired experience*.' The NAACP doubted the commitment of the Army to change: 'the Army's present policy, to which it stubbornly adheres, seems to be a grudging adjustment of the original mobilization plans drawn up well in advance of World War II, which contemplated the use of Negroes under the most limited conditions imaginable.'[101] The NAACP correctly observed how Army policy privileged a sectional position from American society. Its policy disregarded 'successful experimentation carried on in such states as Massachusetts, New York, Indiana and Illinois' to integrate. In these experiments 'the individual human being [is treated] as a human being, and not as a member of an "inferior" or "superior" racial group'. In common with other institutions of the Federal government the 'Army, therefore, focuses upon Negroes "uniformly and without exception" a pattern of racial segregation which legally prevails in a minority of the states of the Union'.[102]

The Air Force, the youngest of the forces, was the most advanced in planning integration and was, according to Lieutenant General Edwards, committed to abolishing racial segregation.[103] This force's policy was the exception.

While aspects of Gillem were implemented much progress remained to be made in 1949, as one exchange before the Fahy Committee reveals:

MR FAHY: Do you have battalions in the United States now which are composed partly of Negro companies and partly of White companies?
MAJOR GENERAL DAHLQUIST: No, we have not.
MR FAHY: Then you have not integrated them on the battalion level.
MAJOR GENERAL DAHLQUIST: No sir.[104]

Some regiments did include White battalions and Black battalions, but that was the lowest organizational unit. Major General Brooks articulated a general commitment to integration but with serious caveats: 'the thing we are concerned with is how we can organize the Army to keep this nation free.' Freedom did not extend to equality of treatment for Black Americans: 'we are not certain—I am not certain personally whether you can have complete integration at this time, but I think it should be tested, and I think it should be done by the Army, Navy, and Air Force right across the board in the National Military Establishment to see what the results are.'[105]

Major General Brooks claimed that the Army was implementing the Gillem Board's[106] recommendations for racial integration. At his testimony to the Fahy Committee, there was disagreement about how the Army had defined the Board's eighteen recommendations and about the pace with which they were being established. In response to Brooks's statement that the changes were occurring 'gradually and progressively', Lester Granger observed that 'the difference of opinion would be as to what "gradually" is, and what is "progressive". Many critics of the Army have felt that the Army's interpretation of the word "gradual" was close to static.'[107] Brooks rejected such an interpretation. Major General Dahlquist acknowledged that the Army had some difficulty in meeting the Gillem Board recommendation that 10 per cent of the Armed Services should be composed of Blacks within existing structures: 'our intake has got to be gauged to the units and installations that we have in being. Our effort has been to keep the units sufficient so that we could take the ratio as it exists in the population.' The level of education of recruits was also judged a problem: 'we had to raise the test score in which we took Negroes in, because we had to have men of adequate basis to take the school training that those men had to get if we were to balance our units with men of all capabilities.'[108]

The Navy's spokesmen claimed a better pattern of racial integration in their appearances before the Fahy Committee. Probing by the Committee members exposed a less sanguine picture. Captain Stickney produced figures to demonstrate the positive effect of the post-1942 widening of Black recruitment: whereas Black Americans constituted 16.8 per cent of the general service ratings (that is, not Steward Branch) on 31 August 1946, two years later they constituted 37.3 per cent.[109] The trend amongst officers was less impressive:

MR FAHY: What are your total officers in the Navy? Do you know that?
CAPTAIN STICKNEY: Forty-five thousand, in round numbers.
MR FAHY: And the number of Negro officers?
CAPTAIN STICKNEY: Five.
MR PALMER: Including a nurse.
CAPTAIN STICKNEY: That includes a nurse.
MR PALMER: What's the ratio?
VICE ADMIRAL FECHTLER: About 2,300.[110]

The opportunities for Black candidates at Naval Academies were notionally egalitarian. The number of Black graduates suggested the hollowness of this principle. For instance, the President's Committee on Civil Rights noted that at Annapolis, 'since 1872 there have been six Negroes accepted into the Academy for midshipman training. Of these, three were dismissed because of studies, one on a disciplinary charge, one resigned and one midshipman is in attendance at present.'[111] In 1950 the NAACP continued to complain to the Secretary of Defense about segregation in the Marine Corps, quoting from an official document issued in January 1950 by the Corps's Assistant Commandant: 'In any area where there is an expressed interest in the formation of a colored Marine Corps Reserve unit and the population is adequate to support such unit, the Reserve District Commander initiates recommendations to effect its organization. Colored officers are made available to these units whenever possible.' As the NAACP noted, this document 'appears to reflect a policy of creating and maintaining Reserve Marine units segregated solely upon the basis of color'.[112]

The Navy was periodically lambasted in the Black press for its restricted recruitment of both Black American men and women,[113] limited promotion prospects for Black recruits, segregated training practices, and the disproportionate concentration of Black recruits in the Navy's bottom ranks.[114] The Navy was slow to appoint Black American women to clerical positions. Two years after the war had ended, the Navy still refused to make such appointments on the grounds that 'there is federal housing for white women only'; and furthermore, according to the Navy, it would be 'undesirable to have Negro girls integrated into such federal housing for white girls'.[115] Such Federal housing was, of course, publicly funded by all taxpayers regardless of race.

A common defence of segregation was the alleged damage integration would cause for Black Americans' promotion. This argument, of course, featured decades earlier during the Wilson administration and was a stalwart of segregationists. Limiting Black recruits to smaller units meant they 'wouldn't be in competition with the white, the tendency by reasons of the lower educational privileges of the Negro generally throughout the nation where they generally gravitate to the lower positions in the unit'.[116] Chief of Staff General Omar Bradley also cited this arrangement as one advantage to the 'Negro soldier . . . [since] . . . he is competing with men who have in general had the same opportunities as to education and development of leadership'.[117] Black American recruits could not easily rectify the inequalities of the education system existing in US society and sustained through patterns of segregated accommodation and community. A remark by the Under Secretary of War illustrates the pernicious consequence of 'separate but equal' educational facilities upon recruits, graded by the Army General Classification Test and the Mechanical Aptitude Test: 'because of the proportionately larger number of highly technical duties required of enlisted men in the Air Force, War Department policy provides that 55 per cent of them qualify by passing the General Classification Test with a grade of 100 or better. The remaining 45 per cent assigned to the Air Forces, who do not meet this qualification are assigned to comparatively unskilled jobs.' The racial pattern was unfavourable for Black Americans: 'experience to date shows that while about 47 per cent of all white enlisted men meet this qualification, the same minimum standard is met by less than 10 per cent of the Negroes inducted.'[118] Consequently the majority of Blacks entering the Armed Services were assigned to unskilled work. The unfavourable labour-market profile of Black Americans was largely reproduced in the military.

TO DESEGREGATE OR NOT?

When President Truman's Committee on the Armed Services convened, its members had to decide whether their brief included recommending desegregation. In a discussion revealing of the times, desegregation was an option contemplated nervously by several members. The Committee's February 1949 meeting began with a lengthy statement from John Sengstacke arguing that allowing segregation to endure would distort Truman's Executive Order. He rejected the claim that 'equality of opportunity' was compatible with ending discrimination: 'the President intends changes far more effective than would be necessary merely to perfect a semblance of equality on a segregated plan.'[119] Ending discrimination in the Armed Services was part of the drive toward civil rights and these latter accrued to individuals, not groups or races: 'the President's order . . . declares equality of treatment and opportunity not for all races, but for all individuals without any attention being paid to race or religion.'[120] Sengstacke argued that 'to suggest that the President, committed to the official public policy of the United States as he is and as he admits, would propose a change from the present practices of our armed forces while at the same time he intends to maintain any system of segregation, is to suggest that he issued Executive Order 9981 with dishonest intent'.[121] In this pre-*Brown* v. *Board* of *Education* era, Fahy could cite the Supreme Court's judgement that the 'Constitution requires equal facilities . . . but not the same facilities for both'.[122]

Fahy declined to support Sengstacke's position or to instruct the Committee's staff that the Executive Order implied desegregation. He judged such discussion 'a little premature in terms of the status of the work of the Committee'.[123] Committee-member Palmer was also unconvinced about the antisegregation view if on rather recondite grounds: 'I feel that if the word "desegregation" was substituted for "equality of treatment and opportunity for all persons" that we wouldn't accomplish what the President's intent is because the word "desegregation" would merely mean that you shall no longer separate them—period.' Articulating an unusual view, he suggested that segregation was better for equality: 'But "equality of opportunity and without respect to race, color, or religion" is more vitally important than merely taking the people and making them up together because there you might reach any kind of an impasse. So, if I were to choose, I would hold on to what the President has said.'[124] No final conclusion was reached at this meeting of four members of the President's Committee (Lester Granger was conspicuously absent), though the consensus appeared to demur from seeking desegregation. The Committee's final report in fact permitted segregation to continue.

In defending segregation, the Army regularly predicted dire effects upon the morale of Whites if units were integrated and if Black officers were placed in charge of White soldiers. According to John McCloy, 'we didn't know what form of resentment might be created by the introduction of the completely integrated unit'. Noting that 'many of the troops were southerners', McCloy worried openly about 'how a colored squadron leader over a bunch of hotheaded southerners would work out, what it would do to the morale of the unit, and the resentments that might arise in the unit might have a depressing effect on the Negro, that the self respect which we thought might be engendered in the smaller unit might be beneficial.'[125] The same barriers to integration and ending segregation were identified by the Secretary of the Army, Kenneth C. Royall, when he appeared before the Fahy Committee. He observed that 'perhaps the most important factor on the question of segregation is the morale of the troops as a whole, their satisfaction with Army life, and the spirit with which they perform Army tasks . . . Effective comradeship in battle calls for a warm and close personal relationship within a unit. We must remember that in close personal relationships such as exist in any Army unit, that in civilian life voluntary segregation is the normal thing.'[126] Royall stressed the high proportion of Southerners amongst volunteers in the Army: 'it is a well-known fact that close personal association with Negroes is distasteful to a large percentage of Southern whites.'[127] Whether Black Americans felt the same about Whites did not win Royall's interest.[128] Concerns about morale were only amplified when the 'question of command arises' according to the Secretary, though he conceded 'two or three instances' when White officers served under Black officers.[129] Royall was unequivocal about the general principle, offering his opinion—and, he believed, 'the opinion of nearly all of the experienced Army men and officers'—that 'it would be most difficult—and unwise from the standpoint of national defense—to require any substantial proportion of white soldiers—whether from the South or other sections of the country—to serve under Negro officers or particularly under Negro non-commissioned officers'.[130] To the charge that the morale of Black soldiers might be adversely affected by segregation, Secretary Royall assured the President's Committee that such an inference lacked 'real substance . . . It is the intention of the Army that every soldier, regardless of race . . . should receive equal treatment in every way.'[131]

Royall's views were echoed in the testimony of Assistant Secretary Gray when he appeared before the Committee. Gray readily shared Royall's contention that segregation was solely a societal problem: 'people in the Army are people just as citizens are people and we have got a long way to go in this country to make it progress.'[132] Gray did not query the appropriateness of the Army maintaining practices so obviously prejudicial to one group of American citizens. Chief of Staff General Bradley favoured desegregation since 'complete integration of units would greatly simplify our administrative problems', but he warned that 'steps toward integration should be taken [only] as fast as our social customs would permit'.[133]

BLACK AMERICAN SOLDIERS IN BRITAIN AND EUROPE

The sham created by rigid military segregation proved most difficult to defend when US troops were stationed overseas, especially in Europe. There the conflict (frequently riotous) between White recruits (often though not exclusively Southerners) and Black recruits was both mystifying and repulsive to Europeans, such as the British. John Schlesinger's otherwise tepid film *Yanks* does convey forcefully the level of tension between Black American and White GIs, and the horror of the English watching the latter's racism. The film's climacteric scene—a brutal brawl in a dance-hall—vividly portrays this violence and racism.[134] That British civilians preferred the Black American to the White GIs is suggested by the Mass Observation study undertaken at the time.[135]

Black American soldiers found themselves charged with crimes in Britain, including rape, at an extraordinarily high rate. The NAACP opened an enormous number of files for cases of alleged rape and other charges served against Black American recruits. Allegations, reported in Congress, about the poor behaviour of Black recruits were sharply disputed by the NAACP in 1946. It maintained that the 'chief fault lies with the War Department itself', because of its policy of consigning 'Negroes to service battalions thus robbing them of any of the incentive which combat troops have'. Furthermore, the invective of White racists was vast: 'prejudiced white Americans carried on an unbelievable campaign of propaganda against Negro troops alleging, that they had tails, were savage and diseased and unworthy of association with human beings. The court-martial procedures were notorious in penalizing any Negro who dared protest against insult, discrimination and segregation.'[136]

A further reason for the tension arose from the efforts of the US military commanders to reproduce the rigid segregated race relations on American bases in Europe, and as much as possible in activities outside the bases. On the bases and at the camps, this could be accomplished through the traditional discipline of MPs. Outside the confines of the bases, segregation was much more difficult to maintain and the US Armed Forces looked to the British Government and police forces to assist in its implementation. Consequently, the arrival of segregated American troops in Britain and Northern Ireland posed a dilemma for the British Government. Principally, was the government going to collude, as strongly requested by the Roosevelt administration, in segregated facilities for the tens of thousands of American troops stationed in the UK?

The War Office proposed unequivocally that Britain should accept and implement a 'colour bar', if only surreptitiously.[137] David Reynolds concludes that the British Government wanted to limit the number of non-White troops in Britain, and this position made them sympathetic to the American view.[138] In fact the government would have preferred that no Black American troops were dispatched to Britain,[139] and this recommendation was telegrammed in late April to the Secretary of War in Washington.[140] Anthony Eden, then Foreign Secretary, voiced concern in the War Cabinet in 1942 that British citizens might be too friendly toward Black American troops, thereby alienating the numerically far larger number of White Americans. The Cabinet feared weakening ties with the US administration, including Congress.

American GIs received some instructions not to express racial prejudices in Britain, and were informed about the absence of a 'colour bar'.[141] To foster an environment favourable to segregated race relations, senior American officers attempted to disseminate a view of their Black American subordinates as inferior amongst British civilians. The senior officer of the Southern Command formulated and distributed a potted history of race relations in the United States for local civilian regional administrators and district commanders, in which the backwardness of Black Americans was stressed. In language reminiscent of congressional debates in 1920s, the status of Black Americans as a 'child race' was rehearsed, and the generosity of Whites towards them in the USA explained.[142] Reynolds reports that whispering campaigns intended to warn British civilians, particularly women, of the dangers of associating with Black GIs were permitted by Whitehall, though the Foreign Office squashed a proposal to associate Black GIs with venereal disease.[143]

The Secretary of State for War, Sir James Grigg, although offended by the Southern Command's paper, had the War Office draft a response for circulation to all serving troops in which discrimination in public would not be permitted but encouraging British troops to share White Americans' attitudes toward Black GIs.[144] This idea was opposed by the Colonial Office, mindful of Britain's own non-White population and their status, and by the Lord Chancellor. Their opposition failed to garner Prime Minister Churchill's support and Grigg's position prevailed. As Reynolds summarizes, 'there was no objection, even from the Colonial Office, to the double-standard policy of covertly supporting US Army segregation as long as the British authorities were not involved in enforcing it'.[145]

Although not lacking in prejudice, few British people had encountered non-Whites because of the group's small population in the UK. Furthermore, the racism of White Americans was considered objectionable by many British people. As the Mass Observation study noted, the 'treatment of the Negro-American by his own countrymen has shocked the Liberal traditions and the tolerant attitude of the people of this country'.[146] Several statements from interviewees were recorded expressing outrage at this overt racism.[147] A survey of attitudes by the Mass Observation found 40 per cent of respondents believing the treatment of Black Americans by White Americans inappropriate, compared with 12 per cent believing it justified; 38 per cent expressed no opinion.[148]

Most controversially, a general order was issued to British troops in 1942 advising them to keep aloof from Black American troops in order not to alienate White Americans.[149] Cities and towns with large garrisons of American troops of both races, such as Bristol and the surrounding area, were encouraged to alternate their facilities for the two races, some pubs becoming designated for Black Americans and others for White American troops. Some dance-halls offered dances for Black American and White American troops on alternate weekends, the system known as 'rotating passes'. None of these measures proved sufficient to preclude numerous violent brawls or to prevent verbal abuse for White British women, from the White Americans, for fraternizing with Black American GIs.

According to Cabinet records the British Government endorsed this *de facto* segregation and urged that Black American troops be kept distant from civilians.[150] This was not the official view, however, as Reynolds correctly notes. In a circular to Chief Constables, the Home Office noted that it was not Government policy to tolerate 'any discrimination as regards the treatment of coloured troops . . . by the British authorities'.[151] If the local American commanders arranged for public places such as pubs, restaurants, or dance-halls to implement rotating schedules according to race, the Chief Constables were instructed not to assist their enforcement (an entreaty which not all constables fulfilled). The Government clearly wanted to have its cake and eat it too, pleased with segregated arrangements but eager to dissociate itself publicly from them. At the War Office, however, a more interventionist approach was adopted, particularly in respect to relations between Black American troops and women members of the ATS.[152]

The NAACP capitalized on the greater popularity of Black American soldiers in Britain and Northern Ireland compared with White soldiers. In a letter to the Secretary of War James Stimson, Walter White explained the concern about the 'friction in England and Ireland caused by southern white soldiers objecting to the presence of American Negro soldiers at entertainments arranged by the British authorities and people for American troops'. White argued that British public opinion was offended and 'alienated by the boorishness and racial bigotry of some of these southern white soldiers, as has been made evident by debates in Parliament and comments by British newspapers, officials and individuals'. White GIs seemed confused about who the enemy was: 'the opinion is apparently growing that at least some of the American troops instead of preparing to fight the Nazis are expending all their energy in warring on their fellow American soldiers because of race.'[153]

In post-war Germany and France, attacks on Black troops by White GIs were common. In a handwritten letter to Walter White, one Black recruit described the atmosphere in Le Havre in grim terms. Of White soliders, he noted that 'their mission finished with the Germans they now return to the rear to attack and murder their long hated enemy, the Negro'. As a result, in Le Havre, 'it is a wind of racial hatred and wanton murder and a river of blood is flowing freely. This being a POE for redeployment through the States, this city is crowded with soldiers returning from the front.' He described the atmosphere on the streets in the evening: 'since V-E Day it has been dangerous for us to walk the streets at night, only in large groups and armed. About 90 per cent of the Colored soldiers are doing area guard duty or guarding prisoners as they work and are armed on duty. Our billets are shaken-down, often for concealed arms, while many whites are permitted to carry arms both on and off duty. As a result many soldiers of both races are being killed.'[154] In 1945 a Navy commander on USS *Croatan* refused (or, in the official parlance, 'declined') to transport a Black quartermaster truck company back from France to the USA. The Secretary of Defense formulated a convoluted and evasive explanation of the Commander's action for the NAACP:

When the Army Officer-in-Charge of the Passenger Branch, Troop Movements Division, at Le Havre informed one of the junior officers of the CROATAN that loading plans had been changed so that 123 Negro troops would be assigned to the ship in place of the 713th M.P. Battalion, this junior officer refused to accept the change until he had consulted the Commanding Officer.

The Commanding Officer, conferring later with the chief of the Army's Passenger Branch, was asked by the Army officer to state his wishes regarding the embarkation of Negro personnel. He said he preferred not to do so.

This statement was not a refusal. Indeed, the Commanding Officer knew his orders did not permit him to refuse. It was merely a preference stated in reply to an inquiry. The Army authorities were not obliged to give any weight to the Commanding Officer's preference, but they evidently elected to do so, moving the 123 Negro troops from the CROATAN's embarkation schedule.[155]

Roy Wilkins reminded the Secretary of Defense of comparable behaviour in 1918: 'shortly after the Armistice on November 11, 1918, it is reported that a Negro regiment, scheduled for return to the United States from a French port on the battleship Virginia, was turned back practically at the gang plank when the captain of the Virginia is reported to have remarked: "No Negroes have ever ridden a U.S. battleship and they could not ride on the Virginia".'[156]

CONCLUSION

The testimony before Truman's investigative committee on the Armed Forces reveals the tenacity of segregation. Segregation enjoyed political support and this support provided a bulwark for its defenders within the military. But segregation was also a source of discrimination, a claim the NAACP diligently documented and publicized. Writing to the Secretary of Defense, Walter White recorded his disappointment upon learning that the 'utilization of Negro manpower in segregated units only is "considered to be in the interest of national defense, and . . . that this is still the case"'. White argued that this Army restriction was short-sighted and discriminatory: 'the NAACP and Americans both Negro and white who believe that democracy at least means equality of treatment of all citizens regardless of race bitterly oppose this discriminatory policy of the United States Army.' Such equality of treatment was patently subverted by the Army, as by the rest of the Federal government: 'it should be unnecessary for me to repeat . . . that the denial of the Federal Government to Negro citizens of equal opportunities to serve their country in all branches of its Armed Forces in our eyes is violative of the fundamental principles upon which this nation was founded.' He continued by identifying the Army's unjustifiable and prejudiced privileging of Southern values: 'the imposition by the Federal Government of such a discriminatory segregation policy upon National Guard Units is particularly abhorrent to the democratic philosophy.' He also noted how even in those circumstances when the Army and Federal government had an opportunity to thwart Southern racism they failed so to do: 'in the past, the Army, when refusing to violate southern segregation customs, has stated that its policy was to conform to local laws, customs and practices. How, then, can the imposition of segregation upon northern states having clear-cut laws and policies in opposition to such practices be justified by the Army?' Without doubt, as White observed, this choice was 'not just a question of segregation but rather clearly involves substantial discrimination against Negroes solely because of race'.[157]

The Second World War placed segregation and discrimination in US government and society under considerable pressure (see Table 4.1), but it did not displace the political coalitions upon which this system rested. The new pressure was insufficient to prevent the resurgence of Jim Crow codes, particularly in the Southern states, once the crisis conditions abated; institutional arrangements can be persistent, especially when they enjoy political and legal support. President Truman attempted exogenously to desegregate by exposing the consequences of segregation within government agencies including the Armed Services. This strategy faced the combined resistance of political coalitions supporting segregation and the internal resistance of segregated institutions to reform. The reticent response of the Army to the recommendations of the Fahy Committee is a good example of the latter.

Confidential memoranda reveal that the Fahy Committee had to expend considerable effort pursuading the Army to end quota restrictions upon the allocation of Black soldiers successfully completing training. At one point, President Truman joined the negotiations. The main source of contention

TABLE 4.1. *The Desegregation of the Armed Services*

Measure	Date
Selective Training and Service Act	16 Sept. 1940
First all-Black-officered regular Army Infantry Regiment (366th) activated	10 Feb. 1941
99th Fighter Squadron activated	22 Mar. 1941
Officer candidate schools open	1 July 1941
First Military Police Battalion (730th) activated	6 Feb. 1942
First Black Pilots (5) commissioned by Army Air Corps	7 Mar. 1942
Black Officer candidates enter Des Moines with First Class	20 July 1942
Black Pilots down their first enemy plane	2 July 1943
War Dept. orders end racially segregated recreational facilities	8 July 1944
Directive for Volunteer Black-integrated Infantry Platoons issued by European Theater	26 Dec. 1944
Gillem Board recommendations announced as post-war policy	4 Mar. 1946
Unification of Armed Forces under National Military Establishment	17 Sept. 1947
National Defense Conference on Black Affairs	26 Apr. 1948
First Black doctor integrated in regular army medical corps	9 June 1948
Pres. Truman issues EO 9981, creating his committee to study equality of treatment and opportunity in the Armed Services	26 July 1948
Lockbourne Air Force base ceases to be concentration of Black Air Force personnel	20 June 1949
President's Committee issues report 'Freedom to Serve'	22 May 1950
Implementation of Air Force racial integration programme practically complete	10 Feb. 1951
Department of Defense announces programme of racial integration in Far East Command	26 July 1951
Last All-Black Regiment (24th) deactivated	1 Oct. 1951
European Command issues directive calling for racial integration	1 Apr. 1952
Department of Navy issues order designed to end racially segregated facilities at all installations	21 Aug. 1953
Last Armed Forces-operated segregated school for dependents of military personnel becomes racially integrated	Sept. 1953

Source: Derived in part from NA RG 12, Records of the Office of Education, Office Files of Ambrose Caliver 1956–62, Box 2, File Attorney General's Policy Materials.

was the Army's determination to maintain a system of quotas for Black soldiers within particular occupations (a process which had previously produced a skewed concentration of Black recruits at the lower end of rankings) and to limit the opportunities for Black soldiers completing training. The Army limited career prospects for Black soldiers by restricting them to Black units, as Fahy noted in his memorandum: 'no matter how high a Negro scored in these world-wide examinations, he was still restricted within his career field to Negro or overhead units.' No modification was contemplated: 'the Army does not propose to change this arrangement . . . even though promotion within the present racial framework defeats in part the purpose of the career guidance program.'[158] Having agreed with the Fahy Committee that 'assignment of qualified personnel to specialist occupations would be on the basis of merit and fitness without regard to race or color', the Secretary of Defense Johnson issued a statement for the Army 'evasive on this point'.[159] The Army was prepared only to end quotas on Black entry into school training but not on allocation. As Fahy appreciated, without the second modification, the first would 'not effect the Committee's intention, which is that the Army make maximum use of its manpower by providing equal opportunity on a truly competitive basis'.[160] The Army's recalcitrance[161] persisted into the next year.[162]

Writing to the President in July 1949, Committee Chairman Fahy was able to report progress in the Army, Navy, and Air Force's equality policies. The Navy agreed to the Committee's recommendation on 'recruiting and on granting to chief stewards the rating of chief petty officers . . . the Air Force's program of integration has been undertaken and some Negro units are now being abolished.'[163] In the same letter, Fahy reported that the Committee had met with the Secretary of the Army and Chief of Staff, holding conversations 'which were exceedingly frank and cordial',[164] and from which certain recommendations were agreed. These recommendations included that all classes of Army jobs be open to any qualified personnel regardless of race, all courses in Army schools be open to any qualified personnel, the termination of the race quota, and the assignment of personnel after completing specialist training without regard to race. Of the final recommendation, Fahy observed: 'the assignment of school-trained men without regard to race, while not requiring at this time the abolition of all Negro units in the Army, would gradually extend the integration already practiced in overhead installation and Army Schools for officers and enlisted men.'[165]

The Fahy Committee remained hesitant about ending segregated units: 'the Committee has not proposed the immediate and complete abandonment of all racial units. It has recommended that qualified Negroes shall be sent to school and assigned where they are needed and qualified without regard to race.'[166] The Committee's wariness was probably informed by its exposure to segregationist values and the recognition that this was the only realistic strategy.

The Korean War had a seminal effect in making integration an urgent issue. Even at this stage, segregation did not evaporate overnight and differences in the degree of desegregation between American troops stationed in Europe and Asia lingered. Writing in January 1953, NAACP administrator

Roy Wilkins reported that the Army began 'integration "around the fringes" as it were, and we do not know of any single large scale changeover within the United States. There are a few Negro officers scattered here and there away from Negro troops.' Of US troops stationed in post-war Germany, Wilkins concluded that desegregation often depended on the whims of 'individual commanders and staffs in the various sectors. If the top command is not sold on the procedure it may be enforced only in a token way, or under some loophole of discretionary powers it may not be enforced at all by certain commanders.' For White Americans that Germany was a caucasian society was more significant than its Nazi legacy: 'then, too, in Germany we have Negro soldiers in the midst of a white population whereas in the Far East they are in the midst of a colored population. The spectacle of unhampered association of these troops with the civilian population, backed up by orders of equality and integration, may be more than some commanders can take.'[167] President Eisenhower finally ordered the end of segregation in the Armed Services which in August 1954 was predicted to 'be completely eliminated within a matter of months. Integration is now nearly complete.'[168] Even at this late date the abolition of segregated institutions required the decisive *Brown* judgements by the Supreme Court in 1954 and 1956, and the exercise of executive authority in its wake. Within the Services, some discrimination persisted. The Commander of the US Air Force issued memoranda in 1958 and again in 1959 reminding all military personnel of the unacceptability of such practices.[169]

Black Americans continued to encounter hostility and prejudice in housing both on military installations and in the community surrounding them. By the 1960s discrimination in the former was significantly curbed but it often flourished in the latter. A report by the US Commission on Civil Rights in 1963 concluded that 'for the Negro serviceman, the already limited supply of decent housing is further restricted by the discriminatory practices of the private housing market. The burden of discrimination, when added to the common housing problems of all servicemen, frequently forces Negro servicemen to choose between living under slum conditions near the base or enduring a family separation.'[170] The Commission criticized the Department of Defense's measures because it accepted only a 'limited obligation to secure equal treatment in housing for servicemen. The services do maintain and implement a policy of nondiscrimination in assignment to Government-owned family housing.' But this policy still failed to benefit Black American recruits because of a different aspect of segregated race relations—their persistent disproportionate concentration in lower ranks: 'this housing is in short supply and its utility to Negro servicemen is even more limited because, as a group, they do not possess sufficient rank to be assigned to such housing under the existing priority system.'[171]

In 1963 the US Commission on Civil Rights issued a study assessing progress toward desegregation since Truman's 1948 committee. The Commission found much to commend but considerable scope for amelioration. While the Army and Air Force had Black recruits in multiple tasks, the Navy, in a lengthy tradition of prejudice, continued to utilize Black recruits 'less in clerical, technical and skilled occupations than is the case in the civilian economy'.[172] The Commission also urged the Department of Defense more fully and effectively to engage with the communities bordering military bases, especially in the South, whose practices were 'galling reminders that second-class citizenship has not been completely eradicated'.[173] Recommendations to improve Black Americans' prospects in the Navy and relations with local communities were formulated by the Commission for the President.

Segregated race relations naturally left a profound mark upon those Black Americans who served in the military under their yoke. Apart from those who died in racial conflicts, many suffered injury from fellow White recruits and the scale of discrimination to which they were subject was exceptional. However, for Black Americans entering the Armed Forces after the 1960s the experience has been largely devoid of discrimination. Once the decision had been finally accepted, the Armed Forces proved capable of rapidly desegregating and of providing equality of treatment to recruits regardless of race.[174] In common with Federal civil service agencies, the military is now an important employer for Black Americans, despite its earlier record of inequality and discrimination.

5

Serving Time with the Government: Federal Penitentiaries

PRISONS are often considered to be instances of 'total institutions' in Erving Goffman's famous sense.[1] Such a characterization was formulated by one warden in the Federal prison system in 1947: 'inmates are enclosed in a prescribed physical area. They must have close contact with the same individuals day after day—persons not of their own choice. They must work with the same men, sleep in the same dormitory or cell house with the same men, eat with the same men and even during recreation associate with the same men. They cannot escape from this situation even for a day.' The consequences of this arrangement were thinly suppressed and controlled tension: 'the general result is frustration, irritability, and emotional tension which may, with little immediate cause, flare up into thoughtless, unreasonable action. All the elements of mob psychology are present in the prison environment.'[2]

In the United States, the totality of Federal prisons acquired its own uniqueness, from the establishment of the Bureau of Prisons in 1930 until the 1960s, through the requirement that prisoners be segregated by race (a practice rigorously enforced in state penitentiaries also).[3] Even in those Federal prisons whose directors believed them racially harmonious, the assumption and practice of segregation permeated their whole character. Speaking in the year of the *Brown* case, the Commissioner of the Bureau of Prisons noted how integral segregation—'the older race relation traditions'—was to Federal penitentiaries: 'the first federal penitentiary was established at Atlanta over 50 years ago. Strict racial segregation became the rule there, located as it was in the South. The pattern was extended to Leavenworth when it opened a few years later, and to other federal prisons as they were operated.' In 1930 when the Bureau of Prisons was established, 'the pattern was set and the tradition firm'. He added also that 'until recent years considerably more than half the federal prison population came from the South'.[4] In common with housing policy (see Chapter 6), penal segregation never received explicit congressional authority, however, as was explained to the Committee against Race Discrimination in the War Effort: 'you ask whether there is any Federal law or regulation segregating Negro prisoners from other prisoners in Federal institutions. There is no such law.'[5] None the less, all Federal prisons were segregated, not just those ones located in the South.

After recording the origins of Federal penitentiaries, I begin this chapter with a statistical profile of the numbers of inmates in Federal prisons before the *Brown* decision, and identify their racial composition. I then consider how the segregated system operated in Federal prisons and how integration was achieved. The Federal system of prisons is an important instance of segregation since these institutions were, to some extent, autonomous from their local political environment, and a direct manifestation of the Federal government's policy. This autonomy varied by area, with the South a more significant presence in the institutions located there, since segregation was in origin Southern.

The Federal prison system potentially enjoyed greater autonomy and independence of the sectional forces in Congress, which were so energetically ensuring that the *Plessy* doctrine was adhered to throughout society in activities such as housing and schooling. Except for the publicity generated by racial conflicts in prisons—which were more common in state and military reformatories—politicians were inclined to leave the Federal penitentiary system alone. Furthermore, in the Bureau of Prisons' Director, James Bennett, the system had a humane man genuinely committed to desegregating these institutions. This aim could be pursued with greater political ease than faced opponents of segregation in more visible and societal activities. Writing to reprimand the Warden of Danbury Correctional Institution, Bennett recalled: 'I am a northerner myself, and while I was in college I lived in a room adjoining that of Fritz Pollard, the negro football star, and we frequently discussed all sorts of problems with the utmost of candor. I am a member of a committee on racial relations here in Washington trying to find practical solutions to some of the difficult problems involved.'[6] 'All sorts of problems' doubtless included discussion of race and segregation.

As a Federal system, the US Bureau of Prisons was able to challenge rather than simply prop up local racial traditions. That it assumed this role seems to me to reflect the personalities and beliefs of its directors. Defences of penal segregation in terms of 'southern practices or customs' were trenchantly challenged by the Bureau of Prisons in Washington. The introduction of a managerial system bringing mobility between institutions across the country ensured the injection of views and attitudes from outside the locality (though lower level personnel were recruited locally and worked in the same institution throughout their career). There were, none the less, important limits to such challenges. Where the guards were predominantly Southern, and even more so where the warden was, then the resentment to non-Southern interference was considerable. Racist beliefs and interests were often in evidence, reflecting staff loyalties, geographic location, the attitude and policy of the serving director, and congressional attention. Within the prisons themselves, Black American inmates were reminded of their inferior status through assignment to the worst jobs, exclusion from prison industries, and separate accommodation and eating facilities. These disadvantages were marked in the South in which the penal tradition was barbaric in general and horrific in its specificity to Black Americans.

In common with many other areas of the US Federal state, the Second World War imposed exogenous pressures upon the functioning of segregation in Federal prisons. In this case, it was the influx of new sorts of prisoners, gaoled under the 1940 Selective Service Act (President Franklin Roosevelt's conscription law), educated, articulate, and determined to engage with prison authorites about race relations, which challenged the segregationist order. In addition, the prison authorities were not unaware of the probable impact of wartime employment for Black Americans' expectations: 'during the war years and the recent almost full employment . . . more negroes than ever before have experienced the benefits of high wages and higher status in the social structure. The possibility of decline in their economic or social status will not be accepted without struggle.'[7]

FEDERAL PENITENTIARIES: ORIGINS AND A PROFILE OF INMATES

Prisons in the United States were almost the exclusive preserve of states until the 1910s. A range of institutions were established throughout the American states, beginning benignly with a Quaker-influenced penitentiary in Philadelphia in the 1680s. Historians consent on dating the period of modern American, state, prisons from 1835 by which date, and 'after many bad starts', the 'American states . . . had finally enjoyed a decade of active prison development'.[8] In the same decade Alexis de Tocqueville was commissioned by the French National Assembly to study American penitentiaries. In the remainder of the nineteenth century, the states reformed and expanded their prison systems, extending the reformatory element. The exception to this pattern was, unsurprisingly, the South where reform had been thwarted by the Civil War. In McKelvey's grim description, 'while the northern prisoner may have grown pale and anemic gazing through the bars in the pale dusk of towering cell blocks, his southern brother dragged his chains through long years of hard labor, driven by brutal physical torture, oftentimes to his grave. A half-century was not sufficient to efface this institutional estrangement.'[9] Where overcrowding and a growing prison population in the North prompted new building of prisons, in the South 'authorities simply lengthened the chains binding man to man',[10] leasing the chained labour out to construction and railroad camps. This tradition owed something to the destruction of prisons during the Civil War, and the failure to build new ones. The leasing arrangement was formalized by the state legislature in Georgia in 1876. Mississippi, Louisiana, Arkansas, Tennessee, and Florida emulated the leasing solution. Federal prisons in the South lingered also under the legacy of slavery and race relations. As McKelvey notes, the 'struggle between the races . . . was so fierce during the first years that cruel penal conditions could have aroused hardly any surprise'. Racial tension created a distinct ethos in Southern prisons: 'in place of the religious and educational ideals that were inspiring the development of the adult reformatories in the North, the old slave system was supplying traditions and customs to the penology of the South. Unfortunately the lease camps never saw the development of the paternalism that had been the saving grace of the old plantation system.' It was Black Americans, newly emancipated, who suffered: 'new laws which horrified idealists in the North gathered the most restless and independent from among the freedmen and gave them hopelessly long sentences. The discipline which had kept the relatively docile slaves in the fields before the war could have no effect now; the penal slaves had to be herded about their camps by armed guards and shackled in the "cribs" at night.'[11] Southern prisons reproduced the racial relations of Southern society and were used as a mechanism to enforce them.

Black Americans achieved no prominent custodial positions in the prisons since it 'was out of the question to hire Negroes'[12] for such vacancies. In 1885 the average death rate in Northern prisons was 14.9 per 1,000, in the South it was a shocking 41.3 per 1,000. Black Americans also received the longest sentences (and sentences handed down by Southern courts themselves were far longer than those in the North): 'everywhere in the South sentences were unreasonably long, and the Negroes got more than their just share. The social hatreds engendered by years of strife were still rampant.'[13] In prison, Black American inmates suffered disproportionately from tuberculosis and other illnesses.

Until 1872 prisoners convicted of specifically Federal crimes were housed in state or local prisons, minimally monitored by the Federal government. In that year the US Department of Justice was made responsible for Federal prisoners, removing this task from the Department of the Interior. The superintendent of prisons in the Justice Department became from 1872 formally responsible for Federal prisons and prisoners. Exclusively Federal prisons were built in the first two decades of this century. In 1915 three Federal prisons—at Leavenworth (Kansas), Atlanta (Georgia), and McNeil Island (Washington), housing 1,514, 1,184, and 239 prisoners respectively[14]—were in existence. These buildings coincided with significant reforms to the internal organization of prisons throughout the USA—for example, recreation and privilege systems became part of the normal order.

In 1928 Congress passed a resolution appointing a special committee to survey and investigate extant Federal penitentiaries. The committee reported in January 1929.[15] Its remit was specifically the circumstances of Federal prisoners 'confined in Federal, State, county, and municipal prisons and jails', the conditions of their confinement, and an assessment of the 'need for additional Federal penal and reformatory institutions to take care of the Federal prisoners'.[16] The three Federal prisons in existence (at Leavenworth, Atlanta, and McNeil Island) housed 18,606 prisoners at the end of 1928, a population which had grown by 10 per cent in each of the preceding ten years. Some Federal prisoners were also held in state, county, and city prisons. The growth in number of inmates had, according to the committee, precipitated a crisis: 'a very serious crisis confronted those who were administering the Federal penal system. Due to the lack of a proper program and to the tremendous increase in the number of persons arrested, convicted and committed for violations of Federal penal laws, the penitentiaries are overcrowded with those sentenced to prisons for more than one year.'[17] Conditions were far worse in the state and city prisons holding Federal prisoners. Both Leavenworth and Atlanta accommodated almost double their designated number of inmates. Consequently, the committee discovered that 'in both of these institutions there exists the vicious practice of "doubling up" or placing two prisoners in single cells. Men are sleeping in dark, ill-ventilated basements, and corridors; improvised dormitories are in use; the kitchen and mess facilities are overloaded to more than twice their proper capacity.'[18]

Amongst its many recommendations, the congressional committee urged the creation of a bureau within the Department of Justice wholly responsible for Federal prisoners. This recommendation prompted the formation of the US Bureau of Prisons in 1930. The committee also recommended that the District of Columbia create facilities to hold prisoners violating District laws, the removal of military prisoners from civilian prisons, the expansion of the work and employment opportunities for Federal prisoners, and more rigorous supervision of Federal prisoners in non-Federal institutions. The construction of additional Federal penitentiaries was strongly promoted: 'there should be two additional penitentiaries established as soon as possible. One should be in the northeastern part of the country, located as near as possible to the center of commitment from the Federal courts, and the other at such a place as a board of experts may determine.'[19] These recommendations were quickly enacted. Significantly, though consistent with the silences created by segregated race relations, the special committee omitted any direct reference to the position of Black American inmates or to any issue of race.

Tables 5.1 and 5.2 provide a summary of the racial profile of prisoners in the Federal system from its foundation in 1930 to the 1950s, the decade of the *Brown* decision. The data in Table 5.1 indicate that Black American inmates remained, in the period covered, a fairly small percentage of the

TABLE 5.1. *Commitments to all Federal institutions by race (Federal penitentiaries in brackets)*

Year	Total	White			Black		
		Total	Male	Female	Total	Male	Female
1931	10,178	8,897			1,138		
1932	10,496	9,112			1,114		
1933	8,775	7,610			906		
1934	8,007	6,891			736		
1935	11,000	9,364			1,378		
1936	11,580	9,519			1,797		
1937	11,488	9,178			2,058		
1938	11,604	9,221			2,117		
1939	11,989	9,195			2,500		
1940	10,632	8,027			2,334		
1945	21,200	16,483	15,799	684	3,993	3,713	280
1951	18,950	13,895	13,519	376	4,443	4,130	313
	(14,676)	(10,540)	(10,284)	(256)	(3,899)	(3,685)	(214)
1954	22,497	17,045	16,418	627	4,667	4,227	440
	(17,448)	(13,196)	(12,904)	(292)	(3,958)	(3,672)	(286)
1955	20,013	14,708	14,229	479	4,523	4,122	401
	(17,456)	(12,783)	(12,500)	(283)	(3,996)	(3,703)	(293)
1960	16,783	11,778	11,366	412	4,224	3,901	323
	(14,833)	(10,487)	(10,157)	(330)	(3,692)	(3,451)	(241)

Source: US Dept. of Justice, Bureau of Prisons: for 1931–40 see *Federal Prisons 1940* (Leavenworth Kan.: US Penitentiary, 1941), 319; for 1945, *Federal Prisons 1945* (Leavenworth Kan.: US Penitentiary, 1945), 50; for 1951, *Federal Prisons 1951* (Leavenworth Kan.: US Penitentiary, 1952), 73; for 1954, *Federal Prisons 1954* (Leavenworth Kan.: US Penitentiary, 1954), 75; for 1955, *Federal Prisons 1955* (Leavenworth Kan.: US Penitentiary, 1955), 69; for 1960, *Federal Prisons 1960* (Leavenworth Kan.: US Penitentiary, 1960), 50.

total prison population. However, the number of Black American prisoners grew substantially in the 1940s, more than doubling by the next decade. The prison population as a whole grew during this period as new sorts of prisoners—principally gaoled under the Selective Service Act—arrived. Table 5.3 reveals the number of Selective Service violators. Between 1943 and 1947 they constituted a significant minority of the prison population, and because they received long sentences their number cumulatively was marked. By 1944 the Bureau of Prisons judged many of these new prisoners 'very troublesome'.[20]

TABLE 5.2. *Average number of Federal prisoners by institution 1939–1954*

Institutions	1939	1941	1946	1948	1954
Penitentiaries for:					
Intractable male offenders					
Alcatraz	288	288	282	246	273
Habitual tractable male offenders					
Atlanta	3,277	2,859	2,223	2,030	2,341
Leavenworth, Kan.	1,359	2,771	2,355	2,323	2,458
Older improvable male offenders					
Lewisburg, Pa.	3,093	1,448	1,273	1,325	1,252
McNeil Island, Wash.	925	964	973	1,016	1,093
Terre Haute, Ind.	—	312	1,040	1,110	1,189
Reformatories for:					
Agricultural-type improvable male offenders:					
Petersburg, Va.	813	747	695	462	704
Younger improvable male offenders:					
Chillicothe, Oh.	1,574	1,288	1,410	1,242	1,161
El Reno, Okla.	1,197	1,023	1,018	1,015	958
Englewood, Colo.	—	195	474	368	
Female offenders:					
Alderson, W. Va.	578	457	477	462	527
Institutions for:					
Male juvenile offenders:					
National Training School for Boys, DC:					
Federal cases	386	289	345	260	227
DC cases	141	102	132	100	205
National Bridge School, Greenlee, Va.			72	58	70
Correctional institutions for:					
Short-term male offenders:					
Ashland, Ky.		265	524	406	
Danbury, Conn.		261	619	428	512
La Tuna, Tex.			627	608	725
Milan, Mich.	576	492	568	528	633
Sandstone, Minn.	254	356	436	153	
Seagoville, Tex.			187	392	460
Tallahassee, Fla.	119	430	460	417	506
Texarkana, Tex.		135	381	404	511

TABLE 5.2. *(Continued)*

Institutions	1939	1941	1946	1948	1954
Prison camps for:					
Minimum-custody-type improvable male offenders:					
Columbia Camp, Wash.			240	43	
McNeil Island, Wash.			316	280	
Mill Point, W. Va.	155	197	213	112	216
Montgomery, Ala.	238	300	221	157	198
Tucson, Ariz.	180	161	203	158	248
Medical Center, Springfield, Mo.:					
Hospital		784	699	714	799
Maintenance unit		166	168	115	213
TOTAL (Bureau of Prisons Institutions)	18,698	17,856	18,698	17,102	19,425
TOTAL (Federal Institutions)			22,709	20,755	24,736

Source: US Dept. of Justice: for 1939, *Federal Prisons 1940* (Leavenworth Kan.: US Penitentiary, 1941), 3; for 1941, *Federal Prisons 1942* (Leavenworth Kan.: US Penitentiary, 1943), 3; for 1946, *Federal Prisons 1947* (Leavenworth Kan.: US Penitentiary, 1948), 9; for 1948, *Federal Prisons 1947* (Leavenworth Kan.: US Penitentiary, 1949), 4; for 1954, *Federal Prisons 1955* (Leavenworth, Kan.: US Penitentiary, 1956), 4.

TABLE 5.3. *Selective Service Act Violators*

Received from the courts into Federal institutions:	1941	1942	1943	1944	1945	1946	1947	Total
COs[a]	129		495	251	214	106	11	1,216
Jehovah's Ws	106		901	1,735	899	409	70	4,120
Others	757		1,368	1,599	1,364	797	658	6,543
TOTAL	982	806[b]	2,764	3,585	2,477	1,312	739	11,879
Median age (years)	28.5	—	29.9	27.4	27.0	26.5	26.9	

Note: Average Length of sentence = 31 months

[a] Conscientious objectors.

[b] Breakdown not available for 1942.

Source: US Dept. of Justice, *Federal Prisons 1947* (Leavenworth Kan.: US Penitentiary, 1948).

SEGREGATION AND RACE IN FEDERAL PRISONS

The potential for discrimination within the framework of 'separate but equal' segregation applied as much to the Federal prison system as to the Federal government. Speaking to the prison wardens' conference in 1948, the Director captured the inherent problem nicely when he used the terms segregation and discrimination synonymously: 'segregation or discrimination—call it what you like—must be minimized.'[21] This compounding of the two conditions alarmed the NAACP in the decades during which this organization campaigned for desegregation. As Thurgood Marshall, NAACP Special Counsel, explained to the same director: 'segregation is in itself discrimination. The moment you tell one citizen that he cannot do what another citizen can do, simply because of his race, you are maintaining a policy of discrimination.'[22] The same points were made, without effect, to President Woodrow Wilson in 1913 as he permitted racial segregation to spread in the Federal government.

What counted as segregation or integration in Federal penitentiaries was often in the eye of the beholder: the frequent attribution of segregation to choice or voluntary actions by inmates might equally well derive from the 'strict racial segregation' inherited by the Federal penal system. The following description of arrangements in Terre Haute, Indiana, in 1951 is instructive:

> there are about 1200 prisoners in the Terre Haute Penitentiary. Of this group approximately 250 are Negroes. The Negro prisoners, as a group, are segregated from the white prisoners in the dormitories, in the mess-hall and at entertainments. All Negro prisoners are confined to cells which are located in a section of the penitentiary which is reserved only for Negroes, while all others, including those of Mexican origin, are confined in cells which occupy the section of the penitentiary reserved only for white prisoners. Negro prisoners as a group and white prisoners as a group enter the mess-hall and the entertainment hall separately and occupy separate sections during meals and entertainments.
>
> Furthermore, various privileges are extended to white prisoners for good behavior which are denied to negro prisoners with equally good behavior. Thus white prisoners who meet prescribed standards enjoy privileges such as the following: Supervision over these prisoners is relaxed. During waking hours the doors to their cells are left unlocked. When not engaged in the performance of their assigned tasks, they are free to repair to a reading room where they are at liberty to engage in conversation, play ping-pong etc. None of these privileges is extended to Negro prisoners who meet the same prescribed standards.[23]

The Warden of Seagoville in Texas wrote that 'we have never had any segregation as to colored inmates here except in housing',[24] thereby assuming that this single practice made his institution a paragon of integrated racial life. Rather like the administrators discussed in Chapter 1, the description of Terre Haute also differed from that provided by the Director of the

Bureau of Prisons in 1951: 'our official position in regard to racial segregation is to work for its eventual and complete abolishment as rapidly as possible.' He documented the extent of its removal: 'at present there is no racial segregation in any of our institutional operations or programs. Negroes and white men work side by side in all of our institutional and industries shops, as well as in all units of our farming operations. Both groups attend the same classes in vocational and educational courses and in many instances are taught by negro instructors. No distinctions are made in the recreational field and both groups participate together in sports and athletic events. We have several negro employees and in one institution, a negro custodial supervisor who is responsible for the work of both white and negro subordinate officers.' However, segregation did exist in one critical area: 'the only situation in which segregation might be said to exist would be in regard to living quarters, especially in the large penitentiaries which have the older type of large congregate housing units.'[25] The physical layout of these cells is conveyed in Don Siegel's film *Riot in Cell Block 11*.[26] The narrative concerns a riot sparked on one of the institution's multiple cell blocks. Before the 1950s each block in a segregated Federal prison, containing numerous cells, was allocated by race. Subsequently, some of the cells within a block were allocated by race, but it was some time before the inmates in a single cell were mixed racially.

From 1944 the question of how to implement racial integration and to end segregation undoubtedly exercised the wardens of Federal prisons. Although some of these institutions were located in communities which were themselves deeply segregated and profoundly racist, Federal status granted their administrators some independence from the local context. In contrast to Federal administrators in most other agencies—for instance, in the housing and public employment agencies—officials in the Bureau of Prisons strenuously avoided an easy accommodation with local 'practices and customs'. Instead, they tried to exploit their autonomy to desegregate. The Director of the Bureau of Prisons assured an inquirer (from the Commission on World Peace of the Methodist Church) that these issues featured at the wardens' annual meeting: 'at our annual conference of federal prison wardens, we have invariably discussed policies and techniques for promoting better racial understanding and breaking down prejudices. For example, last year [1950], several hours were devoted to discussing the report of the President's Committee on Equality of Treatment and Opportunity in the Armed Services as the matters treated therein applied to federal prisons.'[27] The Director, Bennett, was a Northerner unenamoured of Southern racial practices, and progressive in penal reform. Both principles encouraged him to pursue desegregation.

In response to the Supreme Court's *Brown* decision in May 1954, the Bureau of Prisons' Director undertook a survey of the degrees of segregation and integration in Federal prisons, the results of which are summarized in

Table 5.4. These provide a valuable snapshot of segregation by race in Federal prisons. The data in Table 5.4 demonstrate that segregation was characteristic of Federal prisons but, on this evidence, by 1954 less pervasive than might have been anticipated. However, three important areas were strictly segregated across all institutions: housing, dining-rooms, and auditoriums. As the Bureau Director noted, 'these three are closely related since in practically all institutions, until recently at least, men went to the dining room and to the auditorium by housing units. If they were segregated in quarters, they were also segregated in the dining room and auditorium.'[28] As the discussion of Mill Point in the section 'Racial Conflict' below confirms, segregated housing was pivotal to prisoners' understanding of their detention. White prisoners were adamant, and on occasions violent, about its maintenance.

Racial friction and segregation were considered by the wardens again in 1948, though without enthusiasm. Warden Cozart, of El Reno, observed that 'there seems to be some feeling that we shouldn't discuss racial problems very much'.[29] Another warden argued that segregation was a very different problem regionally: 'although we are Federal and cover the whole United States, we are regional in this way: the camp at Montgomery is different from the camp at Tucson. Tallahassee is entirely different from Sandstone. You can eliminate segregation at Sandstone and Tucson but can't eliminate it in Tallahassee.' The warden emphasized the significance of these regional demarcations: 'you are going to have trouble if you try to eliminate segregation in some places, where you won't have any trouble in the Northern institutions with a predominance of Northern people.'[30]

This last comment came from Helen Hironimus, Warden of the Federal Reformatory for Women in Alderson. Some weeks after the conference, the Director of the Bureau wrote to her censoriously to challenge the importance of region: 'now I don't know whether you are a southern institution or not, but you are first and last and all the time a Federal institution and your race problems have got to be in accordance with those of the Bureau regardless of the views of any of your good friends, neighbors or the personnel.' The Director conceded that he was 'speaking quite plainly, I know, and it is meant in all good humor but it nevertheless gives you the facts of life'.[31] Bennett urged the Warden to experiment in desegregation: 'one of the things is the assignment of only colored girls to laundry, which I wish you could somehow break up and get a few white women in there . . . I believe you are the only institution in our system which does not have mixed sports activities. Also, in your school you have separate classes of white and colored girls as I recall it. There is another place where you can immediately begin to have some breakdown in racial segregation.'[32] Director Bennett's commitment to integration was unequivocal and he concluded his letter imploringly: 'please give this matter some thought and let us begin now to do

TABLE 5.4. *Segregation and integration in Federal prisons, 1954*

Integrated	Segregated
Work assignments	
Alcatraz	
Atlanta: for most part	Atlanta: janitor and labour details outside walls; White orderlies for White inmates and Black orderlies for Black inmates
Leavenworth, Kan.: for most part	Leavenworth, Kan.: White in dining-room, servers, and waiters; kitchen orderlies; lawn detail; hospital orderlies
Terre Haute, Ind.	
McNeil Island, Wash.	
Lewisburg, Pa.: for most part	Lewisburg, Pa.: laundry; main corridor; janitors; and officers' mess waiters
El Reno, Okla.: for most part	El Reno, Okla.: cleaners in shops, industries, and administration building are Black
Chillicothe, Oh.	
Alderson, W. Va.: for most part	Alderson, W. Va.: White at dairy and staff food service, Black to piggery
Springfield, Mo.	
Milan, Mich.	
La Tuna, Tex.	
Seagoville, Tex.	
Texarkana, Tex.	
Danbury, Conn.	
Tallahassee, Fla.	Tallahassee: construction cement detail Black
National Training School, DC	
Montgomery, Ala.: some	Montgomery, Ala.: some
Tucson, Ariz.	
Mill Point, W. Va.: for most part	Mill Point, Ariz.: laundry detail is Black
Recreational and sport activities	
Alcatraz	
Atlanta: for most part	Atlanta: ball teams, tennis teams
Leavenworth, Kan.	
McNeil Island, Wash.	
Lewisburg, Pa.: for most part	Lewisburg, Pa.: seating by dormitories in theatre area
Terre Haute, Ind.	
El Reno, Okla.: for most part	El Reno, Okla.: boxing
Chillicothe, Oh.: for most part	Chillicothe, Oh.: seating in theatre
Alderson, W. Va.	
Springfield, Mo.	

TABLE 5.4. *(Continued)*

Integrated	Segregated
Milan, Mich.: for most part	Milan, Mich.: ball teams represent housing units
La Tuna, Tex.	
Seagoville, Tex.	
Texarkana, Tex.	
Danbury, Conn.	
Tallahassee, Fla.: for most part	Tallahassee, Fla.: seating separated by choice
National Training School, DC	
Montgomery, Ala.	
Tucson, Ariz.	
Mill Point, W. Va.	
Visiting room	
All	
Educational activities	
Atlanta: advanced subjects	Atlanta: illiterates and lower grades for which attendance is compulsory
All other institutions	
Hospital	
Montgomery, Ala.	
Springfield, Mo.: psychiatric	Springfield, Mo.: acute mental and medical, tuberculosis
All others	
Seating arrangements in Chapel and Choir	
Alcatraz	
Atlanta: except by request	
Leavenworth, Kan.	
McNeil Island, Wash.	
Lewisburg, Pa.	
Terre Haute, Ind.	
El Reno, Okla.	
Chillicothe, Oh.	
Alderson, W. Va.	
Milan, Mich.	
La Tuna, Tex.	
Seagoville, Tex.: except by request	
Texarkana, Tex.	
Danbury, Conn.	
Tallahassee, Fla: except by request	
National Training School, DC	

TABLE 5.4. *(Continued)*

Integrated	Segregated
Montgomery, Ala.	
Tucson, Ariz.	
Mill Point, W. Va.	
Seating arrangement in auditorium[a]	
McNeil Island, Wash.	
Milan, Mich.	Alcatraz
La Tuna, Tex.	Atlanta
Tucson, Ariz.	Leavenworth, Kan.
Seagoville, Tex. (except by request)	Lewisburg, Pa.
Danbury, Conn.	Terre Haute, Ind.
Tallahassee, Fla. (except by request)	El Reno, Okla.
National Training School, DC	Chillicothe, Oh.
	Alderson, W. Va.
	Springfield, Mo.
	Texarkana, Tex.
	Mongtomery, Ala.
	Mill Point, W. Va.
Dining-room seating	
Danbury, Conn.	Alcatraz
La Tuna, Tex.	Atlanta
Tucson, Ariz.	Leavenworth, Kan.
National Training School, DC	Lewisburg, Pa.
	Terre Haute, Ind.
	El Reno, Okla.
	McNeil Island, Wash.
	Chillicothe, Oh.
	Alderson, W. Va.
	Seagoville, Tex.
	Springfield, Mo.
	Texarkana, Tex.
	Mongtomery, Ala.
	Mill Point, W. Va.
	Tallahassee, Fla.

[a] The prisons which were segregated were segregated because inmates enter by housing units.

Source: NA RG 129, Bureau of Prisons, Central Administrative File 1937–67, Prisoners' Welfare, Box 41, File Segregation: Answers to questionnaire of 10 June 1954 re segregation.

some little things that will make possible the gradual breakdown of these distinctions so that we can look forward to the day when there will be very little segregation or discrimination.'[33] While Bennett's letter encapsulates his view of the Federal government as capable of transcending local racial practices, the attitude of Warden Hironimus plainly reveals an absorption of the latter. There could be little direct advantage to Bennett's confrontation with his wardens, unless he was anxious to integrate. The political rewards of this strategy were not obvious. One possible political motive, however, was recognition that national rather than sectional interests should prevail in Federal institutions funded by all taxpayers, such as penitentiaries.

Warden Lowell Naeve at Danbury received an equally bruising letter from Bennett about his attitude to desegregation: 'instead of trying to help us solve this problem, you resort to coercion rather than persuasion and doing those little things which would help some of the difficulties involved.' He continued, in less-than-elegant prose: 'the solution, Lowell, to the problem is not to wait for us to make a change in our methods, which must take into account the attitude of thousands of prisoners and many hundred civilian employees all over the country as well as the views of millions of taxpayers who feel that they have a right to determine how public institutions should be run.' Instead, the situation required Naeve to cooperate 'in carrying out our policy of equal opportunities for the negro in our sports program, in the field of education, in our paying industries, and in the other privileges we grant our inmates'.[34]

The despondency of Wardens Hironimus and Naeve was countered by other wardens' experience, such as that of the Warden at Terre Haute, of desegregating without violent opposition. Terre Haute also successfully defused conflict arising from the presence of Muslim prisoners in 1960.[35] Other wardens blamed Black inmates for the difficulties: 'in some instances, friction is brought about by aggressive Negroes who have the feeling they are being discriminated against; that their rights are being infringed upon.'[36] The importance of Black American officers was stressed by the Warden at Chillicothe: 'we now have three colored officers. Colored inmates who are racially conscious will accept orders from colored officers when they would resist them from white officers. I recommend that very seriously to anyone. If you get the proper type colored officer, I think it is most helpful.'[37] As for other employees in the Federal government, there are no official statistics about the race of prison officers. A straw poll of wardens present revealed that several Federal institutions employed Black officers or Black employees, though no indication of seniority was recorded: Alderson, El Reno, Petersburg, Leavenworth, Danbury, Tallahassee, Lewisburg, Atlanta. The wardens were urged to desegregate their prison hospitals and chapels as steps toward integration. On their own initiative, several wardens introduced successfully non-racial pre-release units and others desegregated recreation.[38]

In the larger institutions, segregation, propped up with widespread prejudice, remained the norm as the Director himself acknowledged: 'one of the things we should get away from completely is letting the colored fellows get the dirty jobs. That is the next thing we have to work toward. There is no question but what we must deal with a lot of prejudice. I have mine; everyone else has his own; and we have to be careful that we are not unconsciously doing something which shows discrimination.'[39] The Director summarized the position in 1954 thus: 'in housing, only three institutions are completely integrated (Englewood, La Tuna, Tucson). The others range from almost complete integration to almost complete segregation.' Crucially, 'we must admit that the main body of prisoners in the federal prison system are now segregated in living quarters. But each year, particularly since the end of the war, has seen a greater number of housing units in which the races live together.'[40]

The survey results (Table 5.4) also suggested that segregation was unsurprisingly more rooted in those prisons located in the South but also that larger institutions tended to be less integrated: 'the larger institutions have the farthest to go toward integration. By and large, the institutions in the North are farther along than those in the South but that is not always the case.' He gave the example of Seagoville: it was 'closer to full integration than any penitentiary or reformatory. Another point is that integration has been brought about much more rapidly in the institutions having the smaller proportion of negroes. Note the ratios in the institutions where full integration exists—Englewood 8 per cent, La Tuna 4 per cent, and Tucson 4 per cent.'[41] Elsewhere in his assessment the Director concluded, somewhat dispiritedly, that 'no matter where one stands ideologically with respect to racial segregation, it must be admitted that there are real obstacles to integration of quarters in a large prison'. At the core of the problem was segregated accommodation: 'no small part of the obstacle is the fact that fewer than 15 per cent of our inmates are or can be quartered in single cells or rooms, the remainder being in group cells, squad rooms or dormitories.'[42] Multiple cell occupancy immensely complicated integration in prisons, since segregated housing was the most coveted feature of segregation among White inmates.

The task of prison wardens attempting to integrate their inmate populations was made more difficult by a Southern location in which prominent politicians—for example, the Governor of Georgia—were daily expressing, in unequivocal language, their resolve to prevent desegregation in schools and other public activities in the wake of the *Brown* decision. The Warden of the Federal prison in Atlanta noted that the state legislature had enacted 'a private school law to avoid integration of the races in schools, which has aggravated the problem in the prison'.[43] Federal prisons were outside the control of state legislatures and governors but not immune from local pressures.

The Bureau Director recognized that desegregation of living quarters was both the most difficult and the most important stage in the integration process. He suggested a strategy—'some principles and methods'—derived from his experience. First, integration plans had to be 'individualized to meet the special characteristics of the institution, such characteristics including size, location, the type of population, the type and arrangement of living quarters and the stage of development of integration in the institution'. Second, it was important that 'integration plans should be well thought out and each step scheduled and timed so as to avoid disturbance'. However, in his view, 'fear of disturbance' should not become an 'excuse for inaction'. Finally, the Director thought integration should be initiated in the 'admission unit and in honor units'.[44]

The desegregation and integration of Federal prisons did not depend solely upon the attitudes and behaviour of the inmates. It required also the co-operation of prison guards. In 1954 the Bureau did not know how many Black guards were employed in its penitentiaries,[45] but the Director was in no doubt about the importance of guards' attitudes toward integration: 'they are the key to the program. They can speed the process or defeat it.' Because most guards were recruited locally, the 'attitudes of our personnel, by and large, are representative of the attitudes of persons in the communities where they have been raised or where they live'. This pattern produced a predictable dichotomy: 'this means, in general, that there is more feeling, more emotion involved in considering the question in institutions located in the Southern and border states than in those in the Northern or Western states . . . In a number of institutions there is no particular feeling about racial integration . . . In some institutions there are a few personnel who could be considered actively resistant and agitators . . . It is recognised as a real problem in most institutions and particularly so in those located in the South.'[46] There were very few Black guards in Federal prisons before the *Brown* decision (and only one appears to have been given a supervisory position).[47] At the Tallahassee penitentiary there was one Black American officer. According to the 1954 survey, the officer suffered similar treatment to those Black Americans working in Federal agencies during Woodrow Wilson's presidency: 'he has never eaten in the officers dining room. Formerly he had his meal sent to the dormitory where he worked, now he brings his lunch.'[48]

At the correctional institution at Milan, Michigan, a survey in 1958 found some hostility between predominantly Black American inmates and White guards, though the researcher attributed this to previous experiences rather than to bigotry: 'while prejudice might be suspected in the predominantly white staff, our impression was that most inmates simply were not accustomed to communicating easily with whites, a consequence of segregation in their neighborhoods and schools.'[49] The same study found race prejudice to be a poor explanation, in five institutions, of inmate dislike of prison guards, even though the questioners were Black. The percentages identifying race as a cause of hostility at Leavenworth, Terre Haute, Milan, Chillicothe, and Ashland were 3, 13, 21, 2, and 2 respectively.[50]

Prison personnel consisted of three groups:[51] first, those passing a competitive examination of an undemanding type and who lacked other qualifications and were invariably recruited locally; second, those passing the same examination but possessing also professional or technical qualifications; third, those who in addition to holding qualifications successfully passed a special examination in their subject. Once in the service officers were eligible for promotion as they satisfied various course and years-of-experience requirements. Below the level of warden and associate warden five ascending grades operated: correctional officers, instructor, assistant, supervisor, and manager.

A series of steps by which prison personnel could be accommodated to desegregation were identified by the Director, principally the example of the institution's head. Table 5.5 summarizes the attitudes of personnel as reported in the 1954 survey. It demonstrates clearly that the Federal prisons located in the South (Atlanta, Leavenworth, Tallahassee, and Lewisburg) faced serious opposition from their guards toward integration.

In 1947 the Warden of Ashland devoted the entirety of his bimonthly report to the 'racial situation', because 'this problem has been causing me and my staff considerable concern'.[52] The Warden focused on his staff's attempts to assign Black inmates to paying work positions (known as 'Industries'), at the cost of assigning white inmates to orderly jobs, 'formerly performed by negroes'.[53] That this equality of assignment was considered innovative is informative about the previous order prevailing in Federal penitentiaries. The institution also desegregated recreation and entertainment, and although housing was segregated, Black American inmates received one of the more desirable cell blocks. These measures apparently failed to satisfy Black inmates in the way Warden Hagerman had anticipated:

> in spite of the measures we have adopted to break down racial barriers, we are having considerable trouble with the colored military prisoners who want to charge discrimination whenever they are reported for a rules violation. These men have apparently been well indoctrinated with material currently found in all negro publications and have a ready alibi for any personal failure. We have had five colored men within the past two days reported for refusing to work and in every case they charged unfairness and discrimination against colored inmates by the officers who reported them. Careful investigations are conducted by the Disciplinary Board and in no instance was there any circumstance or factor which could cause these men to feel that they were being treated unfairly because of color. Most of these colored military prisoners are arrogant and are seeking to discover issues which could embarrass the administration and spread discontent among the entire colored population. The white inmates for the most part resent the attitude of this group toward the white population and since the majority of our white prisoners come from the south, there is always the possibility of riot.[54]

TABLE 5.5. *Attitudes of Prison Guards and Personnel to Desegregation*

Institution	Attitudes of prison personnel
Alcatraz	No problems reported
Atlanta	Widespread inborn prejudices
Leavenworth, Kan.	Southern-born personnel hostile
McNeil Island, Wash.	Considerable intolerance by White guards
Alderson, W. Va.	Some Black guards facilitating change
Springfield, Mo.	No problems anticipated
Milan, Mich.	No problems anticipated except in housing
La Tuna, Tex.	Black population too small for the issue to matter
Seagoville, Tex.	Unproblematic except for housing
Texarkana, Tex.	No problems anticipated
Danbury, Conn.	Anticipated voluntary segregation by inmates
Montgomery, Ala.	Positive support from personnel
Lewisburg, Pa.	Oppostion anticipated
Terre Haute, Ind.	Opposition or poor compliance anticipated
El Reno, Okla.	Personnel oppose integration but will adhere
Chillicothe, Oh.	Lack of support but not opposition; 3 Black guards
Tallahassee, Fla.	Likely personnel opposition; 1 Black guard
National Training School	Desegregation anticipated without difficulty; 15 Black guards
Tucson, Ariz.	No segregation
Mill Point, W. Va.	Expected cooperation from personnel
Greenlee, Va.	Location in the South an inhospitable context

Source: NA RG 129, Bureau of Prisons, Central Administrative File 1937–67, Prisoners' Welfare, Box 41, File Segregation: Answers to questionnaire of 10 June 1954 re segregation.

The Warden singled out one Black military inmate as exceptionally difficult and asked that no further Black prisoners be sent (of 412 inmates, 87 were Black prisoners). In Milan, a baseball game between a Black team and White team degenerated into a racial fight (provoked by observers rather than participants), causing the Assistant Director of the Bureau to query the wisdom of such games in the South.[55] In Sandstone, Minnesota, the institution adopted 'mixed housing and dining' in the 1930s but this racial harmony was erupted by White military prisoners less keen on such fraternizing: 'since the receipt of the military prisoners, we have had to curtail our mixing . . . As this group grew in numbers, racial tension did develop to some extent.' But in the Warden's judgement, 'the feeling of the white military prisoners against the colored in our population was not directed against them as a group but only toward certain individuals.'[56] This assessment must have been a great source of comfort to the individual victims.

RACE CONFLICT

Federal prison authorities appreciated that racial tension was often a source of conflict in their penitentiaries (though in many respects this was more of a problem in state and military institutions). In 1947 the Director of the Bureau brought this problem to the wardens' conference, coincidentally the year in which a major racial disturbance occurred at Chillicothe.[57] In his amateur sociological style, he identified five factors fostering racial conflict. First, racial tension in the community or society at large such as the race riots occurring in many cities during the Second World War. These tensions infiltrated the penitentiaries. Second, a shift in the racial composition of inmates, and the Director had in mind particularly the increased number of Black prisoners in the 1940s (see Table 5.1), including many aggrieved Black military prisoners. For many years, the percentage of Federal prisoners who were Black was relatively small and this fact limited the scope for conflict. A swelling of their numbers—particularly of Northern Blacks incarcerated in prisons located in the South—altered these dynamics. Third, and more specifically, the Director identified any change in procedures or routines as potentially divisive: 'for example, if negroes and whites had been fed in separate dining rooms, resentment would be created if they were fed in the same dining room, even at separate sittings.'[58] Such changes in dining-room arrangements provoked a riot in Leavenworth. Fourth, either Black American prisoners' belief that they suffered racial discrimination or White prisoners' belief that Black inmates were being advantaged. The former issue was increasingly aired by the new sorts of prisoners received during the war. White prisoners were easily stirred into holding grievances. Fifth, not unlike arrangements in the military, the regional composition of prisoners mattered: 'the mixture in the same institution of northern and southern negroes and northern and southern whites. This admixture, found in many federal institutions, but rarely in state institutions or in outside communities, brings together widely different beliefs, emotions, prejudices and sympathies on racial relations.'[59] It was precisely this diversity which resulted from the types of prisoners received by the Federal system in the 1940s. In the old system, Black prisoners were limited to positions comparable to those they held in society outside the prisons. Although racial disturbances had these undertones it usually required a short-term dynamic to provoke the conflict. The Director also noted the influence of 'inmates who feel strongly about a particular "cause" and will go to any length to promote the cause'.[60]

The Bureau's Director was keen to defuse the potential for such conflicts by programmes to educate and inform and to foster tolerance between the races within prisons. He singled out personnel attitudes as primary to such amelioration: 'officers who demonstrate antipathies toward a racial group or members of it, not only create racial resentment, but also are in no position to create tolerance within the inmate body.' The task of eradicating prejudice daunted the Director: 'admittedly, it is difficult to change attitudes on race or religion. The subject of racial problems and relationships must, however, enter into the training of officers and into staff discussions.'[61] He enunciated ways of dealing with grievances and fostering tolerance amongst inmates.

Predicting riots was obviously close to impossible. In 1952 there were serious riots at Chillicothe and El Reno, and in both cases, according to the Bureau's Director, the 'occurrences were quite unexpected. We thought the morale of the inmates and personnel where the disturbances occurred was excellent and we had no reason to suspect that anything of the kind was brewing. That, of course, naturally leads to the question as to whether we know how to appraise an explosive or dangerous institutional situation when it actually exists.'[62] The Director squarely blamed failure to comply with Bureau regulations as contributing decisively to the riots: 'we should like to give the inmates the opportunities to learn a trade, but if that entails a relaxation of the rules or policies with respect to control of tools, then the need for training will have to take a secondary place.'[63]

In the summer of 1951 a race riot was narrowly averted at the Mill Point Penitentiary in West Virginia.[64] According to the Warden, it was provoked by the presence of five conscientious objectors, one of whom was a highly educated Black American, advocating racial integration. A proposal to designate a 'table where both white and negro inmates could dine together if they wished' stimulated 'racial antagonism';[65] and the request by the conscientious objectors that they be placed in the Black American inmates' dormitory did not win them friends amongst the White prisoners. In a considered reflection on the incident, the Superintendent reported that racial tension had been rare in the prison. However, there was little integration: 'housing has been separate and separation in the dining room has been practiced.'[66] He continued: 'the separation in the dining room, up until April of this year, was maintained by having a so called colored section located on one side in an end. In April, a change was made in this arrangement whereby the colored group were seated by the established rotation of dormitories and the result was that the location of the colored group changed daily, as it does for the white dorms, with separation by tables only.' This arrangement was opposed by White prisoners: 'the white group questioned this procedure and accepted it on explanation, without incident or difficulty of any sort.'[67]

A job assignment which required White men to participate in washing walls in a dormitory assigned to Black inmates was refused by the Whites, on the ground that 'they should not be expected to clean after the colored group. Explanation that the job was a service to overall camp sanitation rather than a service to a group did not change their views.'[68] This incident illustrates the unsurprising ingrainedness of segregation in the Federal prison.

At Mill Point, it was the action of one of the White conscientious objectors in sitting at the Black inmates' table which proved flammable:

> when the officer, Instructor Balzer, returned to the dining room he noted [Conscientious Objector prisoner] Pierce at the colored table but did not move him in the belief that less attention to the incident would result by him leaving there. Occasional mixing of races has occurred on short line without incident. Following the events of the evening, Pierce admitted that he knew he was not supposed to be seated with the colored group but stated that he came in with them on the line and sat down without thinking.[69]

That evening, the White Conscientious Objector prisoners were forcibly ejected from the White inmates' dormitory. A full-blown race riot was adroitly foiled by transferring the Conscientious Objector prisoners to another prison.

Superintendent Thieman speculated from the incident to any initiative aimed at desegregating the Mill Point Penitentiary. It concerned him 'that the present population of Mill Point will not accept changes in the present order of separation of the races. This includes many of the colored group as well as the whites.' Wartime had offered some prospect for racial change but that had ended: 'the type of population here during World War II was quite different, when one dormitory was used for housing both races separated in each end of the building. The present population will go along well together in work and idle time activities without undesirable incident but will not accept changes nor discussion of changes in housing or dining room procedure.' Notions of human commonality transcending race were misplaced and wasted: 'the C.O. philosophy of brotherly love and close association in all activities among the races is over the heads of the majority, both colored and white. It seems that the administration must function on that premise until a more opportune time.'[70] Mill Point was closed down at the end of the 1950s.

THE *BROWN* DECISION AND SEGREGATED PRISONS: 'IT LOOKED LIKE A U.N. GATHERING'

In 1944 the Director of the Bureau of Prisons promulgated a commitment to ending racial discrimination and segregation in Federal penitentiaries. It was a position consistent with his regular articulation of the need for equality of treatment of prisoners irrespective of race, though it meant abandoning any lingering espousal of segregation:[71] 'there is no discrimination on account of race or religion at any of the institutions under the direction of this office. We provide for Negroes the same opportunities for training, work, and recreation as well as other privileges as we do for the white inmates of the

TABLE 5.6. *Percentage of Black prisoners by institution 1954 (selected)*

Institution	%age of black inmates (1948 %ages in brackets)	
Englewood, Colo.	8.1	
El Reno, Okla.	15.7	
Chillicothe, Oh.	22.2	
Atlanta	30.1	(33.4)
Lewisburg, Pa.	30.6	
Petersburg, Va.	43.3	
Alderson, W. Va.	44.2	(25)
National Training School	50.4	
Milan, Mich.	54.4	(36)
TOTAL		

Source: NA RG 129, Bureau of Prisons, Central Administrative File 1937–67, Prisoners' Welfare, Box 41, File Segregation: Wardens' Conference, Leavenworth, Kan., 9 Dec. 1954, minutes and proceedings, 15.

institutions.'[72] The new policy did not end segregation, but it signalled a gradual shift away from both *de jure* and *de facto* practices. The extent of this shift varied across prisons.

The Supreme Court's 1954 ruling that the segregation of public schools was unconstitutional had obvious implications for the Federal prison system. The topic was discussed animatedly at that year's annual wardens' conference.[73] In the main, the wardens welcomed the decision as one speaker commented: since 1944 segregation 'was discussed in greater detail and with more understanding and less tension. Year after year progress reports were made of areas in which segregation had been eliminated and ways in which better understanding between the races had been achieved.' The speaker recalled practices long abandoned: 'several of you have been in the service long enough to recall the time when the only negroes employed in the industrial shops were janitors and when the recreation fields at some institutions had their Mason Dixon lines. That we have made progress, and during the past few years rapid progress, is undeniable.'[74]

By the time of the *Brown* decision, Black American inmates constituted 27.1 per cent of the total prison population compared with 23.4 per cent in 1948, a figure masking significant differences between institutions: the youth institution in Englewood, Colorado, included 8.1 per cent Black inmates whereas in Milan, Michigan, Black prisoners constituted 54.4 per cent (Table 5.6).[75] The percentage of Black inmates in Federal prisons was far higher in 1954 than the percentage of Black recruits in the Armed Services when it integrated, and as the Bureau's superintendent observed, 'it has been generally assumed, and seemingly with reason, that the higher the ratio of the minority group, the greater the problems connected with integration'.[76] At El Reno, the Warden reported a 'little progress in the race situation', but many difficulties: 'some few years ago we had a rather bad situation there. We were even afraid at that time to let the white and colored play together. But we have broken that down entirely.' Significantly the new system was based in the housing: 'the program is set up on a dormitory basis. Our teams are made up of both colored and white. We had an Inmate Council meeting just a short time ago and it consisted of four colored boys, an Indian, a Puerto Rican, and three whites. It looked like a United Nations gathering.' Furthermore, at the prison, 'we have broken down segregation in the hospital. Dr Montroy and Mr Kennedy and I agreed that it was a good time to try. We painted one ward and moved the surgery cases in there. We had a complaint, but one of the doctors pointed out that an appendix doesn't pick out a colored or a white man. When I left we had colored, Puerto Ricans, and whites all there at the same time. We have used a colored officer in the kitchen to supervise the colored line. The kitchen men all live in one dormitory.'[77] By 1956 the Director of the Bureau was ebullient about desegregation: recording 'remarkable, even startling, progress' in the 'integration of white and colored inmates in our institutions'. He continued: 'integration has been completed in Lewisburg, Terre Haute, Petersburg, Englewood, Terminal Island, Texarkana, Chillicothe, McNeil Island, Milan, El Reno, La Tuna, Ashland, Seagoville, National Training School, Alderson, and Tallahassee, which is a pretty good record. Most of this has been accomplished in the past two years, and it is a real accomplishment.' He believed the record superior to other areas of American society: 'I don't know where else in a similar group of institutions this has been achieved so quickly and with so few really serious problems. Now those of you who haven't completed integration and want to get some ideas from those who have, don't neglect to ask them about it.'[78] Commenting in 1964 on some racial incidents, the Bureau's Director again emphasized the importance of prison officers: 'we have asked our personnel to avoid taking umbrage at some of the offensive remarks made by various Negro prisoners . . . We think that most of our personnel will follow this training, but we must concede that there are a few individuals in our Service who are not wholly in sympathy with integration trends. We are keeping them out of situations where they might do something or say something that would complicate our problems.'[79] In 1964 Federal prisons were holding Black Muslim groups, whose members aggressively asserted Black prisoners' rights, and whom the Director plainly did not welcome: 'the representatives of the Black Muslim group too are in the institutions because of their rebellious and violent activities. Some of them are much like our former prisoner, Bayard Rustin, now apparently a moving force in the Civil Rights movement, but as far as our records are concerned, to put it mildly, an extremely unsavory individual with little discernible regard for human decency.'[80]

Formal policy statements about integration and desegregation were not formulated by the Bureau of Prisons until ten years after the *Brown* decision. One major policy statement was issued on 7 August 1964: 'no inmate in any Federal penal institution shall be discriminated against on the grounds of race, color, creed or national origin, in any phase of institutional activities. There shall be no segregation on these grounds in housing, work assignments, eating accommodations, religious, recreational, educational or medical services.'[81] Questioned in 1966 by the American Civil Liberties Union about integration, the Bureau's new director, Myrl Alexander, replied: 'during the past twenty-five years, a policy providing for complete integration in all programs and facilities has evolved within the Federal Bureau of Prisons. While we have encountered occasional individuals who have resisted our efforts in this direction, our problems in implementing this policy have been minimal.'[82] Each prison issued a policy statement for non-discrimination based on the Bureau's position.[83] Inmates were admitted to quarters in the Admission-Orientation unit, classified, and then moved to permanent cells, all of which were integrated. In July 1966 the Bureau of Prisons issued its own policy statement on 'Integration': 'the policy of non-discrimination and full integration in Bureau of Prisons institutions is clear and long standing. The policy applies to all aspects of institutional management relating to inmates and personnel.'[84] The implementation of this policy implied two requirements:

a. In these days of recurring challenges to all aspects of civil rights, including provisions affecting public accommodations, each institution's chief executive is directed to review in detail every aspect of administration to insure that no vestige of discrimination based on race, creed or national origin exists.
b. Each warden and superintendent is requested to reexamine immediately existing policy requirements, survey all institutional operations and certify to this office that his institution is in full compliance with existing policies, in fact and in spirit.[85]

The Bureau received responses from all its institutions assuring, for the most part, their compliance with the policy: Lewisburg, National Training School for Boys DC, El Reno, Montgomery, Danbury, Englewood, Texarkana, McNeil Island, Tallahassee, Seagoville, Sandstone, Ashland, Terre Haute, Springfield, Chillicothe, La Tuna, Milan, and Petersburg.[86] Leavenworth's Warden claimed compliance except for the 'inmate dining room and the multiple cells in A Cellblock'.[87]

Atlanta proved one of the toughest prisons to desegregate. This tenacity reflected its age, the old physical design of the cells, the size of its population, and its regional location. In the 1930s attempts at integration in living quarters failed: 'this experiment of mixing the races was tried out in the old tailor shop to accommodate the dining room men, and was an unsatisfactory experiment, and has convinced us that the two races cannot be mixed in dormitories.'[88] In 1966 in one dormitory there were 33 two-man rooms of which '12 are integrated but 12 of 17 rooms having colored inmates are integrated'.[89] In response to the Director's policy statement, the Warden at Atlanta provided a long memorandum on 1 March 1966, conceding that 'certain areas were not totally integrated'. Efforts to integrate living quarters were halted on 21 February, when 'it was necessary to hospitalize three colored inmates who had been stabbed with some type of sharp instrument'.[90] The Warden elaborated upon the incident from his investigation, which 'revealed that the three colored inmates were involved in some of the integrative moves and one of them (Prater) was scheduled to be moved into the cell occupied by Joseph Donald Nanney, 87849. It is reported that Nanney shook hands with the colored inmate and advised him that everything was fine and to move on over into the cell.' However, Nanney had a welcoming surprise in store for his new cell-mate: 'it is further revealed that at the same time he (Nanney) and others had planned to get Prater into the cell, shut the door, kill him and throw him over the rail to the floor of A Cell House.' This plan fortunately failed: 'they were apparently unable to get inmate Prater into the cell, so they ganged him and the other two on the walkway in front of the cell before officers could reach the scene and break it up. Others over and above Nanney and Terriah . . . were very strongly involved in this incident and were quite active, with many of them wielding knives.'[91] The repercussions of the racial conflict were palpable: 'tension in the institution grew by leaps and bounds, threats were being made, those who had already been moved into integrated cells began to fear for their lives, and it was necessary to bring in a large group of employees on overtime to maintain control.'[92] Integration faced further opposition when resumed three days later but the Warden persevered, and by the end of 25 March, 'I was able to report to Assistant Director Taylor that subsequent integration had now been accomplished in every area within the institution; that we would expect to continue with more integration of cells, but would like to do this in a normal, routine manner rather than a crash program'.[93] While most of the personnel at Atlanta supported integration, the Warden's programme was not assisted by the 'two or three minor indications that employees were not in agreement with the program'.[94] He concluded his report by stating Atlanta's compliance with the integration policy. Such incidents were not confined to Atlanta though they persisted longer at this penitentiary,[95] because of its location and staff, size, and old buildings.

At McNeil Island in the state of Washington, of 40 cells in Number 3 House '16 are integrated. Yet there is only one all Negro cell. Therefore to say 16 out of 40 are integrated presents a distorted picture. It is more accurate (and more favorable) to point out that 16 out of 17 cells having Negroes are integrated.'[96] This memorandum was prepared in response to a query from a US District Judge in Chicago, reviewing an appeal by an inmate challenging segregated policy in a state penitentiary. The Bureau provided the data reported in Table 5.7, and informed the Judge that integration of prisoners was the norm. This latter was qualified in some ways: 'if there are indications that a racial bias on the part of an individual inmate would probably cause serious security or disciplinary problems, we do seek to avoid that situation.' An explanation was given: 'we would not knowingly house a member of the Ku Klux Klan with a Negro inmate, nor would we place a militant Black Muslim in the same cell as a white inmate. However, I should emphasize to you that the happenstance of the color of a man's skin does not itself constitute a consideration in his quarters assignment.'[97] Three penitentiaries had multiple occupancy cells, the focus of the Judge's question, and these are listed in Table 5.7. This information was used to advance desegregation and integration of prisoners in state penitentiaries, where it remained significant in the 1960s more powerfully rooted in local communities and values.[98]

The US Commission on Civil Rights was concerned about segregation in county gaols holding Federal prisoners (see Table 5.8),[99] a problem which had long exercised the Bureau and Department of Justice. In response, the Bureau equivocated, observing of Federal prisoners in segregated gaols, 'we are faced with a difficult problem'. Despite Federal reform, the 'majority of local jails in the United States are segregated. The Bureau itself operates institutions for the pre-trail detention of prisoners only in New York and Arizona.' Solving this conumdrum would require the Bureau to 'maintain federal detention facilities in the majority of the Federal Judicial Districts in the United States. There are obviously no funds available for this purpose.'[100] The Director was not confident about improving this arrangement: 'in a few of the larger segregated jails we have had some success in arranging for the confinement of all federal prisoners in separate non-segregated facilities.' He thought local changes unlikely: 'it is extremely difficult for us to promote changes in local practice, especially in view of the fact that most local jurisdictions would prefer to be relieved of the responsibility for the care of federal offenders, and insistence on compliance with policies of non-segregation would unquestionably result in wholesale termination of contracts.'[101]

This problem persisted, particularly in respect of Southern prisons. Despite the Bureau's opposition to segregation, John Doar in the Civil Rights Division of the Justice Department threatened to support suits against the Bureau for holding Federal prisoners in county gaols.[102] The Bureau agreed, after a meeting between Doar and Director Alexander, to undertake an 'affirmative program to use the influence of the Bureau of Prisons to persuade state officials to change their practices'.[103] Under this pressure, the Bureau inserted a non-discrimination compliance clause in their contracts with local gaols, and directly contacted 226 gaols to explain the modification.[104] This

TABLE 5.7. *Racial composition of prisoners in multi-occupancy prisons*

McNeil Island, Wash.:
- There are 180 Black inmates constituting 19% of the population.
- Cell House No. 3 contains 40 five-man cells. There are Black inmates in a total of 17 cells of which 16 are integrated.
- Cell House No. 4 contains 40 ten-man cells. There are Black inmates in 19 of these cells of which 17 are integrated.
- Cell House 4 also contains 28 two-man cells. There are but four Blacks in this housing, two are in integrated cells and the other two are cellmates.

Leavenworth, Kan.:
- Inmates total 2,042 in number of which 23% are Black.
- Cell Block A contains 101 cells generally housing four to six inmates, 42 of these cells house Black inmates of which 25 are integrated and 17 are all Black.
- There are 600 cells which had been used as double cells but are now in the process of being converted to single cells. Only 60 double cells remain. Because of this change over there have been no reassignments and none are presently integrated.

Atlanta:
- Total population 2,203 of which 25% are Black.
- Cell House A contains 96 six-man cells. There are Blacks in 34 of these cells of which 21 are integrated.
- Cell House B also consists of six-man cells. Blacks are housed in 35 cells of which 20 are integrated.
- Dormitory 3 includes 22 two-man rooms. Blacks are housed in 17 of these rooms of which 12 are integrated.
- Cell House E consists of 184 two-man cells. There are Blacks in 68 of these cells of which 37 are integrated.

Source: NA RG 129 Bureau of Prisons, Central Administrative File 1937–67, Box 41, File Segregation: letter from Dir. Myrl Alexander to Hubert L. Will US District Court, Chicago (26 May 1966).

clause faced many of the same problems of implementation and compliance discussed in relation to non-discrimination in government employment and contracts. In 1968 the Supreme Court, in *Lee* v. *Washington*, overturned an Alabama statute which required segregated prisons as violating the 14th Amendment. The vote was 9 to 0.

CONCLUSION

By 1992 Black prisoners made up a 32.3 per cent of all Federal inmates.[105] These Federal prisoners are arranged in non-segregated arrangements though many examples of segregation by prisoner choice persist.

TABLE 5.8. *Federal prisoners in local prisons 1965*

State	No. of Contract Institutions		Daily average Federal population
	Co. & City	State	
Ala.	17	4	56
Ark.	18		15
Fla.	22		118
Ga.	18		90
Ky.	19	1	73
La.	11		64
Miss.	15		37
NC	24	3	85
SC	14		51
Tenn.	17		66
Tex.:			
Eastern	8		11
Houston, Dall.	3		77
Va.	22		32

Source: NA RG 129 Bureau of Prisons, Central Administrative File 1937–67, Box 41, File Segregation: Memo (3 Feb. 1966).

Three points are worth noting in conclusion. First, the treatment of Black Americans in Federal penitentiaries from the foundation of the US Bureau of Prisons was informed by the ethos and principle of segregation. This principle resulted in most institutions in distinct living, working, and eating arrangements for the two races. As in other agencies and areas of the US Federal government, Black Americans received the worst jobs in prisons disproportionately to their numbers; faced discrimination; and, in the South particularly, experienced Federal prisons as miniature versions of the sectionalism rampant in society. Black Federal prisoners held in non-Federal institutions suffered these abuses for a longer period than those in Federal ones.

Second, these racial practices were undoubtedly stronger in Federal institutions located in the South where several factors held: a brutal state penal tradition, recruitment of most custodial staff and guards—almost exclusively White—from the adjacent communities, and in some cases wardens sharing Southern racial attitudes.

Third, the appointment of the long-serving Director of the US Bureau, James Bennett, had an appreciable impact on the degree of segregation and on the rapidity with which desegregation was undertaken. Bennett filtered and weakened the sectional interests forcing themselves upon all areas of the US Federal government; this reforming tradition was emulated by Bennett's successor Myrl Alexander. The significant role played by this administrator seems to me a useful corrective to the recent tendency amongst scholars to overemphasize the immutability and rigidity of institutional arrangements. It also demonstrates the importance of identifying the individualism around and upon which institutions are constructed, a lesson perhaps better appreciated by historians than social scientists. For instance, the historian Michael Burleigh has reconstructed the harrowing experience of a Nazi asylum's collective identity from individual experiences ensuring that sight is not lost of the individual;[106] while Charles Eagles's dissection of the death of Jon Daniels, a civil rights worker, in Alabama in 1965 is an impressive study of how this outsider was perceived and eventually murdered by the Southern community in Lowndes County, and how his murderer was released under the codes of segregation.[107] Director Bennett seems to have pursued a clear and unwavering policy to humanize race relations through integration in Federal institutions, an initiative which did not of course render these latter exceptionally pleasant places but did begin the process of desegregation before the Supreme Court issued a decisive ruling.

6

The Federal Government in a Segregated Society: Public Employment Exchanges and Housing Programmes

THE election of Franklin D. Roosevelt to the presidency in 1932 on the promise of a 'New Deal' for unemployed and hungry Americans, exposed to the ravages of the Great Depression, signalled a new activism by the Federal government. Working and securing housing are two of the most basic activities in which citizens engage, and it was precisely in these areas that Roosevelt's administration forged a new role for the Federal government.

In 1933 the Congress enacted the Wagner-Peyser Act establishing a national United States Employment Service (USES), intended to help job-seekers find work throughout the United States. The USES vetted workers for positions on the numerous public works programmes created under Roosevelt's New Deal initiative. The USES assumed responsibility, as part of the War Manpower Commission, for placing workers in defence industries. It acquired an important filtering role in helping the unemployed find work in the 1930s and during the Second World War; after 1945 it acted as a labour exchange in the buoyant labour-market. It began as a Federal–state scheme, in which state spending was matched by the Federal government. In 1946 the latter assumed total funding. Congress was responsible for overseeing the USES but it was administered and controlled at the state level. In Congress, the USES was assiduously protected by Southern Congressmen and Senators, alert to any activities detrimental to the *status quo*, as the USES Advisor on Negro Affairs, Lawrence Oxley, discovered in 1938. Congressman John J. Cochran (a Democrat from Missouri) fired off a letter to the USES Director complaining about Oxley's work in Kansas and Missouri. Referring to talks given by Oxley, Cochran declared: 'I do not want Government Employees going around making speeches that cause our Administration trouble.' He warned Oxley to 'be more careful'.[1] Cochran's position as chairman of the House Committee on Executive Departments made his influence over appropriations considerable.

In housing, the government initiated a system of mortgage subsidy to homebuyers and commenced a public housing programme for those unable to buy. Federal programmes reinforced and spread a segregationist residential order. The government's intervention was for too long one which consolidated instead of terminated the racially segregated order. A graphic example of the Federal government's segregationist housing regime was the persistence until the early 1960s of two sections in the FHA's office in Atlanta, one serving Black applicants and staffed by Black employees, the second serving exclusively the needs of Whites.[2] The Chairman of the US Commission on Civil Rights opened a hearing on housing in Washington in 1962 with the observation that 'housing is the one commodity in the American market that is not freely available on equal terms to everyone who can afford to pay'.[3] He continued: 'throughout the country . . . much of the housing market is closed to them [American Negroes] for reasons unrelated to their personal worth or ability to pay, and in the restricted market that is open to them, Negroes generally must pay more for equivalent housing than do the favored majority.'[4] For many Black Americans in the 1940s and 1950s, the inequities of Federal housing policy—both in the loans made available and in the concentration of housing by race—constituted a singularly powerful object of complaint and grievance.[5] The legacy of this residential segregation is apparent to even the most cursory observer of American society.

This chapter treats these two areas of Federal government intervention, marshalling material to illustrate how public policy reinforced segregation in each sphere instead of supplanting it.

THE SEGREGATED USES

The American labour-market was significantly segregated in the 1930s and 1940s. White unionized workers dominated skilled positions while Black workers, frequently unable to obtain union membership or apprenticeships, were concentrated in unskilled, including agricultural, jobs. In the civil service, Black employees were disproportionately concentrated in custodial and menial jobs, marginalized in professional and managerial positions (see Chapter 3). Black American women workers sometimes advanced to clerical jobs. The extent of these patterns was apparent in a survey of selected state labour-markets conducted by Lawrence Oxley in 1937. He examined the service offered by USES offices to Black American job-seekers in fifteen states, in whose jurisdictions lived eight and a half million Blacks. He consistently found that Black workers were concentrated in the worst jobs and excluded from the better ones. For example, from his study of occupational profiles in Indianapolis, Oxley concluded that Black Americans worked as chauffeurs, truck and tractor drivers; labourers on roads and streets, steam railroads, coalyards and lumber yards, public service; porters and helpers in stores; janitors and sextons; porters in domestic and personal service; servants; waiters; barbers; hairdressers; charwomen and cleaners; housekeepers and stewardesses; laundresses and laundry operatives; and hairdressers and manicurists. But they were unrepresented in several industries including: printing, publishing, and photo engraving; all types of lumber and timber industries; electrical machinery, apparatus, and supplies; motor vehicle bodies and parts. The USES did not arrest or ameliorate this pattern by sending Black American job-seekers to positions from which they were historically excluded. Oxley believed the USES should help Black Americans achieve a foothold in these latter sectors.[6] Of employment exchanges, he observed: 'there is still room to give particular consideration and attention to the employment needs of the Negro group.'[7] Crucially, the reluctance of officials to classify Black American job-seekers for vacancies other than menial ones, regardless of the applicant's qualifications, perpetuated the labour-market position of Black workers. The only special attention accorded Black job-seekers was likely to be harmful rather than advantageous to their prospects. In Baltimore, Oxley learned from the Manager of the Employment Center that the 'placement of Negro white collar and professional workers and Negro skilled workers on construction work offered the two main problems to his office'.[8] The record of the USES's local offices in helping Black American job-seekers find positions was unimpressive. The USES was frightened to challenge the constraints imposed by Congress (for instance, in the insistence that the District of Columbia's offices be segregated). It compromised a nominal commitment to equality of placement with the acceptance of discriminatory job orders (even after 1941) and failed to tackle the profound inequalities present in Southern offices.

In Southern states, such as Georgia, Alabama, Louisiana, Texas, Arkansas, and Tennessee, employment opportunities were predictably severely limited.[9] Black Americans living in these states faced abject poverty, in large part a function of their marginal labour-market position.[10] Oxley identified Chicago as the city in which Black American workers had made the greatest inroads into skilled trades and professional white-collar jobs. Despite this progress, in Chicago the 'mass of Negroes remain as laborers, and to a large extent, as laborers in classes of work which are common to the Negro throughout the country . . . Even in those industries which are peculiar to the sections of the country and to the city the Negro, though he participates to a large extent, continues to appear as a laborer and in the heaviest industries.'[11] Oxley's analysis and agenda were framed by segregation. Writing in 1940, with several years' experience, and appreciating the significance of wartime for Black Americans' employment, caution and deference shaped his prognosis.

Black Offices in the USES

The USES was established to help job-seekers find employment, irrespective of race or religion.[12] This precept was violated by its organization, which was segregated: each office was divided into a White section and a Black section. In a speech in 1940, the Illinois Commissioner of Placement rejected claims that this division created inequality: '*the place of the Negro in the Employment Service program is, and must be, the same as that of any other citizen.* No one has or can have any prior or privileged claim to the benefits of its provisions over and above that of any other citizen.'[13] In fact, the consequences of segregated facilities for the services offered Black job-seekers were frequently scandalous. The arrangement enabled USES officials to limit the positions to Blacks. On a visit to Kentucky, Oxley discovered that the 'Negro Divisional office in Louisville was an utter disgrace to the Service from the standpoint of housing, physical equipment, location and personnel'.[14] Oxley contrasted the differences in equipment available to it and to the White office. In the local White office, the 'entire equipment was absolutely new and modern, while the Negro office is forced to use not only obsolete equipment but is faced also with the handicap of not being adequately supplied with even this type of furniture'. Equipment at the Black section relied parlously upon 'pot luck'.[15]

Most employment offices for staff interviewing Black American job-seekers were inferior to those for Whites (Baltimore offering a partial exception).[16] For example, in Charlotte, North Carolina, Oxley found that the 'Negro Divisional office', located in the Star of Zion Building, Second and Brevard Streets, presented 'one of the most inadequate physical setups for a public Employment Service office that I have seen on any of my field visits. The offices are located in the basement of a publishing house, and one of the interviewing rooms was formerly used by an undertaker as a mortuary: twelve chairs, three tables and 24 card application files 5 × 8 and 4 × 5 constituted the sum total of office furniture and equipment.'[17] Similar conditions were reported for the Winston-Salem and Durham Negro Division offices. In response to Oxley's complaints, the USES prevaricated, a strategy not disguised by a special memorandum prepared two months later: 'it has been impossible to find a suitable location for this office. The condition which exists in this and many other cities of North Carolina has prevented the leasing of desirable quarters for the Negro Division.' 'Condition' was a happy euphemism for segregation and prejudice: 'this condition is the unwillingness on the part of landlords to rent desirable property for the maintenance of such an office and the inclusion in at least some of the leases of a clause which prevents the North Carolina State Employment Service from using property already under lease for this purpose.'[18]

Black employment offices were frequently located at remote points in cities. Consequently, in many cities, Black job-seekers were inadequately served by the USES. For instance, in Chicago the State Director of the USES observed to Oxley that although Black Americans constituted 20 per cent of the population on the West Side and North Side 'there is not an employment office within three or four miles of this section—in any direction. This is the greatest need of the Negro—the most pressing in the Cook County and Chicago area.'[19]

A recurrent difficulty for many Black American job-seekers was the refusal of USES staff to register them for any positions other than menial ones regardless of their qualifications. In California, Oxley found that Black job-seekers were disproportionately classified by USES officers as physical labourers or service workers.[20] Writing to the WMC in 1943, the NAACP reported: 'complaints have been received from various sections of the country by the Association in which Negroes complain that local offices of the USES refuse to furnish applications, or consider them, for skilled, professional, or white-collar jobs in war industries. Negroes are required to use separate entrances and are interviewed in segregated offices.'[21] Two instances were included, complaints from Mrs Demaris V. Alston and J. Henry Alston, of 'discriminatory practices' in the Fort Worth offices. Mrs Alston, a college graduate and a teacher of mathematics, 'was refused an application by the Fort Worth office for employment in war industries for any classification above that of maid or waitress'. She was informed by the interviewer that 'jobs for "mechanics for the assembly line at Warrent Field or Consolidated Aircraft (plants) were not available for Negroes"'. Mr Alston, who held a Master of Arts degree, was 'informed by a Mr Riggs of the Fort Worth office "that there was nothing open but common labor, railroad labor, and construction labor jobs"'.[22] Alston described his experience in a formal complaint to the FEPC:

> at the US Employment Office, which is housed with the Texas Employment Office, Negroes are enrolled in a side office upstairs. Just beside this entrance is another marked Federal Work. When I entered I was told that all jobs open to Negroes were handled upstairs. Entering this jim crow entrance, I ascended the stairs and was told by the gentleman, Mr Riggs, that there was nothing open but common labor.
>
> I insisted on filing my application for one of the defense jobs but after registering the clerk very politely told me that there was no defense work open just now . . . I went downstairs and saw the white men coming away with papers and application blanks for toolmakers and other branches of mechanics.[23]

In New Jersey, a complaint from the NAACP on behalf of a Black American woman seeking non-domestic work was vigorously disputed by the state office of the USES. According to the NAACP, the office registered Black American women exclusively for domestic housework. Its director gave a tortuous and contorted explanation: 'I think the explanation is that in the confusion the term "register" was used when, actually, the sense of the statements by the Manager and the Interviewer had reference to the act of offering a job opportunity, which is known in this service as "referral".' He claimed the discriminatory practice did not exist: 'I will now add my own denial that any such instructions to only register colored women for housework were ever sent from my office . . . This would be unthinkable, not only because of the unfairness to persons who possess training and experience which would equip them for other or higher types of employment, but also because the question of such discrimination . . . has been passed around in New Jersey at least for the past several years.'[24] The Director went on to argue that since the applicant's most recent work experience was in housecleaning (for one week) and two years' work on a WPA sewing project it was reasonable to assign her to domestic work. However, the same applicant also had five years' teaching experience! White officials working in USES offices were normally unwilling to send Black American workers to job openings. A member of the Michigan—notably not a Southern state—staff of the USES explained the general perception to Oxley in 1937: 'Mr Verner stated that in many of the Michigan State Employment offices there was a tendency on the part of the Referral Departments to assume that white workers were preferred to Negroes.'[25] This illustrates how segregated race relations reinforced segregation in the labour-market.

Black Staff and the USES

In the three decades after its founding in 1933, segregation rarely extended to USES staff. Instead, staff working in the Black sections were usually White, and almost always so in the South. Hiring Black Americans to work in Southern state employment offices was divisive and conflictual. Objecting to the firing of Black American workers in Georgia in a memorandum in 1938 to the Chairman of the USES's Federal Advisory Council, Lawrence Oxley advocated such employment, urging the staff to consider the 'appointment of Negro personnel in southern states'. He argued that for the 'separate but equal' doctrine 'to be consistent', it required that 'when Negroes have qualified for positions in the state employment services they should be appointed *to at least serve Negroes*'. He again noted that these offices were financed and monitored by the Federal government: 'it cannot be forgotten that federal funds are used also to supplement local employment service activities.'[26] Such requests were blatantly and intentionally ignored.

The reluctance to appoint Black staff was justified tendentiously by a USES official in response to the woeful conditions in North Carolina. Writing in response to criticisms by Oxley, Lyle Garlock explained: 'if Negro Interviewers and Clerks were employed in offices of this type the Director would lose the mobility of staff that is so essential to efficient operation in North Carolina.' 'Mobility of staff' equated with employing Whites exclusively: 'a tabulation of the offices in NC shows that thirty-two of the forty-five offices have six or less employees on the Employment Service staff. These thirty-two offices employ 128 persons and none of them have Negro

Interviewers or Clerks. If Negro personnel were used in these offices, it would be impossible for the Director to transfer them to other offices needing temporary help, whenever such offices or divisions of such offices were dealing exclusively with white applicants. Therefore, for operating reasons, Negro personnel in all offices must be kept to that minimum which is always needed in the particular city concerned.'[27] These opaque 'operating reasons' meant reproducing segregated race relations in the government which mirrored those in society. As for appointing Black staff, Garlock observed candidly and simply: 'the responsible officials in North Carolina believe that it would be unwise to make such appointments in their State.'[28] A not dissimilar point was articulated more subtly in Chicago where the Director of the Illinois office of the USES openly acknowledged racism amongst White staff: 'some of my white interviewers are not fit by temperament and training to serve Negro applicants. These I am weeding out as fast as they are discovered.'[29]

Throughout his memoranda, reports, and recommendations, Oxley stressed the urgency of appointing Black staff to serve the needs of Black job-seekers, evidently unpersuaded of the willingness of White staff to refer Blacks to positions other than the most menial with the least attractive conditions. This view was strongly endorsed by the NAACP.[30] From his study of St Louis, Oxley concluded that 'there should be competent Negroes, selected on the basis of merit, integrated as members of staff of the St Louis Employment Service'. An appropriately located office was also required: the 'most effective service related to registering, referrals, and placement of Negro workers will be realized through the opening of an adequately staffed branch office located strategically in the center of St Louis' Negro population. A wise beginning would be the appointment of at least two Negroes as members of the central Employment Office, and when they have become sufficiently trained in employment service techniques they could consistently be named to supervise such Negro branch office as may be set up.'[31] Speaking to a special meeting with the Kansas Urban League about the local office of the USES, Oxley confessed that, in his view, the 'Negro in Missouri at the present time, from a standpoint of employment, is in a terrible mess'.[32] Oxley urged Black Americans to sit the examinations for appointment to positions in the USES.

The results of sitting entrance examinations were not always propitious, however. In May 1935 the NAACP complained about the failure to hire Black American candidates successful in the examinations. Even appointment did not guarantee equality of treatment (see Chapter 3). Commending the reorganization of the District of Columbia office of the USES in July 1934 (including the appointment of some Black staff), the NAACP objected to the replacement of a Black supervisor by a White one, insufficiently acquainted with Black American job-seekers' needs: 'the colored woman placed in charge of the colored domestics did not make good. You removed her, and have since placed in charge of this Section, a young, inexperienced white woman who knows nothing of the problems of colored people.' There were problems in another division: 'the colored section of the Industrial Division is in charge of a white man whose conduct thereof has been unsatisfactory and distasteful to intelligent colored people.' He failed to treat his Black subordinates respectfully: 'he has under him a colored woman who has grown children; yet he lacks sufficient respect for colored womanhood to call her "Mrs McCullough". Colored men, seeking employment in his office, must submit to his calling them by their first names.'[33] The NAACP then placed these problems in the context of Washington, the administrative heart of the American Federal government, illustrating how segregation meant unequal race relations. Since Washington was a city 'in which the races live separate and apart, it is almost impossible for white people to learn enough about colored people to properly serve them without intelligent colored advisors'. Segregated race relations induced separation and inequality: 'excepting janitors and messengers, you do not have, anywhere in this Center, colored people looking after the interests of the white public. Unless this practice works both ways, it will discourage colored youths and stifle their ambition.'[34] This racist culture in the nation's capital was a principal concern of the Committee on Civil Rights established by President Truman, which reported in 1947.

Discrimination was common in local USES offices, as the NAACP carefully documented. Responding to one NAACP letter in 1940 about practices in Tennessee, the chief of that office acknowledged that 'at present there are no Negro personnel in the Tennessee employment service divisions serving Negro workers'. He provided a standard explanation: 'there are no qualified eligible Negro applicants on the existing civil-service registers for that State and from which applicants must be selected to fill openings in the local offices.'[35] This latter system of civil service recruitment was subsequently trenchantly criticized by Black Americans. Rather than constituting an explanation of the absence of qualified Black applicants, it was symptomatic of the general problem.

Oxley made similar points in reverse order. In his view, Black workers knew all too much about Whites' conditions and psychology in the District of Columbia, because of the intrinsic lopsidedness of segregation: 'most Negroes have worked for or under the direct supervision of white people. In most instances because of the Negro's social background, this work has been done as an industrial or domestic worker.' This experience informed Black Americans' perceptions of Whites: 'he knows the white man and his psychological and racial reactions as an employer. He also knows the attitudes, reactions and characteristics of the Negro as an employee, due to his own personal work, experience, and social relation with other Negro employees.' The experience of Whites was different and rarely reciprocated: 'few white people have been associated with the Negro as an employer or on an equal status as an employee; and, not having the Negro's experience and difficulties as a result of social handicaps, are not in a position to know or to appreciate his problems and difficulties encountered as an employee.' This inequality of race relations meant that 'the white person as an interviewer or put in a supervisory capacity of placement work over Negroes fails to appreciate, through lack of knowledge plus experience, the problem and difficulties of employment as it relates to Negroes'.[36] The position of the District of Columbia remained anomalous, but its segregated codes were vigorously upheld by Congress. As the Secretary of Labor, Lewis Schwellenbach, explained to a member of Congress in 1946, the District's segregated offices were maintained by congressional instruction: 'the problem of providing service to white and non-white applicants in the District of Columbia has been a matter of grave concern to the USES for many years.' Efforts to reform this system foundered: 'in 1942 the USES was advised by the House Committee on Appropriations that, in the judgment of Congress, the customs of the District of Columbia required that segregated services be maintained for white and non-white applicants.' These nebulous customs constituted, in Schwellenbach's view, an impregnable barrier to integration: 'the USES experienced considerable difficulty in going contrary to the customs of a community and, in many instances, any effort to do so reduces the assistance the USES might otherwise give in promoting equality of job opportunities.'[37]

That some White Americans supported segregated race relations vehemently was demonstrated pellucidly in the 1940s and 1950s when Department of Labor officials tried to desegregate the District of Columbia offices. In a dispiriting memorandum the Director of the USES outlined the resistance of two AFL members to such reforms; they 'strongly defended the policy of segregation in the local D.C. office on the basis that that was what this community wanted overwhelmingly'. The two spokesmen, Mr Howard and Mr Conaty, disingenuously cited segregation to justify this argument: 'the practice in the building trades, district schools, theatres, restaurants and other local institutions was cited by them as indicating that the community favored segregation. They argued further that the colored people themselves, insofar as the building trades were concerned, favored segregation.' Concluding on a threatening note, 'Mr Howard and Mr Conaty expressed the fear that we would precipitate racial riots if the attempt were made to eliminate segregation in the local office'.[38] Such defenders of segregation could happily cite supporting legislation. Congressional appropriations to the USES had been accompanied by commitments to segregation, as Secretary of Labor Schwellenbach explained in a letter to Congressman Gordon McDonough: 'in 1942 the United States Employment Service was advised by the House Committee on Appropriations that, in the judgment of Congress, the customs of the District of Columbia required that segregated services be maintained for white and non-white applicants.'[39] The Department of Labor was unprepared, and indeed unable, to counter such strong pressures.

An earlier meeting with the AFL, held by the Director of the District of Columbia USES, produced equally fierce opposition to desegregation—'the [AFL] group pointed out, in no uncertain terms, that they were emphatically opposed to changes of any kind'—and the considerable threat to mobilize congressional support. The Director, Fred Hetzel, reported that it threatened to '1. notify every Congressman, particularly those of the Appropriation Committee, of the local AF of L's opposition to any policy remotely resembling integration [and] 2. notify employers of the District of Columbia that it was the feeling of the AF of L that the USES locally, was attempting to set a community pattern rather than follow the pattern already in existence.'[40] The AFL's enthusiasm for segregation was not shared by many affiliates of the CIO. Its Washington branch vigorously opposed the institution. In 1946 the local CIO President requested a meeting with the Secretary of Labor 'to discuss the urgency of the abolition of segregation in the Washington office of the USES . . . The purpose of our meeting with you would be to correct the systematic distortion of the facts in the situation on the part of some USES officials, as well as to propose specific steps for the elimination of segregation in the local office.'[41] The CIO arranged pickets outside the offices of the USES in Washington to protest the persistence of segregation. Unfortunately, the USES was more responsive to the threats of the AFL than to the demands of abolitionists such as the CIO or the NAACP. Given the AFL's greater political strength, political influence in Congress, and traditional links with the US Department of Labor, this reaction was hardly surprising.

In 1937 an officer in the New York office of the USES argued that reforms were required urgently to offer a proper service to Black job-seekers. William Wilkinson, Staff Supervisor at the National Reemployment Service in New York City, maintained that 'impartial administrative judgment must inevitably realize that the public employment service in New York State has not given equal service to Negroes'.[42] Wilkinson recommended improvements in staff within the employment offices and ensuring that openings for Black workers were identified and notified to the USES. On the former issue he suggested a range of measures including ensuring that Blacks were not discouraged, however subtly, from applying.[43] These proposals, however, found no support in the USES.

The USES and Discrimination

Anti-discrimination Policy

Monitoring discrimination against Black American job-seekers was a task the USES was compelled to address, if unenthusiastically, soon after its foundation. Before the Second World War the Negro Placement Service Unit (later renamed the Racial Relations Unit) was created to assist in the placement of Black American job-seekers. The position was transformed in 1941 into a special Consultant on Racial Relations to the Director of the USES. In 1942, when the Service was temporarily integrated into the WMC, the Minority Groups Service was established. The USES was required to report to the President's FEPC (see this section, below) about its efforts to end discrimination through the use of 'persuasion' upon employers. In 1940 the NAACP stressed the illegality of a federally funded service discriminating by race (as it did also in respect of other Federal programmes).

The USES's own operating manual, issued in 1942, compromised the commitment to non-discriminatory notices: 'the primary objective of the USES in the present emergency is to provide manpower necessary for maximum production in essential industry.' All labour was to be utilized regardless of race: 'therefore it is the policy of the USES: 1. To make all referrals without regard to race, color, creed or national origins *except when an employer's order includes these specifications which the employer is not willing to eliminate*.'[44] Challenging this latter clause with the Administrator of the USES, the NAACP was informed that 'the USES found that a statement of a non-discriminatory policy in itself will not remove the discriminatory barriers of the labor market'. The USES pleaded a lack of sanctions: 'the USES has no way of compelling an employer to accept any worker it may refer to him.'[45] The Administrator concluded plaintively that because the USES 'is charged with the responsibility of maintaining an orderly labor market on the one hand, and of promoting the effective use of all labor on the other, and must do this within the relatively unconfined limits of a free labor market, the course it charts must be one designed to do both jobs'. The result was far from satisfactory or resolute: 'we realise that the operations bulletin in question, which is one phase of the agency's responsibility, has some imperfections. I am advised that these imperfections are being eliminated as rapidly as possible.'[46] Imperfections persisted after the Second World War, despite an awareness within the USES that facilitating the labour-market opportunities for Black Americans was important.[47] This national concern was ignored by many local offices.[48] The Federal government controlled a significant part of the budget of the local offices of the USES and could have used this resource as a mechanism to 'compel' acquiescence.

To cooperate with the FEPC, the USES established procedures for dealing with discriminatory notifications from employers. Bulletin No. USES C-45, issued on 1 July 1942, required local USES offices to forward reports about employers submitting discriminatory specifications in any vacancy notices they received. These reports were copied to the FEPC.[49] In practice, USES offices in the (mainly Southern) states with the most notorious discrimination failed to submit reports. The limitations of this strategy were conceded in a memorandum by the USES Director: 'two WMC regions which included the States of Texas, Louisiana, New Mexico, Virginia, West Virginia, Maryland, and North Carolina, and the District of Columbia never submitted a single report of discriminatory hiring practices. Other regions submitted few reports.'[50]

The processing of job orders specifying racial requirements persisted after 1945. The Denver, Colorado, USES office listed positions for the Navy as available to 'whites only' in 1949.[51] The NAACP's Labor Secretary, Clarence Mitchell, characterized the attitude of the Federal Security Agency officials, who advertised positions through the USES, thus: 'those in that agency are very much opposed to any plan for abandoning discriminatory orders or wiping out segregation in southern states.'[52] Mitchell was reacting to a letter from the Agency,[53] which included an explicit refusal to decline discriminatory job orders on wholly spurious grounds: 'in our considered judgment the refusal of such job orders would not produce the remedy, but would, in the final analysis, deprive minority groups of job opportunities which might otherwise be made available to them by maintaining contact with employers and making concrete efforts to persuade them to remove such discriminatory hiring specifications.'[54] Some USES state and local offices were reluctant to cooperate with the Federal agencies charged with regulating discrimination by employers using USES files.[55]

In 1946 USES Director Goodwin authored what was heralded as the USES's first major antidiscrimination statement. It included providing equality of opportunity to job applicants and refusing to take vacancy orders with discriminatory components.[56] Ensuring compliance with these instructions was much more difficult, especially in highly segregated states. The abolition of the FEPC and the termination of the WMC removed powerful Federal agencies with jurisdiction in these matters. Goodwin conceded these weaknesses. During the war, he noted that both the FEPC and WMC possessed 'effective whips to combat discriminatory hiring practices'. However, from 1946 'these no longer obtain. Employers are no longer required to hire through public employment offices. The USES post-war program for service to minority groups must, therefore, be based upon persuasion and education.'[57] The interests of minority groups applying for jobs through the USES were supposed to be protected by the Minority Groups Section Director. It was his or her responsibility to coordinate this programme of 'persuasion and education'. Elsewhere, Goodwin characterized the USES's minority groups programmes as principally an 'educational appeal to employers, unions, and workers'. Each group was addressed differently: 'the appeal to employers is that it is sound economic and personnel practice to hire the best qualified worker from the total labor supply. The appeal to ES staff is that of indicating what a professional worker does in a professional public service. The appeal to workers is that of fair play and avoidance of depressing the labor standards of the total labor market by discriminatory practices.'[58] Goodwin maintained that the USES could not go beyond this 'maximum policy and program . . . The USES has no authority to dictate to employers the terms upon which they shall hire, nor any authority to police or enforce non-discrimination clauses of procurement contracts to which the USES is not a party.'[59] Such methods were unsuccessful. The embeddedness of the problem can be inferred from one CIO affiliate's claims of discrimination in the Department of Labor in Washington (though it considered the USES less reprehensible than other parts of the Department).[60] Labor was one of the executive departments consistently failing to return survey data about their number of Black employees to the FEPC (see Chapter 3).

The USES itself chose not to specify a non-discriminatory clause in its regulations. This weakened its role as an agent of equality of opportunity and treatment, a point noted by the FEPC and its successor bodies. The USES's Assistant Director, A. V. Motley, was questioned about this practice by the Fair Employment Board, especially in relation to supplying candidates for positions in government agencies the Civil Service Commission was unable to fill: 'it seems to some of us that when one Federal agency certified to another Federal agency on a discriminatory basis, that Federal agency is a party to the discrimination.' Motley cited equivocation at higher levels to defend his approach: 'we were criticised by some of the members of our Advisory Council that we had not adopted that policy before now, and others thought we had gone far enough.'[61] Earlier in the meeting the Minority Groups Consultant of the Labor Department explained USES policy in response to a question from the Board's Executive Secretary: 'As I understand it, the general policy now with respect to the Employment Service precludes or forbids a notation as to whether the applicant is a Negro or a white man?' The Consultant replied: 'the policy is that we will promote the equitable employment of all persons coming into the Employment Service offices and we shall make an effort by persuasion with employers that hiring specifications be based on qualifications only.' He recognized that this was a 'minimum policy'. In those eleven states with fair employment practice commissions, 'job orders containing discriminatory requirements are not serviced [in eight of them]. There are 27 cities in which there are non-discrimination ordinances.'[62] The weakness of such procedures, lacking Federal enforcement, was conceded by the Assistant Director of the USES himself: 'we realize that during the height of the recruitment for the defense effort that certain agencies were doing their recruiting in states where their selection would be made for them rather than in other states.' The USES was aware of dishonesty in hiring: 'we could see how it was being planned to get around this. For instance, a certain Federal agency would not recruit in New York State which has an FEPC law so that all qualified applicants would be referred to that particular employer without any prior screening.'[63]

When the USES issued a new minority groups policy in 1953, its non-discrimination ambitions remained ones of exhortation, not compulsion.[64] The policy focused particularly upon recruitment for Federal agencies through USES offices. The policy had two elements: first, a ban on 'racial, color, religious or nationality discrimination in the filling of job orders placed by Federal establishments with the public employment service. The second point calls for cooperation by the USES with other Federal agencies in securing compliance with nondiscrimination clauses of government contracts.'[65] Indicative of the USES's reluctance to adopt a tougher stance is a memorandum from Robert Goodwin in 1948. This recommended against the adoption of an explicit regulation opposing discrimination in the USES's Regulations for several reasons,[66] but principally because 'the practical and political effect of incorporating in the USES Regulations, a prohibition against discrimination will do much more *damage to the USES and its program than it can possibly accomplish by way of benefit to minority groups*'.[67] Goodwin recommended a weaker statement, with which the 1953 statement was consistent.

Serving the Federal Government

The Fair Employment Board was understandably alarmed that the USES offices continued to accept discriminatory job orders from Federal agencies. The same offices also supplied applicants when the civil service lists did not have eligibles, as a USES official explained to the Board: 'thru arrangements we have with the Civil Service Commission, when civil service lists are exhausted, Federal agencies can go into the open market and they utilize the Employment Service for recruiting Federal workers.' This source was substantial: 'in 1951, 35 per cent of all accessions to the Federal rolls were recruited thru the Employment Service. That was during a period when the civil service lists were about exhausted.'[68] Practice in the Baltimore office of the USES was a particular concern:

> the Executive Director called attention to the complaint which the Board had received some time ago from the NAACP to the effect that the Employment Service office in Baltimore was accepting discriminatory job orders from Federal agencies. It was his impression that the local offices of the USES had already been advised not to accept discriminatory job orders from Federal establishments. He recalled that at the time of the complaint regarding the Baltimore office there was a discussion of the possibility of having the Board advised when local USES offices receive discriminatory job orders from Federal agencies in order that the Board could refer the matter to the appropriate Fair Employment Officer. The Executive Secretary was of the opinion that the Board should submit to the Bureau of Employment Security a request that the local USES office be advised that all referrals of applicants to Federal agencies must be made on a non-discriminatory basis; and that at the same time the Board should request that it be advised of the details upon receipt of any discriminatory job orders from Federal agencies.[69]

It is remarkable that some local USES offices, financed entirely with Federal funds, should have been accepting discriminatory job orders from Federal agencies as late as 1953. It suggests the limited impact of appointing Fair Employment Officers in each department. Weak or non-existent enforcement procedures and sanctions and a commitment to segregation fuelled this pattern. The acceptance of discriminatory job orders from Federal agencies when the Civil Service Commission lacked suitable candidates was an obvious concern, and it led eventually to a policy statement from the Secretary of Labor in 1953. In April 1954 clear instructions were issued by the USES to local offices that discriminatory requests should not be accepted. However, the new institutions were not supported by new sanctions.

In this context, a decision by the President's Committee on Government Employment Policy, established in 1955, to coordinate with the USES in monitoring discriminatory job orders from Federal agencies might have seemed unpromising. Such an arrangement was reached in early 1957, modelled on the USES's comparable arrangement with the President's Committee on Government Contract Compliance.[70] The USES Director issued a circular to all local offices in 1957, prohibiting the acceptance of discriminatory jobs orders from Federal agencies.[71] In the light of this circular, the President's Committee of Government Employment Policy felt it appropriate to take 'no further action . . . to require a report to the Committee when such [discriminatory] job orders are received from Federal agencies'.[72] Whether this latter decision was justifiable given the scale of discrimination in Federal employment is questionable.

The Failure of Anti-Discrimination Policy

The regulatory procedures failed for several reasons.

1. There was the 'traditional practice of local employment offices comply[ing] with local attitudes toward minority groups'.[73] In less subtle language, the racism of a community was reproduced in and upheld by the local office of the USES. Few Black Americans were employed in them, and the jobs offered to Blacks were the worst.

2. There was the 'relative autonomy of State administrators in applying or refusing to apply USES standards of operation'. In exercising this 'relative autonomy' administrators were concerned mainly with the reactions of employers. Officials in local offices of the USES considered employers their main constituency and feared that 'strict adherence to a nondiscrimination policy would drive employers to recruit elsewhere than through public employment offices, and bring about disruption of the labor market'.[74] This defence was used to justify a myriad of dubious practices. USES officials constantly stressed the importance of retaining employer confidence to receive notifications about job vacancies. Thus, the USES's Federal Advisory

Council maintained in 1953 that 'an employment service can be effective only if it is used by both employers and workers. If employers are not serviced satisfactorily they will cease using the services. Then, if employers cease using the Employment Service, it will not be able to service qualified workers of any type.'[75] The Council also cited weak fair-employment practice legislation at the Federal level to support its strategy: indeed, the fact that Congress failed to enact such reform could be cited. Without such legislative authority, 'progress in eliminating minority discrimination from employment service operations can be best achieved by education and persuasion'.[76] This strategy implied trying to persuade employers to drop their discriminatory hiring specifications without any sanctions if they declined to change—a lukewarm approach at best.

3. The absence of sanctions made 'enforcement of the policy' against 'recalcitrant employers' problematic.[77] Strikingly, Congress took no interest in ensuring that a Service funded partly by Federal tax income was offered equally to all citizens, irrespective of race. It did not authorize sanctions to use against recalcitrant employers.

4. Dilatory Federal oversight of the USES and its return to state control in 1947 each corroded its reputation for impartiality. The Director's initiative failed to reduce discrimination in local offices. The brief period of weakened state control during the Second World War, in response to national labour needs, ended after 1946 as pre-war practices returned. As a consequence, the NAACP resumed its lengthy and frustrating correspondence with the Social Security Board and Department of Labor about discrimination in the USES. As a memorandum recording a meeting between Walter White and the USES reports, old habits revived. The NAACP Secretary reported a case in Nashville, Tennessee: 'there are two employment offices, one labelled for "skilled workers" and the other for "unskilled and domestic workers". All whites are registered at the former and all Negroes at the latter. Even at the Jim Crow office in Nashville, Negroes, whatever their training or experience, are registered as unskilled workers and obtain a second classification on the basis of their skill only when the individual Negro worker knows his rights and insists upon them.' Requests for skilled labour were retained exclusively by the White office: 'even then no requests for skilled workers are ever referred to the Negro office until every available man has been employed from the white office.'[78] Comparable inequities were unearthed by the NAACP in St Louis, Missouri, two years after the war ended. The White applicants' office was located 'in the heart of the business center, and the Negro office is located at 3140 Olive Street, in the Negro section of town'. The two facilities differed: '*central office* is in a large government building in the business center and occupies at least two floors. There is a great deal of room and much seating equipment. The office is well lighted and modern. Some interviewing is done on the second floor and elevator service is provided.' By

contrast, the '*colored office* is located on Olive Street which has a bus line but is not near the main Negro business center. It is in a two-storey modern building, with the offices of the unemployment compensation bureau on the ground floor and the employment service on the second floor. No elevator is available. There seemed to be little accommodation for seating applicants and the offices were not well lighted.'[79]

These administrative flaws and inadequate sanctions were exploited by the USES and its congressional defenders. Despite Federal funding, the local officials of the USES enjoyed considerable independence, confident that Southern Democrats in Congress would protect their interests, and confident of gubernatorial support. The USES state system reflected local politics, and local officials cherished the power they derived from this segregated system. For them, segregated local offices were an important means of maintaining segregated race relations, and ensuring that 'separate but equal' rested upon inequality. The Federal Security Agency reflected these local pressures: 'those in that agency are very much opposed to any plan for abandoning discriminatory orders or wiping out segregation in southern states.'[80]

Not surprisingly, the NAACP opposed the return of the USES to the states after 1946 and advocated a vigilant Federal role. It argued that unless a state promulgated procedures which outlawed discriminatory job orders and ensured that Black American job-seekers were referred to positions for which they were qualified and that separate offices for White job-seekers and Black job-seekers were abolished, no Federal funding should be granted.[81] The NAACP wrote to all the state governors in October 1946 requesting their assurance and support that USES offices would practice non-discrimination once returned from Federal control; it received bland reassurances from most gubernatorial offices.[82] A coalition under the National Citizens' Political Action Committee documented the need to retain Federal control of the USES if discrimination was to end. Amongst other concerns the Committee predicted that 'return of the Employment Service to the states will automatically remove any responsibility on the part of the federal government for a continuation of a policy of non-discrimination and will automatically make it possible for local employment services to revert to prewar practices of discrimination'.[83] Less than a year after the USES had been returned to the states, the NAACP Labor Secretary, Clarence Mitchell, was reporting widespread discrimination to Congress: 'more than a thousand NAACP branches throughout the country have had first hand experience with state employment service discrimination against colored job applicants.'[84] In 1951 Mitchell wrote to the FEB about the Alabama office of the USES, alleging discrimination toward Black job-seekers. In Birmingham, Alabama, the USES office refused, as an explicit policy, 'to permit Colored People to file applications for defense employment, and also refuses to give job information to Colored people who make inquiries'. Many instances of this bias were reported. A Mr Ernest Henderson of Birmingham, Alabama, reported his visit to the USES office in Birmingham to answer an employment announcement for skilled mechanics and helpers to fill defence-plant jobs. Henderson was informed by 'a Mr Smith at the Alabama State Employment Service [that] no announcement had been made, then said if there was a call the jobs would only be open for certain "types of color of people"'. One large corporation advertised in 1951 in the *Birmingham News* that 'it had good jobs for men, apply at the Alabama State Employment Service Office, 1800 First Avenue, North Birmingham'. Men, however, was not a race-neutral designation: 'several Colored men answered this advertisement and were told by Mr E. B. Head of the Alabama State Employment Service Office that the company requested "white applicants only".'[85] The FEB decided, in response to Mitchell's charges, that 'no action should be taken on the matter'.[86]

FEDERAL HOUSING POLICY

In 1932 President Herbert Hoover convened a conference on housing which resulted in the creation of the Federal Home Loan Bank Board and the HOLC to assist home-buyers to acquire mortgages. With these initiatives, the Federal government commenced its fiscal and programmatic engagement in public housing (Table 6.1). The National Housing Act of 1934 created the FHA, which became the principal instrument of Federal housing policy in both public and private units. In 1965 this organization was replaced by the Department of Housing and Urban Development which also took responsibility for the array of programmes enacted by Congress to provide financial assistance through mortgage guarantees for prospective home-owners.

Federal Housing Programmes and Segregation

The Federal government's housing programmes had two dimensions. First, from the 1930s, in a variety of schemes, it provided guarantees to mortgage lending institutions to stimulate house building and home ownership. The agencies responsible for this work were gathered under the FHA. Second, also dating from the 1930s (and expanding significantly in the 1940s and 50s), were Federal programmes financing directly the construction of low-rent public housing dwellings. These buildings were coordinated with slum clearance programmes. Both dimensions rested upon an unquestioned assumption of segregated race relations.

The *Plessy* doctrine dominated the first two decades of Federal housing programmes. This influence was explained by the FHA's Racial Relations

TABLE 6.1. *Federal housing initiatives*

Year	Legislation	Components
1933	Home Owners' Loan Act	HOLC created
1934	Housing Act	Created FHA
1937	Housing (Wagner–Steagall) Act	Created US Housing Authority and provided Federal funds for local housing agencies and slum clearance
1949	Housing Act	Title I: Slum Clearance and Community Redevelopment, authorizes HHFA to give Federal aid in loans and grants to local communities to assist them in clearing their slums and encourage redevelopment by private developers. Title III: authorizes Public Housing Administration to make loans and annual contributions to local communities to assist them in remedying unsafe and insanitary housing conditions and in providing dwellings for low-income families
1956	Voluntary Home Mortgage Credit Program	Stimulated private investors in FHA-insured and VA-guaranteed home loans

Adviser, Joseph Ray, in 1954: 'from its inception, the public housing program accepted the "separate-but-equal" doctrine and, through its racial equity policy, undertook to insist upon uniform enforcement of the "equal" while allowing local communities to decide upon the "separate"'.[87] The *Plessy* doctrine had even persisted after the 1948 Court outlawing of racial covenants: 'as the result of discussions held among Agency officials and with public interest group leadership in 1948, it was clearly evident that both groups understood that FHA sanction of locally enforced segregation by race in Federally subsidized public housing projects had no supportable legal authority.' This influence of *Plessy* was odd since use of the 'separate but equal' precept was of dubious authenticity in housing policy in Ray's view: 'it was tacitly understood that FHA application of the *Plessy* v. *Ferguson* theory of "separate but equal" in the Federally subsidized public housing program rested upon no sound legal theory or pertinent application to real property but rather reflected "political expediency".'[88] This Federal government agency directly participated, therefore, in the maintenance and dissemination of segregated race relations in American society,[89] uncritically sharing the assumption of 'separate but equal' arrangements.

The FHA's mirroring of racist attitudes in society was accomplished principally through the instructions included in its *Underwriting Manual* until 1947. It explicitly identified Black Americans as unreliable and undesirable buyers, a clause removed only in 1948.[90] It also included a model racial covenant.

The *Underwriting Manual* framework distinguished four types of residential area and graded their relative desirability. It was this framework which perhaps most forcefully committed Federal programmes to fostering segregation:

> the First Grade or A areas are, in nearly all instances, new well-planned sections, not yet fully developed, and almost synonymous with the area where good mortgage lenders with available funds are willing to make their maximum loans to be amortized over a 10–15 year period. They are homogeneous and in demand as residential locations in 'good times' or 'bad'; hence on the up-grade. The Second Grade or B areas, as a rule, are completely developed. Within recent years they have reached their peak, but should continue to be stable and remain desirable places in which to live for a number of years. The Third Grade or C areas are often characterized by age, obsolescence, and change of style; expiring restrictions or lack of them; infiltration of a lower grade population; the presence of influences which increase sales resistance such as inadequate transportation, insufficient utilities, heavy special assessments, poor maintenance of homes, etc. 'Jerry' built areas are included, as well as neighborhoods lacking homogeneity and those within such a low price or rent range as to attract an undesirable element. Generally, these areas have reached the transition period, having seen their best days. The Fourth Grade or D areas represent those neighborhoods in which the things that are now taking place in the C neighborhoods have already happened. They are characterized by detrimental influences in a pronounced degree, such as undesirable population or an infiltration of it; often, a low percentage of home ownership; poor maintenance of homes; possible vandalism; unstable income which often makes collection difficult etc. These areas are broader than the so-called slum district.[91]

There was no great mystery about what kind of racial elements contributed to a problematic 'fourth Grade or D' rating. Writing of the Kansas City (Kan.) area the appraisers opined: 'a large negro population is scattered over all parts of the city which is one of the reasons for the preponderance of D or fourth class grade security areas. This is a heritage of the Civil War days when Kansas was admitted as a free state and negroes were given more latitude of freedom than in adjoining Kansas City, Missouri.'[92] In all city surveys, the HOLC appraisal department commented on the presence or absence (and number) of Black residents as it did for other ethnic groups and immigrants. The HOLC appraisers were struck by the contrast between German-born immigrants and Black migrants in the Missourian city of St Louis, unsubtly judging the former an asset—the 'attraction to the area of high-type foreign immigrants'—and the latter a liability—'location of the area with respect to southern negro populations resulting in a constant migration of persons of that race to St Louis'.[93]

It was unfortunate that Federal housing programmes did not challenge segregation and racism because these were already endemic in the private sector. Lending institutions were distinctly unenthusiastic about lending money to Black families wishing to buy a house, and the 'majority made an arbitrary decision not to lend on Negro properties as they were considered undesirable'.[94] This bias was reinforced by the FHA's *Underwriting Manual*. The findings of the President's Advisory Committee on Housing Policies and Programs, which reported in 1953, suggest how significant these biases were. It concluded that 'too often, the opportunities of minority group families to obtain adequate housing are extremely limited or non-existent'.[95] The lack of sufficient financial support for Black Americans wishing to purchase housing was one important way in which these citizens were affected by the Federal government.[96]

The Voluntary Home Mortgage Credit Program was created to assist Black (and other) Americans receive mortgages, by channelling private investment funds into FHA-insured home loans for eligible families. The administration of these programmes was scathingly criticized by Black interest groups. One group wrote to the Director of the Federal Public Housing Administration in 1956 about a matter of 'grave concern': the 'lack of action by your agency in safeguarding the rights of citizens of minority groups in regard to existing and planned public and publicly subsidized housing'.[97] Similar views were expressed to President Eisenhower by the National Committee Against Discrimination in Housing, a coalition of interest groups: 'Federal housing programs continue to reinforce and spread segregation. In federal public housing close to 85 per cent of the projects are segregated. Urban renewal developments receive federal approval and funds, despite plans for new segregated housing'. It urged Eisenhower 'to issue a policy statement that federal authority, money, and aid will not be used for segregated housing facilities'.[98] One Congressman from California wrote to the HHFA complaining that 'in Long Beach . . . any attempt by a member of a minority group to purchase one of the F.H.A. insured homes meets with either exorbitant demands or with downright rebuffs. They are forced to buy old homes in undesirable locations, paying higher prices for them and then forced to spend high sums of money to have the homes improved.'[99] He noted that the 'problem exists all over the country'. In October 1954, the NUL, long an advocate of reform in Federal mortgage schemes,[100] sent a telegram to President Eisenhower claiming that 'in guaranteeing mortgage loans for housing which is not open to Negro occupancy, the Federal Housing Administration is violating the broad principle of non discrimination which the President of the United States has adopted and so successfully implemented in the Armed Forces and in many agencies of the Federal government . . . The Federal government has the . . . right and power and duty to require non discrimination in FHA mortgage insurance.'[101] The same view was communicated to the President by the American Jewish Congress: 'enactment of the new Housing Act of 1954 provides appropriate opportunity for careful reconsideration of the effect of our Federal housing laws on discriminatory practices.'[102] A critical study in 1955 identified similar problems and issues:

> of 2,761,172 units which received FHA insurance during the years 1935–1950 an estimated 50,000 units were for Negro occupancy. This amounts to 2 per cent of the FHA total. Moreover, half of the 50,000 is accounted for by 25,000 units built with racially designated priorities during World War II under the defense housing program which provided special advantages to builders during a period of controls and shortages. Thus, during 1935–1950, while the FHA insured 30 per cent of all new construction, the nonwhite 10 per cent received only 1 per cent of the benefits of normal FHA operations. The South has a greater than proportionate share of this small amount of housing. All of the Southern units were in strictly segregated Negro projects.[103]

The authors of this study argued that despite paying lip-service to minority housing, FHA programmes provided shockingly little mortgage insurance to Black American house-purchasers: 'throughout the country are housing developments, large and small, for sale or rent, which receive the highly important assistance of FHA and VA programs yet exclude anyone whose skin happens not to be white.'[104]

Prior to the 1930s, the restriction of Black home-owners' options was maintained by the lease contract and racially limiting covenants, instruments popular throughout the United States. Under the former, a lease-purchase plan was agreed on a piece of property whereby the buyer made small monthly payments, paying more in aggregate for the property than with a normal downpayment lump-sum agreement. Covenants were legally sanctioned clauses in property deeds, prohibiting certain categories of people owning or living in the property concerned.[105] They were outlawed by the Supreme Court in 1948; however, covenants existing prior to the ruling affected Black American buyers' choices—a crippling legacy especially since the FHA demonstrated no inclination to challenge them. It took the FHA two years after the Court's ruling to ensure that Federal funds would no longer be available for properties with racially restricting covenants.

The Supreme Court judgements should have resulted in the Federal government sharply dissociating its programmes from these segregationist efforts. But they were not so used. In a letter to the Commissioner of the Public Housing Administration, the NAACP's Counsel Thurgood Marshall stressed the legal context: 'the decisions in the case of Buchanan v Warley [in 1948] and the restrictive covenant cases make it clear that no state or federal agency can require segregation in housing. The Buchanan case made it clear that municipal ordinances requiring segregation in housing were invalid. The covenant cases made it clear that courts could not enforce voluntary agreements requiring segregated housing.' These decisions meant that the 'Public Housing Administration has no authority whatsoever to grant to local housing authorities the power to segregate in housing projects'.[106]

Although the FHA's role in maintaining the segregation justified in *Plessy* lacked unequivocal legal authority, it had a powerful effect in structuring government–society relations. Since the Supreme Court never explicitly applied the 'separate but equal' doctrine to public housing,[107] FHA policy suggests the attitude of Federal officials toward segregated race relations, and how they acted even in the absence of explicit guidelines.

Many organizations petitioned the FHA to assume a more forceful role in integrating housing. Meeting in 1950, the NAACP urged the FHA, and in particular its Division of Slum Clearance and Urban Redevelopment, to withhold funds from those local communities which organized housing on a segregated basis or discriminated.[108] In 1950 the NAACP wrote to the Director of this Division about the redevelopment programme in Baltimore, maintaining that the proposed restructuring would result in fewer houses for Black buyers because of the unwillingness of the Federal housing authorities to overrule unwritten restrictive covenants: 'the President and the Department of Justice say that restrictions based on race are contrary to the policy of the United States. In this they are supported by the US Supreme Court.' However, the agency concerned, the HHFA, 'although it is fully aware of the fact that its assistance will promote racial restrictions in housing, seems bent on doing the exact opposite of what the President, the Supreme Court, and the Department of Justice say is the policy of our Government'.[109]

As in respect of the USES, so in housing, Congress was a defender of Jim Crow practices, and an unwilling critic of segregation. Federal authority was not deployed with sufficient force in either area to tackle discrimination. In the same year as the *Brown* ruling, Congress declined to include in the Housing Act a requirement that private redevelopers be compelled to administer their private property free of racial discrimination.[110] Given its political composition in 1954, Congress was unlikely to extend Federal authority so substantially. Of nine million new private dwelling units constructed between 1935 and 1950 in the United States, less than 1 per cent were open to purchase by non-white Americans.[111] This statistic illustrates how the US Federal government acted to insulate the segregated order: 'by granting mortgage insurance to private builders who follow a known discriminatory policy [and] in effect are zoning racially', the FHA and VA were deploying 'government aid to operate racially segregated housing, [and lent] government process to enforce unwritten, but nevertheless understood, race restrictive covenants'. The FHA thereby empowered a 'private person to do what the government itself cannot do—use criteria of race . . . Just as Presidential action was required in the matter of discrimination under government contracts, civil service, and the armed services, so action by the President is necessary in the case of government housing programs.'[112]

Without a sustained attack upon residential segregation it was by definition impossible to produce sufficient numbers of dwelling units to absorb all those displaced by urban renewal programmes in the 1950s. This was a problem recognized by George Nesbitt, Racial Relations Adviser in the HHFA, and one he made several times to his superiors. Writing in 1953, Nesbitt observed that 'in the absence of a sufficiently expanding new housing production, the enforcement program's nonwhite displacees will do what they must, find rehousing in other areas already minority-occupied. The patent risk is an increment in existent overcrowding and a contribution to quickened slum growth.'[113] This patent risk fully materialized.

Federal Housing Programmes and Desegregation: 'Never to Dictate or Coerce'

Between the 1940s and the late 1960s Federal housing authorities were under increasing fire for the racial consequences of their programmes. In the 1950s the Administrator of the FHA was questioned by several senators critical of its policy. In a letter in May 1956 to Senator Bush, he attempted to exculpate the FHA's record, beginning with a weary complaint about the familiarity of the charges. The Administrator, Albert Cole, blandly identified several areas of the FHA's work to justify his defence. First, 'in 1954 I conducted a conference on housing for minority groups'.[114] Second, the FHA had tried to encourage builders and investors to fund housing for minorities: 'through January 1956, the Voluntary Home Mortgage Credit Program had placed a total of 12,000 loans. Of these loans, nearly 1,800 were for housing specifically available to members of minority groups.'[115] Third, 'in all public housing first preference for occupancy goes to families displaced from slum housing. Since racial minorities constitute a high proportion of slum dwellers, these circumstances orient the low-rent program significantly to serve their needs.'[116] The Urban Renewal Administration was supposed to monitor displaced families and ensure they were housed in the new buildings.[117] Cole dismissed the National Committee Against Discrimination's proposal that a precise agreement be inserted in grants of urban renewal aid to local recipients, committing the latter to eliminating racial segregation and to integration: 'to the extent that it were possible to put teeth into such a requirement I am convinced that the result, in many parts of the country, would be a sharp cutback in the rate of housing production, and of our capacity to meet the housing needs of all the people.' He claimed that local authorities would prefer to forfeit the funds than adopt this criterion.[118] This choice plainly posed an important problem for Federal administrators mindful to modify residential segregation, though there seem to have been strikingly few with this propensity.

The FHA was unwilling to use its substantial housing grants to liberalize the residential racial segregation common to most American cities. Cole was writing only two years after the *Brown* case, but evidently had little interest in using the 'power of the purse' to foster racial integration. Cole articulated his view of the limited capacity of Federal authority thus: 'the role of the Federal Government in the housing program is to assist, to stimulate, to lead, and sometimes to prod, but never to dictate or coerce, and never to stifle the proper exercise of private and local responsibility.' He was not unhappy with this circumscribed strategy: 'this is as it should be, not only because housing needs and problems are peculiarly local but also because undue Federal intervention is incompatible with our ideas of political and economic freedom.'[119] In fact the Federal grants constituted an ideal fiscal instrument for 'prodding' local agents. But writing to another senator in the same year, Cole again offered a minimalist and cautious conception of the FHA's role: 'neither the President nor the Housing and Home Finance Agency has any specific authority to compel a private lender to extend a home loan to any particular person.'[120] But it did have the power to ensure that the terms of loans were equitable. In an approach not dissimilar to the FEB, the FHA was reluctant to take measures toward non-discrimination apart from educational ones.

Officials at the FHA truculently defended their commitment to racially equitable housing and mortgage policy. In correspondence with another senator (from West Virginia), the Commissioner of the FHA informed him that a development in Charleston must adhere to a racially equitable distribution of public housing.[121] Writing to the NAACP in 1954, Administrator Cole rejected the charge that some builders and owners of housing insured by FHA refused to sell or rent property to Black citizens: 'present policy renders FHA insurance of mortgages "unavailable for assistance in the financing of a property for which any instrument or agreement of record is executed after February 15, 1950, whereby the occupancy or sale thereof is restricted on the basis of race, color or creed." This policy, however, does not attempt to control any owner in determining what tenants he shall have or to whom he shall sell his property.' Cole then distanced the Federal government from substantial action: 'I am sure you know that neither the President nor any Federal agency has any specific authority to force a private lender, builder, or individual to lend, rent, or sell to any particular person.' He then gave a statement of aspiration: 'But I can assure you that it is the desire of the President and the policy of this Agency . . . within the limits of our authority, to encourage and assist both private and public resources to expand and improve the local housing supplies available to all segments of housing needs to the end of equalizing the opportunity for decent housing among all our citizens.'[122] Without effective Federal action, these aspirations would remain simply aspirations.

Addressing the President's CGCC, Cole did concede that 'minority group families have been disadvantaged in obtaining FHA or other good homes'.[123] This admission differed from his concession to Senators. To make amends, he cited the FHA's cooperation with the National Association of Home Builders and the Mortgage Bankers' Association to secure loans and other measures increasing local officials' discretion. Such cooperation was complicated, however, by the same Association's members' policy of charging higher interest rates for mortgages to Black home-buyers. A year after writing to Senator Bush, Cole was criticized by the Director of Minorities of the Republican National Committee. He provided a twelve-page letter defending the HHFA's policies.[124] The letter included little of substance to support Cole's defence of the FHA's programmes for non-White buyers. In November 1958 the HHFA Administrator, Albert Cole, was reported as stating at a press conference that the HHFA had no role in enforcing racial desegregation in housing. His remarks provoked wide criticism and concern from interest groups. It provoked letters to President Eisenhower from the State Park Citizens' Committee for Housing and Planning, Illinois; the National Council of the Churches of Christ; and Algernon Black, representing the National Committee Against Discrimination in Housing. A plainly irritated White House aide, Rocco Siciliana, informed Cole that 'as you can suspect, we have been getting a lot of questions and criticism on your alleged statements, and I expect that the President may be asked questions in his next press conference. Accordingly, I think it is not only appropriate but needed that you write directly to Mr Black.'[125] Cole's letter to the interest groups restated yet again his glowing version of the Federal government's housing programme.[126]

Within the HHFA itself, the Racial Relations Adviser worried that Federal policies had perpetuated racial segregation patterns, an opinion somewhat at variance with Cole's complacency. Local housing authorities exploited 'tenant selection requirements' (in the Housing Act of 1949) to 'apply criteria on the basis of race, permitting eligible Negro tenants to exercise these legislative rights only in designated "Negro" projects. While FHA has earnestly sought, through administration, to countenance the "separate" and insist on the "equal," it may be charged that FHA has conditioned by race a requirement of the organic legislation itself.'[127] Tenant-selection criteria were, of course, not designed to be used in this discriminatory way.

The Urban Renewal Administration appreciated the implications for both residential segregation and the position of minorities arising from its responsibility to clear slums and to rehouse their occupants. In a memorandum in 1950 for the FHA's field representatives, George Nesbitt identified the constraints influencing such measures, principally the attitudes of the local community and authorities: 'while recognizing that clearance and redevelopment of slum areas is subject to "local determinations and aspirations" it [the Housing Act of 1949] also recognizes that in the locality the operating feasibility as well as the legal validity of what is attempted may turn upon how the question of "what to do with the minorities" is handled.' This issue was crucial because, Nesbitt argued, the 'success of the whole national program, in turn, may hinge upon the same crucial question'.[128] The memorandum instructed field representatives (of the Slum Clearance and Urban Renewal programme) to emphasize 'racial considerations' implicit or explicit to policies in their locality. Its author stressed the role of the FHA as a representative of the Federal government acting on behalf of all citizens, an emphasis notably missing from subsequent policy and half-heartedly supported by Administrator Cole: 'if the local officials obtain indications as to Federal racial policy only by questions and cross-questions, the inevitable impression will be that the Federal concern is not real but a "passing display of concern", apologetic, defensive or even hypocritical.'[129] Unfortunately, Nesbitt's fears were frequently realized. Federal policy solidified segregated race relations.

In 1951 one NAACP leader accused the FHA of systematically funding discriminatory housing schemes. In a searing denunciation, he stated: 'what the courts have forbidden state legislatures and city councils to do and what the Ku Klux Klan has not been able to accomplish by intimidation and violence, the present Federal Housing Policy is accomplishing through a monumental program of segregation in all aspects of Housing which receive Government aid.'[130] Clarence Mitchell, the speaker, accused the officials of defining the federal role modestly and timidly, instead of identifying their responsibilities as fostering housing integration through the judicious distribution of aid: 'the Housing Agencies, on the advice of their lawyers and after counseling with White House advisers, have taken the position that the Federal Government cannot require those who build housing with Federal assistance to refrain from segregating or excluding tenants or buyers solely because of race.' As a consequence, segregated race relations were privileged: 'the Housing Program of the Federal Government as currently administered in the entire South, all of the border states, and in a few northern communities, is one of the greatest single factors in underwriting segregation with tax money.'[131] Mitchell called for both presidential and congressional action to attach non-segregation requirements to housing legislation. A memorandum reflecting on his speech prepared for the FHA Administrator supported Mitchell's analysis. Its author, Frank Horne, noted that 'this same [point] has been raised before in reference to FHA operations'; and he continued: 'during the last two years, the tendency toward enforced racial segregation under Federal programs has also increased.'[132]

In sum, Federal housing policy reinforced, and partially fostered, residential segregation. While this outcome reflected in part congressional pressures and the intractability of local communities, it also arose from the decisions of Federal government administrators, reluctant to alienate private developers by deploying federal aid as a mechanism of reform. The presence of racial relations advisers in the FHA offered a consistent reminder of these consequences. The advisers' effects on the meticulous racial coding of FHA surveyers were regrettably slight.

CONCLUSION: THE PERSISTENCE OF SEGREGATION AFTER *BROWN*

Segregated race relations persisted in the USES. A report in 1971, the NUL's 'Falling Down on the Job', depicted profligate neglect and inadequacy. The problems were clearly described in an NAACP study two decades earlier: 'in Southern and border states many employment services are presently operated on a segregated basis, i.e., separate offices are maintained for white and Negro job-seekers and employers are permitted to specify in their job orders whether they wish to have white or Negro employees.' Elsewhere, integrated offices did not prevent discriminatory job orders being accepted: 'in other states where Negro and white applicants are served by the same offices, discriminatory job orders are accepted and filled. In general, these segregated offices notify each other of orders in which an employer indicates willingness to take either white or colored employees.' Whites were always referred to employers first: 'in the St. Louis employment service, at least, the Negro office makes a practice of checking with the white office to see whether a sufficient number of white workers have been sent out to fill a job on which whites or Negroes will be accepted before sending any Negro workers. A comparable check is not made by the white office before referring white job applicants.' In segregated offices, facilities for White job-seekers remained superior to those provided for Black Americans: 'in general, the white offices are larger and more centrally located and it may be expected that employers more readily place their orders at the white office.'[133] Discrimination featured in policy discussion at the end of the Eisenhower administration. In June 1959 Eisenhower's Secretary of Labor was advised to announce publicly 'a non-segregation policy for all public employment facilities and begin action to achieve this objective with all deliberate speed'.[134] The problem of the USES was brought by the Secretary of Labor to the Cabinet at the end of 1959. He reported that in the 'solid South there are still four or five states where USES has not been able to eliminate the segregation of its offices. Persuasion may be our only resource since otherwise it might mean a complete abandonment of the USES in the areas involved.'[135]

Remarkably little had changed by the mid–1960s. A task force established by Congress in 1965 observed that 'it is not sufficient . . . merely to reaffirm existing laws and policies as they relate to this agency. Instead, Employment Service personnel at every level must make a positive effort to understand

and cope with the special problems that confront members of racial minorities in the labor market.'[136] The BES sent a circular to all state employment agencies in 1964 stressing the importance of placing Black Americans and of tackling prejudice. In particular, the practice of failing to register Black Americans for 'nontraditional jobs' persisted because: '(1) they may have been classified only for "traditional" jobs, even though qualified for other jobs; or (2) they may not have registered at the local office because they felt the nontraditional jobs were not open to them.'[137] President Kennedy instructed his Secretary of Labor, Willard Wirtz, to eliminate racially discriminatory practices in state employment service offices. In an interim report to Lyndon Johnson at the beginning of 1964, Wirtz reported 'good progress' toward this end but identified three cases in which an impasse had been reached: Alabama, Louisiana, and North Carolina. These states had defeated the Eisenhower administration also. Of Alabama, Wirtz reported that 'there clearly is racial discrimination in the hiring and promotional practices of the Alabama employment service'. A 'long series of conferences' with state officials made it 'clear that the State offices are [unchanged] and officials are not going to change their position in response to the kind of Federal efforts exerted so far'.[138] Why the Administration did not consider terminating the state's Federal funding is unexplained.

The USES's record in serving Black Americans remained under fire even in the 1970s. According to the study by the National Urban Coalition, instead of striving to eradicate prejudice amongst employers, the USES sedulously mirrored it: 'the chief weakness of the ES with regard to minorities is that it mirrors the attitudes of employers in the community.' Instead of constituting an institution promoting equality of opportunity in the labour market and eradicating prejudice, the USES 'is frequently a passive accessory to discriminatory employment practices; it is widely viewed in that light by the minority community'.[139] Many state agencies continued to use written testing to determine job classification. This practice was contrary to a Department of Labor directive issued to end the discrimination associated with such testing.

The state offices of the USES were able to maintain their deplorable racial practices for several reasons. Locally, they received strong political support empowering the USES to act in almost quasi-autonomous fashion. Nationally, the decision to give the USES 100 per cent Federal funding from the unemployment trust fund, a tax levied on employers, exempted the USES from the annual Federal budget appropriation process and obligatory hearings. These exemptions seriously eroded congressional oversight of the USES, as was intended by its supporters. Consequently, USES officials were able further to disregard the needs of their constituents, including Black Americans. In Congress, the USES's strength rested on solid Southern Democratic support. In particular, Congressman John Fogarty, Chairman of the House HEW-Labor Appropriations Subcommittee, and the legendary House Ways and Means chairman, Wilbur Mills, were its indefatigable defenders. Fogarty's death in 1967 permitted tighter congressional oversight of the USES but as the evidence above suggests any amelioration in the facilities offered job-seekers had by the early 1970s failed, largely, to benefit Black Americans. An agency established during the New Deal era of Federal government activism to help Americans find jobs, and to facilitate employment on the public works programmes of that decade, reproduced the ethos and codes of segregation. These customs and practices were particularly prominent in local and state offices, whose officials and overseers recognized an opportunity further to entrench the segregation to which Black Americans were subject from the 1890s. Thus USES offices were organized on segregated lines, White officials served over Blacks in the sections for Black job-seekers, and Black offices were located in shabby facilities often removed from the centres of economic activity or housing. If these disadvantages were not sufficient to demonstrate the separate and unequal nature of segregation, then the USES offices' practice of not classifying Black American job-seekers for any but a limited range of jobs was. USES officials were for too long unwilling to refer Black workers to White employers, including government agencies filling vacancies. It was unfortunate that segregation was so thoroughly accepted by the USES and its local affiliates, since it proved a tenacious embrace. It significantly damaged the capacity of this publicly funded arm of the Federal government to improve the employment prospects of Black Americans or to challenge instead of maintain a segregated labour-market.

At the end of 1959 the Commission on Civil Rights proposed that the President issue an executive order about housing in which the Federal government's commitment to equity and alleviating the needs of Black Americans was stressed.[140] The National Committee Against Discrimination in Housing telegrammed the President urging him to implement this recommendation.[141] Senator Jacob Javits, a longtime advocate of desegregation, wrote to the President and the HHFA in support of the idea. To Eisenhower, Javits argued: 'there is substantial evidence that discrimination against minority groups continues in Federally-aided housing activities. [T]he housing program's . . . operation has strongly influenced the racial pattern of residence mainly in the direction of retarding racial desegregation.' Residential segregation denuded the effect of the Supreme Court's school desegregation decision (which led later to the bussing decisions). Furthermore, it was Black Americans who were most affected by urban renewal: 'in view of the fact that most families displaced by urban renewal projects are members of minority groups, relocation under the Urban Renewal Program has been particularly severe in imposing hardships on such groups, particularly in the light of the fact that new construction is often segregated in effect.'[142] The proposal was implacably opposed by the FHA Administrator, Norman Mason. Mason claimed the 'issuance of an executive order in housing might seriously interrupt and restrict the full cooperation of a large sector of private enterprise in our effort to provide this important opportunity for all the citizens'.[143] This 'full cooperation' had produced remarkably few results in housing integration, however. Writing to Senator Javits, Mason maintained that 'the purposes for which the Executive Order was proposed are already being achieved in an enduring, practical way, and for this reason the Administration has felt that no additional constructive results would be achieved by the issuance of such an order at this time'.[144] Mason claimed that progress had been made in building housing for minorities, but he did not address the issue of *de facto* residential segregation identified by Javits and unmistakably evident to any observer of American cities. Such residential segregation persists.

Federal housing programmes were designed and implemented in a way which favoured White home-buyers and ensured that Black Americans continued to be restricted in their choice of area in which to live. The pre-1948 *Underwriting Manual* of the FHA illustrates these propensities. Federal housing programmes were segregated at their cores, in two senses. First, they were unable to overcome the prejudice and segregation embraced by numerous local communities. It was unthinkable for certain local communities to condone integrated housing (or to permit the intermingling of Black job-seekers with Whites in USES offices). FHA policy was never considered an instrument to promote desegregation. Second, in Washington, administrators addressed the discriminatory consequences of programmes operated on the 'separate but equal' precept reluctantly and indolently. As the Director of the FHA wrote in 1956 to a senator: 'I am sure I do not need to remind you that the problems of racial discrimination are also peculiarly local. In addition, they are complex and deeply rooted in local traditions, institutions and emotions.'[145] Segregated race relations undoubtedly reflected deeply rooted local traditions but it was not the Federal government's role uncritically to accommodate such attitudes.

PART IV

The Legacies of Segregated Race Relations

7

Conclusion

WHAT I hope the preceding chapters have demonstrated is how the Federal government, in a range of areas, colluded in the maintenance of segregated race relations in the half-century before the Civil Rights Act of 1964. Federal authority was used either to impose or to accommodate segregated race relations in government departments and public policies. In Chapter 2, the transformation of the US Civil Service Commission from an agent of meritocratic appointment at its establishment in 1883, to a discriminating barrier from 1914, was explained and the consequences for Black Americans investigated. As the evidence in Chapter 3 revealed, Black Americans working in the Federal government between 1914 and the 1960s rarely achieved positions in the professional or senior administrative classes, and were disproportionately confined to clerical, janitorial, or custodial positions. The restriction of Black employees to such grades was aided immensely by the decision in 1914 to require applicants for government positions to attach photographs to their application forms. This practice quickly undermined the impartiality of the 'rule of three' appointment criterion proudly extolled by the US Civil Service Commission. The abolition of the photograph requirement in 1940 coincided with the expansion of the Federal government necessitated by wartime. After 1945 the Civil Service Commission's enforcement of the 'rule of three' system continued to evoke protest from Black American interest groups as Black applicants continued to encounter discrimination in the 1950s. One consequence of these trends was to stunt and trammel the potential for equality of treatment by race in the Federal government. If Black American citizens could not look to the national government to act impartially on their behalf, but rather witnessed it reproducing narrow racist interests from society, then their prospects were indeed circumspect.

The pervasiveness of the Federal government's support of segregated race relations was examined in Chapters 4, 5, and 6. These chapters demonstrated the extent to which segregation was not merely a system of separation but in reality a mechanism for the domination of Black Americans by Whites. The 'separate but equal' framework did not preclude the daily interaction of Black Americans and Whites—whether in a government department, branch of the Armed Forces, prison, or job centre—but segregation did dictate the terms on which these interactions occurred. Injustices and discriminatory behaviour had to be protested by Black Americans. It was Whites who could object to working with Blacks. Thus, segregated race relations were inherently unequal, and sat with a national politics which between the 1890s and 1960s denied equality to Black Americans: in the South this denial was often sufficiently explicit to include disenfranchisement; in the North the right to vote did not remove discrimination and prejudice in a range of areas such as employment and housing. Chapters 4 and 5 explicated the discriminations and inequalities coexisting with segregated race relations in the Armed Forces and Federal penitentiaries, illustrating how Federal authority of segregation extended into all areas of the government. Chapter 6 examined the way in which Federal support of segregated race relations permeated into a segregated society. I argued that the USES did little to challenge or supplant discrimination in the labour-market. Its employment offices were segregated and many administrators were reluctant (if not unwilling) to register Black job-seekers for any positions other than menial or domestic ones. Remarkably, this reluctance—and the related one of accepting 'Whites only' vacancy notices—extended to the USES's supply of candidates for Federal government department posts. In Federal housing programmes, the government's own criteria for evaluating the value of different properties and neighbourhoods incorporated explicit racial assumptions mirroring those effected in society through racial covenants and prejudice. Government policy reinforced, and on occasion engendered, segregated residential housing.

Black Americans' employment experience of the Federal government has altered dramatically since the middle of the 1960s and passage of the Civil Rights Act (see Table A5.1).[1] The Civil Rights Act of 1964 was the most important legislation in the field since Reconstruction and empowered the US Department of Justice extensively to investigate and prosecute discrimination and other abuses of citizens' rights.[2] Section 717 of the Act referred to 'nondiscrimination in federal government employment'. It declared that 'all personnel actions affecting employees' throughout the Federal government and military should be 'free from any discrimination based on race, color, religion, sex or national origin'. The US Civil Service Commission was charged with monitoring and enforcing this directive, by investigating complaints and issuing judgements. The 1964 Act created the EEOC to regulate discrimination in employment but gave it modest enforcement powers. Consequently, to pursue recalcitrant employers, Congress was compelled to strengthen the powers of the EEOC in the Equal Employment Opportunities Enforcement Act in 1972. The EEOC was empowered to sue employers in the Federal district courts who failed to respond to orders. In 1978, this responsibility was transferred from the EEOC. Each department and agency was directed to formulate and implement an 'equal employment opportunity plan' which included affirmative employment action for Federal employees. This arrangement was not uncriticized and in October 1992 the EEOC issued new regulations to improve the system under which Federal employees (including applicants for positions) charging discrimination could seek redress.[3]

The tables in Appendix 3 include some data documenting the improvement in the employment position of Black Americans in the Federal government. Table A3.8 shows significant increases between 1961 and 1965 in the number of Black Americans working in general schedule categories, a trend confirmed in table A3.9: this reports that by the end of the 1980s Black American employees constituted over 16 per cent of total government employees. The trend in general schedule positions is particularly important since this category covers many professional positions. Table A3.10 reports that between 1963 and 1974 the percentage of Black American employees in these grades rose from 9.2 to 12.7 per cent. However, Table A3.13, which records Black American employment in the general schedule by grade level, shows that while Blacks had made significant advances in the middle and lower grades, their presence in the senior grades by 1980 was less impressive. This issue concerned a congressional committee in 1978 which, in its report, noted that 'government wide statistics show a concentration of minorities in the lower salary grade ranges (GS 1–4 and WG 1–4) in 1975 with only a very slight improvement in 1977. Individual Agencies also show this same disproportionate concentration in the lower salary grade levels.'[4] This trend is supported by Tables A3.14 and A3.15. But in aggregate terms, the number of Black American employees in the Federal government had undoubtedly increased significantly by the 1980s compared with the half-century preceding the Civil Rights Act. Black American employees had also made substantial inroads into the middle ranks of the civil service grades, though less so at the senior levels. Discrimination and equality of opportunity are pursued vigorously.

Of the multiple legacies of the Federal government's collusion in maintaining segregated race relations for contemporary American politics three are notable.

First, major areas of American public policy have a fundamental racial dimension which springs directly from the way in which Federal government programmes were formulated. Residential housing is massively segregated in the United States and this has profound consequences for labour-market participation and equality.[5] In Federal welfare and training programmes, the continuing effect of discrimination and segregation derived from their initial administration is apparent.[6] The marginalization of Black Americans from the Social Security Act of 1935, and the stigmatization associated with welfare benefits—initially through the ADC and later AFDC programmes—is a fundamental aspect of modern citizenship in the United States.[7] The new emphasis upon training and apprenticeship programmes by the Clinton administration (an enthusiasm shared with many other advanced industrial democracies) is constrained and diluted by the historically discriminatory stance of Federal agencies and labour unions toward Black Americans.[8] However, as Sniderman and Piazza rightly stress, the place of and attitudes about race in such a range of policies differs: 'a distinguishing mark of the contemporary politics of race is the number of fundamentally different arguments being conducted over race at the same time. The clash over affirmative action is not the same as the conflict over more conventional forms of government assistance, and differences of opinion over an issue like fair housing have their own dynamic.'[9] Sniderman and Piazza, in the same major study, stress how political attitudes about policy areas—or what they term agendas—structure preferences: 'the contemporary politics of race has as much to do with politics as with race.'[10] This view needs also to be complemented by an appreciation of how racial biases were built into many important Federal programmes. Federal government programmes which assumed or privileged segregated race relations have, by institutionalizing inequality and second-class citizenship, contributed to the terms of these contemporary debates. Instead of squashing such distinctions by race the Federal government gave a basis for their persistence. The NAACP, and other groups working in behalf of Black Americans, repeatedly and patiently explained to the Federal administrators, with whom they tirelessly corresponded, that citing Black Americans' acceptance of segregation was an inappropriate defence of this practice: it was not the role of the Federal government to foster and sustain such distinctions between its citizens, since this would emulate practices in society. Thus, the NAACP Special Counsel, Thurgood Marshall, protested to the US Bureau of Prisons in 1942 about the latter's uncritical acceptance of the notion of 'self-segregation' amongst Black inmates:

> you mentioned in your letter that it is impossible to allow the prisoners to choose with whom they may associate. It is interesting to note that several other officials of state institutions have made the statement that they separate the races 'because Negroes like to be by themselves.' Both of these reasons, to my mind, are without bearing on the particular protest. It is not a question of whether or not a Negro wants to be associated with a particular white individual. The only problem is whether or not the Federal Government is justified in segregating Negro Americans as a group and as a race.[11]

Segregation meant inequality and this is the legacy which Federal programmes confront.

Second, to what extent affirmative action programmes should be instituted to compensate for the pernicious and inegalitarian effects of a half-century of segregated race relations is a question of profound importance.[12] The problems now faced were presciently anticipated in the 1960s by the Executive Secretary of the President's Committee on Government Employment

Policy, as he entered the minefield of discrimination created by segregation. He wondered: how should the incidence of discrimination be established? 'A mere head count showing the absence of negro personnel simply is not enough information upon which to make a judgment, for the reason may be, and in many situations is, the absence of Negroes on certificates which the agency is using.' Consequently, any blame for discrimination should be directed at the Civil Service Commission and not individual departments: 'the Committee has not charged agencies with discriminatory practices even when such information has been at hand.' He understood the mounting pressure for affirmative action:

> Our critics would then say that the hiring practices of the agencies should be reviewed. But to do this either we or the agencies must be able to identify, through a review of certificates, those Negroes who have been considered and determine whether or not they have been passed over. With the absence of any identifying racial information on the certificates, it becomes impossible to review past practices. The only possibility lies in a current review on a day-by-day basis, based almost entirely on identifying those Negroes who appear for personal interviews. Even if such identifications are made (and it may be possible to do so) there remains the further problem of determining the relative qualifications of those Negroes passed over as compared with the whites who were hired before any finding of discrimination can be made. On any large scale this would be a very involved process.

To rectify such a pattern required a different course: 'the only alternative to this difficult process that I can see at present is simply to take the position that where there are no Negroes there ought to be some, and direct the agencies to find and employ them.' But this strategy was also problematic: 'this comes close to the "quota" idea, and in any event would put the program in the position of deliberate preference for Negroes. There are, of course, many who believe that the situation now demands such preference if Negro employment in the South is to increase.'[13] This analysis accurately foresaw many of the problems in ensuring equal opportunity for Black Americans in the Federal government. Unfortunately, the record of inequality arising from segregation gave the nebulously specified critics not inconsiderable grounds for their views. Sniderman and Piazza's careful research also confirms how fissural an issue affirmative action remains.

Finally, there is considerable irony, and indeed paradox, in the now quotidian claim that government policy to address issues such as poverty and inequality is inherently flawed and doomed to fail, a view commonly expressed on the political right in the United States. As the material in this book has demonstrated, for over half a century the Federal government played a significant role in shaping and reinforcing the system of race relations which disadvantaged Black American citizens. Furthermore, it was resources deployed by the same Federal government which brought democracy to the South in the 1960s and which tackled discrimination in hiring both in government and outside.[14] Contrary to the common view that the US Federal state is a weak one,[15] at both of these stages the Federal government proved powerful and effective. It is unclear why the conviction that the Federal government cannot be harnessed through its public programmes to the pursuit of equality of opportunity and treatment, for example in the housing- and labour-markets and in training schemes, has become so commonplace in the final decade of the twentieth century. Such a view certainly imputes an inconsequentiality to the Federal government belied by the historical record of its role in upholding the fiction of 'separate but equal' segregated race relations.

In Chapter 1, I drew attention to the partisan and judicial sources of segregated race relations. The Federal government tolerated these relations within their own agencies and permitted their extension into society, in large part, because of the dominant partisan interests in Congress and the executive. One good example of this partisan grip was the consistently weak anti-discrimination measures established by the executive and the hostility of many members of the Congress to such initiatives. Thus, Franklin Roosevelt's agreement to found the FEPC in 1941 did not include many of the other measures sought by A. Philip Randolph and the March on Washington Movement, such as Executive Orders to abolish discrimination in government defence training programmes, impose substantial sanctions with which to penalize discriminators in receipt of government contracts or in government departments, and abrogate segregated race relations in Federal government departments. Congress would have thrown out proposals which moved toward these reforms. The executive bodies created after the demise of the FEPC faced comparable limits. This political and partisan context dictated the Federal government's role in maintaining segregated race relations in the state and in society. Since this constellation of political and electoral forces was able to use the Federal government to protect and accommodate segregated race relations, it is far from self-evident that a different configuration or coalition of political interests could not deploy Federal authority to address the enduring inequalities and disadvantages which remain for Black Americans.[16]

Appendix 1

The Politics of Segregation in the United States

TABLE A1.1. *Presidents and party balances 1876–1969*

Years	Congress	President and party	House		Senate	
			Majority	Minority	Majority	Minority
1877–81	45th	Rutherford Hayes	153 D	140 R	39 R	36 D
	46th	R.	149 D	130 R	42 D	33 R
1881	47th	James A. Garfield	147 R	135 D	37 R	37 D
		R.				
1881–5	48th	Chester A. Arthur	197 D	118 R	38 R	36 D
		R.				
1885–9	49th	Grover Cleveland	183 D	140 R	43 R	34 D
	50th	D.	169 D	152 R	39 R	37 D
1889–93	51st	Benjamin Harrison	166 R	159 D	39 R	37 D
	52th	R.	235 D	88 R	47 R	39 D
1893–7	53rd	Grover Cleveland	218 D	127 R	44 D	38 R
	54th	D.	244 R	105 D	43 R	39 D
1897–1901	55th	William McKinley	204 R	113 D	47 R	34 D
	56th	R.	185 R	163 D	53 R	26 D
1901–9	57th	Theodore Roosevelt	197 R	151 D	55 R	31 D
	58th	R.	208 R	178 D	57 R	33 D
	59th		250 R	136 D	57 R	33 D
	60th		222 R	164 D	61 R	31 D
1909–13	61st	William H. Taft	219 R	172 D	61 R	32 D
	62nd	R.	228 D	161 R	51 R	41 D
1913–21	63rd	Woodrow Wilson	291 D	127 R	51 D	44 R
	64th	D.	230 D	196 R	56 D	40 R
	65th		216 D	210 R	53 D	42 R
	66th		240 R	190 D	49 R	47 D

1921–3	67th	Warren Harding	301 R	131 D	59 R	37 D
		R.				
1923–9	68th	Calvin Coolidge	225 R	205 D	51 R	43 D
	69th	R.	247 R	183 D	56 R	39 D
	70th		237 R	195 D	49 R	46 D
1929–33	71st	Herbert Hoover	267 R	167 D	56 R	39 D
	72nd	R.	230 D	214 R	48 R	47 D
1933–45	73rd	Franklin Roosevelt	310 D	117 R	60 D	35 R
	74th	D.	319 D	103 R	69 D	25 R
	75th		331 D	89 R	76 D	16 R
	76th		261 D	164 R	69 D	23 R
	77th		268 D	162 R	66 D	28 R
	78th		218 D	208 R	58 D	37 R
1945–53	79th	Harry S. Truman	242 D	190 R	56 D	38 R
	80th	D.	245 R	188 D	51 R	45 D
	81st		263 D	171 R	54 D	42 R
	82nd		234 D	199 R	49 D	47 R
1953–61	83rd	Dwight Eisenhower	221 R	211 D	48 R	47 D
	84th	R.	232 D	203 R	48 D	47 R
	85th		233 D	200 R	49 D	47 R
	86th		283 D	153 R	64 D	34 R
1961–3	87th	John F. Kennedy	263 D	174 R	65 D	35 R
		D.				
1963–9	88th	Lyndon B. Johnson	258 D	177 R	67 D	33 R
	89th	D.	295 D	140 R	68 D	32 R
	90th		247 D	187 R	64 D	36 R

TABLE A1.2. *Chairmen of selected Senate and House Committees 1933–1965*

Democrat		Republican	
Chair	Year	Chair	Year
SENATE			
Agriculture and Forestry			
Ellison D. Smith (SC)	1933–44		
Elmer Thomas (Okla.)	1945–6		
		Arthur Capper (Kan.)	1947–9
Elmer Thomas (Okla.)	1949–51		
Allen J. Ellender (La.)	1951–3		
		George D. Aiken (Vt.)	1953–5
Allen J. Ellender (La.)	1955–71		
Appropriations			
Carter Glass (Va.)	1933–45		
Kenneth McKellar (Tenn.)	1946		
		Styles Bridges (NH)	1947–9
Kenneth McKellar (Tenn.)	1949–53		
		Styles Bridges (NH)	1953–5
Carl Hayden (Ariz.)	1955–69		
Military Affairs			
Morris Sheppard (Tex.)	1933–40		
Robert B. Reynolds (NC)	1941–4		
Elbert D. Thomas (Ut.)	1945–6		
renamed Armed Services			
		Chan Gurney (S. Dak.)	1947–9
Milliard E. Tydings (Md.)	1949–51		
Richard B. Russell (Ga.)	1951–3		
		Leverett Saltonstall (Mass.)	1953–5
Richard B. Russell (Ga.)	1955–69		
District of Columbia			
William H. King (Ut.)	1933–40		
Robert B. Reynolds (NC)	1941		
Pat McCarran (Nev.)	1942–4		
Theodore G. Bilbo (Miss.)	1945–6		
		C. Douglass Buck (Del.)	1947–9
J. Howard McGrath (RI)	1949–51		
Matthew M. Neely (W. Va.)	1951–3		
Francis Case (S. Dak.)	1953–5		
Matthew M. Neely (W. Va.)	1955–9		
Alan Bible (Nev.)	1959		

TABLE A1.2. *(Continued)*

Democrat		Republican	
Chair	Year	Chair	Year
Finance			
Pat Harrison (Miss.)	1933–41		
Walter F. George (Ga.)	1942–6		
		Eugene D. Millikin (Colo.)	1947–9
Walter F. George (Ga.)	1949–53		
		Eugene D. Millikin (Colo.)	1953–5
Harry Flood Byrd (Va.)	1955–65		
Expenditures in the Executive Departments			
J. Hamilton Lewis (Ill.)	1933–9		
Frederick Van Nyus (Ind.)	1940		
Lester Hill (Ala.)	1941–6		
		George D. Aiken (Vt.)	1947–9
John L. McClellan D (Ark.)	1949–52		
renamed Government Operations			
John L. McClellan (Ark.)	1952–3		
		Joseph R. McCarthy (Wis.)	1953–5
John L. McClellan (Ark.)	1955–72		
Civil Service			
William J. Bulow (SC)	1933–42		
Sheridan Downey (Calif.)	1943–6		
Post Offices and Post Roads			
Kenneth McKellar (Tenn.)	1933–45		
Dennis Chavez (N. Mex.)	1946		
combined as Post Office and Civil Service			
		William Langer (N. Dak.)	1947–9
Olin D. Johnston (SC)	1949–53		
		Frank Carlson (Kan.)	1953–5
Olin D. Johnston (SC)	1955–65		
A. S. Mike Monroney (Okla.)	1965–9		
HOUSE OF REPRESENTATIVES			
Agriculture			
Marvin Jones (Tex.)	1933–40		
Hampton P. Fulmer (SC)	1941–4		
John W. Flanagan Jr. (Va.)	1945–6		
		Clifford R. Hope (Kan.)	1947–9
Harold D. Colley (NC)	1949–53		
		Clifford R. Hope (Kan.)	1953–5
Harold D. Colley (NC)	1955–67		

TABLE A1.2. *(Continued)*

Democrat		Republican	
Chair	Year	Chair	Year
Appropriations			
James P. Buchanan (Tex.)	1933–7		
Edward T. Taylor (Colo.)	1938–41		
Clarence Cannon (Mo.)	1942–6		
		John Taber (NY)	1947–9
Clarence Cannon (Mo.)	1949–53		
		John Taber (NY)	1953–5
Clarence Cannon (Mo.)	1955–64		
George H. Mahon (Tex.)	1964–77		
Military Affairs			
John J. McSwain (SC)	1933–6		
Lester Hill (Ala.)	1937–8		
Andrew J. May (Ky.)	1939–46		
renamed Armed Services			
		Walter G. Andrews (NY)	1947–9
Carl Vinson (Ga.)	1949–53		
		Dewey Short (Mo.)	1953–5
Carl Vinson (Ga.)	1955–65		
L. Mendel Rivers (SC)	1965–71		
District of Columbia			
Mary T. Norton (NJ)	1933–7		
Vincent L. Palmisano (Md.)	1938		
Jennings Randolph (W. Va.)	1939–45		
John L. McMillan (SC)	1946		
		Everett M. Dirksen (Ill.)	1947–9
John L. McMillan (SC)	1949–53		
		Sid Simpson (Ill.)	1953–5
John L. McMillan (SC)	1955–73		
Expenditures in the Executive Departments			
John J. Cochran (Mo.)	1933–40		
James A. O'Leary (Wy.)	1941–4		
Carter Manasco (Ala.)	1945–6		
		Clare E. Hoggman (Mich.)	1947–9
William L. Dawson (Ill.)	1949–52		
renamed Government Operations			
William L. Dawson (Ill.)	1952–3		
		Clare E. Hoggman (Mich.)	1953–5
William L. Dawson (Ill.)	1955–71		

TABLE A1.2. *(Continued)*

Democrat		Republican	
Chair	Year	Chair	Year
Civil Service			
Lamar Jeffers (Ala.)	1933–4		
Robert Ramspeck (Ga.)	1935–45		
Jennings Randolph (W. Va.)	1946		
Post Office and Post Roads			
James M. Mead (NY)	1933–8		
Milton A. Romjue (Mo.)	1939–42		
Thomas G. Burch (Va.)	1943–5		
George D. O'Brien (Mich.)	1946		
combined as Post Office and Civil Service			
		Edward H. Rees (Kan.)	1947–9
Tom Murray (Tenn.)	1949–53		
		Edward H. Rees (Kan.)	1953–5
Tom Murray (Tenn.)	1955–67		
Ways and Means			
Robert L. Doughton (NC)	1933–46		
		Harold Knutson (Minn.)	1947–9
Robert L. Doughton (NC)	1949–53		
		Daniel A. Reed (NY)	1953–5
Jere Cooper (Tenn.)	1955–7		
Wilbur D. Mills (Ark.)	1958–75		

TABLE A1.3. *Congressional bills to segregate Black workers from White workers, 57th–70th Congresses*

Congress	Session and date	Bill	Sponsor	Committee
57th–62th	1902–12	—		
63rd	1st 1913	HR 5968	J. Aswell (La.)	Reform in the Civil Service
	2nd 1914	HR 13772	C. Edwards (Ga.)	Reform in the Civil Service
	3rd 1915	HR 20329	C. Vinson (Ga.)	Reform in the Civil Service
64th	1st 1915–16	HR 11	C. Vinson (Ga.)	Reform in the Civil Service
		HR 539	J. Aswell (La.)	Reform in the Civil Service
		HR 5797	C. Edwards (Ga.)	Reform in the Civil Service
	2nd 1915–16	—		
65th	1st 1917	HR 1682	C. Vinson (Ga.)	Reform in the Civil Service
	2nd 1918	—		
	3rd 1919	—		
66th	1st 1919	—		
	2nd 1920	—		
	3rd 1921	—		
67th	1st 1921	S 1795	T. H. Caraway (Ark.)	Military Affairs
67th–70th	1922–9	—		

Sources: *Congressional Record*: for HR 5968—63rd Congress 1st sess., vol. l (10 June 1913), 1985 (a bill 'to effect certain reforms in the civil service by segregating clerks and employees of the white race from those of African blood or descent'); for HR 13772—63rd Congress, 2nd sess., vol. li pt. 3 (23 Feb. 1914), 3814; for HR 20329—63rd Congress 3rd sess., vol. lii pt. 1 (23 Dec. 1914), 631; for HR 11—64th Congress 1st sess., vol. iii pt. 1 (6 Dec. 1915), 14; for HR 579—64th Congress 1st sess., vol. iii pt. 1 (6 Dec. 1915), 25; for HR 579—64th Congress 1st sess., vol. iii pt. 1 (15 Dec. 1915), 295; for HR 1682 *Congressional Record*, 65th Congress 1st sess., vol. lv pt. 1 (4 Apr. 1917), 299; for S 1795—67th Congress 1st sess., vol. lxi pt. 2 (14 May 1921), 1449 ('a bill prohibiting the enlistment of any member of the Negro race in the military or naval services of the United States of America, and directing the discharge of all members of the Negro race now serving in any branch of the military or naval service of the United States').

TABLE A1.4. *Bills introduced to establish a Committee on Fair Employment Practice 1946–1964*

Year	Bill	Progress
1945	HR 2232	Reported by House Labor Com. 20 Feb. but blocked by House Rules Com.
	S 101	Reported by Senate Education and Labor Com. 24 May: 18-day filibuster and closure motion rejected 9 Feb. 1946.
1947	S 984	Reported by Senate Labor and Public Welfare Subcom. to full Com. Reported to Senate 5 Feb. but Republicans declined to bring to the floor. No House action.
1949	HR 4453	House Education and Labor Com. reported bill 2 Aug. but no floor action.
	S 1728	Senate Labor and Public Welfare Com. reported bill 17 Oct. but no floor action.
1950	HR 4453	In House floor debate the compulsory element was replaced with one to create a voluntary FEPC with no enforcement powers. Bill passed on 23 Feb.: 240–177 [D 116–34; R 124–42; Ind. O-1].
	S 1728	Two attempts to invoke closure failed, and Truman indicated unwillingness to accept voluntary FEPC.
1951	—	—
1952	S 3362	Bill reported by Senate Labor and Public Welfare Com. to create Equality of Opportunity in Employment Com. with powers of enforcement; did not reach floor.
1953	—	—
1954	S 692	Bill reported by Senate Labor and Public Welfare Com. 28 Apr. to outlaw discrimination in employment; not voted on by Senate.
1955–9	—	
1960	Civil Rights Act	Clause to establish a permanent Com. on Equal Job Opportunity under Govt. Contracts was deleted in the Senate after successful opposition by Southerners. Defeated in Senate Judiciary Com. and by Senate as a whole 1 Apr., 48–38 (D 27–27; R 21–11).
1961		—
1962	HR 10144–H Rept 1370	Bill reported by House Education and Labor Com. 21 Feb outlawing discriminatory practices by employment agencies, unions, or employers and creation of an Equal Opportunity Commission. Bill and measure failed to reach House floor.
1963		—
1964	Civil Rights Act	Title VII—Equal Employment Opportunity established EEOC, with enforcement powers. (Acquired powers to take employers to federal district courts only in the

Appendix 2

Segregation in Government

The data in Appendix 2 is less than complete. This reflects the material available and its standard. Segregation by race was a category never officially compiled by the Federal government or Civil Service Commission. Rather, our knowledge about its incidence and diffusion depends upon either individual administrators' diligence or outside groups such as the NAACP documenting trends or incidental material collected for other purposes. Likewise, in respect of Federal government employment by race, official data is haphazard before the 1970s, generally compiled by agencies established—such as the FEPC—to monitor discrimination, and which often failed to win the full cooperation of individual departments. These points should be borne in mind when examining the ensuing tables.

TABLE A2.1. *Black employment in the Federal government 1893*

Department	No.	Total Salaries ($)
Executive Mansion	5	5,880
Public Buildings and Grounds:		
the Commissioner employs	53	21,234
State:		
consuls	4	5,500
messengers	5	3,660
labourers	7	4,620
Treasury:		
Total (excluding below)	168	
Bureau of Engraving and Printing	146	
Coast Survey	17	
Collectors of custom	3	229,219
Interior:	354	284,208
Recorder of Deeds in DC (Hon. Blanche Bruce)		18,000
War	174	116,340
Navy	8	6,040
Post Office:	70	49,540
Mail-bag repair	42	18,480
Agriculture	37	19,760
Smithsonian Institute	29	14,880
Public Printing Office:		
The Public Printer	204	138,831
United States Senate	36	27,175
House of Representatives:		
Capitol police and architect's office	27	820
Librarian of the House	1	2,000
Library of Congress	4	4,120
Commissioners of the District:		
Labourers, clerks, teachers, superintendents, assessors, etc.	1,000	304,428
Office of Recorder of deeds, DC:		
permanent	14	
temporary	5	
Washington City post office	68	40,900
Total in executive depts. and other branches of govt.	2,393	1,370,623

Source: US Civil Service Commission, *Ninth Report of the U.S. Civil Service Commission July 1 1891 to June 30 1892* (Washington: Government Printing Office 1893), 236–7. The text begins: 'the Commission is indebted for the following statement to Hon. John M. Langston: "I find much on which to congratulate the colored race when I consider the advances they have been making during the last several years. Some time ago I began the collection of data showing the number of colored people employed in the public service . . . The figures I have gotten are as follows."'

TABLE A2.2. *Segregation in government departments (selected) 1928*

Separate rooms occupied by Black employees:

1. Registrar's Office, Room 308, Liberty Loan checking Division, 15 Black clerks under a Black section chief.
2. US Veterans Bureau, Room 219, 15 Black clerks under a Black section chief.
3. GAO, Room 427, 4 Black clerks.
4. Division of Statistics, Room 614, 2 Black men.
5. Navy Dept., Room 3747–50, 11 Black clerks who are a part of the Enlisted Personnel Division of the Bureau of Navigation. The grouping here is distinct, the races being separated by large filing cabinets.
6. Dept. of the Interior, Miss Gretchen McRae, Black stenographer, is the sole occupant of a room on the 1st floor, 3rd wing.
7. Government Post Office Building, Room 720, 8 Black Women. Room 728, 5 Blacks. In section including rooms 721–31, 6 Black men operating punching and tabulating machines.
8. Treasury Dept., Room 341, 5 Black male clerks.

Black employees and White employees working in the same room in racially divided groups:

1. Government Printing Office, North Wing, Column 503, Black Women working as punchers; North Wing, Column 520, separate groups doing the same work. North Wing, Column 416, Black Women grouped as stitchers; White girls in same vicinity doing the same work.
2. Dept. of the Interior, 5th floor, 3rd wing, 5 Black male clerks are grouped at the south end of one of the rooms while White clerks occupy the rest of the rooms. 6th floor, 3rd wing, 2 Black male clerks have desks at the south end of the room, the balance of the room being used by White clerks.

Govt. depts. where segregation is practised in cafeteria service:

1. Cooperative cafeterias:
   (*a*) Bureau of Engraving and Printing: tables in rear of room used solely by Blacks. Same steam tables and both races stand in line together.
   (*b*) Government Printing Office, Blacks assigned separate tables; also separate steam tables.
2. Cafeteria operated by govt. depts.:
   (*a*) Navy Dept., cafeteria is operated by Bureau of Supplies and Accounts. Blacks assigned three tables in rear of room. Other tables in immediate vicinity used exclusively by White employees who because of their dirty clothes do not care to go to other part of room.
3. Cafeterias operated by concessionaries:
   (*a*) Dept. of the Interior: separate room assigned to Blacks with a separate steam table.
   (*b*) Washington City Post Office: separate tables assigned to Black clerks and carriers.
   (*c*) US Post Office Building: separate tables assigned and separate steam tables.
   (*d*) GAO: separate tables assigned.

TABLE A2.2. *(Continued)*

Separate lockers:
1. For Women:
   (*a*) Bureau of Engraving and Printing.
2. For Men:
   (*a*) Bureau of Engraving and Printing.
   (*b*) Washington City Post Office.

Separate toilets:
1. For Women:
   (*a*) Bureau of Engraving and Printing.

Source: LC NAACP, Group I, Box C403, File: Segregation—Federal Service, 6 Mar. 1928–21 Feb. 1929: 'Segregation in Government Departments', reports of investigations made by W. T. Andrews & W. White NAACP (1928).

TABLE A2.3. *Black employees in the US Department of Agriculture 1914 (by bureau)*

Bureau	Black employees and position	
	Washington office	Field
Accounts and Disbursements	—	—
Animal Industry	43 unskilled labourers 7 charwomen	6 veterinary inspectors 5 meat inspectors 34 inspectors' assistants 4 stock examiners 2 clerks 2 messengers 1 cement finisher 1 laboratory helper 3 charwomen
Biological Survey	1 charwoman	—
Chemistry	11 unskilled labourers 9 laboratory helpers 1 laboratory technician 7 charwomen	8 laboratory helpers 1 messenger
Chief Clerk	2 clerks 1 messenger 32 labourers 7 firemen 6 elevator conductors 8 watchmen 1 carriage driver 9 charwomen	—
Crop Estimates	2 labourers 2 charwomen	—
Division of Publications	1 skilled labourer 2 labourers 5 charwomen	—
Entomology	1 unskilled labourer 4 charwomen	1 mechanic 2 unskilled labourers
Experimental Stations	3 unskilled labourers 1 charwoman	—
Federal Horticultural Board	—	—
Forest Service	3 clerks 3 minor clerks 3 messengers 2 messenger boys 2 watchmen 5 unskilled labourers 12 charwomen	1 packer 2 unskilled labourers 2 messenger 1 janitor 1 messenger boy 1 charwoman

TABLE A2.3. *(Continued)*

Bureau	Black employees and position	
	Washington office	Field
Insecticide and Fungicide Board	1 labourer	—
Library	1 messenger	—
	2 charwomen	
Office of Markets	—	—
Office of Rural Organization	—	—
Office of the Solicitor	—	—
Plant Industry[a]	1 gardener	
	2 clerks	
	3 skilled labourer	
	55 unskilled labourers	
	32 agents	
	23 charwomen	
	11 collaborators	
	1 collaborating clerk	
Public Roads	1 assistant chemist	—
	1 laboratory helper	
	4 unskilled labourers	
	1 charwoman	
Soils	2 laboratory helpers	—
	5 unskilled labourers	
	1 labourer	
Weather	3 skilled artisans	2 assistant observers
	2 watchmen	2 messengers
	2 firemen	1 messenger boy
	11 unskilled labourer	1 unskilled labourer
	1 skilled labourer	
	2 charwomen	

Note: Several of these categories, particularly 'labourer' and 'unskilled labourer', for convenience combine a number of subgroups divided according to salary.

[a] The Bureau of Plant Industry did not distinguish their employees by field or Washington offices.

Source: NA RG 16, Office of the Sec. of Agriculture, General Correspondence, Negroes 1909–23, Box 1, Folder: Negroes 1914.

TABLE A2.4. *Black employees in the Department of Agriculture 1914 (by position)*

Position	Number
Veterinary inspector	6
Agent	32
Assistant Chemist	1
Assistant Observer	2
Collaborator	11
Meat Inspector	5
Inspectors' assistants	33
Stock examiner	4
Clerk (stenographer & typewriter)	3
Clerk	6
Minor clerk	3
Collaborating clerk	1
Laboratory helper	21
Laboratory technician	1
Skilled labourer	17
Classified labourer	1
Messenger	12
Messenger boy	4
Watchman	12
Fireman	9
Carriage driver	1
Packer	1
Janitor	1
Gardener	1
Elevator conductor	6
Mechanic	1
Skilled artisan	3
Cement finisher	1
Unskilled labourer	130
Labourer	39
Charwoman	79
TOTAL	447[a]

[a] By 1923 the total had risen to 806 (529 Washington, 277 field) (NA RG 16, Office of the Sec. of Agriculture, General Correspondence, Negroes 1909–23, Box 1, Folder Negroes 1923).

Source: NA RG 16, Office of the Sec. of Agriculture, General Correspondence, Negroes 1909–23, Box 1, Folder Negroes 1914.

Appendix 3

Statistical Profile of Black American Employees in the Federal Government

The data in Appendix 3 are less than complete. This reflects the material available and its standard. Segregation by race was a category never officially compiled by the Federal government or Civil Service Commission. Rather, our knowledge about its incidence and diffusion depends upon either individual administrators' diligence or outside groups such as the NAACP documenting trends or incidental material collected for other purposes. Likewise, in respect of Federal government employment by race, official data is haphazard before the 1970s, generally compiled by agencies established—such as the FEPC—to monitor discrimination, and which often failed to win the full cooperation of individual departments. These points should be borne in mind when examining the ensuing tables.

TABLE A3.1. *Black employees in Federal government 1923 and 1928*

Agency	1923	1928
Alien Property Custodian	16	16
American Battle Monuments Com.	—	1
Capitol	47	187
Chief Coordinator	—	1
Claims Com. (US and Mexico)	—	2
Congressional Lib.	38	69
Department of:		
Agriculture	806	1,086
Commerce	629	686
Interior	560	459
Justice	44	68
Labor	114	92
Navy	5,213	5,427
State	77	76
Treasury	5,221	5,407
War	5,205	5,914
District of Columbia govt.	2,687	3,674
Federal Board for Vocational Education	14	11
Federal Reserve Board	17	22
Federal Trade Com.	9	7
GAO—Treasury	178	143
Government Printing Office	782	934
Inland Waterways Corporation	—	3
International Boundary Com.	—	1
Interstate Commerce Com.	64	15
National Advisory Com. for Aeronautics	4	17
Mixed Claims Com.	—	2
National Military Home	—	181
Panama Canal Office	8,178	23
Pan American Sanitary Bureau	—	1
Personnel Classification Board	—	2
Post Office Dept.	20,391	23,390
Public Buildings and Parks	—	1,189
Smithsonian Institution	157	161
US Board of Tax Appeals	—	9
US Botanic Garden	4	7
US Bureau of Efficiency	3	3
US Civil Service Com.	19	12
US Employees' Compensation Com.	2	2
US Railroad Administration	36	1
US Railroad Labor Board	1	
US Shipping Board	6	7

TABLE A3.1. *(Continued)*

Agency	1923	1928
US Shipping Board—Merchant Fleet Corporation		34
US Soldiers' Home	62	27
US Tariff Commission	7	7
US Veterans' Bureau	341	495
War Finance Corporation	21	1
White House, the	10	10
TOTAL	51,805	51,882

Sources: 1923: NA RG 16, Office of the Sec. of Agriculture, General Correspondence, Negroes 1924–39, Box 2, Folder. Negroes, 1925: letter from Sec. of Labor to Sec. of Agriculture Howard Gore (11 Feb. 1925) with memorandum 'Negroes in United States Service at Close of Fiscal Year 1923'. 1928: LC NAACP, Group I, Box C403, File Segregation—Federal Service, 1928: 'Negroes in the US Service at Close of FY Ended June 30, 1928'. The data was compiled by the Dept. of Labor on the basis of returns from individual depts. and agencies, and issued by Labor.

TABLE A3.2. *Federal civil service employees*

Year	Employees	
	Black	Total
1923 (June)	51,805	548,531
1928	51,882	568,715
1930	54,684	608,915

Source: NA RG 228, Records of the FEPC, Office Files of Joy Davis, Box 405, Folder Employment of Negroes in Federal Govt.: 'Negroes in Federal Service', news release by Sec. of Labor (n.d.).

TABLE A3.3. *Black employees in Federal government 1943*

Department	Employees								
	Total	Black		Professional		Clerical and administrative fiscal		Crafts, protective custodial	
		No.	%	No.	%	No.	%	No.	%
State	2,671	238	8.9	—	—	50	21.0	188	79.0
Treasury	32,271	7,401	22.9	1	—	2,401	32.4	1,828	24.7
Justice	9,120	165	1.8	2	1.2	40	24.3	123	74.5
Post Office	1,489	100	6.7	—	—	42	42.0	58	58.0
Interior	3,980	427	10.7	7	1.6	254	59.5	144	33.7
Commerce	11,218	1,392	12.5	17	1.2	770	55.7	582	34.9

Source: NA RG 228, Office Files of Joy Davis, Box 405, Folder Employment of Negroes in Federal Govt.: President's FEPC, Division of Review & Analysis 'Table and Summary of Employment of Negroes in Federal Government' (Dec. 1943), table 3 (confidential).

TABLE A3.4. *Black employment by grade 1945*

Agencies	Employees			
	Total Black junior employees	Professional	Subprofessional	Clerical
Board of Govt. Fed. Reserve	31	—	—	9
Bureau of Budget	24	—	—	2
Civil Aeronautics Board	12	—	—	7
Civil Service Com.	647	6	1	552
Commerce	2,249	37	86	826
Dept. Agriculture	384	11	22	99
Dept. Justice	165	2	—	49
Dept. Labor[a]				
Fed. Commerce Com.	114	—	—	84
Fed. Deposit Insurance Corp.	57	—	—	11
Fed. Housing Admin.	22	—	—	2
Fed. Power Com.	33	—	3	15
Fed. Security Agency	1,052	9	25	790
Fed. Works Agency	7,593	3	2	408
Food and Drug Admin.	29[b]			
Foreign Economic Admin.	1,535	2	2	872
GAO	1,252	—	—	974
Govt. Printing Office	2,505	—	—	44
Interior	512	15	26	324
Interstate Commerce Com.	65	—	—	39
Nat. Advisory Com. for Aeronautics	10	—	—	9
NA	49	4	14	1
Nat. Capital Housing Authority	51	3	1	15
Nat. Housing Authority	305	8	2	208
Nat. Labor Relations Board	62	1	—	46
Nat. War Labor Board	143	8		122
Navy	3,346	14	32	101
Office of Censorship	19	—	—	8
Office of Defence Transport	77	—	—	59
Div. of Central Ad. Serv.	663	1	4	437
Office of Govt. Reports	90	—	—	90

TABLE A3.4. *(Continued)*

Agencies	Employees			
	Total Black junior employees	Professional	Subprofessional	Clerical
Office of Land Lease	25	—	—	8
OPA	412	15	—	351
Office of Scientific Research and Development	65	—	—	49
Office of Strategic Service	99	—	—	44
Post Office	111	—	1	69
Railroad Retirement Board	8	—	—	1
Reconstruction Finance Corp.	153	—	—	—
Securities and Exchanges Com.	25	—	—	13
Small War Plants Corp.	27	—	—	19
Smithsonian Inst.	115	—	3	1
State	257	—	—	65
Tariff Com.	11	—	—	5
Treasury	7,730	—	1	3,117
Tax Court of US	9	—	—	2
US Employment Compensation Com.	8	—	—	7
US Maritime Com.	364	—	—	252
VA	1,135	7	—	873
War	7,638	22	20	5,937
War Manpower Admin.	245	13	—	197
War Shipping Admin.	147	—	—	133

[a] No report ever submitted.

[b] No breakdown.

Source: NA RG 188, Records of OPA, Racial Relations Adviser, Box 3, Folder Employment Services: 'Professional and Clerical Negro Employees in Federal Agencies in Washington DC' (1945).

TABLE A3.5. *Black employees in the OPA, Jan. 1946*

Region	Board members		Black %age of	
	Total	Black	Members	Population
1	3,808	2	0.05	1.2
2	6,809	86	1.3	5.9
3	5,899	36	0.6	5.0
4	8,372	84	1.0	31.5
5	10,850	7	0.06	20.1
6	7,085	47	0.7	2.4
7	2,853	0	0	1.0
8	2,690	11	0.4	1.3
TOTAL	48,366	273	0.6	9.8

Source: NA RG 188, Records of OPA, Records of Racial Relations Officer, Box 1, Folder Analysis of Negro Participation, War Price and Rationing Boards: 'Number of Local Boards Having Negro Participation is Exceedingly Low' (Jan. 1946, confidential and not to be released).

TABLE A3.6. *Black employees by grade 1956 and 1960*

No. by GS grade	All areas		Washington		Chicago		Mobile	
	1960	1956	1960	1956	1960	1956	1960	1956
1	1,074	604	827	517	114	53	0	0
6	326	141	280	129	9	7	0	0
7	316	157	236	137	35	17	0	0
8	40	16	30	13	10	2	0	0
9	140	71	109	58	24	7	0	0
10	8	1	5	0	2	0	0	0
11	81	31	52	23	19	6	0	0
12	32	8	24	6	5	2	0	0
13	15	0	14	0	1	0	0	0
14	0	0	0	0	0	0	0	0
15	1	1	1	1	0	0	0	0
TOTAL no. of Blacks	2,033	1,030	1,578	884	219	94	0	0
TOTAL employees	50,411	52,571	30,966	31,314	7,600	10,293	723	611

Source: NA RG 220, President's Com. on Govt. Employment Policy 1955–61, Surveys 1956–61, Box 5: 'Survey: Employment of Negroes in Selected Metropolitan Areas', report (31 Mar. 1960), 3.

TABLE A3.7. *Black employees in the National Capital Housing Authority 1950*

Grade	No. of employees		
	White	Black	Total
GS-1	—	—	—
GS-2	7	7	14
GS-3	9	5	14
GS-4	18	7	25
GS-5	13	6	19
GS-6	6	2	8
GS-7	8	2	10
GS-8	—	—	—
GS-9	6	7	13
GS-10	—	—	—
GS-11	4	—	4
GS-12	3	1	4
GS-13	3	—	3
GS-14	2	—	2
GS-15	1	—	1
SUB TOTAL	80	37	117
CPC-2	3	66	69
CPC-3	—	5	5
CPC-4	1	63	64
CPC-5	—	11	11
CPC-6	8	37	45
CPC-7	2	3	5
CPC-8	1	3	4
CPC-9	—	1	1
SUB TOTAL	15	189	204

Source: NA RG 146, Civil Service Agencies, FEB, Correspondence with Agencies 1948–54, Box 5 Folder National Capital Housing: Letter from James Ring Fair Employment Officer, National Capital Housing Authority to James Houghteing chairman FEB (27 June 1950).

TABLE A3.8. *Black employees in the Federal government 1965*

Pay Category	1965			Change from 1961		
	Total No.	Black		Total No.	Black	
		No.	%		No.	%
Total all-pay plans	2,233,615	308,675	13.5	91,255	26,059	9.2
GS-1–4	335,642	64,651	19.3	19,804	409	0.6
GS-5–8	310,681	29,697	9.6	23,239	10,010	50.3
GS-9–11	264,699	9,090	3.4	49,083	4,472	96.8
GS-12–16	213,259	2,818	1.3	59,316	1,781	171.7

Source: LC NAACP, Group III-A, Box A144, Folder Government, National Civil Service 1958–65: Derived from table attached to letter to Roy Wilkins NAACP from Lee White, Special Counsel to the Pres. (13 Nov. 1965).

TABLE A3.9. *Total employees in Federal government agencies 1969–1990*

Year	Employees			
	Total full time	Total full-time Black	Total Black GS	Black % of total
1969	2,601,611	389,251	137,918	15.0
1975	2,419,520	384,652	175,164	15.9
1976	2,418,540	384,515	180,372	15.9
1977	2,414,034	387,630	185,640	16.1
1978	2,418,151	394,642	192,577	16.3
1979	2,419,047	402,358	199,512	16.6
1980	2,438,906	414,345	211,336	17.0
1982	2,008,605	311,131	222,020	15.5
1984	2,023,333	317,875	231,669	15.7
1986	2,083,985	339,770	253,628	16.3
1988	2,125,148	350,052	267,693	16.5
1990	2,150,359	356,867	272,657	16.6

Sources: Derived from US Civil Service Com., *Federal Civilian Workforce Statistics: Equal Employment Opportunity Statistics 1976* (Washington: GPO, 1976); US Civil Service Com., *Federal Civilian Workforce Statistics: Equal Employment Opportunity Statistics 1977* (Washington: GPO, 1977); US Civil Service Com., *Federal Civilian Workforce Statistics: Equal Employment Opportunity Statistics 1978* (Washington: GPO, 1978); US Office of Personnel Management, *Federal Civilian Workforce Statistics: Equal Employment Opportunity Statistics 1979* (Washington: GPO, 1979); US Office of Personnel Management, *Federal Civilian Workforce Statistics: Equal Employment Opportunity Statistics 1980* (Washington: GPO, 1980); US Office of Personnel Management, *Federal Civilian Workforce Statistics: Affirmative Action Statistics 1984* (Washington: OPM, 1984); US Office of Personnel Management, *Federal Civilian Workforce Statistics: Affirmative Action Statistics 1986* (Washington: OPM, 1986); US Office of Personnel Management *Federal Civilian Workforce Statistics: Affirmative Action Statistics 1988* (Washington: OPM, 1988).

TABLE A3.10. *Black employment in Federal agencies by aggregate occupation as a percentage of total employment 1963–1974*

Category	%ages							
	1963	1964	1965	1966	1967	1971	1972	1974
GS	9.2	9.3	9.5	9.7	10.5	11.3	11.9	12.7
Total Wage Board	19.0	19.3	19.7	20.6	20.4	20.4	20.8	20.9
Total Postal Field Service	15.3	15.4	15.7	15.9	18.9	18.7	18.8	20.7
Total other pay plan	8.1	8.1	12.9	12.1	5.9	6.4	6.9	6.1

Sources: US Civil Service Com.: *Study of Minority Group Employment in the Federal Government 1967* (Washington: GPO, 1967), *Minority Group Employment in the Federal Government 1971* (Washington: GPO, 1971), *Minority Group Employment in the Federal Government 1972* (Washington: GPO, 1972), and *Minority Group Employment in the Federal Government 1974* (Washington: GPO, 1974).

TABLE A3.11. *Total Black employees in GS by grade 1969–1980*

Year	Total	GS grades (%ages)					
		1–4	5–8	9–11	12–13	14–15	16–18
1969	137,918	48.8	34.7	11.8	3.9	0.8	—
1975	175,164	36.1	41.4	14.5	6.1	1.5	0.1
1976	180,372	34.5	41.4	15.6	6.8	1.6	0.1
1977	185,640	33.9	41.3	15.9	7.1	1.7	0.1
1978	192,811	32.6	41.7	16.4	7.5	1.8	0.1
1979	199,512	32.2	41.5	16.6	7.9	1.8	—
1980	211,336	31.1	41.6	16.9	8.4	2.0	—

Sources: US Civil Service Com., *Federal Civilian Workforce Statistics: Equal Employment Opportunity Statistics 1976* (Washington: GPO, 1976), p. xi; US Civil Service Com., *Federal Civilian Workforce Statistics: Equal Employment Opportunity Statistics 1977* (Washington: GPO, 1977), p. xiii; US Civil Service Com., *Federal Civilian Workforce Statistics: Equal Employment Opportunity Statistics 1978* (Washington: GPO, 1978), p. xiv; US Office of Personnel Management, *Federal Civilian Workforce Statistics: Equal Employment Opportunity Statistics 1979* (Washington: GPO, 1979), p. xxii; US Office of Personnel Management, *Federal Civilian Workforce Statistics: Equal Employment Opportunity Statistics 1980* (Washington: GPO, 1980), p. xv; US Office of Personnel Management, *Federal Civilian Workforce Statistics: Affirmative Action Statistics 1982* (Washington: OPM, 1982).

TABLE A3.12. *Distribution of Black employees by type of pay system (percentages) 1976–1990*

Pay system	%age									
	1976	1977	1978	1979	1980	1982	1984	1986	1988	1990
All Pay Systems	15.9	16.1	16.3	16.6	17.0	15.5	15.7	16.3	16.5	16.6
GS	12.8	13.0	13.4	13.9	14.5	14.7	15.2	15.9	16.3	16.5
Total Executive				4.0	5.0	4.3	4.2	4.2	4.3	4.7
Total Wage Systems	21.1	20.5	20.7	20.8	20.7	20.2	19.6	19.8	19.5	19.7
Other Wage Systems	26.2	17.6	16.6	16.9	16.5	22.0	21.6	21.7	18.7	24.2
Total Postal Service	20.9	21.0	21.0	20.9	21.3					
Postal Headquarters	21.0	21.6	20.3	23.7	24.4					
Postal Field	20.9	21.0	21.0	20.9	21.3					
Rural Carriers	0.6	0.8	0.8	0.4	0.4					

Sources: US Civil Service Com., *Federal Civilian Workforce Statistics: Equal Employment Opportunity Statistics 1976* (Washington: GPO, 1976); US Civil Service Com., *Federal Civilian Workforce Statistics: Equal Employment Opportunity Statistics 1977* (Washington: GPO, 1977); US Civil Service Com., *Federal Civilian Workforce Statistics: Equal Employment Opportunity Statistics 1978* (Washington: GPO, 1978); US Office of Personnel Management, *Federal Civilian Workforce Statistics: Equal Employment Opportunity Statistics 1979* (Washington: GPO, 1979); US Office of Personnel Management, *Federal Civilian Workforce Statistics: Equal Employment Opportunity Statistics 1980* (Washington: GPO, 1980); US Office of Personnel Management, *Federal Civilian Workforce Statistics: Affirmative Employment Statistics 1982* (Washington: OPM, 1982); US Office of Personnel Management, *Federal Civilian Workforce Statistics: Affirmative Action Statistics 1984* (Washington: OPM, 1984); US Office of Personnel Management, *Federal Civilian Workforce Statistics: Affirmative Action Statistics 1986* (Washington: OPM, 1986); US Office of Personnel Management, *Federal Civilian Workforce Statistics: Affirmative Action Statistics 1988* (Washington: OPM, 1988).

TABLE A3.13. *Percentage of Black employees by selected Federal agency 1965–1967*

Agency	GS grade 1–4		5–8		9–11		12–18	
	1965	1967	1965	1967	1965	1967	1965	1967
Dept. of Army	14.9	14.5	9.7	10.8	3.6	4.4	1.4	1.7
Sec. of Defense	25.5	22.1	15.6	15.8	7.4	5.5	2.1	2.1
Treasury	24.8	26.8	9.9	11.5	3.6	4.0	1.3	1.8
State	47.2	48.2	33.2	41.0	9.4	15.2	2.0	3.0
Smithsonian	46.2	51.3	21.7	25.3	6.4	9.4	0.8	1.7
National Labor Relations Board	23.4	26.5	19.8	25.1	7.7	8.0	2.3	2.7
Interstate Commerce Com.	35.8	51.5	9.9	18.4	1.0	1.3	—	0.4
Small Business Admin.	15.3	19.5	10.9	16.2	3.5	8.3	2.2	0.8
Information Agency	28.6	41.9	27.4	36.9	6.4	7.3	1.3	1.5
Civil Service Com.	41.3	36.4	24.7	23.0	3.0	4.9	1.3	3.1
Selective Service System	8.2	11.5	3.3	5.2	4.8	5.4	—	—
Govt. Printing Office	56.0	67.0	19.7	29.9	2.6	8.2	—	—
Atomic Energy Com.	14.4	14.7	3.8	5.9	2.9	4.7	0.6	0.6
VA	32.8	34.6	12.7	16.8	7.1	8.6	1.9	2.3
Nat. Aeronautics and Space Admin.	5.8	5.7	4.8	4.8	2.2	2.7	0.7	0.8
General Service Admin.	31.4	34.2	15.6	19.3	3.8	6.0	1.6	1.8
Transportation	—	18.1	—	8.0	—	2.2	—	1.0
Housing and Urban Development	28.8	37.4	16.4	22.4	3.8	5.5	2.8	4.5
Health, Education and Welfare	30.3	35.3	18.7	20.6	5.6	7.3	2.2	3.8
Labor	41.7	49.9	28.7	32.6	9.0	15.0	4.5	6.8
Commerce	31.0	37.5	14.9	18.4	4.7	5.8	1.4	3.0
Agriculture	7.0	11.7	4.3	6.1	1.2	1.9	0.6	0.9
Interior	5.0	7.5	3.8	5.5	1.8	2.8	0.5	0.6
Post Office	59.9	46.9	15.6	24.9	4.4	8.7	2.0	3.4
Justice	12.4	19.2	4.3	6.7	1.5	2.0	0.6	0.9
Air Force	8.3	7.2	5.2	5.3	2.4	2.5	1.4	1.6
Navy	13.8	12.6	8.7	9.0	3.2	3.4	1.4	1.7

Source: US Civil Service Com., *Study of Minority Group Employment in the Federal Government 1967* (Washington: GPO, 1967).

TABLE A3.14. *Black employees in Federal government*

Grade	Employees					
	1975			1977		
	Total	Black	% Black	Total	Black	% Black
GS 1–4	256,489	57,929	22.59	255,629	56,188	21.98
GS 9–12	429,589	29,101	6.77	454,313	33,841	7.45
GS 13–15	177,890	6,249	3.51	188,551	7,324	3.88
GS 16–18	4,737	147	3.10	5,240	159	3.03
WG 1–4	50,181	24,320	48.46	48,909	23,362	47.77
WL 6–10	8,291	1,035	12.48	7,988	1,054	13.19
W$ 9–12	19,559	1,004	5.13	19,181	1,060	5.53
W$ 16–19	298	3	1.01	229	3	1.31

Source: Subcommittee on Employment Opportunities of the Com. in Education and Labor US House of Representatives, *Staff Report Comparing Figures for Minority and Female Employment in the Federal Government, 1975 and 1977, and in Forty-four Selected Agencies, 1977*, May 1978 (Washington: GPO, 1978), 6–7.

TABLE A3.15. *Government service employment (000s)*

Year	Employees			
	Total	White	Total minority	Black
1973	3,809	3,115	693	523
1975	3,899	3,102	797	602
1976	4,369	3,490	880	664
1977	4,415	3,480	935	705
1978	4,447	3,481	966	723
1979	4,576	3,568	1,008	751
1980	3,987	3,146	842	619
1981	4,665	3,591	1,974	780
1983	4,492	3,423	1,069	768
1984	4,580	3,458	1,121	799
1985	4,742	1,952	1,179	835
1986 *Total*:	4,779	3,549	1,230	865
breakdown:				
Officials/administrators	260	226	34	23
Professionals	1,005	812	194	119
Technicians	459	360	99	65
Protective service	736	586	150	105
Paraprofessional	364	228	136	113
Office/clerical	868	626	242	165
Skilled craft	401	312	98	57
Service/maintenance	686	400	286	219

Source: Derived from *Statistical Record of Black America* compiled and ed. by Carrell Peterson Horton and Jessie Carney Smith (Detroit: Gale Research Inc. 1990), 292.

Appendix 4

Strikes settled by the FEPC 1943–1944

TABLE A4.1. *Strikes settled by FEPC July 1943–Dec. 1944*

Causes	No. of		
	Strikes	Workers affected	Man days lost
Opposition by White workers to the promotion of Black workers	10	69,927	75,732
Opposition by White workers to the hiring of Black workers	5	9,634	330
Opposition by White workers to the non-segregated facilities	2	4,337	39,017
Opposition by White workers to Blacks in the training school	1	3,468	15,055
Opposition by Black workers to conditions of employment	7	50,601	10,400
Opposition by Black workers to a policy of non-promotion	7	84,237	695
Opposition by Black workers to discriminatory transfers	3	50,307	1,297
Opposition by Black workers to wage differential	4	13,194	395
Opposition by Black workers to discriminatory discharge	1	304	
Opposition by White workers to discrimination against Black workers	1	585	6,048

Source: NA RG 228, Records of the FEPC, Office Files of Joy Davis, Box 204, Folder Annual Report Data.

Appendix 5

Civil Rights Laws 1957–1991

TABLE A5.1. *Selected Civil Rights Legislation 1957–1988*

Year	Act	Main provisions
1957	Civil Rights Act HR 6127 PL 85-315	Outlawed actions preventing citizens from voting in Federal elections; Attorney Gen. was empowered to sue persons preventing others from voting.
1960	Civil Rights Act HR 8601 PL 86-449	Expanded the enforcement powers of the 1957 Act and introduced criminal penalties for obstructing the implementation of Federal court orders.
1964	Civil Rights Act HR 7152 PL 88-352	Fundamental legislation prohibiting discrimination throughout public facilities such as housing and schools; created EEOC to monitor employment in public and private sectors; and provided additional capacities to enforce voting rights.
1965	Voting Rights Act S 1564 PL 89-110	Empowered the Attorney Gen. with extensive powers to investigate voting in Federal elections.
1968	Fair Housing Act HR 2516 PL 90-284	Prohibited discrimination in the sale or renting of property; extended to almost 80% of all property.
1988	Fair Housing Act Amendments PL 100-430	Strengthened the powers of enforcement granted to Housing and Urban Development Dept. in the 1968 Fair Housing Act.
1989	Civil Rights Act HR 3532 PL 101-180	Extension of the U.S. Commission on Civil Rights.
1991	Civil Rights Act S 1745 PL 102-166	Limited the impact of Supreme Court decisions which made it more difficult for workers to mount and win lawsuits charging job discrimination.

Notes

PREFACE

1. Within Federal agencies those appointed as racial advisers in the 1930s (beginning with an appointment in the Dept. of the Interior in 1934) wanted to influence policy positively for Black Americans: they were able to 'affect the formulation of policy on racial questions and to get remedy for specific ills, especially in the War Department. In FEPC Negroes participated as equals in policing, formation and administration.' NA RG 228, Records of the FEPC, Office Files of John A. Davis, Box 358, Folder Civil Service—Negro: 'The Wartime Enforcement of the Non-Discrimination Policy in the Federal Government: Techniques and Accomplishments' (n.d.), 3. See also NA RG 12 Records of the Office of Education, Papers of Ambrose Caliver 1956–62, Box 2, File Attorney General's Policy Materials: 'Experiences of the Department of the Interior in Relation to Use of Public Facilities by Persons of Diverse Racial Groups', 8–9.

   As early as 1935 the Advisor on Negro Affairs in the Dept. of the Interior, Robert C. Weaver, conducted a study of the TVA to assess the opportunities it was providing for Black workers, concluding that 'the greatest defect of the program as far as Negroes are concerned is the absolute lack of policy for Negro participation'. NA RG 183, Records of the BES/USES, Papers of Lawrence A. Oxley, Correspondence with Govt. Agencies, Box 3, Folder Discrimination against Negroes on TVA: letter from Weaver to Dr Arthur E. Morgan, chairman Board of Directors TVA (12 Nov. 1935), 1.

CHAPTER 1

1. NA RG 318, Records of the Bureau of Engraving and Printing, Central Correspondence File 1913–39, Box 6, File Segregation, 1913: memorandum from Mr Williams for Mr Ralph, Director Bureau of Engraving and Printing (3 Apr. 1913). Ralph replied: 'I could not put in writing many things in regard to the matter referred to by you which it would be well to take up, but will discuss the same with you when you call at this Bureau.' The Bureau was a large organization, almost all of whose employees were recruited through civil service examinations, rather than by patronage, making practices within it extremely significant.
2. For this term see C. V. Woodward, *The Strange Career of Jim Crow* (New York: Oxford University Press, 3rd edn. 1974). Woodward describes it thus:

   > the public symbols and constant reminders of his [the Negro's] inferior position were the segregation statutes, or 'Jim Crow' laws. They constituted the most elaborate and formal expression of sovereign white opinion upon the subject . . . [The segregation] code lent the sanction of law to a racial ostracism that extended to churches and schools, to housing and jobs, to eating and drinking. Whether by law or by custom, that ostracism extended to virtually

all forms of public transportation, to sports and recreations, to hospitals, orphanages, prisons and asylums, and ultimately to funeral homes, morgues and cemeteries.

3. This segregation of Black American employees proved tenacious in the Bureau of Engraving and Printing. Responding to a woman complaining about intermixing of the races in 1920, the Bureau's Director was able to assure her that the 'assignment of these people' was arranged so as not to 'offend the sensibilities of either the white or colored people', a description of segregated race relations. NA RG 318, Records of the Bureau of Engraving and Printing, Central Correspondence Files 1913–39, Box 64, Folder Employees—Colored, 1920: letter from James L. Wilmeth, Dir., to a Miss Ellen E. Converse (8 Oct. 1920).
4. For segregation in TB hospitals see the useful discussion in B. Bates, *Bargaining for Life: A Social History of Tuberculosis 1876–1938* (Philadelphia: University of Pennsylvania Press, 1992), ch. 16.
5. Although the 1954 Supreme Court *Brown* decision was seminal, the inferior position of Black Americans was rectified fully only in the 1964 Civil Rights Act and 1965 Voting Rights Act. For details of the latter Act's implementation see the essays in B. Grofman and C. Davidson (eds.), *Controversies in Minority Voting* (Washington: Brookings Institution, 1992).
6. See also Washington Urban League, *Race Relations in the Nation's Capital 1939–1940*, First Annual Report (Washington: Washington Urban League, 1940); and NA RG 48, Records of the Dept. of the Interior, Records of Sec. H. Ickes, General Subject File 1933–42, Box 10, Folder Misc. correspondence relating to Negroes: letter from George W. Goodman, Executive Sec., Washington Urban League to Commissioner John R. Young (17 Apr. 1940), in which Goodman offers many instances of prejudice and discrimination against Black Americans in the District.
7. The report of the President's Com. on Civil Rights, *To Secure These Rights* (Washington: Government Printing Office, 1947), 89. In 1946 the Interior Dept.'s Recreation Association discovered the hotel they had booked for the annual dance refused to admit Black American couples, who were unable to participate in the social occasion: see NA RG 48, Records of the Dept. of the Interior, Office of the Sec., Central Classified Files, 1937–53, Box 2968, Folder Racial Discrimination pt. 4: letter from Asst. Sec. Warner Gardiner to Irving Schulman, Pres. United Public Workers of America (20 Sept. 1946).
8. In 1934 the National Capital Housing Authority (initially called the Alley Dwelling Authority) was established by EO 6868 to reclaim slums in DC. During W.W.II the agency's name was changed and it was made responsible for providing housing for war workers under the Lanham Act. In 1936 the Authority held a conference in Washington about housing for Black Americans. See NA RG 302, Records of the National Capital Housing Authority, Administrative Records 1935–51, Box 12, File Negro Housing Conference: report of the Conference on Better Housing among Negroes pub. by Washington Committee on Housing (18 Apr. 1936, pp. 40).
9. Americans use the terms 'agencies' and 'departments' interchangeably when discussing the Federal bureaucracy. The British term 'ministry' is rarely used.
10. A survey of fourteen departments in Apr. 1942 found that of a total of 171,103 personnel, 9.1 per cent were Black, of whom a mere 2.3 per cent were in positions other than junior or custodial ones. 'Sixty-two percent of the Negro employees . . . were in custodial classifications—an extremely disproportionate ratio.' HSTL,

Papers of Philleo Nash, Box 20, Folder Official Documents, Nash File: Memo from FEPC to heads of govt. depts. and independent establishments (10 Aug. 1942), 3. The FEPC requested in Apr. 1942 that heads of all eighty-three govt. depts. and independent establishments furnish a progress report 'indicating steps taken to open opportunities for employment to Negroes and a statement of the number of Negroes employed'. Six months later fourteen depts., including Justice and Labor, had failed to reply and several who had promised reports failed to deliver. See ibid.

11. In fact, the US Army had been segregated since the War of Independence, when Black Americans—initially excluded from joining—were allowed to enlist.
12. LC, Papers of the NUL, I—Administrative Series, Box 16, Folder FEPC 1942–3: conference on scope and powers of the FEPC held with representatives of minority group organizations (19 Feb. 1943), 10.
13. For this last case see NA RG 48, Records of the Dept. of the Interior, Records of Sec. H. L. Ickes, General Correspondence File 1933–42, Box 10, Folder Misc. correspondence relating to Negroes: 'The Negro and National Parks: A Discussion before the Superintendents of the National Parks', by W. J. Trent Jr., Advisor on Negro Affairs (9 Jan. 1939).
14. See V. O. Key Jr., *Southern Politics* (New York: Vintage, 1949); R. F. Bensel, *Sectionalism and American Political Development 1880–1980* (Madison: University of Wisconsin Press, 1984); J. M. Kousser, *The Shaping of Southern Politics: Suffrage Restriction and the Establishment of the One-Party South 1880–1910* (New Haven: Yale University Press, 1974); and I. Katznelson, K. Geiger, and D. Kryder, 'Limiting Liberalism: The Southern Veto in Congress 1933–1950', *Political Science Quarterly*, 108 (1993), 283–306.
15. The support of segregated race relations by the Federal govt. was not confined to its benign neglect of the South, but embedded in its internal organization and in its public policies. This point was made as late as 1939 in relation to National Parks by the Advisor on Negro Affairs at the Interior Dept.: the problem of discrimination and segregation is 'not localized in any one (geographic) area. It is probably more acute in some than others, but discriminatory practices have been widespread.' NA RG 48, Records of the Dept. of the Interior, Records of Sec. H. L. Ickes, General Correspondence File 1933–42, Box 10, Folder Misc. correspondence relating to Negroes: 'The Negro and National Parks: A Discussion before the Superintendents of the National Parks', by W. J. Trent Jr., Advisor on Negro Affairs (9 Jan. 1939), 8.
16. In this study I use a number of definitional terms interchangeably: Federal government, Federal state, Federal polity, and Federal civil service. My delineation of 'Federal state' is intentionally broad, partly in recognition of the fragmented character of the US system. It includes the Federal civil service located in Washington with field offices throughout the country, the US Armed Services, and Federal programmes defining relationships between citizens and the government. It excludes state and local governments.
17. *Reconstruction: America's Unfinished Revolution 1863–1877* (New York: Harper and Row, 1988), 603.
18. There has been growing scholarly attention to the diversity of the American political tradition, and to the need to recognize more than the liberal strand so eloquently identified by L. Hartz in *The Liberal Tradition in America* (New York: Harcourt,

Brace and World, 1955), and, to some extent, restated by J. D. Greenstone in *The Lincoln Persuasion* (Princeton: Princeton University Press, 1993), in which the author distinguishes between 'humanist liberalism' and 'reform liberalism'. A more sustained account of the diversity of the US political tradition is developed by R. M. Smith in 'Beyond Tocqueville, Myrdal, and Hartz: The Multiple Traditions in America', *American Political Science Review*, 87 (1993), 549–66.

19. As W. J. Trent observed in relation to the National Parks:

> the Federal Government should not lend itself to discriminating against or segregating any race or religious group. To do such allows a contradiction in democratic government. The pattern should be set by the Federal agencies and in cooperative enterprises, the Federal agencies should urge and insist that local social patterns be continually liberalized.

NA RG 48, Records of the Dept. of the Interior, Records of Sec. H. L. Ickes, General Correspondence File 1933–42, Box 10, Folder Misc. correspondence relating to Negroes: 'The Negro and National Parks: A Discussion before the Superintendents of the National Parks', by W. J. Trent Jr., Advisor on Negro Affairs (9 Jan. 1939), 2.

20. LC NAACP Records Group I, Box C403, File Segregation—Federal Service 12 July–24 Aug. 1913: letter to Pres. Woodrow Wilson on Federal Race Discrimination from the NAACP (15 Aug. 1913), 1.
21. Ibid., Box C273, File Discrimination—Employment, Federal Service 1924: Letter to NAACP New York branch from Moorfield Storey (2 Dec. 1924), 1.
22. NA RG 16, Office of the Sec. of Agriculture, General Correspondence, Negroes 1940–55, Box 3, Folder Negroes: 'Negroes in a Democracy at War', Survey of Intelligence Materials No. 25, Office of Facts and Figures, Bureau of Intelligence, (27 May 1942), 27.
23. For an outstanding account see G. M. Frederickson, *The Black Image in the White Mind* (Hanover, NH: Wesleyan University Press, 1987). On public opinion see H. Schuman, C. Steeh, and L. Bobo, *Racial Attitudes in America* (Cambridge, Mass.: Harvard University Press, 1985).
24. *Papers of Woodrow Wilson*, xxviii (Princeton: Princeton University Press, 1978), 88–9: letter from Thomas Dixon Jr. to Wilson (27 July 1913).
25. Dixon's literary outpourings included a novel alluringly titled *The Clansman: An Historical Romance of the Ku Klux Klan* (1905). This novel was the basis for W. B. Griffiths's film *The Birth of a Nation*, in which the Klan was represented rather favourably. With such 'best friends' Wilson was ill-placed to ensure the equality of Black Americans' rights of citizenship. In an NAACP pamphlet about the film, Dixon is quoted as declaring that the motive for this work was 'to create a feeling of abhorrence in white people . . . against colored men'. Quoted in *Fighting a Vicious Film: Protest Against 'The Birth of a Nation'* (Boston: Boston Branch of the NAACP, 1915), 1 (copy in LC, Papers of Moorfield Storey, Box 13, Folder 1915). For the context and background see Frederickson, *The Black Image in the White Mind*, 275–82.
26. Following V. O. Key Jr., the South alludes to those eleven states which seceded from the Union in the 1860s and whose representatives in Congress acted in solidarity on racial issues: Alabama, Arkansas, Florida, Georgia, Louisiana, Mississippi, North Carolina, South Carolina, Tennessee, Texas, and Virginia: Key, Jr., *Southern*

Politics, 10. Key notes that 'if the critical element in the southern political system has been solidarity in national politics, there is logic in defining the political South in terms of consistency of attachment to the Democratic party nationally'.

27. See Bensel, *Sectionalism and American Political Development 1880–1980*; Key Jr., *Southern Politics*; Kousser, *Shaping of Southern Politics*; id., 'The Voting Rights Act and the Two Reconstructions', in B. Grofman and C. Davidson (eds.), *Controversies in Minority Voting* (Washington: Brookings Institution, 1992). See also D. Rueschemeyer, E. H. Stephens, and J. D. Stephens, *Capitalist Development and Democracy* (Chicago: University of Chicago Press, 1992).
28. As Bensel correctly observes: 'less durable than sectional conflict, the major political institutions that control the course and strength of the central state have been crucially influenced by regional competition': *Sectionalism and American Political Development 1880–1980*, 24.
29. Segregation practices, so-called Jim Crow laws, reflected the values and assumptions of many White Americans in the Southern states; as Goldfield has recently argued, the origins of segregation lie in the South. D. Goldfield, *Black, White and Southern: Race Relations and Southern Culture 1940 to the Present* (Baton Rouge, La.: Louisiana State University Press, 1990).
30. As R. M. Smith notes, 'sophisticated doctrines of racial inequality were dominant in American universities and public opinion through much of U.S. history': 'Beyond Tocqueville, Myrdal and Hartz', 555. See also E. Foner, 'Blacks and the US Constitution 1789–1989', *New Left Review*, 183 (1990), 63–74; and C. H. Wesley, 'The Concept of Negro Inferiority in American Thought', *Journal of Negro History*, 25 (1940), 540–60.

    Whilst it is not unusual to point to Northern indifference toward race relations in the South, the Federal govt.'s contribution to these relations nationally is less familiar. Furthermore, proponents of Progressivism in the first two decades of this century often assumed an inferior position for Black Americans, exemplified in the beliefs of Pres. Theodore Roosevelt and later embraced by Pres. Woodrow Wilson. On Progressivism and race see N. J. Weiss, 'The Negro and the New Freedom: Fighting Wilsonian Segregation', *Political Science Quarterly*, 84 (1969), 61–79. See also J. M. Blum, *The Republican Roosevelt* (Cambridge, Mass.: Harvard University Press, 1977).
31. 'Seeds of Failure in Radical Race Policy', in F. A. Bonadio (ed.), *Political Parties in American History*, ii. *1828–1890* (New York: G. P. Putnam's Sons, 1974), 734.
32. Ibid.
33. A position entrenched by most labour organizations which denied membership to Black American workers, even in the Reconstruction decade.
34. Ibid. 735. On this tradition see also E. Foner, *Free Soil, Free Labor, Free Men: The Ideology of the Republican Party before the Civil War* (New York: Oxford University Press, 1970).
35. Woodward, 'Seeds of Failure in Radical Race Policy', 735.
36. *Reconstruction: America's Unfinished Revolution 1865–1877*, 369. Foner also documents important advances in the establishment of equal rights for Black Americans at the height of Reconstruction in the North, though he concludes that 'despite the rapid toppling of traditional racial barriers, the North's racial Reconstruction proved in many respects less far-reaching than the South's': ibid. 471.

In George Frederickson's judgement on the 1890s, 'the Negro became the scapegoat for the political and economic tensions of the period', with the result that Jim Crow laws were enacted, lynchings increased, and Black Americans were legally disenfranchised in the South: *The Black Image in the White Mind*, 266.

37. *Politics, Parties and Pressure Groups* (New York: Thomas Y. Crowell Co., 3rd edn. 1952), 189. See also S. M. Scheiner, 'Theodore Roosevelt and the Negro, 1901–1908', *Journal of Negro History*, 47 (1962), 169–82.
38. R. W. Mullen, *Blacks in America's Wars* (New York: Monad Press, 1973), 41–2.
39. *The Black Image in the White Mind*, 299.
40. Ibid. 301.
41. N. J. Weiss, *Farewell to the Party of Lincoln: Black Politics in the Age of FDR* (Princeton: Princeton University Press, 1983).
42. They resonated powerfully with the prejudices and attitudes openly expounded in the 1890s and 1900s in the South. For details see Frederickson, *The Black Image in the White Mind*, ch. 9.
43. *Congressional Record*, 67th Congress 4th Sess., vol. lxiv pt. 2 (20 Jan. 1923), 2082. The occasion of Lankford's intervention was to praise a decision by the President of Harvard University prohibiting White and Black students to board in the same dormitory—'Negroes ought not to attend his school [Harvard] at all.' For the background to the Harvard Dormitories issue see LC, Papers of Moorfield Storey, Box 4, Folder Harvard Dormitories.
44. *Congressional Record*, 70th Congress 1st Sess., vol. lxix pt. 4 (7 Mar. 1928), 4284–5. Tarver accused the NAACP Pres. of 'going around the country spreading among members of the Negro [race] . . . this rotten, indeed indecent doctrine on marriage between the white and African races'. Howard Univ. was (and is) a federally funded institution.
45. Ibid. pt. 6 (10 Apr. 1928), 6149. There are several pages incorporating the Senator's exchanges with the Civil Service Commission.
46. See D. S. King, *Actively Seeking Work? The Politics of Unemployment and Welfare Policy in the United States and Great Britain* (Chicago: University of Chicago Press, 1995), ch. 1. See also NA RG 228 FEPC Records, Office Files of George M. Johnson, Box 76, Folder H. R. Northrup: H. R. Northrup, 'An Analysis of the Discriminations against Negroes in the Boiler Makers Union' (n.d.); id., *Organized Labor and the Negro* (New York: Harper, 1944); and J. Quadagno, *The Color of Welfare* (New York: Oxford University Press, 1994), esp. ch. 3.
47. See King, *Actively Seeking Work?*, ch. 1.
48. A riot in Detroit in June 1943 left 34 dead, over 700 injured, and significant loss in war production. H. Sitkoff, 'Racial Militancy and Interracial Violence in the Second World War', *Journal of American History*, 58 (1971), 674.
49. See K. T. Jackson, *Crabgrass Frontier: The Suburbanization of the United States* (New York: Oxford University Press, 1985), and Quadagno, *The Color of Welfare* (New York: Oxford University Press, 1994), ch. 4.
50. *Papers of Woodrow Wilson*, xxviii. 408: letter to Wilson from Oswald Garrison Villard, NAACP Pres., enclosing a report by May Childs Nerney, NAACP Sec. on segregation in government departments (14 Oct. 1913).
51. See amongst others G. Myrdal, *An American Dilemma: The Negro Problem and American Democracy* (New York: Harper and Row, 1944); Frederickson, *The Black*

Image in the White Mind; id., *White Supremacy* (New York: Oxford University Press, 1981); M. Banton, *Racial Theories* (Cambridge: Cambridge University Press, 1987), esp. 32–46; B. J. Fields, 'Ideology and Race in American History', in J. M. Kousser and J. M. McPherson (eds.), *Region, Race and Reconstruction* (New York: Oxford University Press, 1982); J. S. Haller, Jr., *Outcasts from Evolution: Scientific Attitudes of Racial Inferiority 1859–1900* (Urbana, Ill.: University of Illinois Press, 1971); and A. Smedley, *Race in North America: Origin and Evolution of a World View* (Boulder, Colo.: Westview Press, 1993). Such attitudes were manifest e.g. in sterilization policies: See Channel 4 documentary in Secret History Series, 17 Feb. 1994, *The Lynchburg Case*.

52. This behaviour was carefully recorded by one writer to the NAACP in 1913: 'the great majority of the white people here hold the Southern view of the negro, and as for the Northerners here, it takes but a little while for them to become infinitely more anti-negro than any Southerner.' *Papers of Woodrow Wilson*, xxviii. 349: Letter from John Palmer Gavit to Oswald Garrison Villard, 1 Oct. 1913.
53. e.g. the Dir. of the Bureau of Engraving and Printing informed May Childs Nerney of the NAACP that 'in this Bureau there has always been a segregation of the two races in the assignment of dressing and locker rooms, and a limitation as to the divisions in which they are employed'. NA RG 318, Records of the Bureau of Engraving and Printing, Central Correspondence File 1913–39, Box 6, Folder Segregation 1913: Letter from J. E. Ralph to Nerney (29 July 1913). See also Nerney's letter to Ralph (26 July 1913). Evidently this segregation had not been introduced effectively into work arrangements before 1913, hence the memorandum quoted at the beginning of this ch.
54. This had been pointed out to the Pres. a year previously: 'We protested such segregation as to working positions, eating, toilets, dressing rooms, rest rooms, lockers, and especially public toilets in government buildings. We stated that such segregation was a public humiliation and degradation, entirely unmerited and far-reaching, in its injurious effects, a gratuitous blow against ever-loyal citizens.' *Papers of Woodrow Wilson*, xxix (Princeton: Princeton University Press, 1979), 298–9: Address to the Pres. by William Monroe Trotter, 12 Nov. 1914.

    Writing to NAACP Pres. Oswald Villard, May Childs Nerney noted the changed atmosphere occasioned by the Democrats' election, giving greater significance to earlier prejudices: 'in saying they favor segregation, many white employees seem not to be expressing their own convictions so much as to be reflecting what they regard as the spirit of the new administration. Those who have been appointed in previous administrations apparently think that if they do not put themselves on record as approving this policy, the danger of losing their positions is thereby increased.' Ibid. xxviii. 403: letter (30 Sept. 1913).
55. Ibid. 165: letter to Wilson from Moorfield Storey [NAACP Pres.] and Others (15 Aug. 1913).
56. NA RG 16, Records of the Office of the Sec. of Agriculture, General Correspondence, Negroes 1909–13, Box 1, Folder Negroes July–Sept. 1913: Letter from the Chicago branch of the NAACP to David A. Houston, Sec. of Agriculture (12 Sept. 1913), 1.
57. This trend was anticipated presciently and accurately by the editor of the *Congregationalist and Christian World*: 'the movement [to segregation] once started

in the government service is likely . . . to force colored people out of the higher positions and down into the lower positions where they would bear the stamp of inferiority.' LC NAACP, Group I, Box C403, File Segregation—Federal Service, 27–31 Aug. 1913; see also letter from the associate editor to Oswald Villard (27 Aug. 1913).

58. NA RG 318, Records of the Bureau of Engraving and Printing, Central Correspondence File 1913–39, Box 6, File Segregation, 1913: Letter from J. E. Ralph Dir. of the Bureau to Miss Rose Miller, Wetting Division, (23 July 1913); see also Miller's letter (19 July 1913). For another instance of White workers objecting to working alongside Black employees see ibid., File Segregation 1914: memorandum of 10 Nov. 1914 to the Bureau Dir.

59. USBP, Archives Division, Proceedings of the Federal Prison Wardens' Conference (1948), 32.

60. NA RG 129, Bureau of Prisons, Central Administrative File 1937–47, Prisoners' Welfare, Box 41, File Segregation: Letter from Marshall to Dir. James Bennett (1 Sept. 1942).

61. NA RG 318, Records of the Bureau of Engraving and Printing, Central Correspondence File 1913–39, Box 6, File Segregation, 1913: Letter from J. E. Ralph Dir. of the Bureau to Sec. of the Treasury William G. McAdoo (6 Dec. 1913), 2.

62. HSTL, President's Com. on Equality of Treatment and Opportunity in the Armed Services, Box 10, Minutes (28 Mar. 1949), 39.

63. For partial exceptions see S. Krislou, *The Negro in Federal Employment: The Quest for Equal Opportunity* (Minneapolis: University of Minnesota Press, 1967); and also M. E. Belknap, *Civil Rights, the White House and the Justice Department 1945–1968*, iv. *Employment of Blacks by the Federal Government* (New York: Garland, 1991). Belknap's vol. reproduces a selection of documents from the Truman, Eisenhower, Kennedy, and Johnson presidential libraries. The criteria for inclusion are unclear and the introductory text rather brief. For an author who does appreciate the significance of the sectional divide for the US state, though he does not address directly the position of Black employees, see Bensel, *Sectionalism and American Political Development 1880–1980*. Early studies of Black employees under segregation include N. J. Weiss, 'The Negro and the New Freedom: Fighting Wilsonian Segregation', *Political Science Quarterly*, 84 (1969) 61–79; K. L. Wolgemuth, 'Woodrow Wilson's Appointment Policy and the Negro', *Journal of Southern History*, 24 (1958), 457–71; and A. Meier and E. Rudwick, 'The Rise of Segregation in the Federal Bureaucracy 1900–1930', *Phylon*, 28 (1967), 178–84. See also relevant entries to P. P. Van Riper, *History of the United States Civil Service* (Evanston Ill.: Row, Peterson and Co., 1958). The substantial exception to this neglect is the military: there have been several scholarly studies of segregation in the armed forces which are cited in Ch. 4, below.

64. *Papers of Woodrow Wilson*, xxviii (Princeton: Princeton University Press, 1978), 491–2: letter from William Monroe Trotter, Sec. of the NIPL, to Wilson, 6 Nov. 1913 (my emphasis).

65. 'Outside the government service the whole race would suffer an added stigma and handicap because of the government's attitude toward the race.' LC NAACP, Group I, Box C403, File Segregation—Federal Service 27–31 Aug. 1913, see also letter from the associate editor to Oswald Villard (27 Aug. 1913).

66. e.g. twenty-three years after segregation was introduced to the Bureau of Engraving and Printing, the NAACP wrote repeatedly complaining about the failure of Black American employees to be promoted, a charge obfuscated in the Bureau's response: NA RG 318, Records of the Bureau of Engraving and Printing, Central Correspondence File 1913–39, Box 243, Folder Employees—Colored, 1936: Correspondence between the Bureau and NAACP (2 and 7 Oct. 1936).
67. NA RG 16, Records of the Office of the Sec. of Agriculture, General Correspondence, Negroes 1909–13, Box 1, Folder Negroes July–Sept. 1913: Letter from the Chicago branch of the NAACP to David A. Houston, Sec. of Agriculture (12 Sept. 1913), 2.
68. *Papers of Woodrow Wilson*, xxviii. 492: letter from William Monroe Trotter to Wilson (6 Nov. 1913).
69. Ibid. 245: letter to NAACP Sec. Oswald Garrison Villard from Wilson (29 Aug. 1913).
70. Ibid. 265: letter to Howard Allen Bridgeman from Wilson (4 Sept. 1913).
71. Ibid. 65: letter from Wilson to Oswald Garrison Villard (23 July 1913). The Black Americans with whom Wilson had consulted were principally clergy, notably Bishop Alexander Walters (head of the National Colored Democratic League and a bishop in the African Methodist Church).
72. Ibid. xxix. 302: Remarks by Wilson and a Dialogue, 12 Nov. 1914.
73. NA RG 318, Records of the Bureau of Engraving and Printing, Central Correspondence File 1913–39, Box 6, File Segregation, 1913: Letter from J. E. Ralph Dir. of the Bureau to Sec. of the Treasury William G. McAdoo (6 Dec. 1913), 2–3.
74. McAdoo was a close Southern conservative contender for the Democratic party presidential nomination in 1924.
75. NA RG 318, Records of the Bureau of Engraving and Printing, Central Correspondence File 1913–39, Box 6, File Segregation, 1913: Letter from J. E. Ralph Dir. of the Bureau to Sec. of the Treasury William G. McAdoo (6 Dec. 1913), 3 (emphasis added).
76. Ibid.; memorandum from J. E. Ralph Dir. of the Bureau to Asst. Sec. of the Treasury Williams (12 July 1913), 1.

    The same administrator denied that a Black woman, Mrs Belle C. La Follette, was removed from her post for raising the question of racial segregation; rather her departure arose 'from an ordinary case of insubordination which was handled and acted on in exactly the same way as a great number of other cases have heretofore been treated, without regard to the race of the person involved or her connection with the race segregation matter'. Ibid.: Letter from J. E. Ralph Dir. of the Bureau to Sec. of the Treasury William G. McAdoo (6 Dec. 1913), 1–2.
77. LC NAACP, Group I, Box C403, File Segregation—Federal Service Oct.–Nov. 1928: letter from Mellon (18 Oct. 1928).
78. NA RG 129, Records of the Bureau of Prisons, Central Administrative Files 1937–47, Prisoners' Welfare, Box 41, Folder Segregation: Letter from James Bennett to Thurgood Marshall, Special Counsel NAACP (22 Aug. 1942).
79. *Papers of Woodrow Wilson*, xxviii. 453: letter from William Gibbs McAdoo to Oswald Garrison Villard, 27 Oct. 1913. McAdoo added, 'The failure of Patterson's appointment caused the abandonment of the experiment [to create a distinctively colored section].'

80. *Papers of Woodrow Wilson*, xxix. 361–2: letter from Sec. McAdoo to F. I. Cobb, ed. of the *World*, 26 Nov. 1914.
81. LC NAACP, Group I, Box C403, File Segregation—Federal Service, 1928: Letter from Sec. of the Treasury Andrew Mellon to James Johnson Sec. NAACP (16 May 1928), 2–3 (my emphasis).
82. Ibid.: letter from NAACP to Sec. Mellon (26 Sept. 1928).
83. NA RG 48, Records of the Dept. of the Interior, Office of the Sec., Central Classified File 1937–53, Box 2967, Folder Racial Discrimination: letter from Phineas Indritz, Asst. Solicitor Dept. of the Interior, to the Public Printer (25 Jan. 1940).
84. Ibid. Indritz continued: 'I am sure that no law of Congress requires segregation of the Negro employees from the white employees either in the cafeteria or in any other part of the Government Printing Office . . . The Government, above all other organizations or persons, should be reluctant to sanction any policies which appear to lend approval to discriminations against its citizens, since policies of discrimination on the basis of race or color are directly opposed to the permanent aims of this Nation.'
85. Ibid.: letter from the Public Printer, Augustus E. Giegengack, to the Sec. of the Interior (2 Feb. 1940):

    the Government Printing Office cafeteria is not a Government organization in any sense of the word. It is operated solely by the employees of the Government Printing Office for the employees of the Government Printing Office. The cafeteria is managed by a general board elected by the employees of the Office. On this governing board there are several colored men and women. The employees feel they have one of the best cafeterias in the city from every standpoint . . . The employees deeply resent criticisms of this nature by an outsider who has no knowledge of the daily existing conditions and no understanding of its policy or the reasons therefor. The employees feel that it does not behoove an outsider who has accepted their hospitality apparently without invitation to criticize it in the manner indicated in the attached correspondence.

86. NA RG 16, Records of the Office of the Sec. of Agriculture, General Correspondence, Negroes 1940–55, Box 3, Folder Negroes: letter to Claude A. Barnett, Associated Negro Press from Paul Appleby, Under Sec. Dept. of Agriculture (7 May 1941); see also Barnett's letter (17 Feb. 1941).
87. As one activist, Robert Wood, explained in a letter to Pres. Woodrow Wilson (5 Aug. 1913), 'however necessary and important the enforced segregation of the races may be to the voters in rural communities in Alabama or Mississippi and to their candidates for office, it is not a business in which this great nation can engage with any profit to the people as a whole, and it can be productive only of evil and ill will among a large and important minority'. *Papers of Woodrow Wilson*, xxviii. 118.
88. Ibid. 408: letter to Wilson from Oswald Garrison Villard, NAACP Pres., enclosing a report by May Childs Nerney, NAACP Sec. on segregation in govt. depts. (14 Oct. 1913).
89. Ibid. xxix. 304–5: Remarks by Wilson and a Dialogue (12 Nov. 1914).
90. In a clever ruse, a Black activist set out fourteen points necessary for civil rights for Black Americans to parallel those Wilson was pursuing as the basis for world peace. They were: (1) Universal suffrage; (2) Better educational facilities in the South; (3) Abolition of the so-called 'Jim Crow' system; (4) Discontinuance of

unjust discriminatory regulations and segregation in the various depts. of the govt.; (5) The same military training for Black youth as for White; (6) The removal of an imaginary deadline in the recognition of fitness for promotion in military and naval service; (7) The removal of the peonage system in the South; (8) An economic wage to be applied to White and Black alike; (9) Better housing conditions for Black employees in industrial plants; (10) Better sanitary conditions in certain sections of US cities and towns; (11) Reform in the penal institutions of the South; (12) A fair and impartial trial by jury instead of lynching; (13) Recognition of Blacks' right and fitness to sit on juries; (14) Fair play. Cited in M. White Ovington, 'Reconstruction and the Negro', *Crisis*, 17 (Feb. 1919), 169. The points were formulated by an NAACP member.

91. TABLE. The Growth of the Federal Bureaucracy

Year	No. of Employees
1901	235,756
1905	300,615
1910	384,088
1915	476,363
1920	691,116
1925	564,718
1930	608,915
1932	572,000
1939	920,000
1950	2,600,000
1982	2,900,000

Derived from R. J. Stillman II, *The American Bureaucracy* (Chicago: Nelson-Hall, 1987), 49, 56; and *Statistical Abstract of the United States*. The figures for 1905 to 1930 are taken from L. D. White, *Trends in Public Administration* (New York: McGraw Hill, 1933); 243. For a thorough, though slightly dated, study of the Federal govt., see Van Riper, *History of the United States Civil Service*. For a good contemporary account of the Federal bureaucracy see J. W. Fesler and D. F. Kettl, *The Politics of the Administrative Process* (Chatham, NJ: Chatham House Publishers, 1991).

92. For the major exceptions see Krislou, *The Negro in Federal employment*; and also Belknap, *Employment of Blacks by the Federal Government*. On the pre-1930s period see also Weiss, 'The Negro and the New Freedom', 61–79; K. L. Wolgemuth, 'Woodrow Wilson's Appointment Policy and the Negro', 457–71; A. Meier and E. Rudwick, 'The Rise of Segregation in the Federal Bureaucracy 1900–1930', *Phylon*, 28 (1967), 178–84; and Van Riper, *History of the United States Civil Service*, esp. 158, 161–2, 241–2, 333, 438.

93. For a discussion of American historians and Black history see the admirable A. Meier and E. Rudwick, *Black History and the Historical Profession 1915–1980* (Urbana, Ill.: University of Illinois Press, 1986).

94. Key Jr., *Politics, Parties and Interest Groups*, 382–91.

95. On the effects of the merit system after 1883 see A. Hoogenboom, 'The Pendleton Act and the Civil Service', *American Historical Review*, 64 (1959), 301–18.
    Bernard Silberman's recent comparative study constructs an elegant explanation of the distinctive character of the US bureaucracy, yet oddly gives no consideration to how this institution both facilitated and reified the exclusion of Black Americans; in common with many observers, he writes as if this characteristic of the US Federal govt. were invisible: *Cages of Reason* (Chicago: University of Chicago Press, 1993), see esp. chs. 8 and 9 for the USA and chs. 1–3 for the theoretical framework.
96. See L. C. Dodd and R. L. Schott, *Congress and the Administrative State* (New York: John Wiley, 1979), ch. 3, on the historical development of congressional powers and institutions.
97. *Plessy* v. *Ferguson* 163 US 537 (1896). For a detailed analysis of the case see C. A. Lofgren, *The Plessy Case* (New York: Oxford University Press, 1987).
98. For one good account see H. J. Abraham, *Freedom and the Courts* (New York: Oxford University Press, 5th edn. 1988).
99. One justice did not participate in the decision.
100. Furthermore, the Court held that upholding the appeal would necessitate integration in public educational facilities, to which public opinion and custom were alleged to be opposed (as indeed they were in certain parts of the country). Justice Henry Billings Brown, writing the majority view, noted that the 14th Amendment did abolish inequality before the law on grounds of race but 'it could not have been intended in the nature of things . . . to abolish distinction based upon color or to enforce social, as distinct from political equality'. *Plessy* v. *Ferguson* 163 US 537 (1896), 544.
101. Ibid. 559.
102. The Court ordered that the plaintiff Gaines should be admitted to the all-White state education institution. It rejected the state's offer to pay out-of-state fees for the student as an inadequate defence of a citizen's equal protection clause under the 14th Amendment. The 6 to 2 decision (the late Justice Cardozo had not yet been replaced) did not negate the 'separate but equal' doctrine but marked an inroad upon it. *Missouri ex rel. Gaines* v. *Canada* 305 US 337 (1938).
103. *Sweatt* v. *Painter* 339 US 629 (1950). Upholding Sweatt's equal protection right under the 14th Amendment required his admittance to the all-White state university law school.
104. *McLaurin* v. *Oklahoma State Regents for Higher Education* 339 US 637 (1950).
105. *Morgan* v. *Virginia* 328 US 373 (1946). Four years later in 1950, the Court held that any segregation on interstate railways contravened the Interstate Commerce Act: *Henderson* v. *United States* 339 US 816 (1950).
106. *Smith* v. *Allwright* 321 US 649 (1944).
107. *Brown* v. *Board of Education of Topeka Kansas* (I) 347 US 443 (1954).
108. NA RG 60, Records of the Dept. of Justice, Records of John Doar, Asst. Attorney General, Civil Rights Div. 1960–7, Box 1, File Legal Memos—Schools: 'Leading Civil Rights Cases: School Desegregation' (anon.).
109. On education see NA RG 12, Records of the Office of Education, Div. of Equal Educational Opportunities, Records relating to desegregation in education, Box 3, File Desegregation: G. W. Foster, 'Guidelines for Southern School Desegregation'

(22 Feb. 1965). For a different interpretation of the case see M. J. Klarman, 'How *Brown* Changed Race Relations: The Backlash Thesis', *Journal of American History*, 81 (1994), 81–118.

110. For one account see H. D. Graham, *The Civil Rights Era: Origins and Development of National Policy 1960–1972* (New York: Oxford University Press, 1990).
111. Only finally addressed in the Civil Rights Act of 1968.
112. See NAACP, *The Decision of the US Supreme Court in the Louisville Segregation Case (Buchanan vs. Warley 245 US 60.)* (New York: NAACP, 1917) (copy in LC, Papers of Moorfield Storey, Box 14, Folder 1917).
113. NA RG 207, Records of the Dept. of Housing and Urban Development, Urban Renewal Admin., General Subject Files 1949–60, Box 330, File Racial Relations: Memorandum by George B. Nesbitt to Nathaniel Keith Dir. Slum Clearance and Urban Redevelopment, 'Basic Approaches to Racial Considerations' (9 Mar. 1950), 9–10.
114. As the NAACP noted in its annual report for 1925, such covenants—'private agreements among white property owners not to sell their property to Negroes nor allow it to be occupied by Negroes'—were adopted throughout the country after the 1917 decision: 'this policy and practice spread rapidly, especially in northern communities, until now the point is reached where the Supreme Court decision in the Louisville Case will be practically nullified unless this manner of enforcing segregation is checked and defeated.' *Sixteenth Annual Report of the National Association for the Advancement of Colored People for the year 1925* (New York: NAACP, 1926), 7.
115. *Shelley* v. *Kraemer* US 1 (1948), 22.
116. NA RG 129, Bureau of Prisons, Central Administrative File 1937–67, Prisoners' Welfare Box 41, File Segregation: Wardens' Administrative Session, Leavenworth, Kan. (7 Dec. 1954), see esp. pp. 14–26.
117. NA RG 207, Records of the Dept. of Housing and Urban Development, HHFA Subject Files 1947–60, Box 96, File Racial Relations: Memorandum for the Commissioner 'Observations Regarding Implications of Decisions of the US Supreme Court for HHFA Programs and Policies' (1 July 1954).
118. Ibid.: telegram from Robert W. Dowling Pres. of the Board of Trustees of the NUL to Pres. Eisenhower (21 Oct. 1954). The telegram was passed by the White House to the Commissioner of the FHA for a response.
119. LC NAACP, Group I, Box C403, Folder Segregation—27–31 Aug. 1913: letter from Sen. John D. Norks to Miss Florence Kelley in New York (16 Oct. 1913).

    In holding such views, Woodrow Wilson did not deviate from attitudes prevailing in the USA, and he should not be held in judgement on that account. He was a product of his times—doctrines of White supremacy were widespread and often uncritically accepted, even by Progressives, and race relations were premissed on the inferiority of Black Americans. D. W. Griffith's film *The Birth of a Nation*, distributed in 1915, wallowed in and celebrated such views.
120. See *Congressional Record*, 63rd Congress, 1st and 2nd Sessions, entries under 'District of Columbia' and 'Colored People'; US House of Representatives, 63rd Congress, 1st and 2nd Sess., House Committee on Reform in the Civil Service, *Segregation of Clerks and Employees in the Civil Service*, hearings on HR 5968 and HR 13772 1914. In the 1st sess. HR 5968, and in the 2nd sess. HR 13772 and HR 17541 each proposed segregation by race in the civil service. On DC see Hearing

before the Committee on the District of Columbia, 64th Congress 1st sess. on HR 12, HR 13, HR 274, HR 326, HR 618, HR 715, and HR 748 (11 Feb. 1916), 'Intermarriage of Whites and Negroes in the District of Columbia and Separate Accommodations in Street Cars for Whites and Negroes in the District of Columbia' (copy located in LC, Papers of Moorfield Storey, Box 13, Folder 1913). On the civil service see also NA RG 233 Records of the US House of Representatives, 63rd Congress, Committee on the Civil Service, Box 484, and M. Sasna, 'The South in the Saddle: Racial Politics during the Wilson Years', *Wisconsin Magazine of History*, 54 (1970).

121. *Congressional Record*, 63rd Congress, 2nd sess., vol. 55 pt. 2, (27 June), 11278, HR 17541 introd. by Sen. Park to the Com. on Military Affairs.
122. Ibid. 1st sess., vol. 50 pt. 2 (10 June 1913), 1985. Assigned to the Com. on Reform in the Civil Service.
123. Hearings before the Com. on the District of Columbia, House of Representatives 64th Congress, 1st sess. on HR 12, HR 13, HR 274, HR 326, HR 618, HR 715, and HR 748 (11 Feb. 1916). 'Intermarriage of Whites and Negroes in the District of Columbia and Separate Accommodations in Street Cars for Whites and Negroes in the District of Columbia'.
124. Opponents of segregation in the Federal govt. generally lacked a majority: LC NAACP Group I, Box C403, File Segregation—27–31 Aug. 1913: see letters to the NAACP from Congressman Andrew Peters (29 Aug. 1913); Sen. Theodore E. Burton (1 Sept. 1913); and Sen. Lawrence Y. Sherman (3 Sept. 1913). One Republican Sen., Theodore E. Burton, responding to NAACP protests about segregation in the government, explained the partisan source of its introduction: 'you will notice that this order has been issued under a Democratic Administration.' Ibid.; letter to Frank Morgan in Cleveland, Oh. (10 Sept. 1913).
125. National Com. on Segregation in the Nation's Capital, *Segregation in Washington* (report) (Chicago: National Com. 1948).
126. *Congressional Record*, 63rd Congress 1st sess., Sen., vol. 51 pt. 12 (8 July), 11798.
127. Ibid. vol. 50, pt. 7 (29 Oct. 1913), 411.
128. Ibid.
129. The Congressman explained the urgency of these issues to the perpetuation of the White race, accusing the Republican party of indulging in a misguided policy of 'racial equality': 'every informed and right-thinking white man, while sympathizing with and anxious to help the negro in his place, recognizes the necessity of preserving the integrity of and the supremacy of the white race.' He warned, in unabashed terms, of the consequences of failing to maintain White supremacy: 'No nation ever destroyed itself, except by amalgamating with an inferior race.' Aswell believed his country had a leading role nationally in racial matters: 'The United States is peculiarly commissioned to lead all other nations, not only in the purity of race-quality but in world problems of just and wise Government . . . It is our duty to help the negro . . . by giving this child race a correct idea of his proper circumscribed position in society and in the Republic.' Ibid.
130. Ibid.
131. The language of 'child race' was a further inheritance from *fin de siècle* discourse in the South, particularly amongst politicians and activists bitterly hostile toward

Reconstruction: see the discussion in Frederickson, *The Black Image in the White Mind*, 283–97.

132. LC NAACP, Group I, Box C403, File Segregation—Federal Service 1928: 'Hoover Ends Segregation in Commerce Department' press release (6 Apr. 1927). See article 'Hoover Changes Racial Policy in Census Office—Colored Clerks Now in all Departments', *Washington Post* (31 Mar. 1928).
133. *Congressional Record*, 70th Congress, 1st sess., vol. lxix pt. 6 (10 Apr. 1928), 6150.
134. Ibid. pt. 10 (29 May 1928), 10657.
135. Ibid. pt. 6 (10 Apr. 1928), 6175.
136. Ibid. (16 Apr. 1928), 6487. Blease inserted letters from disgruntled employees in the Record. See also remarks by Sen. Reed Smoot of Utah pointing out that all the 'villians' identified were Democrats, ibid. pt. 7, 2 May 1928, p. 7593.
137. Key Jr., *Politics, Parties and Pressure Groups*, 697.
138. See also Katznelson, Geiger, and Kryder, 'Limiting Liberalism', 283–306. James Patterson has constructed an index of the most conservative Democrats serving in the House and Senate between 1933 and 1939, defined by their opposition to Administration policy. His lists include several of the chairmen featured in Table A1.1. In the Senate it includes Smith (SC) on Agriculture and Forestry, who voted against the Administration 44 per cent of the time; Glass (Va.), chairman of Appropriations, who voted against 81 per cent; Bulow (S. Dak.) on the District of Columbia committee who voted against 28 per cent; and King (Ut.) chairman of DC who voted against 25 per cent. J. T. Patterson, *Congressional Conservatism and the New Deal* (Lexington, Ky.: University of Kentucky Press, 1967), 248–9.
139. NA RG 183, BES (USES), Papers of Oxley [Negro U], Box 3, Folder Missouri SES: Letter from Cochran to Persons, 19 Mar. 1938, p. 2.
140. On pre-war patterns of segregation and discrimination see, amongst others, C. S. Johnson, *Patterns of Negro Segregation* (New York: Harper, 1943), chs. 2–6, and esp. Myrdal, *An American Dilemma*, pt. 4. For long-term trends see G. D. Jaynes and R. M. Williams (eds.), *A Common Destiny: Blacks and American Society* (Washington: National Academy Press for the Com. on the Status of Black Americans, National Research Council, 1989).
141. 'Whatever action programs are undertaken should be publicized in such a way as to encourage a more favorable attitude towards minority participation in the war; and to bring home the war issues more clearly to minority members.' HSTL, Papers of Philleo Nash, Box 29, Folder Race Tensions: memo from Nash to Jonathan Daniels Admin. Asst. to the Pres. (7 Aug. 1943).
142. In 1941 A. Philip Randolph, Pres. of the Brotherhood of Sleeping Car Porters, threatened a mass march of Black American workers in Washington if Pres. Roosevelt failed to issue EOs ensuring that they benefited from the expansion of defence contracts to industry and of the armed forces. HSTL, White House Central File, Confidential File, Box 21, Folder Justice Dept. [6 of 10]: FBI, *Survey of Racial Conditions in the US* (16 Oct. 1946), 479. According to the FBI their information revealed that 'thousands of Negroes agreed with A. Philip Randolph', ibid. On the Movement generally see H. Garfinkel, *When Negroes March: The March on Washington Movement in the Organizational Politics of the FEPC* (Glencoe, Ill.: Free Press, 1959); L. C. Kesselman, *The Social Politics of FEPC: A Study in Reform Pressure*

Movements (Chapel Hill, NC: University of North Carolina Press, 1948); and the discussion in J. B. Kirby, *Black Americans in the Roosevelt Era* (Knoxville, Tenn.: University of Tennessee Press, 1980). For a recent assessment of Randolph see W. H. Harris, 'A. Philip Randolph as a Charismatic Leader 1925–1941', *Journal of Negro History* 64 (1979), 301–15.

Randolph also received strategic support from Eleanor Roosevelt, who was unsupportive of the tactic but not of the cause: see LC, Papers of Eleanor Roosevelt, Reel 15: letter to A. Philip Randolph (10 June 1941).

143. HSTL, President's Sec. Files, Box 119, Folder Fair Employment Practice: Memo from FEPC to the Pres. (18 Sept. 1945), 1. It was chaired by Malcolm Ross. The other members were Boris Shishkin, Charles H. Houston, Sara E. Southall, and Milton P. Webster. See Kesselman, *Social Politics of the FEPC*; and L. Ruchames, Race, *Jobs and Politics: The Story of FEPC* (New York: Harper, 1953). Ross was not the first chairman but the longest-serving and *in situ* at the end of the war.
144. This process was aided by the Racial Relations Unit of the USES and a unit within the National Defense Advisory Com.: together they implemented the 'policy of non-discrimination adopted by their respective agencies'.
145. HSTL, Papers of Philleo Nash, Box 20, Folder Official Documents: 'Minority Groups Service', Clarence Johnson (1944), 1.
146. HSTL, President's Com. on Civil Rights, Box 12, Folder Proceedings of the Com.—Transcripts: Data from FEPC 1945, Report cited by Thomas Richardson CIO before the Com. (1 Apr. 1947), 37. See also D. M. Johnson and R. R. Campbell, *Black Migration in America* (Durham, NC: Duke University Press, 1981), 103.
147. See H. Sitkoff, 'Harry Truman and the Election of 1948: The Coming of Age of Civil Rights in American Politics', *Journal of Southern History*, 37 (1971), 597–616.
148. He added: 'Clint, I would think that the Department of Agriculture had more important work to do in behalf of the farmers of this country than to spend the tax payers money by hiring a caste of people to prepare such damned insulting articles as this and then incorporate them in some bulletins to be issued by the Department.' NA RG 16, Records of the Office of the Sec. of Agriculture, General Correspondence, Negroes 1940–55, Box 3, Folder Negroes 1945: correspondence between McGehee and Anderson (15 Nov. 1945).
149. As Bensel writes:

> ideally, the political interests of legislative committees are best served by the creation of permanent central bureaucracies with broad discretionary mandates. During the New Deal, the maturing committee system attempted to turn emergency, temporary programs into permanent bureaucracies. Thus, committees tended to favor civil service provisions over patronage, centrally controlled over federal–state administrative structures, and discretionary language over well-articulated statutes.

Sectionalism and American Political Development 1880–1980, 172.

150. For an account see King, *Actively Seeking Work?*, ch. 3; and I. Katznelson and B. Pietrykowski, 'Rebuilding the American State: Evidence from the 1940s', *Studies in American Political Development*, 5 (1991), 301–39.
151. They were mobilized through the ICESA (the principal representative of the states and, despite Federal funding, effectively an interest lobby). Janoski maintains that

the ICESA 'even opposed raising state workers' salaries for doing the same work as more highly paid federal workers during World War II; it was also accused of lobbying against appropriation bills for the employment service in 1947. T. Janoski, *The Political Economy of Unemployment* (Berkeley and Los Angeles: University of California Press, 1990), 77.

For a discussion of this organization see DDEL, Papers of James P. Mitchell, Box 77, Folder 1955—Administrative—John Gilhooley: Statement on Interstate Conference (July 1955).

152. On Labor's view see NA RG 174, Records of the Dept. of Labor, Subject Files of the Sec., Box 3, Folder AFL 1945: letter from AFL Pres. William Green to Sec. of Labor Schwellenbach (27 Sept. 1945) opposing returning the USES to the states.
153. HSTL, President's Official File, Box 1392, Folder 552 (Jan. 1946) includes an example of this form. The same folder includes numerous letters urging Truman to keep the USES under Federal control.
154. See D. W. Brady, *Critical Elections and Congressional Policy-Making* (Stanford, Calif.: Stanford University Press, 1988).
155. In 1945 Dirksen succeeded in attaching an amendment to the Rescission Bill (HR 4407) in the House Appropriations Com. requiring the USES to be defederalized within thirty days of enactment. The bill was vetoed by Truman.
156. HR 6793, PL 79–549.
157. The distribution of power between the Federal and state govts. limited the former's capacity to influence organization or personnel in the USES: 'the states were responsible for administration. They hired the people and fired them. We required that they do that through a merit system, but we could not substitute our judgment for theirs in the selection of people or getting rid of people. In those areas they had full control.' Local control undoubtedly assisted the persistence of the USES's segregated practices. HSTL, *Oral History of Robert C. Goodwin* (1977), 9.
158. Two bills were introduced in 1946, the Dirksen bill and the Murray-Wagner bill (HR 4437 and S 1848), a social democratic measure which posited the USES as part of a national full employment strategy. The former, which was successful, returned the USES to the states and, significantly, allowed for the USES's financing exclusively by the Federal govt. without state matching funds. 'The Question of Federal or State Control of the Employment Services', *Congressional Digest*, 25 (Apr. 1946).
159. Figures cited in Katznelson and Pietrykowski, 'Rebuilding the American State', 335. The states were required to maintain Federal employees but were empowered to dismiss them when they failed to satisfy state merit systems. By 1950 the vast bulk of the USES's budget was transferred directly to the states—$176 million from a budget of $184 million. Figures from the Federal Security Agency, *Annual Report 1949* (Washington: Government Printing Office), and cited in Katznelson and Pietrykowski, 'Rebuilding the American State', 333.
160. See also National Com. on Segregation in the Nation's Capital, *Segregation in Washington* (report).
161. HSTL, Papers of Philleo Nash, Box 37, Folder WH Files—Civil Rights: Memo from Carr to Truman's Com. on Civil Rights with Background Statement of Civil Rights in DC prepared by Milton Stewart and Rachel Sady (24 Apr. 1947), 3.

162. *Congressional Record*, 67th Congress, 4th sess., vol. lxiv pt. 6 (3 Mar. 1923), 5414.
163. LC NAACP, Group II, Box B102, Folder National Com. on Segregation in the Nation's Capital: letter from U. S. Grant, chairman, to Hon. Arthur G. Klein HR (19 Oct. 1948), 1, 2.
164. Kousser, *Shaping of Southern Politics.*
165. R. Farley and W. R. Allen, *The Color Line and the Quality of Life in America* (New York: Russell Sage Foundation, 1987). On the Ku Klux Klan in the 1920s, see N. MacLean, *Beyond the Mask of Chivalry: The Making of the Second Ku Klux Klan* (Oxford: Oxford University Press, 1994).
166. *Papers of Woodrow Wilson*, xxviii. 350 (letter from John Palmer Gavit to Oswald Garrison Villard, 1 Oct. 1913). The correspondent of the NAACP noted, before 1913, 'the white men and women in the Government service always have resented being compelled to associate with the negroes'. Little was done to accommodate this resentment before the Democratic party success, however. Gavit also noted that the new practices were 'done on the initiative of subordinate chiefs who would like to have done it long ago but dared not, or who, mostly newly-appointed Southerners, took the first opportunity', ibid.
167. Though perhaps a less dramatic break in relation to Black Americans than often assumed. By 1912 the NAACP was openly criticizing the Taft administration's failure to advance Black Americans' interests, and in the case of the Post Office, hindrance of them. See *Crisis* (Feb. 1912).
168. Segregation became 'known as the policy of the present government'. *Papers of Woodrow Wilson*, xxviii. 402: letter to NAACP Pres. Oswald Villard from May Childs Nerny NAACP Sec. (30 Sept. 1913).
169. LC NAACP, Group I, Box C402, File Segregation—Federal Service, 12 July–24 Aug. 1915 (copy in this folder). This direct instruction was unusual. In a study prepared for the NAACP in 1913, May Nerney concluded that the introduction of segregation in govt. agencies rarely reflected explicit instructions but was rather an insidious process: 'no orders have been issued segregating colored people in their work, yet the practice goes on . . . The only official order issued in regard to segregation related to lavatories . . . in force in the Post Office Division, the Treasury Department and the Bureau of Engraving and Printing.' Working by stealth, and in the absence of explicit direction, middle managers actively segregated Black employees with a single outcome in mind: 'Generally the excuse is a readjustment in the work to increase efficiency. In this reorganization clerks are moved from one room to another and when the process is completed the colored clerks always find themselves in some mysterious way together.' *Papers of Woodrow Wilson*, xxviii. 409: letter to Wilson from Oswald Garrison Villard, NAACP Pres., enclosing a report by May Childs Nerney, NAACP Sec. on segregation in govt. depts. (14 Oct. 1913).
170. The Bureau's own director denied that an order existed in a letter to a Congressman enquiring about the segregationist practice: 'I am unable to furnish you with the copy requested as there has been no such formal order issued, but I would add that for a great many years past separate dressing-rooms and wash-rooms have always been provided for the colored employes in this Bureau and recently, in conformity with this custom and because it is a more satisfactory arrangement, separate toilets were assigned for the exclusive use of the colored employes.' NA RG 318, Records

of the Bureau of Engraving and Printing, Central Correspondence File 1913–39, Box 6, File Segregation, 1913: letter from J. E. Ralph Dir. to Congressman E. F. Kinkead (14 Aug. 1913).

171. Ibid.: letter from J. E. Ralph Dir. of the Bureau to Sec. of the Treasury William G. McAdoo (6 Dec. 1913), 2.
172. LC NAACP, Group I, Box C403, File Segregation—Federal Service 27–31 Aug. 1913, contains many letters received during the preparation of the survey. In what follows I draw on various excerpts and summaries from the NAACP study, though I have not seen a complete copy of the report. The LC NAACP papers do not include a copy. Nor does the LC itself.
173. LC NAACP, Group I, Box C403, File Segregation—Federal Service 12 July–24 Aug. 1913: circular letter from NAACP (18 Aug. 1913).
174. It told Woodrow Wilson that 'the colored people everywhere are greatly stirred up over what they consider the hostile attitude of the Administration in regard to colored employees in the government departments'. *Papers of Woodrow Wilson*, xxviii. 60: letter to Wilson from Oswald Garrison Villard (21 July 1913). See also ibid. 209–12: letter from Alfred B. Cosey to Joseph Patrick Tumulty (12 Aug. 1913).
175. Ibid. 403–4: letter to Wilson from Oswald Garrison Villard, NAACP Pres., enclosing a report by May Childs Nerney, NAACP Sec. on segregation in govt. depts. (14 Oct. 1913).
176. LC NAACP, Group I, Box C273, File Discrimination—Government, Federal Service 1925 includes 'Memorandum on Segregation of Civil Service Employees' which documents several cases of segregation. See also the correspondence with individual departments about discrimination in LC NAACP, Group I, Box C403, File Segregation—Federal Service June–Sept. 1928. It includes letters to and from the Office of the Postmaster General, the Sec. of the Treasury, and the Dir. of Public Buildings. In 1925 it appointed a journalist to establish the scale of segregation. The exercise was to be kept 'absolutely secret' until all the 'information that is necessary of that can possibly be secured'. LC NAACP, Group I, Box C273, File Discrimination—Employment, Federal Service 1925: letter from NAACP Sec. to Miller (10 Jan. 1925).
177. LC NAACP, Group I, Box C403, File Segregation—Federal Service 1927: press release by NAACP (19 Aug. 1927) including the letter.
178. Ibid.: letter from Storey to Sec. Work (14 Oct. 1927).
179. Ibid.: letter from NAACP to Coolidge (7 Dec. 1927).
180. Ibid., File Segregation—Federal Service, 6 Mar. 1928–21 Feb. 1929: 'Segregation in Government Departments', Reports of Investigations made by W. T. Andrews and Walter White NAACP (1928).
181. Ibid., File Segregation—Federal Service, 1928: memorandum from Walter White to the Board of Directors NAACP (21 Sept. 1928). He subsequently offered a four-point strategy for ascertaining data about these phenomena, including writing to appointing officers and to leading Black Americans in Washington, and interviewing the Civil Service Com. Ibid.: memorandum from Walter White to the Conference of Executives NAACP (17 Oct. 1928).
182. National Com. on Segregation in the Nation's Capital, *Segregation in Washington* (report), 63. For the background to this study see LC NAACP, Group II, Box A386,

File National Com. on Segregation in the Nation's Capital 1942–9, which includes minutes of the meeting at which the study was agreed upon. In particular see the meeting of 23 Oct. 1946 which includes a detailed plan for the report's remit.

183. LC NAACP, Group I, Box C403, File Segregation—Federal Service, 1928: letter from Col. U. S. Grant, Dir. of Public Buildings to James Johnson Sec. NAACP (4 June 1928). For Johnson's reply see ibid.: letter (19 June 1928).
184. Ibid., File Segregation—Federal Service Oct.–Nov. 1928: Letters from Chief, Division of Personnel GAO to NAACP (3 Oct 1928); Sec. of the Navy (8 Oct. 1928); and Dept. of the Interior (16 Oct. 1928).
185. LC Papers of Eleanor Roosevelt Reel 19: letter from Roy Wilkins to Eleanor Roosevelt (20 May 1935). Wilkins continued: 'the NRA benefited them little, if at all; from the PWA they secured a very small amount of employment; from the AAA the black tenants and sharecroppers have thus far received little consideration; the FERA has benefited them some, but there has been a great deal of discrimination in its administration.' Writing to the Sec. of the Interior Harold Ickes in 1934, the Boston branch of the NAACP reported 'widespread belief . . . among the Negroes of New England that there is discrimination against them in the allotment of federal, state and municipal monies conducted under the authority and direction of your department.' NA RG 48, Records of the Dept. of the Interior, Office of the Sec., Central Classified File 1907–36, Box 506, Folder Racial Discrimination—General: letter (23 Jan. 1934).

    It was suggested to Ickes on several occasions that an advisory committee for Black Americans be appointed to monitor the New Deal programmes but without action: see correspondence in NA RG 48, Records of the Dept. of the Interior, Records of Sec. H. L. Ickes, General Subject File 1933–42, Box 10, Folder Misc. correspondence relating to Negroes. However, Clark Foreman was appointed in the Interior Dept. to oversee the interests of Black Americans.

    For general accounts see amongst others Patterson, *Congressional Conservatism and the New Deal*; R. Wolters, *Negroes and the Great Depression* (Westport, Conn.: Greenwood, 1970); R. J. Bunche, *The Political Status of the Negro in the Age of FDR* (1940; Chicago: 1973); and Bensel, *Sectionalism and American Political Development 1880–1980*, chs. 4, 5. See also K. T. Jackson, *Crabgrass Frontier*.
186. *Pittsburgh Courier* (15 Apr. 1939.) See NA RG 16, Records of the Office of the Sec. of Agriculture, General Correspondence, Negroes 1924–39, Box 2, Folder Negroes 1939.
187. NA RG 228 Records of the FEPC, Office Files of John A. Davis, Box 358, Folder Civil Service—Negro: 'The Wartime Enforcement of the Non-Discrimination Policy in the Federal Government: Techniques and Accomplishments' (n.d.), 3.
188. An interdepartmental group 'concerned with the special problems of Negroes', established in the mid-1930s, spent much of their time monitoring and worrying about the limited employment opportunities proffered Black Americans on New Deal programmes: see NA RG 48, Records of the Dept. of the Interior, Records of Interior Dept. Officials, Records of Sec. Harold L. Ickes, General Subject File 1933–42, Box 10, Folder Misc. correspondence relating to Negroes: minutes of the second and third meetings of the interdepartmental group concerned with the special problems of Negroes (1934). The minutes of these and other meetings

record extensive discussion of two topics: discrimination against Black workers on public works projects, and the baneful effect of trade unions for the employment opportunities of Black Americans.

189. As Richard Bensel writes: 'the enrollment of Roosevelt appointees in the civil service after 1936 increased core dominance of the central, Washington-based bureaucracy by raising educational standards beyond the reach of the periphery's young adults (who were the product of an impoverished, substandard educational system) and by further reducing bureaucratic sensitivity to political influence.' *Sectionalism and American Political Development 1880–1980*, 152.
190. LC NAACP, Group II-A, Box A237, Folder Discrimination and Segregation–Government Agencies 1941–55: letter to Walter White from Roy Wilkins (2 Mar. 1942).
191. Ibid.: letter from Tomy Jones to the ed. *Crisis* (16 Feb. 1942).
192. Ibid.: letter from Roy Wilkins NAACP to Lieut. Col. A. F. White Chief Machine Records Branch War Dept. (9 Mar. 1945).
193. Ibid.: letter from Roy Wilkins NAACP to Harold Ickes Sec. Dept. of Interior (14 Apr. 1943).
194. LC NAACP, Group, II-B, Box B183, Folder TVA General 1940–5: letter to Walter White from Gordon R. Clapp Gen. Manager TVA (24 Sept. 1945), 1.
195. NA RG 228, Records of the FEPC, Office Files of the Chairman, Box 63, Folder D: memorandum from Daniel Donovan and Elmer Henderson to Lawrence Cramer, 'Employment of Negro Women at Norfolk Navy Yard, Portsmouth, Virginia' (29 Sept. 1942), 2.
196. Ibid., Office Files of Cornelius Golightly, Box 398, Folder Race: 'Philadelphia Transportation Company Employees' Strike' (7 Aug. 1944).
197. Harvard Sitkoff records the popular slogan of Black recruits, epitomizing their resentment toward segregation: 'here lies a black man killed fighting a yellow man for the glory of a white man': 'Racial Militancy and Interracial Violence in the Second World War', 666–7.
198. Key Jr., *Politics, Parties and Pressure Groups*, 137.
199. NA RG 228, Records of the FEPC, Office Files of John A. Davis, Box 358, Folder Civil Service—Negro: 'The Wartime Enforcement of the Non-Discrimination Policy in the Federal Government: Techniques and Accomplishments' (n.d.), 3.
200. Ibid., Office Files of Malcolm Ross, Box 69, Folder Reports to the Pres.: see memorandum from Malcolm Ross chairman FEPC to Pres. Truman (1 Mar. 1946), commenting on the race riot in Columbia, Tenn.; Woodward, *The Strange Career of Jim Crow* (New York: Oxford University Press, 3rd edn. 1974), 114; and Sitkoff, 'Racial Militancy and Interracial Violence', 674.
201. HSTL, Papers of Philleo Nash, Box 29, Folder Race Tensions; Memo from Nash, Ass. to Deputy Dir. Office of War Information to Jonathan Daniels Admin. Asst. to the Pres. 'Certain Angles of the Minorities Problem' (7 Aug. 1943).
202. For one discussion see W. Z. Foster *et al.*, *The Communist Position on the Negro Question* (New York: New Century Publishers, 1947).
203. NA RG 228, Records of the FEPC, Office Files of Malcolm Ross, Box 67: letter from Acheson to Ross (8 May 1946).
204. NA RG 16, Records of the Office of the Sec. of Agriculture, General Correspondence,

Negroes 1940–55, Box 3, Folder Negroes 1952: text of speech by Eugenie Anderson, American Ambassador to Denmark (16 Jan. 1952), 1. The speech consisted principally of a historical lecture.

205. HSTL, Papers of Philleo Nash, Box 29, Folder 1943–5: memo for David Niles (n.d.), prepared by Philleo Nash, Asst. to Deputy Dir. Office of War Information.
206. He wrote: 'a considerable number of loyal and qualified employees have been refused transfer and reemployment by employing agencies solely because of race and creed. This condition is a violation of civil service rules which have been issued by the President and in violation of existing rules.' HSTL, Papers of David Niles, Box 26, Folder Civil Rights/Negro Affairs 1945–7: Circular from Truman (18 Dec. 1945).
207. Ibid.: memo from Truman (18 Dec. 1945).
208. See also NA RG 228, Records of the FEPC, Office Files of George M. Johnson, Box 74, Folder John A. Davis: memorandum from John A. Davis to Will Maslow, 'Resistance of White Workers to Negro Workers because of Fear of Job Security after the War' (21 Aug. 1943).
209. NA RG 174, Records of the Dept. of Labor, Office of the Sec., Subject Files, Schwellenbach Box 31, Folder Discrimination: letter from chairman Roy Patterson to Sec. of Labor (16 Dec. 1947), 5. In response Schwellenbach restated the Department's anti-discrimination policy to staff in Jan. 1948. The hiring officer was Mr Lester S. Kellogg.
210. Ibid.: letter from Roy Patterson to Sec. of Labor (16 Dec. 1947), 6.
211. HSTL, Papers of David Niles, Box 26, Folder Civil Rights/Negro Affairs 1945–7: letter from Truman to Clark (20 Sept. 1946).
212. Ibid. The letter was copied to Niles. In *Quest and Response* (Lawrence, Kan.: Univ. Press of Kansas, 1973), 481 D. McCoy and M. Ruetten confirm that this meeting stimulated the commission proposal though initially Truman planned to ask Congress to establish it, a strategy likely to be blocked, predicted NAACP leader White.
213. H. Sitkoff, 'Harry Truman and the Election of 1948: The Coming of Age of Civil Rights in American Elections', *Journal of Southern History*, 37 (1971), 597–616.

CHAPTER 2

1. See H. Parris, *Constitutional Bureaucracy: The Development of British Central Administration since the Eighteenth Century* (London: Allen & Unwin, 1969).
2. See B. S. Silberman, *Cages of Reason* (Chicago: University of Chicago Press, 1993).
3. A Hoogenboom, 'The Pendleton Act and the Civil Service', *American Historical Review*, 64 (1959), 302.
4. Named after its prime senatorial sponsor Sen. George Pendleton of Ohio. For details see S. Skowronek, *Building a New American State* (New York: Cambridge University Press, 1982); and P. P. Van Riper; *History of the United States Civil Service* (Evanston, Ill.: Row, Peterson and Co., 1958), ch. 5.
5. *Congressional Record*, House, Proceedings and Debates, 47th Congress, 2nd Sess., vol xiv (12 Dec. 1882), 226–30.

6. *Congressional Record*, Proceedings and Debates, 47th Congress, 2nd Sess., vol. xiv (4 Jan. 1883), 860–1.
7. Ibid. (12 Dec. 1882), 204.
8. Ibid.
9. Ibid. He gave examples from the Treasury again and other unidentified depts.
10. Ibid. 205.
11. Ibid. 206.
12. Pendleton stated:

    We do know now that so great has been the increase of the powers of this Government and the number of officers under it that no President, no Cabinet, no heads of bureaus, can by possibility know the fitness of all applicants for the subordinate offices of the Government. The result has been, and under the existing system it must always be, that the President and his Cabinet and those who are charged with the responsibility have remitted the question of fitness to their own partisan friends, and those partisan friends have in their turn decided the question of fitness in favor of their partisan friends. The Administration has need of the support of members of Congress in carrying out its work. It therefore remits to members of Congress of its own party the questions of appointment to office in various districts. These gentlemen, in the course of their political life, naturally (I do not find fault with them for it) find themselves under strain and pressure to secure a nomination or election, and they use the places to reward those whose friends and families and connections and aids and deputies will serve their purposes.

    (Ibid.)
13. Ibid.
14. Ibid.
15. Ibid. 208.
16. It replaced the Grant Civil Service Com., known as the Advisory Board of the Civil Service, established under an Act of 1871.
17. See the discussion in N. Miller, *Theodore Roosevelt: A Life* (New York: Quill William Morrow, 1992), ch. 10; and Hoogenboom, 'The Pendleton Act and the Civil Service', 301–18.
18. Thus, of the Com.'s first seventeen years, Skowronek observes:

    from the administration of Chester Arthur through that of William McKinley, the Civil Service Commission struggled for recognition at the periphery of power. It supervised examinations, made investigations, recommended rules to govern federal personnel, and requested disciplinary action; but enforcement depended entirely on the President and the department heads. The problems the commission faced in American government during these years reflected the contradictions of its creation. By its very nature it challenged the power base of party professionals; its raison d'etre was to place administrative offices outside the sphere of party politics. Yet, its fate was in the hands of officials who were nothing if not good party men.

    (*Building a New American State*, 68.)
19. Ibid. 68–9. I draw upon this analysis for this para.
20. US Civil Service Com., *Eleventh Report of the US Civil Service Commission July 1 1893 to June 30 1894* (Washington: Government Printing Office, 1895), 143.
21. Skowronek, *Building a New American State*, 69; he puts the figure at 113,161. His source is D. H. Smith, *The United States Civil Service Commission* (Baltimore: Johns Hopkins University Press, 1928), 37.
22. Skowronek, *Building a New American State*, 69.

23. Ibid. 83.
24. US Civil Service Com., *Eleventh Report July 1 1893 to June 30 1894*, 20.
25. Even Leonard White, a tirelessly sanguine chronicler of the Federal bureaucracy, is provoked into a critical assessment of this service: 'faithful enforcement of the merit system was a constant problem, and no one could assert that the Post Office had been taken out of politics. Congressmen (or referees) continued in substance to name local postmasters, normally for political reasons. It was a great advance when McKinley adopted the policy of not removing fourth-class postmasters until their four-year terms had expired. Clerks, moreover, continued to rely on congressional aid in time of trouble. In return they did favors for the members from their districts.'

    L. D. White, *The Republican Era 1869–1901* (Chicago: University of Chicago Press, 1958), 269. See also discussions and reports in NA RG 146, Records of the US Civil Service Commission, Minutes 1886–1929, boxes 1–32. There are no post-1929 records in the NA.
26. Van Riper, *History of the United States Civil Service*, 187–9.
27. *Building a New American State*, 186.
28. The report continued:

    > Of the 159,399 persons whose positions are not subject to competitive examination under the civil service rules, 10,397 are presidential appointees, 8,228 being postmasters of the first, second, and third classes; 36,228 are fourth-class postmasters; 12,850 were reported in 1907 as clerks at post offices having no free-delivery service; 28,191 are minor employees; 729 are employees of the Department of Commerce and of Labor, most of them in the Census Bureau, all appointed through examination or some other method prescribed by the Thirteenth Census act; 18,788 unclassified employees in the field service, and 2,056 in Washington are in the main mere unskilled laborers; and approximately 25,000 are mechanics and laborers at Navy yards, subject to appointment under navy-yard regulations.

    US Civil Service Com., *Twenty-Ninth Annual Report of the US Civil Service Commission for the FY ended June 30 1912* (Washington: GPO, 1913), 10–11.
29. NA RG 146, Records of the US Civil Service Commission, Minutes 1886–1929, boxes 1–32. See LC: Papers of Joseph Tumulty (esp. box 124 which contains the 'black book' documenting all patronage appointments) and the Papers of Albert S. Burleson.
30. US Civil Service Com., *Thirty-First Annual Report of the US Civil Service Commission for the FY ended June 30 1914* (Washington: GPO, 1915), 16.
31. NA RG 228, Records of the FEPC, Office Files of John A. Davis, Box 358, Folder Civil Service: 'The Wartime Enforcement of the Non-discrimination Policy in the Federal Government: Techniques and Accomplishments', 2.
32. US Civil Service Com., *Eighth Report of the US Civil Service Commission July 1 1890 to June 30 1891* (Washington: GPO, 1891), 6.
33. US Civil Service Com., *Eleventh Report July 1 1893 to June 30 1894*, 319–21.
34. Ibid.
35. Ibid. 319.
36. Ibid. 321.
37. *The Letters of Theodore Roosevelt*, ed. E. E. Morison, J. M. Blum, and J. J. Buckley, 8 vols. (Cambridge, Mass.: Harvard University Press, 1951–4). Letter from Roosevelt to Hugh McKittrick, 21 Feb. 1895, ibid. i. 427–8, cited in Hoogenboom, 'The Pendleton Act and the Civil Service', 307.

38. Van Riper, *History of the United States Civil Service*, 284–5; and see F. M. Stewart, *The National Civil Service Reform League* (Austin, Tex.: University of Texas, 1929).
39. *Building a New American State*, 69.
40. NA RG 146, Records of the US Civil Service Commission, Minutes 1886–1929, Box 21: Minutes of the meeting (27 May 1914), 228.
41. LC NAACP, Group I, Box C272, File Discrimination—Employment, Federal Service: see letters to the Com. from Wilson and Waters, lawyers (27 July 1914). In another letter (20 Aug. 1914), the same firm noted: 'the reason given by the Commission for the photograph scheme—"namely, to assist in the identification of applicants when they present themselves for examination"—does not appear in any publication issued by the Commission to date.'
42. NA RG 146, Records of the US Civil Service Commission, Minutes 1886–1929, Box 21: Minutes of the meeting (27 May 1914), 228.
43. LC NAACP, Group I, Box C272, File Discrimination—Employment, Federal Service 1913–15: letter from NAACP Chairman to Wilson (23 Mar. 1915).
44. Van Riper, *History of the United States Civil Service*, 241.
45. LC NAACP, Group I, Box C273, File Discrimination—Employment, Federal Service, 1924: letter from Prof. Kelly Miller to William Dudley Foulke, Pres. of the Civil Service Reform Association (18 Sept. 1923).
46. Ibid.: reported in *Washington Post* (22 Dec. 1924).
47. LC NAACP, Group I Box C403, File Segregation—Federal Service, 6 Mar. 1928–21 Feb. 1929: 'Segregation in Government Departments', reports of Investigations made by W. T. Andrews and Walter White NAACP (1928), 2.
48. Figures from L. J. W. Hayes, *The Negro Federal Government Worker* (Washington: Howard University, 1941), 37–58, cited in Van Riper, *History of the United States Civil Service*, 242.
49. *History of the United States Civil Service*, 242.
50. e.g. the NAACP was increasingly critical of Pres. Taft as his presidency unfolded. Its view was expressed in *Crisis*, 3 (Feb. 1912), 141:

    > President Taft has again indicated his hostility toward Negroes by signing an executive order, providing that in the case of all free rural delivery appointments, three eligibles shall be certified in each instance to the appointing office instead of one, as in the past. This appears to be done for the purpose of preventing colored men who pass the examinations from being appointed.

    The position of rural carriers was one which Black Americans could hope to acquire.
51. NA RG 228, Records of the FEPC, Office Files of John A. Davis, Box 358, Folder Civil Service—Negro: 'The Wartime Enforcement of the Non-Discrimination Policy in the Federal Government: Techniques and Accomplishments' (n.d.), 3.
52. 76th Congress, 1st sess., HR 186, 'A Bill to prohibit the President of the United States and the United States Civil Service Commission, or any branch thereof from requiring, as a condition precedent to the taking of an examination for a position in the classified civil service or as a condition precedent to an appointment in such a service, a photograph of applicants for such examinations.' The bill was introduced on 3 Jan. 1939 by Congressman Mitchell. NA RG 233, Records of the US House of Representatives, HR 76A–D5 (HR 27–10728), Box 14975, Folder 76th Congress: Accompanying Papers Com. on the Civil Service D5 (1), HR 27–4219.

53. NA RG 233 Records of the US House of Representatives, HR 76A–D5 (HR 27–10728), Box 14975, Folder: 76th Congress: Accompanying Papers Com. on the Civil Service D5 (1), HR 27–4219. Letter from Harry B. Mitchell, Pres. US Civil Service Com. to Representative Robert Ramspeck (8 Jan. 1940), 1.
54. Ibid. 2.
55. Ibid.
56. For details see US Civil Service Com., *Annual Report* (Washington: GPO, 1923), 127–35; 'Congress Provides New Classification for Civil Service Employees', *Congressional Digest* (Apr. 1923), 206–12; and Van Riper, *History of the United States Civil Service*, ch. 12 esp. 296–304. The Act created the following services: Professional and Scientific Service; Subprofessional Service; the Clerical, Administrative and Fiscal Service; the Custodial Service; and the Clerical-Mechanical Service. Within each service grades were specified rising in importance.
57. See US Civil Service Com., *Fifty-fifth Annual Report of the US Civil Service Commission for the FY ended June 30 1938* (Washington: GPO, 1939), 28–33: 'Early Historical Background of the Classification Act of 1923'.
58. In 1928 the Welch Act was passed by Congress amending the 1923 legislation, requiring the Personnel Classification Board to undertake a survey of field positions, and raising salaries. The former exercise had been abandoned in 1923. The field survey was not implemented but according to Van Riper its recommendations served 'as the principal examples available for the guidance of federal personnel officers until the end of World War II'. Van Riper, *History of the United States Civil Service*, 303.
59. See R. J. Bunche, *The Political Status of the Negro in the Age of FDR* (1940; Chicago: University of Chicago Press, 1973), esp. 115–16.
60. Van Riper writes: 'by 1930 the merit system seemed as firmly entrenched as it had appeared to be in 1913. More than 80 percent of federal public employees occupied competitive positions within the classified service, leaving only 100,000 or so positions outside the merit system. This group represented both the highest and the lowest of the federal positions, with the bulk of the exempt positions specifically excluded from the merit system by the terms of the Pendleton Act.' *History of the United States Civil Service*, 312.
61. US Civil Service Com., *Fiftieth Annual Report of the US Civil Service Commission for the FY ended June 30 1933* (Washington: GPO, 1933), 2.
62. *History of the United States Civil Service*, 320.
63. US Senate, 85th Congress 1st sess., Report to the Com. on Post Office and Civil Service, 'Administration of the Civil Service System' (1957), 38.
64. EO 7916 of 24 June 1938 provided for the inclusion within the classified civil service of all positions in the executive branch. Sect. V of the EO instructed the Civil Service Com. to 'initiate, supervise and enforce a system as uniform as practicable for the recruitment, examination, certification, promotion from grade to grade, transfer and reinstatement of employees in the classified Civil Service . . . which system shall so far as practicable be competitive with due regard to prior experience and service'. HSTL, Papers of Philleo Nash, Box 4, Folder Civil Service Com.—Non-discrimination: cited in memo for the files (8 Apr. 1947).
65. HSTL, President's Com. on Civil Rights, Box 5, Folder Civil Service Com.: letter from Mitchell US Civil Service Com. to Carr (19 Mar. 1947), 2–3.

66. NA RG 46, Records of the US Civil Service Com., Minutes of Proceedings, Boxes 1–31.
67. See also NA RG 228, Records of the FEPC, Office Files of Malcolm Ross, Box 64, Folder Civil Service: letter from Harry B. Mitchell Pres. US Civil Service Com. to Ross (19 July 1944).
68. House of Representatives, 78th Congress, 1st sess. on H Res 16 Hearing before the Com. on the Civil Service, 'A Resolution to Authorize the Committee on the Civil Service to Investigate Various Activities in the Departments and Agencies of the Government', pts. 1, 2, and 3 (Mar. 1943): 10 Mar. 1943 p. 16. See also NA RG 233, Records of the US House of Representatives, HR 76A–D5 (HR27–10728), Box 14975, Folder 76th Congress: Accompanying Papers Com. on the Civil Service D5 (1) HR27–4219, letter from Harry Mitchell, Pres. US Civil Service Com. to Representative Robert Ramspeck (9 Jan. 1940), explaining the origins of the system and opposing its reform.
69. NA RG 318, Records of the Bureau of Engraving and Printing, Central Corrrespondence Files 1913–39, Box 64, Folder Employees—Colored, 1920: Resolution of the DC NAACP branch (1919).
70. NA RG 228 Records of the FEPC, Office Files of George M. Johnson, Box 74, Folder Employment of Negroes in the Federal Govt.: FEPC Division of Review and Analysis, 'The Wartime Employment of Negroes in the Federal Government' (Jan. 1945), 27.
71. LC NAACP, Group I, Box C228, File Civil Service Cases B–C: Letter from Borras to Charles Houston Special Counsel NAACP (30 Dec. 1936).
72. Ibid.: letter from Charles Houston Special Counsel NAACP to James A. Farley Postmaster Gen. of the USA (5 Jan. 1937).
73. Ibid.: letter to Charles Houston Special Counsel NAACP from W. W. Howes 1st Asst. Postmaster Gen. of the USA (14 Jan. 1937).
74. Ibid.: letter from Charles Houston Special Counsel NAACP to W. W. Howes 1st Asst. Postmaster Gen. of the USA (19 Jan. 1937).
75. Ibid.
76. Ibid.: letter to Charles Houston Special Counsel NAACP from W. W. Howes 1st Asst. Postmaster Gen. of the USA (27 Jan. 1937).
77. NA RG 174, Records of the Dept. of Labor, Office of the Sec. (Perkins), General Subject Files, Box 127, Folder FEPC 1942: memorandum from Robert Smith to the Sec. of Labor (16 Apr. 1942).
78. LC NAACP, Group I, Box C273, File Discrimination—Employment, Federal Service 1932: 'Discrimination US Customs Service', memorandum about Cunningham. The problem was linked to a Southern appointee in the Civil Service Commission: 'during the twelve years of Mr Coles' incumbency no colored man has been appointed, though there are three colored inspectors who were appointed prior to Mr Coles assuming his present position.' Ibid. 1.
79. NA RG 233 Records of the US House of Representatives, HR 76A–D5 (HR27–10728), Box 14975, Folder 76th Congress: Accompanying Papers Committee on the Civil Service D5 (1), HR 27–4219: letter from Harry Mitchell, Pres. US Civil Service Commission to Representative Robert Ramspeck (9 Jan. 1940).
80. House of Representatives, 78th Congress, 1st sess. on H Res 16, Hearing before the Com. on the Civil Service, 'A Resolution to Authorize the Committee on the Civil

Service to Investigate Various Activities in the Departments and Agencies of the Government', pts. 1, 2, and 3 (Mar. 1943): (10 Mar. 1943), 32; Congressman Arthur G. Klein speaking.

81. Ibid.
82. LC NAACP, Group II-A, Box A234, Folder Discrimination, Civil Service—Henry Alston 1940–3: Letter from Alston to FEPC (9 Feb. 1943), 1.
83. Ibid.: see Alston's original handwritten letter to Thurgood Marshall (4 Jan. 1940).
84. Ibid.: letter from E. H. Jennings District Manager Tenth US Civil Service District to Henry Alston (28 Jan. 1941).
85. Ibid., Box A194, Folder Civil Service General 1940–55: 'Statement Proposing an Investigation of a Concentration of Negro Eligibles on the Civil Service Certificates Prior to Displacement by New Releases' (Aug. 1940), 1, 2.
86. HSTL, Papers of Philleo Nash, Box 4, Folder Civil Service Commission—Non-discrimination: Nash to Niles (8 Apr. 1947), 1.
87. Ibid.
88. NA RG 228, Records of the FEPC, Office of the Com. Box 1, Folder Minutes: President's FEPC (18 Jan. 1942), 1–2.
89. NA RG 188, Records of OPA, Records of Racial Relations Advisor, Box 13, Folder Statistics—Negro E: Elmer W. Henderson, 'The Employment of Negroes in the Federal Government', FEPC (1 Mar. 1943), 1.
90. LC NAACP, Group II-A, Box A194, Folder Civil Service General 1940–55: memorandum to Mrs Anna Rosenberg, Regional Dir. WMC from John Beecher, Regional Representative, President's FEPC 'Governmental Discrimination Against Negroes' (5 Nov. 1942), 1.
91. NA RG 146, Civil Service Agencies, FEB, Correspondence with Agencies 1948–54, Box 3, Folder Labor Dept.: Summary of Discussion of the 110th Meeting of the FEB (18 May 1951), 1.
92. LC NAACP, Group II-B, Box 9, Folder Civil Service 1948–9: FEB Informational Bulletin, 1 (24 Aug. 1949), 1.
93. Ibid. 2.
94. LC NAACP, II-A, Box A194, Folder Ramspeck Bill 1940: letter from Harry Mitchell to Sen. Mead (20 Nov. 1940).
95. NA RG 228, Records of the FEPC, Office Files of Malcolm Ross, Box 68: 'Report A' attachment to a letter from Arthur Flemming, Acting Pres. of the US Civil Service Com. to Ross (1 Apr. 1946).
96. *History of the United States Civil Service*, 333.
97. HSTL, President's Com. on Civil Rights, Box 5, Folder Civil Service Com.: letter from Harry Mitchell Pres. US Civil Service Com. to Robert Carr (19 Mar. 1947).
98. Ibid. 6.
99. LC NAACP, Group II-A, Box A194, Folder Civil Service Gen., 1940–55: memorandum prepared for Walter White (19 Nov. 1942).
100. Ibid.: memorandum to Mrs Anna Rosenberg, Regional Dir. WMC from John Beecher, Regional Representative, President's FEPC 'Governmental Discrimination Against Negroes' (5 Nov. 1942), 1–2.
101. NA RG 228, Records of the FEPC, Office Files of George M. Johnson, Box 293,

Folder Field Reports: memorandum from G. James Fleming to Lawrence Cramer, executive Sec. (19 Sept. 1942), 1.

102. Ibid.
103. LC NAACP, Group II-A, Box A194, Folder Civil Service: letter from White to Roosevelt (12 Sept. 1941), 1.
104. HSTL, President's Com. on Civil Rights, Box 10 Folder NAACP: letter from White (21 Apr. 1947), 1.
105. LC NAACP, Group II, Box A653, Folder USES 1940–2, General: affidavit of Luella Thompson (17 May 1940). The District Manager was Mr W. R. Leath.
106. HSTL, President's Com. on Civil Rights, Box 10, Folder NAACP: letter from White to Truman (21 Apr. 1947), 2.
107. Ibid.: memo from Carr to David Niles (30 Apr. 1947).
108. LC NAACP, Gorup II-A, Box A194, Folder Civil Service—President's Com. on Civil Service Improvement 1940: letter from W. A. Hunton, Spokesman for the Delegation to the US Civil Service Com. (6 Aug. 1940), 1.
109. NA RG 146, Civil Service Agencies, FEB, Correspondence with Agencies 1948–54, Box 3, Folder Labor Dept.: letter from James Houghteling, chairman FEB, to Robert Goodwin (25 May 1951).
110. HSTL, President's Com. on Civil Rights, Box 10, Folder National Com. on Segregation in the Nation's Capital: memo 'Implementing Non-Discrimination in Federal Employment' (19 July 1947), 1.
111. Ibid.: memo from Bradbury to Stewart (19 July 1947), 1.
112. Ibid.: memo from Bradbury to Carr (19 July 1947), 2.
113. There were three subcommittees dealing with (1) Federal laws and the remedy of their inequities or inadequacies; (2) social, economic, and public relations dimensions of civil rights; and (3) factors responsible for the denial or weakening of civil rights.
114. HSTL, President's Com. on Civil Rights, Box 12, Folder Proceedings of the Com.—Transcripts (20 Mar. 1947), 3.
115. See also NA RG 228, Records of the FEPC, Office Files of John Davis, Box 361, Folder memoranda: memorandum from John A. Davis to FEPC Postwar Planning Com. (22 Sept. 1944).
116. HSTL, President's Com. on Civil Rights, Box 12, Folder Proceedings—Transcripts (1 Apr. 1947), 12.
117. For a general discussion of the often hostile position of US trade unionists toward civil rights see P. S. Foner, *Organized Labor and the Black Worker 1619–1981* (New York: International Publishers, 2nd edn. 1982).
118. HSTL, President's Com. on Civil Rights, Box 12, Folder Proceedings (1 Apr. 1947), 35–6 (Testimony of Thomas Richardson, International Vice-Pres. of the United Public Workers section of the CIO).
119. Ibid. 36.
120. Ibid. 37.
121. Ibid. 38.
122. Ibid. 39.
123. Ibid. 40.
124. Ibid. 45.

125. In his testimony to the Civil Rights Com., CIO officer George Weaver (later appointed Asst. Sec. of Labor by Kennedy) stressed the potential of the USES in advancing Black Americans' employment:

> in light of our experiences, we feel [the USES] is one of the key government agencies. If properly utilized, it could be of tremendous aid in advancing democracy in industry. The discriminatory practices which have and still do prevail in USES highlight the need for state and federal fair employment practice legislation.

Ibid. 65–6.

126. Ibid. 48.
127. NA RG 183, Records of the BES/USES, Records of Lawrence A. Oxley, Reports of Investigation of Negro Unemployment and Public Placement Facilities for Negroes 1937–9, Box 1, Folder Birmingham AL (Discrimination). The letter's author was a Mr Emory O. Jackson who wrote on 3 May. Oxley replied on 5 May promising to investigate the matter. See also the letter from Flora P. Carter of 10 May 1938 complaining about failure to gain work in the USES.
128. Truman seemed initially to support the proposal to maintain Federal control of the USES but a powerfully orchestrated campaign by the USES state offices with the support of key congressional members ensured that the state control was re-established in 1946. A year later the NAACP Labor Sec., Clarence Mitchell, was reporting discrimination to the Congress: 'more than a thousand NAACP branches throughout the country have almost all had first hand experience with state employment service discrimination against colored job applicants.' LC NAACP, Group II, Box A653, Folder USES Discrimination 1944–7: NAACP press release (25 Apr. 1947), 1. The state employment offices' pressure group, the ICESA, received powerful support from the House of Representatives Health, Education Welfare–Labor Appropriations Subcommittee whose chairman, John Fogarty, was an indefatigable defender of the USES and of its decentralized organization.
129. See NA RG 228, Records of the FEPC, Office Files of Malcolm Ross, Box 68, 'Report A' attachment to a letter from Arthur Flemming, Acting Pres. of the US Civil Service Commission to Ross, 1 Apr. 1946.
130. Ibid., Office Files of John A. Davis, Box 358, Folder Civil Service—Negro: 'The Wartime Enforcement of the Non-Discrimination Policy in the Federal Government: Techniques and Accomplishments' (n.d.), 2.
131. Ibid. 4–5.
132. Ibid., Folder Agreements with Other Agencies, 1.
133. Ibid., Office Files of Malcolm Ross, Box 64, Folder Civil Service: memorandum to all FEPC Regional Directors from Will Maslow Director of Field Operations' 'Civil Service Commission' (11 Aug. 1944).
134. Ibid., Office Files of John A. Davis, Box 358, Folder Civil Service—Negro: 'The Wartime Enforcement of the Non-Discrimination Policy in the Federal Government: Techniques and Accomplishments' (n.d.), 5.
135. G. Goodwin Jr., 'The Seniority System in Congress', *American Political Science Review*, 53 (1959), 433. In the Senate the Com. on DC was ranked lowest; in the House Veterans Affairs.
136. J. P. Harris, *Congressional Control of Administration* (Washington: Brookings Institution, 1964), 165.

137. US Civil Service Com., *69th Annual Report* (Washington: Government Printing Office, 1952), 20.
138. US Congress House of Representatives, 84th Congress, 2nd sess., *The Civil Service Commission*, House Report No. 1844 (Mar. 1956).
139. HSTL, President's Com. on Civil Rights, Box 12, Folder Proceedings of the Com.—Transcripts: Confidential minutes (1 Apr. 1947), 2, 3.
140. 'We say that the mere existence of a Federal policy of non-discrimination is not effective. The national wartime policy of non-discrimination was not cancelled by the enforcement agency, FEPC, going out of the picture. That is still there, but it is not observed.' Ibid. 4.
141. HSTL, Papers of Philleo Nash, Box 20, Folder Official Documents—Nash Files: 'Minority Groups Service—War Manpower Commission', Clarence Johnson (1944), 3.
142. HSTL, President's Com. on Civil Rights, Box 15, Folder NUL: 'Civil Liberties Implications of the Employment, Housing and Education Problems of Minorities' (1 Apr. 1947), 1.
143. Ibid. 4.
144. Ibid., Box 16, Folder Discrimination in Govt. Employment: memo from Carr to the Com. by Stewart and Murtha (23 June 1947), 1.
145. Ibid.
146. NA RG 220, President's Com. on Govt. Employment Policy 1955–61, Agency Files, Box 13, File Civil Service Commission: US Civil Service Com. Interagency Advisory Group, Summary of 132nd Meeting (3 Nov. 1960), esp. 3–4.
147. Ibid.: letter from Ross Clinchy, Com. Executive Dir., to John W. Macey, chairman US Civil Service Com. (1 Feb. 1961), 1–2.
148. Ibid. 2.
149. Ibid.
150. LC NAACP, Group III-A, Box A144, Folder Govt., National Civil Service Com. 1958–65: letter from Arthur J. Chapital New Orleans Chapter NAACP to Louis Lyon Regional Dir. Civil Service Com. 8th Region (13 Nov. 1961), 1.
151. Ibid. 2.
152. Ibid.:, letter from Louis Lyons Regional Dir. to Arthur J. Chapital New Orleans Chapter NAACP (24 Dec. 1961), 1.
153. Ibid. 2–3.
154. The NAACP assisted many Black Amerians to file complaints with the President's Com. on Govt. Employment Policy charging racial discrimination. See LC NAACP, Washington Bureau, Boxes 84 and 85.
155. See the extensive files, ibid., Boxes 29–32. A failed applicant for the job of Investigator-Trainee wrote to the NAACP in 1952 that 'you will note that listed among the requirements for the position is one to the effect that the appointee "must be able to meet all segments of the public." It is my belief that they are interpreting that provision in a manner which discriminates against Negroes.' Ibid., Box 29, File Civil Service Com.: letter from Arthur L Lane to Clarence Mitchell, 2 May 1952.
156. EO 11246.
157. US Civil Service Commission, *Eighty-Sixth Annual Report for 1968* (Washington: US Civil Service Commission, 1968), 15.

158. LC NAACP, Washington Bureau, Box 29, File Civil Service Commission 1964–5: letter from John Macey Jr., chairman to James D. Williams (29 Oct. 1965).

CHAPTER 3

1. NA RG 228, Records of the FEPC, Legal Division, Box 329, Folder Verbatim Transcript, 19 Feb. 1942: Minutes of Proceedings before the FEPC in the matter of the complaint of Leslie S. Perry (19 Feb. 1942), 6.
2. Perry wrote to the Sec. of the Treasury in 1937 about his non-promotion: 'during my five years of employment in the government service my efficiency grades have been uniformly good—my record clear but I seem wholly unable to obtain a promotion to higher type of work. I have made numerous efforts to secure an appointment or transfer to branches of the field force maintaining offices in more liberal sections of the country, without success.' LC NAACP, Group I, Box C273, File Discrimination—Employment, Federal Service 1937: letter from Perry to Sec. Henry Morgenthau, Jr. (12 Jan. 1937).
3. LC NAACP, Group II-A, Box A237, Folder Discrimination and Segregation—Govt. Agencies 1941–55: NAACP press release (5 Mar. 1943). The Dir. was Arthur Altmeyer.
4. Most of the Com.'s work was concerned with injustices perpetrated by defence industry contractors. For details see NA RG 228, FEPC Records, Office Files of George M. Johnson, Box 292, Folder Personal and Confidential: memorandum from Robert P. Patterson Under Sec. of War to the Chiefs of all Supply Arms and Services, 'Procedure in cases involving discrimination by War Department contractors and subcontractors' (12 Sept. 1941).
5. NA RG 16, Records of the Office of the Sec. of Agriculture, General Correspondence, Negroes 1924–39, Box 2, Folder Negroes, 1932: letter from Sec. of Agriculture to Congressman Louis Ludlow (12 Dec. 1932).
6. Ibid., Negroes 1940–5, Box 3, Folder Negroes, 1940: letter from Dir. of Personnel to Miss Mable Alston, Afro-American Newspaper (5 Aug. 1940).
7. e.g. responding to complaints from the NAACP about the failure to promote Black American employees, the Bureau of Engraving and Printing claimed promotions were made 'impartially, regardless of race': NA RG 318, Records of the Bureau of Engraving and Printing, Central Correspondence Files 1913–39, Box 243, Folder Employees—Colored, 1936: letter from Administrative Sec. to the Sec. of the Treasury to DC branch, NAACP (7 Oct. 1936). However, two years later the same bureau informed a researcher that 'there is only one negro employed here as offset pressman . . . There are, however, a number of colored employees assigned as skilled helper, press helper etc.' Ibid., Box 269, Folder Employees—Colored 1938: letter from Acting Dir. C. R. Long to Vernon Lewis (21 July 1938). Lewis was a graduate student undertaking a dissertation about Black American employment. In 1939 Long informed an enquirer that 'there are no Negroes employed in this bureau as engravers', that is, in the skilled positions: Ibid., Box 281, Folder Employees—Colored 1939: letter from Long to the Universal Negro Improvement Association, 22 Aug. 1939.

8. Cited in NA RG 188, Records of the OPA, Records of the Racial Relations Officer, Box 1, Folder Analysis of Report on Negro Employment in the National Office: 'Analysis of a Report on Negro Employment in the National Office' (31 Mar. 1945), 1.
9. NA RG 228, Records of FEPC, Office Files of Malcolm Ross, Box 64, Folder Agenda: 'The President's Committee on Fair Employment Practice: Beginning and Growth' (n.d.), 4.
10. Ibid. 2.
11. LC NAACP, Group II-A, Box A251, Folder FEPC—Reports: Report of the President's FEPC (May 1943, confidential), 56.
12. Presidential intervention, with Committee implementation, has been effective in bringing about a noticeable modification of federal employment practice. By Nov. 1942 the proportion of Negroes had risen from 9 per cent to more than 17 per cent of total personnel in the departmental (Washington) services, almost one-half (48 per cent) of whom were in clerical, administrative, fiscal and professional classifications. In the field service Negroes still constituted only 5 per cent of total employees of whom about two-fifths (38 per cent) were in other than custodial classifications.

    Ibid. 57.
13. NA RG 228, Records of the FEPC, Legal Division, Box 329, Folder Verbatim Transcript, 19 Feb. 1942: Minutes of Proceedings before the FEPC in the matter of the complaint of Leslie S. Perry (19 Feb. 1942).
14. Ibid.
15. Ibid. 2–3.
16. NA RG 228, Records of the FEPC, Office Files of George M. Johnson, Box 74, Folder Employment of Negroes in the Federal Govt.: FEPC Division of Review and Analysis, 'The Wartime Employment of Negroes in the Federal Government' (Jan. 1945), 24.
17. NA RG 228, Records of the FEPC, Legal Division, Box 329, Folder Verbatim Transcript, 19 Feb. 1942: Minutes of Proceedings before the FEPC in the matter of the complaint of Leslie S. Perry (19 Feb. 1942), 3.
18. This point was made in correspondence between the FHA and Bureau of Engraving and Printing: see NA RG 318, Records of the Bureau of Engraving and Printing, Central Correspondence File 1913–39, Box 269, Folder Employees—Colored, 1938: letter from FHA, 20 June 1938.
19. Prior to the creation of the FEPC, concern about the position of Black American employees in Federal agencies, particularly in the expanded New Deal programmes, led to investigative work by an interdepartmental group created in 1934. NA RG 48, Records of the Dept. of the Interior, Office of the Sec., Central Classified File 1907–36, Box 506, Folder Racial Discrimination, General: Minutes of the 1st meeting of the interdepartmental group concerned with the special problems of the Negro population (7 Feb. 1934). The group appears to have been the initiative of Clark Foreman, Adviser on Economic Status of Negroes in the Interior Dept. The following were in attendance: Dept. of Agriculture: Dr E. H. Shinn, Extension Service; Agricultural Adjustment Admin.: Mr Phil Campbell; Attorney Gen.'s Office: Mr Robert L. Vann, Asst. to Attorney Gen.; Civil Works Admin.: Mr Forrester B. Washington, Dir. of Negro Work; Dept. of Commerce: Mr Eugene Kinckle Jones, Advisor on Negro Affairs; Emergency Conservation Work: Mr J. J. McEntee, Asst. Dir.; Farm

Credit Admin.: Mr H. A. Hunt, Asst. to the Governor; Dept. of Labor: Mr Edward F. McGrady, Asst. Sec.; National Recovery Admin.: Dr Charles F. Roos, Research and Planning; Navy: Mr William D. Bergman, Chief, Appointment Division; TVA: Mr G. R. Clapp, Asst. Dir. of Personnel; Treasury Dept.: Mr W. H. McReynolds, Administrative Asst. to the Sec.; War Dept.: Mr W. D. Searle, Chief, Civilian Personnel Division; Interior Division: Dr Clark Foreman, Advisor on Economic Status of Negroes, Dr Robert C. Weaver, Housing Division, WPA. That the work of this group was rarely above the anodyne is suggested by the summary of Dr Bergman's statement about the Navy: 'the Navy Department had no Negro problem as far as he knew . . . There are 146 Negroes in the Department itself . . . Their personnel problems, he reported, show no race issues to be involved', ibid. 6. The evidence in Ch. 4 rather refutes this complacency. Subsequent meetings were more useful, though the group served principally as a forum for a discussion of common problems—esp. regarding discrimination against Black Americans on New Deal projects—and less as a formulator of policy or enforcement agency. See ibid., minutes of the inter-departmental group meeting (1 June 1934).

20. In 1936 the Racial Advisor at the Dept. of the Interior, Robert C. Weaver, attempted to collect data about Black American employment from other depts.: see NA RG 318, Records of the Bureau of Engraving and Printing, Central Correspondence File 1913–39, Box 243, Folder Employees—Colored 1936: letter from Weaver (13 May 1936).
21. NA RG 228, Records of FEPC, Office Files of Malcolm Ross, Box 64, Folder Agenda: 'The President's Committee on Fair Employment Practice: Beginning and Growth' (n.d.). The FEPC subsumed the earlier Office of Production Management, established for similar purposes. For one earlier review of the Federal govt. see NA RG 46, Records of the US Senate, 77th Congress, Special Com. to Investigate Civil Service System, 17 boxes. This com., chaired by Sen. Allen J. Ellender (La.) was concerned principally with inequities in the promotion system. Its copious correspondence included a number of complaints from Black American employees about their status: see Box 1, Folder Colored—complaints.
22. For details see LC, Papers of A. Philip Randolph, Boxes 23–6. For accounts see *Pittsburgh Courier* (17 May 1941).
23. A. Randolph Phillip, Pres. of the Brotherhood of Sleeping Car Porters threatened a mass march on Washington in 1941 if Roosevelt failed to ensure equality of employment in defense industries. HSTL, WHCF, Confidential File, Box 21, Folder Justice Dept. [6 of 10] FBI: *Survey of Racial Conditions in the US* (16 Oct. 1946), 479. See also H. Garfinkel, *When Negroes March: The March on Washington Movement in the Organizational Politics of the FEPC* (Glencoe, Ill.: Free Press, 1959); L. C. Kesselman, *The Social Politics of the FEPC: A Study in Reform Pressure Movements* (Chapel Hill, NC: Univ. of North Carolina Press, 1948); J. B. Kirby, *Black Americans in the Roosevelt Era* (Knoxville, Tenn.: Univ. of Tennessee Press, 1980), and the account provided in *No Ordinary Time: Franklin and Eleanor Roosevelt: The Home Front in World War II* (New York: Simon & Schuster, 1994) by D. K. Goodwin who stresses Eleanor Roosevelt's role as an intermediatory in pursuading the Pres. to act.
24. NA RG 228, Records of FEPC, Office Files of Malcolm Ross, Box 64, Folder Agenda: 'The President's Committee on Fair Employment Practice: Beginning and Growth' (n.d.). Of the civil service the report observes:

Negroes have also made considerable gains in the Federal civil service. The 1938 report by L. J. W. Hayes showed that Negroes composed 8.4 per cent of Federal employees in Washington, and that 90 per cent were in custodial jobs. In contrast, a study by the Division of Review and Analysis of FEPC, involving a sample which covered 1,957,858 Government employees, showed that 12.5 per cent of these workers were colored. According to this study, in the departmental service Negroes composed 18 per cent of the total personnel. A large number, 50 per cent or more in some agencies, were employed in the clerical, administrative, fiscal category, although in the field service most Negroes were still in custodial classifications.

Ibid. 9.

25. This is made clear in a memorandum to the Com.'s Southern Regional Dir.: 'I am afraid that you would do poorly in a debate with Senator Russell conducted in the Atlanta papers and would expose yourself to harmful attacks which would interfere with our work. We have found from experience that the only time an answer is justified is when there is an error of fact which can be corrected. Otherwise leave the answering of such attacks to friendly groups such as the Urban League etc. They can reply without the restraint which is incumbent upon any Government officer.' Ibid., Office Files of the Chairman, Box 63, Folder D: memorandum from Will Maslow FEPC office to Witherspoon Dodge, Regional Dir. (23 Nov. 1944).
26. For details see ibid., Office Files of George M. Johnson, Box 294, Folder To be refiled 'Thumbnail History of FEPC' (n.d.).
27. For details see ibid.
28. Ibid., Office Files of the Chairman, Box 61, Folder C: letter from Malcolm Ross to Hon. Clarence Cannon chairman House Appropriations Com. (11 May 1944).
29. *Politics, Parties and Interest Groups* (New York: Thomas Y. Crowell Co., 3rd edn. 1952), 136.
30. NA RG 228, Records of FEPC, Office Files of Malcolm Ross, Box 64, Folder Agenda: 'The President's Committee on Fair Employment Practice: Beginning and Growth' (n.d.), 3.
31. It defined war industries as: '(1) employers engaged in the production of war materials, and (2) employers engaged in activities necessary for the maintenance of the production or utilization of war materials.' HSTL, President's Sec. Files, Box 119, Folder Fair Employment Practice: memo from FEPC to the Pres. (18 Sept. 1945), 1.
32. See NA RG 228, Records of the FEPC, Division of Review and Analysis, Office Files of Joy Davis, Box 204, Folder Handbook for the Negro Worker (n.d.).
33. The Com. reached agreement with several wartime Federal agencies about both their internal procedures for addressing complaints of discrimination and referring complaints to the FEPC. These included: the Maritime Com., the US Civil Service Com., the National War Labor Board, the Office of Labor Production, the War Shipping Administration, the War Dept., and the Navy Dept. Ibid., Office Files of John A. Davis, Box 358, Folder Agreements with Other Agencies.
34. Ibid., Office Files of the Deputy Chairman, Box 72, Folder F: see e.g. letter from George M. Johnson FEPC asst. executive sec. to the Fax Co. (27 Mar. 1943) about its hiring practices.
35. The FEPC was initially chaired by Mark Ethridge, publisher of the *Louisville Courier-Journal*, with Lawrence Cramer appointed executive sec. (a position he retained until the Com.'s termination). The other members were Boris Shishkin,

Charles H. Houston, Sara E. Southall, and Milton P. Webster. Ross was the last chairman but had the longest tenure. Ethridge was replaced by Mgr. Francis J. Haas as chairman, who was in turn succeeded by Malcolm Ross in Oct. 1943, previously with the National Labor Relations Board. See NA RG 228, Records of FEPC, Office Files of Malcolm Ross, Box 64, Folder Agenda: 'The President's Committee on Fair Employment Practice: Beginning and Growth' (n.d.). See also Kesselman, *Social Politics of the FEPC*; and L. Ruchames, *Race, Jobs and Politics: The Story of FEPC* (New York: Harper, 1953).

36. HSTL, Papers of Philleo Nash, Box 20, Folder Official Documents 'Minority Groups Service': Clarence Johnson (1944), 1.
37. HSTL, President's Com. on Civil Rights, Box 12, Folder Proceedings of the Com.—Transcripts: Data from FEPC 1945 Report cited by Thomas Richardson CIO before the Com. (1 Apr. 1947), 37. See also D. M. Johnson and R. R. Campbell, *Black Migration in America* (Durham, NC: Duke University Press, 1981), 103.
38. See e.g. NA RG 228, Records of the FEPC, Office Files of Malcolm Ross, Box 70, Folder UEW–FEPC Agreement: 'Agreement between the United Electrical, Radio and Machine Workers, CIO and the Committee on Fair Employment Practices' (7 Nov. 1945).
39. LC NAACP, Group II-A, Box A251, Folder FEPC—Reports: Report of the President's FEPC (May 1943, confidential), 8.
40. Ibid. 9.
41. Ibid. 9–10.
42. Ibid. 10.
43. Ibid. 11.
44. Issued on 18 Jan. 1955.
45. Under EO 10925 (6 Mar. 1961).
46. For details see NA RG 60, Justice Dept. Records, Records of John Doar, Asst. Attorney Gen., Civil Rights Division 1960–7, Box 1, File Legal Memos—Employment: Memorandum for the Acting Attorney Gen. re 'New Government Contract Regulations the Department of Labor Proposes to Issue on November 19 1966' (11 Apr. 1966).
47. The expansion in govt.-funded employment during the 1930s amplified the disadvantages confronting Black job-seekers. In 1930, of 608,915 Federal civil servants, 54,664 were Black. NA RG 228, Records of the FEPC, Office Files of Joy Davis, Box 405, Folder Employment of Negroes in Federal Govt.
48. The Com. had some difficulty extracting the germane information from govt. agencies and received bland assurances that efforts to employ more Black Americans were under way. Many depts. failed to provide information about field establishments, where under-representation of Blacks was glaring. See NA RG 174, Dept. of Labor Records, Perkins, General Subject Files, Box 127, Folder FEPC 1943. Memorandum from the FEPC to Heads of all Depts. and Independent Establishments 'Analysis of present status of Negro employment in the Federal Government' (17 Aug. 1942).
49. HSTL, Papers of Philleo Nash, Box 20, Folder Official Documents—Nash Files: memo from FEPC to Heads of all Depts. and Independent Establishments (10 Aug. 1942).
50. Ibid. 3.

51. NA RG 188, Records of OPA, Records of Racial Relations Advisor, Box 13, Folder Statistics—Negro E: Elmer W. Henderson, 'The Employment of Negroes in the Federal Government' FEPC (1 Mar. 1943), 2. Created in 1923, the civil service divisions were: professional and scientific service; subprofessional service; the clerical, administrative, and fiscal service; the custodial service; and the clerical-mechanical service.
52. NA RG 228, Office Files of Joy Davis, Box 405, Folder Employment of Negroes in Federal Govt.: President's FEPC, Division of Review & Analysis 'Table and Summary of Employment of Negroes in Federal Government' (Dec. 1943, confidential).
53. Ibid. 1.
54. Ibid. 2.
55. NA RG 228, Records of the FEPC, Office Files of George M. Johnson, Box 74, Folder Employment of Negroes in the Federal Govt.: FEPC Division of Review and Analysis 'The Wartime Employment of Negroes in the Federal Government' (Jan. 1945), 4.
56. Ibid. 13.
57. Ibid. 14–15.
58. Ibid. 21–2.
59. Ibid. 24.
60. Ibid. 25.
61. Ibid.
62. Ibid. 26.
63. These factors included:

    the extent to which Negroes qualify when the Civil Service Commission returns to the practice of holding open competitive examinations for appointments conferring classified Civil Service status . . . The extent to which the statutory 'rule of three' governing selection of employees is not abused by considerations of race or color. The 'rule of three' as applied to persons having no disqualifications defined by law or Civil Service Rules and Regulations, states that the appointing officer shall make selection for the first vacancy from the group of the three highest eligibles willing to accept appointment. For the second vacancy, selection must be made from the group consisting of the two remaining eligibles considered for the first vacancy and the next highest available eligible. The same procedure must be followed in filling additional vacancies until each eligible willing to accept appointment has been considered in connection with three actual appointments. The appointing officer need not consider further any eligible whom he has previously considered for three separate vacancies. This rule permits the rejection of any nonpreference eligible regardless of his earned rating and makes possible the complete exclusion of Negroes from appointments except in those cases where all in the group of three highest eligibles are colored.

    Ibid. 27.
64. The chairman was Archibald Carey, an attorney in Chicago. He was joined by Charles Kendell, Gen. Counsel Office of Defense Mobilization; J. Ernest Wilkins, Asst. Sec. Dept. of Labor; and W. Arthur McCoy, former chairman of the FEB.
65. NA RG 220, President's Committee on Government Employment Policy 1955–61, Surveys 1956–61, Box 3 A Five-City Survey of Negro-American Employees of the Federal Govt. (1956).
66. Ibid. 2–3.
67. Ibid. 4.

68. Ibid. 5.
69. NA RG 228, Office Files of Joy Davis, Box 405, Folder Employment of Negroes in Federal Govt.: President's FEPC, Division of Review & Analysis 'Table and Summary of Employment of Negroes in Federal Government' (Dec. 1943, confidential), 3.
70. Ibid. 4.
71. NA RG 188, Records of OPA, Records of Racial Relations Advisor, Box 13, Folder Statistics—Negro E: Elmer W. Henderson, 'The Employment of Negroes in the Federal Government' FEPC (1 Mar. 1943), 3.
72. Ibid. 1.
73. Ibid. 3.
74. Ibid.
75. It continued: 'The National War Labor Board reported that it employed 13 Negroes in professional capacities.' NA RG 228, Office Files of Joy Davis, Box 405, Folder Employment of Negroes in Federal Govt.: President's FEPC, Division of Review & Analysis 'Table and Summary of Employment of Negroes in Federal Government' (Dec. 1943, confidential), 3.
76. Ibid. 4.
77. Ibid. 5.
78. Ibid. 6.
79. Ibid. 7.
80. NA RG 228, Records of FEPC, Office Files of George M. Johnson, Box 74, Folder Employment of Negroes in the Federal Govt.: 'Tables and Summary of Employment of Negroes in the Federal Government', FEPC Division of Review and Analysis (Dec. 1943), 7.
81. Ibid. 12.
82. National Committee on Segregation in the Nation's Capital, *Segregation in Washington* (report) (Chicago, 1948), 68.
83. NA RG 188, Records of OPA, Records of Racial Relations Advisor, Box 1, Folder Analysis of Report on Negro Employment in the National Office: memorandum from Chester Bowles (5 Nov. 1945), attached to 'Analysis of a Report on Negro Employment in the National Office' (31 Mar. 1945).
84. Ibid., Folder Analysis of Negro Participation, War Price and Rationing Boards: 'Number of Local Boards Having Negro Participation is Exceedingly Low' (Jan. 1946, confidential and not to be released).
85. Ibid., Box 6, Folder Negro Employment—Field Offices: 'Analysis of Reports on Negro Employment in all Field Offices' (30 Nov. 1945).
86. Ibid., Box 1, Folder Analysis of Reports on Negro Participation, War Price and Rationing Boards: see memorandum from Tom Donnelly to Regional Administrators 'Reports on Negro Participation in the Work of War Price and Rationing Boards' (24 Aug. 1945).
87. Ibid., Box 5, Folder Negro Activity in OPA: memorandum from Frances Williams to Jack O'Brien 'OPA and the Negro' (12 June 1944), 1.
88. NA RG 228, Records of FEPC, Office Files of Malcolm Ross, Box 69, Folder Reports to the Pres.: FEPC Report to the Pres. (27 Aug. 1945), 3.
89. Malcolm Ross observed:

> one usually very reliable source indicates that we have about returned to prewar status in types of industrial jobs now open to Negroes. In other words, that most of the gains which have

> been made during the war have been lost, or are in the process of being lost. Heavy work, hazardous work and dirty work in iron and steel are still open to negroes, but not much else. Even jobs which have been considered the prerogative of Negroes are being challenged, in the service trades. Employers who have taken untrained Southern whites into even such jobs as dishwashers find that they are thereby unable to employ Negroes. Clerical and commercial jobs where the workers deal with the public are practically nonexistent.

Ibid., Box 66, Folder West Coast Material: letter from Ross to Dr Laurence Hewes, Jr. American Council On Race Relations (15 Mar. 1946), 2.

90. LC NAACP II-B, Box B9, Folder Civil Service 1941–7: see letter to Walter White from Eliot Kaplan, executive sec. Civil Service Reform Assoc. (25 Oct. 1944).
91. The Civil Service Com. did not collect data about employment by race: see NA RG 318, Records of the Bureau of Engraving and Printing, Central Correspondence File 1913–39, Box 269, Folder Employees—Colored, 1938; letter from Douglas Cannon FHA to Bureau Dir. (20 June 1938).
92. For an inventory of the FEPC's formal representation see NA RG 228, Records of the FEPC, Office Files of George M. Johnson, Box 74, Folder John A. Davis: memorandum from Davis to Malcolm Ross, 4 Mar. 1946, 'Status of our Relationships with other Government agencies: an Inventory of Progress to date and Projects Proposed by the Programming Committee'.
93. According to Ross,

> it is the position of the Committee that jurisdiction over agencies of the Government derives from paragraphs four and five of the Order and extends to all of the various agencies; that paragraph four authorizes it to make recommendations in implementation of general policies, such recommendations necessarily being general in nature too; that paragraph five . . . in effect authorizes the Committee to issue findings and directives based upon specific complaints of discrimination by the agencies; that such findings are conclusive upon the agencies and such directives mandatory, within the limits of their respective authorities.

Ibid., Office Files of the Chairman, Box 63, Folder B: Memorandum from Ross to Hon. Attorney Gen. Francis Riddle 'Jurisdiction of the President's Committee on Fair Employment Practice over Federal Departments and Agencies' (29 Sept. 1944), 2.

94. Ibid., Legal Division, Box 329, Folder Verbatim Transcript 19 Feb. 1942: Minutes of Proceedings before the FEPC in the matter of the complaint of Leslie S. Perry, (19 Feb. 1942), 3.
95. LC NAACP, Group II-A, Box A194, Folder Civil Service General 1940–55: memorandum to Mrs Anna Rosenberg, Regional Director WMC from John Beecher, Regional Representative, President's FEPC 'Governmental Discrimination Against Negroes' (5 Nov. 1942), 1.
96. NA RG 228, Records of the President's FEPC, Legal Division, Box 329, Folder Verbatim Transcripts: Verbatim Transcripts of Proceedings (14 Dec. 1942, Washington), 2.
97. Ibid. 2–3.
98. Ibid. 3.
99. Ibid. 4.
100. Ibid. 7.
101. Ibid. 8–9.
102. Ibid. 10.
103. Ibid. 14.

104. Ibid. 18–19.
105. Ibid. 21–2.
106. Ibid. 26–7.
107. Ibid. 33.
108. Ibid. 34–5.
109. Ibid. 40.
110. Ibid. 44.
111. Ibid. 47.
112. Ibid. 53.
113. Ibid. 62–3.
114. NA RG 228, Records of the FEPC, Office Files of George M. Johnson, Box 290, Folder FEPC Misc: Summary of Hearing on Complaints of Negro Workers Against the Personnel Classification Division of the US Civil Service Com. with Intermediate Findings and Recommendations, 3.
115. Ibid. 3–4.
116. Ibid.: letter from L. A. Moyer US Civil Service Com. to FEPC executive sec. (28 Apr. 1943), 4.
117. Ibid.: letter from FEPC chairman to L. A. Moyer US Civil Service Com. (20 July 1943), 1.
118. An interdepartmental committee created by EO 10308 of 3 Dec. 1951. It was composed of eleven members to study the rules, procedures, and practices of the contracting agencies of the govt. as they relate to obtaining the compliance with govt. contract provisions prohibiting racial or religious discrimination against employees or applicants for employment. NA RG 325, Records of the CGCC, Correspondence with Agencies 1952–3, Box 2, Entry 10, File Department of Justice: memorandum to the Attorney Gen. from J. Lee Rankin, Asst. Attorney Gen. Office of Legal Counsel (3 June 1953).
119. HSTL, Files of Philleo Nash, Box 17, Folder Equal Economic Opportunity: CGCC Report. (12 Jan. 1953), 2.
120. Ibid.
121. Ibid.
122. PL 308 75th Congress.
123. NA RG 183, Records of the BES/USES, Oxley Papers [Correspondence with Govt. Agencies] Box 2, Folder Apprenticeship Training: Federal Com.: 'Apprenticeship Information' (25 Oct. 1937). The Fitzgerald Act was signed on 6 Oct. of the same year.
124. Quoted ibid.
125. HSTL, Papers of Philleo Nash, Box 17, Folder Equal Economic Opportunity: CGCC Report (12 Jan. 1953), 61.
126. Ibid. 62.
127. Ibid. 63.
128. Ibid. 64.
129. Ibid. 77.
130. Ibid.
131. Ibid. 78.
132. Ibid.

133. NA RG 325, Records of the CGCC, Correspondence with Federal Agencies 1952–3, Boxes 1–3.
134. Ibid., Box 2, Entry 10, File Dept. of Justice: memorandum to the Attorney Gen. from J. Lee Rankin, Asst. Attorney Gen. Office of Legal Counsel (3 June 1953), 6.
135. Ibid.
136. See H. Walton, Jr., *When the Marching Stopped* (Albany, NY: State University of New York Press, 1988).
137. NA RG 228, FEPC Records, Legal Division, Box 329, Folder Verbatim Transcripts, 13 Apr. 1942: text of letter from FEPC included in Hearing of the President's FEPC on Discrimination in Defense Training (13 Apr. 1942), 1.
138. Ibid. 10. The speaker was Pres. of the Julius Rosenberg Fund.
139. Ibid. 12.
140. Ibid. 13.
141. Ibid. 26.
142. Ibid. 32.
143. Ibid. 34.
144. NA RG 228, FEPC Records, Office of George M. Johnson, Box 293, Folder Summaries: Summary, findings, and directions in the National Training Program Alabama, Tennessee, and Georgia (June 1942), 1.
145. Ibid., Legal Division, Box 329, Folder Verbatim Transcripts, 13 Apr. 1942: Hearing of the President's FEPC on Discrimination in Defense Training (13 Apr. 1942), 49.
146. Ibid.
147. NA RG 228, FEPC Records, Office of George M. Johnson, Box 293, Folder Summaries: Summary, findings, and directions in the National Training Program Alabama, Tennessee, and Georgia (June 1942), 6–7.
148. Ibid. 7.
149. Ibid. 8.
150. Ibid.
151. LC NAACP, Group III-A, Box A180, Folder Labor, Apprenticeship Training: NAACP, 'Negro Wage Earners and Apprenticeship' (NAACP, 1960), 4.
152. For details see D. S. King, *Actively Seeking Work? The Politics of Unemployment and Welfare Policy in Britain and the United States* (Chicago: University of Chicago Press, 1995), ch. 4.
153. LC NAACP, Group III-A, Box A180, Folder Labor, Apprenticeship Training: NAACP, 'Negro Wage Earners and Apprenticeship', 12.
154. Ibid. 14.
155. Ibid. 19.
156. Ibid. 20.
157. Ibid. 57.
158. Ibid. 58.
159. Ibid. 67.
160. LC NAACP, Group III-A, Box A146, Folder Govt.—National, Dept. of Labor 1960–5: circular to all state employment security agencies from the BES, 'Implementation of Policy and Procedure With Respect to Serving Minority Groups' (12 Mar. 1964); and see King, *Actively Seeking Work?*

161. e.g. the Comptroller-General of the GAO replied as follows:

> On November 10 1948 pursuant to Executive Order No 9980 I designated Mr Donald G. Dudley as Fair Employment Officer for the General Accounting Office, with full operating responsibility, under my immediate supervision, for carrying out the fair employment policy stated therein. Coincident therewith, there was issued over my signature General Accounting Office Administrative Order No 67 which set forth the policy of the Office with regard to all personnel actions and the procedures through which allegations of discrimination are to be presented, heard and adjudicated. A copy of such order was furnished each employee.

NA RG 146, Civil Service Agencies, FEB, Correspondence with Agencies 1948–54, Box 3, Folder General Accounting: letter to James L. Houghteling chairman FEB (16 Nov. 1950).

162. See ibid.: correspondence to the FEB.
163. Ibid., Folder Interior Dept.: letter from Dan H. Wheeler Fair Employment Officer to James L. Houghteling (18 Jan. 1952), 2.
164. Ibid.
165. See e.g. ibid., Box 4, Folder VA: Summary Minutes of the 110th Meeting of the FEB (18 May 1951), at which the difficulty of obtaining information from the VA was discussed.
166. Ibid., Box 5, Folder Post Office Dep.: letter from E. B. Jackson Fair Employment Officer to the FEB (23 Nov. 1951).
167. US Senate, 82nd Congress, 2nd sess., Committee on Labor and Public Welfare, Subcommittee on Labor and Labor Management Relations, *Discrimination and Full Utilization of Manpower Resources*, Hearings on S. 1732 and S. 551 (8 Apr. 1952), 75; the speaker was Fred Coxton.
168. NA RG 146, Civil Service Agencies, FEB, Correspondence with Agencies 1948–54, Box 3, Folder Labor Dept.: see minutes of 110th Meeting of the FEB, 18 May 1951 when this system was discussed and concern was expressed about its effect upon eligible Black candidates.
169. Ibid., minutes of 122nd Meeting of the FEB (31 Oct. 1951), 1.
170. An exception was the Justice Dept. which revealed that of forty-five typists, stenographers, and clerks employed in 1951, none were Black. Ibid., Folder Justice Dept.: letter from C. W. Palmer Fair Employment Officer, Justice Dept. to the FEB (27 Mar. 1951).
171. NA RG 220, President's Com. on Government Employment Policy 1955–61, Appeals Files, Box 35. This box includes two notebooks listing many of the appeals considered by the Committee. Unfortunately, the lists are not complete and the basis on which details were recorded changed over time, making comparison very difficult.
172. Ibid.
173. Ibid., Box 47, File Cecil E. Golder: see letter from Ross Clinchy executive dir. to Sec. of the Navy Thomas S. Gates, Jr. (24 Oct. 1958), and 'Brief on Complaint of Cecil E. Golder'; for exx. of unsuccessful complaints see the cases of Lonzo A. Gregory (against the Army) and Eloise M. Goins (against the Immmigration and Naturalization Service in the Dept. of Justice), both also in Box 47.
174. NA RG 220, President's Com. on Government Employment Policy, Reports and Summaries of Area Conferences and Meetings, Box 26: Southern Regional Council, 'The Federal Executive and Civil Rights' (Atlanta: Southern Regional Council, Jan. 1961), 12.

175. Ibid., File Meetings with Employment Policy Officers.
176. Ibid., Southern Regional Council, 'Federal Executive and Civil Rights', 13.
177. Ibid. 15.
178. Report to the Pres. by the President's EEOC (Washington: GPO, 1963), 104–5.
179. Ibid. 105.
180. Ibid. 106.
181. LC NAACP, Washington Bureau, Box 65, File President's EEOC: letter from J. Francis Pohlhaus, Counsel NAACP Washington Bureau to the President's Com. with a 5-page memorandum from the affected workers (11 Apr. 1961).
182. Ibid., Box 66, File President's EEOC 1960: see memorandum to Lawrence J. Powers, Employment Policy Officer, GAO from the affected workers (17 Mar. 1964). The grievances concerned the Reports Group at the GAO.
183. E. Goffman, *Asylums* (1961; Harmondsworth: Penguin Books, 1991).

CHAPTER 4

1. LC NAACP, Group II-A, Box A644, Folder US Army, General 1940–4: letter from Mr Bernard Randolph (7 Jan. 1940), 1.
2. Ibid.: letter from Roy Wilkins Asst. Sec. NAACP to Mr Bernard Randolph (1 Feb. 1940).
3. Cited in D. G. Mandelbaum, *Soldier Groups and Negro Soldiers* (Berkeley and Los Angeles: University of California Press, 1952), 91.
4. W. B. Hartgrove, 'The Negro Soldier in the American Revolution', *Journal of Negro History*, 1 (1916), 110–31.
5. F. A. Shannon, 'The Federal Government and the Negro Soldier, 1861–1865', *Journal of Negro History*, 11 (1926), 563–83.
6. L. D. Reddick, 'The Negro Policy of the United States Army, 1775–1945', *Journal of Negro History*, 34 (1947), 9–29.
7. The distinguished Black American leader W. E. B. Du Bois encouraged Black Americans to 'close ranks' with White Americans for the period of the war.
8. NAACP, *Freeing America: Seventh Annual Report of the National Association for the Advancement of Colored People* (New York: NAACP, 1917), 1.
9. NA RG 16, Office of the Sec. of Agriculture, General Correspondence, Negroes 1940–55, Box 3, Folder Negroes: 'Negroes in a Democracy at War', Survey of Intelligence Materials No. 25, Office of Facts and Figures, Bureau of Intelligence (27 May 1942), 2.
10. Ibid. 1. This report is enclosed with a letter from John R. Fleming Deputy Dir., Office of Facts and Figures to Sam Bledsoe, Asst. to the Sec., Dept. of Agriculture, 13 June 1942. Fleming observed: 'we don't circulate these intelligence surveys very widely but this one is so important and I know you are so interested in the subject that I thought you ought to have a copy.' He added: 'you will appreciate the necessity for discretion in the use of this material.'
11. NA RG 16, Office of the Sec. of Agriculture, General Correspondence, Negroes 1940–55, Box 3, Folder Negroes: 'Negroes in a Democracy at War', Survey of Intelligence Materials No. 25, Office of Facts and Figures, Bureau of Intelligence (27 May 1942), 1.

12. Ibid. 21.
13. Ibid. 21–2.
14. Ibid. 25. The report added: 'it is significant in this connection that one-tenth of the poor whites felt that the Negroes would fare no worse under German domination than they do under American democracy.'
15. Ibid. 6.
16. Amongst a large literature see R. M. Dalfiume, 'The "Forgotten Years" of the Negro Revolution', *Journal of American History*, 55 (1968), 90–106.
17. NA RG 16, Office of the Sec. of Agriculture, General Correspondence, Negroes 1940–55, Box 3, Folder Negroes: 'Negroes in a Democracy at War', Survey of Intelligence Materials No. 25, Office of Facts and Figures, Bureau of Intelligence (27 May 1942), 10.
18. Ibid. 12.
19. Ibid. 14.
20. Ibid. 15.
21. Ibid. 20–1.
22. R. J. Stillman II, *Integration of the Negro in the US Armed Forces* (New York: Praeger, 1968), 27.
23. C. T. Rowan, *Breaking Barriers* (London: Little Brown, 1991), 60, 61.
24. LC NAACP, Group II-A, Box 643, Folder US Army Camp Stewart Ga 1942–3.
25. Ibid. (20 Dec. 1942), 1.
26. Ibid. 2.
27. Ibid., Memo No. 4 from Nesbitt (24 Jan. 1943), 4.
28. *New York Times* (23 Mar. 1948), 21.
29. HSTL, Official File, Box 442, Folder OF 93-B: letter from David Niles, the key person in the White House dealing with the Com. on Civil Rights to Matthew Connolly (20 July 1948).
30. H. Sitkoff, 'Harry Truman and the Election of 1948: The Coming of Age of Civil Rights in American Elections', *Journal of Southern History*, 37 (1971), 597–616.
31. V. O. Key, Jr., *Southern Politics* (New York: Vintage, 1949), 330–2.
32. HSTL, President's Official File, Box 1509, Folder 596 (1947–Mar. 1949): Press release 29 Oct. 1947.
33. Pres. Truman established his Com. on Equality of Treatment and Opportunity in the Armed Services in 1948 under EO 9981 with Charles H. Fahy, a former US Solicitor General, as chairman to determine existing practices in the Armed Services toward minorities. HSTL, President's Official File, Box 1651, Folder President's Com. on Equality of Treatment and Opportunity in the Armed Services (1948–Apr. 1950): letter from Truman to Fahy (18 Sept. 1948). The other members were: Dwight Palmer, pres. of General Cable Corp.; John Sengstacke, publisher of the Chicago *Defender*; Charles Luckman, pres. of Lever Brothers; Lester Granger, executive sec. of the NUL; William Stevenson, pres. of Oberlin College; and Alphonus Donahue, pres. of A. J. Donahue Corp.
34. Ibid.: minutes (12 Jan. 1949), 1, 2 (editorial emphasis).
35. Established in Nov. 1947. For details see L. D. Reddick, 'The Negro Policy of the American Army since World War Two', *Journal of Negro History*, 38 (1953), 196–215.
36. On this and related campaigns see LC NAACP, Group II-B, Box B191, Folder US

Army—General 1948–9: memorandum to Thurgood Marshall re 'Campaign to resist military segregation' (21 Sept. 1948).

37. *New York Times* (1 Apr. 1948), 1.
38. Ibid. (3 Apr. 1948), 3. Eisenhower retained this position during his presidential years.
39. LC, Records of NUL, Papers of Lester Granger, Box 157, Folder Navy, General 1947: letter from Granger to James Forrestal (23 Apr. 1948).
40. But in Stillman's view 'the process of getting the legislation through Congress had enabled Negro voices to be heard': *Integration of the Negro in the US Armed Forces*, 29.
41. Ibid. 23.
42. Ibid. 35.
43. HSTL, Papers of Philleo Nash, Box 37, Folder WH—Civil Rights—President's Committee: memo from Robert K. Carr to President's Com. on Civil Rights 'Negroes in the Armed Forces', prepared by Milton D. Stewart and Joseph Murtha (10 June 1947), 2.
44. Ibid. 3.
45. H. Sitkoff, 'Racial Militancy and Interracial Violence in the Second World War' *Journal of American History*, 58 (1971), 669.
46. NA RG 16, Office of the Sec. of Agriculture, General Correspondence, Negroes 1940–55, Box 3, Folder Negroes: 'Negroes in a Democracy at War', Bureau of Intelligence, Office of Facts and Figures, Survey of Intelligence Materials No. 25 (27 May 1942), 20.
47. Ibid.
48. HSTL, Com. on Equality of Treatment and Opportunity in the Armed Services, Box 7, Folder Army—Utilization of Negroes: Survey and Recommendations concerning the Integration of the Negro Soldier into the Army, submitted to the Sec. of War by the Civilian Aide to the Sec. of War (22 Sept. 1941).

    For secondary accounts of military integration see, amongst others, R. M. Dalfiume, *Fighting on Two Fronts: Desegregation of the Armed Forces* (Columbia, Mo.: University of Missouri Press, 1969); J. D. Foner, *Blacks and Military in American History* (New York: Praeger, 1974); M. J. MacGregor, Jr., *Integration of the Armed Forces 1940–1965* (Washington: US Army, 1985); Mandelbaum, *Soldier Groups and Negro Soldiers*; R. W. Mullen, *Blacks in America's Wars* (New York: Monad Press, 1973); and Stillman II, *Integration of the Negro in the US Armed Forces*.
49. HSTL, Com. on Equality of Treatment and Opportunity in the Armed Services, Box 10, Minutes (17 Mar. 1949), 40.
50. Ibid. 42.
51. Ibid., Box 7, Folder Army—Utilization of Negroes: Survey and Recommendations concerning the Integration of the Negro Soldier into the Army (22 Sept. 1941). Pressure from the NAACP and NUL forced the Air Force to abandon its segregated group of fighter pilots at Tuskegee, Ala.
52. See e.g. the account in Rowan, *Breaking Barriers*, 53–8, of one of thirteen Black officers commissioned by the Navy at the Great Lakes Naval Training Center.
53. HSTL, Com. on Equality of Treatment and Opportunity in the Armed Services, Box 7, Folder Army—Utilization of Negroes: Letter from Under Sec. of War Robert Patterson to Wilbur La Roe (26 Mar. 1943). These points are conceded by Patterson.

54. Ibid.: memo from Truman K. Gibson to Charles Poletti, Special Asst. to the Sec. of War (22 Mar. 1943).
55. LC NAACP, Group II-A, Box A644, Folder US Army, General 1942–3: letter from Wilkins to Col. Fred C. Milner Asst. Air Adjutant General Army Air Forces (9 Mar. 1942), 1.
56. HSTL, Com. on Equality of Treatment and Opportunity in the Armed Services, Box 7, Folder Army: memorandum from Gibson to Poletti (22 Mar. 1943).
57. W. Hastie, *On Clipped Wings* (Washington: NAACP, 1943).
58. See e.g. LC NAACP, Group II-A, Box A130, Folder William Hastie 1943–5: statement of William H. Hastie, former Civilian Aide to the Sec. of War, occasioned by an answer recently made by the War Dept. to charges of racial discrimination in the Air Corps (1943).
59. HSTL, Com. on Equality of Treatment and Opportunity in the Armed Services, Box 7, Folder Army—Utilization of Negroes: Letter from Under Sec. of War Patterson to Wilbur La Roe, Com. on Civic Affairs of the Washington Federation of Churches (26 Mar. 1943), 2.
60. Ibid.
61. Ibid. 3.
62. The replacement in 1944 of Frank Knox by James Forrestal as Sec. of the Navy produced a change in policy toward using Black recruits and the Navy dropped its segregated training first for advanced training and then in 1945 for basic training.
63. Race as a general category underpinned the endogenous value system of segregation but its specification was profoundly ideological. Barbara Fields dismisses the 'assumption that race is an observable physical fact, a thing, rather than a notion that is profoundly and in its very essence ideological'. B. J. Fields, 'Ideology and Race in American History', in J. M. Kouser and J. M. McPherson (eds.), *Region, Race and Reconstruction* (New York: Oxford Univ. Press, 1982), 144. See also M. Banton, *Racial Theories* (Cambridge: Cambridge Univ. Press, 1987); and A. Smedley, *Race in North America* (Boulder, Colo.: Westview Press, 1993).
64. Granger instanced some cases of Puerto Ricans in the Army recruited in New York City. He added that he 'would like to know what the policy is about admission of dark skinned Puerto Ricans in the Army—I mean dark skinned Puerto Ricans who are as Negro as myself, who are in White units because they speak Spanish and they presented themselves as being Puerto Rican'. HSTL, Com. on Equality of Treatment and Opportunity in the Armed Services, Box 10, Minutes (13 Jan. morning), 13–17.
65. For relevant background material see amongst others E. Foner, *Reconstruction: America's Unfinished Revolution 1863–1877* (New York: Harper and Row, 1988); id., 'Blacks and the US Constitution 1789–1989', *New Left Review*, 183 (1990), 63–74; B. J. Fields, 'Slavery, Race and Ideology in the United States of America', *New Left Review*, 181 (1990), 95–118; and G. Frederickson, *White Supremacy* (New York: Oxford Univ. Press, 1981).
66. 'Only if *race* is defined as innate and natural prejudice of colour does its invocation as a historical explanation do more than repeat the question by way of answer. And there an insurmountable problem arises: since race is not genetically programmed, racial prejudice cannot be genetically programmed either but, like race itself, must

arise historically.' Fields, 'Slavery, Race and Ideology in the United States of America', 101.

67. HSTL, Com. on Equality of Treatment and Opportunity in the Armed Services, Box 10, Minutes (17 Mar. 1949), 38.
68. Ibid. 36–7.
69. Ibid. 38.
70. Stillman II, *Integration of the Negro in the US Armed Forces*, 27.
71. See LC NAACP, Group II-B, Box B195, Folder US Navy, Guam racial conflict and courtmartial: proceedings of the Court of Inquiry.
72. Ibid.: letter from White to Sec. Forrestal (16 July 1945), 1.
73. NA RG 16, Office of the Sec. of Agriculture, Gen. Correspondence, Negroes 1940–55, Box 3, Folder Negroes: 'Negroes in a Democracy at War', Survey of Intelligence Materials No. 25, Office of Facts and Figures, Bureau of Intelligence (27 May 1942), 15.
74. NA RG 228, Records of the FEPC, Office Files of Clarence Mitchell, Box 459, Folder Transportation Systems: speech by George M. Johnson, Asst. Executive Sec. FEPC, 'Equal Employment Opportunity for Negroes in Local Transportation Systems' (23 May 1943).
75. LC NAACP, Group II-A, Box A646, Folder US Army, Truman Gibson: letter from Roy Wilkins to Gibson, Acting Civilian Aide to the Sec. of War (1 Apr. 1943), 1.
76. Recalled in Channel 4's *Liberators* (12 Sept. 1993).
77. LC NAACP, Group II-B, Box B153, Folder Soldier Morale, Gen. 1941–5; NAACP press release (13 Sept. 1941), 1.
78. LC NAACP, Group II-B, Box B153, Folder Stimson, Soldier Morale: memorandum on Morale of Negro Soldiers in Certain Army Camps (17 Nov. 1941).
79. See ibid., Box B192, Folder US Armed Forces, War Dept. building segregation 1941–3: letter from Leon Ransom, NAACP lawyer to Walter White describing the Dept.'s efforts to persuade the Association to 'soft-pedal' the success.
80. Ibid., Box A646, Folder US Army, Truman K. Gibson: letter to Gibson from Wilkins (9 Feb. 1944), 1.
81. HSTL, Com. on Equality of Treatment and Opportunity in the Armed Services, Box 10, Minutes (13 Jan. 1949, morning), 73.
82. LC NAACP, Group II-A, Box A644, Folder US Army, Conference on Negroes in the Armed Services 1948–9: Report of Conference on Racial Policy of the Armed Services held in Washington DC (26 Apr. 1948), 4.
83. HSTL, Com. on Equality of Treatment and Opportunity in the Armed Services, Box 10, Minutes (13 Jan. 1949, morning), 74.
84. Ibid. 70.
85. Ibid. 71.
86. LC NAACP, Group II-B, Box B195, Folder US Navy, Discrimination, Dr Harold Franklin 1941: letter from Franklin to Frank Reeves Legal Research Asst. NAACP (26 Sept. 26 1941), 2.
87. Ibid.: letter to Franklin (17 Oct. 1941), 1.
88. Ibid.: letter from Franklin to Sec. of the Navy (20 Oct. 1941), 1.
89. Ibid.: memorandum to the Executive Staff (23 Oct. 1941).
90. HSTL, Papers of Philleo Nash, Box 37, Folder WH—Civil Rights: memo from Carr

to the President's Com. on Civil Rights, 'Negroes in the Armed Forces', prepared by Stewart and Murtha (10 June 1947), 4.

91. HSTL, Com. on Equality of Treatment and Opportunity in the Armed Services, Box 10, Minutes (13 Jan. 1949, morning), 79–80.
92. In assessing the Fahy Report, Dr Ambrose Caliver, Specialist for Higher Education of Negroes and Advisor on Related Problems to the US Commissioner for Education, observed in 1953 that 'special note should be made of the fact that the chairman of this Committee, Charles Fahy, is a native of Georgia, and was reared in the tradition of the South'. NA RG 12, Records of the Office of Education, Office Files of Ambrose Caliver 1956–61, Box 2, Folder Attorney Gen.'s Report, pt. 11, p. 14.
93. Stickney claimed that regarding progress he was alluding 'primarily to the fact that we had been able to double the number of Negroes in our general service rating in the Navy in two years'. HSTL, Com. on Equality of Treatment and Opportunity in the Armed Services, Box 10, Minutes (13 Jan. 1949, morning), 81.
94. NA RG 16, Office of the Sec. of Agriculture, Gen. Correspondence, Negroes 1940–55, Box 3, Folder Negroes: 'Negroes in a Democracy at War', Bureau of Intelligence, Office of Facts and Figures, Survey of Intelligence Materials, No. 25 (27 May 1942), 14.
95. LC, Records of the NUL, Papers of Lester Granger, Box 157, Folder Navy, General 1948: letter from Gilbert Johnson to Granger (17 Apr. 1947), 3.
96. HSTL, Papers of Philleo Nash, Box 37, Folder WH—Civil Rights: memo from Robert Carr to Members of the President's Com. on Civil Rights 'Negroes in the Armed Forces', prepared by Stewart and Murtha (10 June 1947), 8.
97. LC NAACP, Group II-A, Box A647, Folder US Army, Gillem Report: 'Analysis and Recommendations on the Army (Gillem) Report on Negroes in the Army' (n.d.), 1.
98. Ibid.: memorandum from Leslie Perry, summarizing conversation with Hastie, to Walter White (1 Nov. 1945).
99. Ibid.: letter from White to Gillem (15 Oct. 1945).
100. LC NAACP, Group II-A, Box A644, Folder US Army, Conference on Negroes in the Armed Services 1948–9: Report of Conference on Racial Policy of the Armed Services, held in Washington DC (26 Apr. 1948), 8.
101. Ibid. 9.
102. Ibid.
103. HSTL, Com. on Equality of Treatment and Opportunity in the Armed Services, Box 10, Fahy Com. Minutes (28 Mar. 1949, morning), 31–3.
104. Ibid. (13 Jan. 1949, morning), 59.
105. Ibid. 61–2.
106. The recommendations of the Gillem Board were circulated on 27 Apr. 1946 in a War Dept. Circular 124, though the Board's final report was submitted before that date.
107. HSTL, Com. on Equality of Treatment and Opportunity in the Armed Services, Box 10, Minutes (13 Jan. morning), 9.
108. Ibid. 10, 11.
109. Ibid. 75.
110. Ibid. 76–7.

111. HSTL, Papers of Philleo Nash, Box 37, Folder WH—Civil Rights: memo from Carr to the President's Com. 'Negroes in the Armed Forces', prepared by Stewart and Murtha (10 June 1947), 4.
112. LC NAACP, Group II-A, Box A646, Folder US Army, General 1950–5: letter from Wilkins to Sec. of Defense Louis A. Johnson (27 Feb. 1950), 1.
113. Black American women were not allowed to serve in the Waves, Spurs, and Marines—a discrimination for which the Navy was regularly excoriated by Black political leaders and newspapers. HSTL, Papers of Philleo Nash, Box 29, Folder 1943–5: confidential memo to Nash from Mrs Thomasina W. Johnson, 'Admission of Negro Women to the Waves, Spurs and Marines' (29 Sept. 1944).
114. Ibid., Folder Race Tensions: Office of War Information, 'Navy Department and Negro Press' (23 Oct. 1943), 1–4, documents these press campaigns.
115. LC, Records of NUL, Papers of Lester Granger, Box 157, Folder Navy, Jan.–Apr. 1947, General: quoted in letter from NUL's Vocational Sec. Frances Kornegay to Sec. Forrestal (17 Jan. 1947), 1.
116. HSTL, Com. on Equality of Treatment and Opportunity in the Armed Services, Box 10, Minutes (17 Mar. 1949), 42. This view was supported by Gen. Gillem when he appeared before the Com.: 'I think that if nearly two-thirds of them were white in a particular unit, the educational advance would be far more on the part of the whites, and they would not be placed in the proper positions etc. I think they would have a better advantage in units composed of their own people.' Ibid. 23.
117. Ibid. (28 Mar. 1949, afternoon), 69.
118. Ibid., Box 7, Folder Army—Utilization of Negroes: letter from Robert Patterson to Wilbur La Rose, Com. on Civic Affairs of the Washington Federation of Churches (26 Mar. 1943), 1.
119. Ibid., Box 10, Minutes (21 Feb. 1949, morning), 4–5.
120. Ibid. 6.
121. Ibid. 8.
122. Ibid. 15.
123. Ibid. 19.
124. Ibid. 21–2.
125. Ibid. (17 Mar. 1949), 43. Chief of Staff General Bradley also cited morale as a problem of integration in his testimony (28 Mar. 1949), 71.
126. Ibid. (28 Mar. 1949), 5, 6.
127. Ibid. 7.
128. Stillman reports a meeting in Apr. 1948 between Royall and sixteen Black leaders at which the former insisted that 'any improvement must be made within the framework of segregation': *Integration of the Negro in the US Armed Forces*, 40.
129. HSTL, Com. on Equality of Treatment and Opportunity in the Armed Services, Box 10, Minutes (28 Mar. 1949), 7.
130. Ibid. 8.
131. Ibid.
132. Ibid. (25 Apr. 1949), 28.
133. Ibid. (28 Mar. 1949, afternoon), 68.
134. *Yanks* (1979), dir. John Schlesinger. See also J. Gardiner, *'Over Here': The GIs in Wartime Britain* (London: Collins & Brown, 1992), ch. 14.

135. MOA, File Report 1569, 22 Jan. 1943: 'Feelings about America and the Americans', 31–41. Covers interviews with subjects in Bristol principally. Regarding attitudes toward the Americans, the diary reports (p. 35): 'on interviews it has been said that the black Americans are preferred to the white.'
136. LC NAACP, Group II-A, Box A633, Folder Truman 1946–69: statement by NAACP on Charges of Misconduct by Negro Troops by George Meader, Counsel to the Sen. War Investigating Com. (12 Dec. 1946), 1.
137. For accounts see D. Reynolds, 'The Churchill Government and the Black American Troops in Britain during Word War II', *Transactions of the Royal Historical Society*, 5th ser., 35 (1985), 113–33; G. Smith, *When Jim Crow Met John Bull: Black American Troops in World War II in Britain* (London: I. B. Taurus and Co., 1987); and T. E. Hachey, 'Document: Jim Crow with a British Accent: Attitudes of London Government Officials toward American Negro Soldiers in England during World War II', *Journal of Negro History*, 59 (1974), 65–77.
138. Reynolds, 'Churchill Government and Black American Troops in Britain', 115. I draw heavily upon this article in this section.
139. This view was expressed by the British Chiefs of Staff in Washington: PRO, Cabinet Office Papers, CAB 79/20 COS 126 (42) 11, 21 Apr. 1942, and CAB 80/62 COS (42) 104 (0).
140. DDEL, US War Dept., Operations Division Diary, summary of telegram from Chaney reporting Gen. Staff com. recommendations as to priorities for US troop shipments to War Department, 25 Apr. 1942: 'it does not favor shipment of colored units', p. 2.
141. Instructions were issued by Gen. Dwight Eisenhower to this effect on 16 July and 5 Sept. 1942, both cited in Reynolds, 'Churchill Government and Black American Troops in Britain', 117.
142. PRO CAB 66/29 WP (42) 441, 'Notes on relations with coloured troops'.
143. Reynolds, 'Churchill Government and Black American Troops in Britain', 119.
144. Grigg observed that 'while there can be no official discrimination, it is considered desirable that the British troops . . . should understand the American background of this matter in order that they may so regulate their conduct as not to give cause for offense either to the white or to the coloured troops.' Memorandum by Sec. of State for War Sir Percy James Grigg (n.d. Sept. 1942), Premier 4/26/9, reprod. in Hachey, 'Jim Crow with a British Accent', 68.
145. Reynolds, 'Churchill Government and Black American Troops in Britain', 122.
146. MOA, Topic Collection: Town and District Survey (Portsmouth) 17/E (14 Jan. 1944), 1.
147. Ibid., *passim*. However, this report does include a discussion of the contrast between the public and private views of many of the respondents, acknowledging that although they publicly abhor prejudice they quite frequently recognize it in their private opinions and views.
148. MOA, File Report 1569 (22 Jan. 1943), 'Feelings about America and the Americans', 32.
149. Document Two, War Office Paper 12154–1, London, Nov. 1942, reprod. in Hachey, 'Jim Crow with a British Accent', 71–4.
150. See PRO War Cabinet minutes, 10 and 31 Aug. 1942, CAB 65/27, WM (42) 109/6 and 119/6.

151. Home Office circular, 4 Sept. 1942, annexe to PRO CAB 66/29, WP (42) 456.
152. 'Notes on relations with coloured troops', PRO CAB 66/29, WP (42), 441.
153. LC NAACP, Group II-B, Box B153, Folder Stimson, Soldier Morale: letter from White to Stimson (2 Oct. 1942).
154. LC NAACP, Group II-A, Box A643, Folder US Army, Camp Conditions 1944–6: letter from PFC James P. Stanley to White (19 July 1945), 1–2.
155. LC NAACP, Group II-B, Box B195, Folder US Navy, Discrimination Gen. 1943–6: letter from Forrestal to Wilkins (28 Dec. 1945), 1.
156. Ibid.: letter from Wilkins to Sec. Stimson (5 Dec. 1945), 1.
157. Ibid., Box A644, Folder US Army, Conference on Negroes in the Armed Services 1948–9: letter from Walter White to Sec. Forrestal (17 Feb. 1948), 1, 2.
158. HSTL, Official File, Box 1651, Folder Com. on Equality of Treatment and Opportunity in the Armed Services: confidential memorandum from Fahy to Sec. of the Army (25 July 1949), 4.
159. HSTL, Papers of David Niles, Box 27, Folder Civil Rights/Negro Affairs 1949–52: memo from David Niles to Truman (5 Oct. 1949), 1.
160. HSTL, President's Official File, Box 1651, Folder Com. on Equality of Treatment and Opportunity in the Armed Services: confidential memorandum from Fahy to Sec. of the Army (25 July 1949), 1.
161. David Niles anticipated the Pres. being questioned at a Press Conference about the Army's position and advised Truman to 'reply to the effect that Secretary Johnson's release is a progress report only; that it is not final; and that the Fahy Committee is studying the program and will make some recommendations in the near future.' HSTL, Papers of David Niles, Box 27, Folder Civil Rights/Negro Affairs 1949–52: memo from Niles to Truman (5 Oct. 1949), 2.
162. Ibid.: memo from Niles to Truman (7 Feb. 1950) and letter from Sec. of the Army Gordon Gray to Truman (1 Mar. 1950).
163. HSTL, President's Official File, Box 1651, Folder Com. on Equality of Treatment and Opportunity in the Armed Services: letter from Fahy to Truman (27 July 1949), 1.
164. Ibid.
165. Ibid. 3.
166. Ibid.: confidential memorandum from Fahy to Sec. of the Army (25 July 1949), 5.
167. LC NAACP, Group II-A, Box A643, Folder US Army, Case—Complaints 1952–3: letter from Wilkins to Prof. Ralph Harlow (27 Jan. 1953), 1. For a more positive response see LC NAACP, Group II-B, Box B192, Folder US Air Force, Desegregation Plans 1949: memo to Roy Wilkins and Thurgood Marshall from Robert Carter 'Reaction of the Lockbourner Army Air Base to Prospective Integration in the US Air Force' (Mar. 1949).
168. DDEL, President's Official File, Box 137, Folder 6 Releases: talk by Asst. Sec. of Labor Wilkins (2 Aug. 1954), 3. The Korean War had a decisive impact on ending segregation: see D. McCoy and M. Ruetten, *Quest and Response* (Lawrence, Kan.: University Press of Kansas, 1973); and Stillman II, *Integration of the Negro in the US Armed Forces.*
169. NA RG 220, President's Com. on Govt. Employment Policy 1955–61, Agency Files, Box 15, File Air Force: memorandum from Col. Leon E. Bell Jr, Commander

USAF, to all military personnel (25 July 1958); and memorandum from Bell to Deputy Employment Policy Officers (25 Mar. 1959).

170. US Com. on Civil Rights, *Family Housing and the Negro Serviceman* (Washington: US Com. on Civil Rights, 1963), 34.
171. Ibid.
172. Ibid., appendix A: Summary and Recommendations, 'The Negro in the Armed Forces', *1963 Report of the US Commission on Civil Rights*, p. 40.
173. Ibid.
174. See W. N. Eskridge, Jr., 'Race and Sexual Orientation and the Military', *Reconstruction*, 2 (1993), 52–7.

CHAPTER 5

1. E. Goffman, *Asylums* (1961; Harmondsworth: Penguin, 1991). See also id., 'On the Characteristics of Total Institutions: The Inmate World' and 'On the Characteristics of Total Institutions: Staff-Inmate Relations', both in D. R. Cressey (ed.), *The Prison: Studies in Institutional Organization and Change* (New York: Holt, Rinehart and Winston, 1961).
2. USBP, Archives Division, Washington, Proceedings of the Federal Prison Wardens' Conference 1947, 'Discipline, Morale and Problems of Racial Relations', 11.
3. For historical accounts of the development of American penitentiaries and penal systems see *inter alia* D. J. Rothman, *The Discovery of the Asylum* (Boston: Little Brown, 1971); J. Jacobs, *Stateville: The Penitentiary in Mass Society* (Chicago: University of Chicago Press, 1977); O. F. Lewis, *The Development of American Prisons and Prison Customs 1776–1848* (1922; Montclair, NJ: Patterson Smith, 1967); B. McKelvey, *American Prisons* (Montclair, NJ: Patterson Smith, 1977); D. Clemmer, *The Prison Community* (New York: Holt, Rinehart and Winston, 1940); and A. J. Hirsch, *The Rise of the Penitentiary* (New Haven: Yale University Press, 1992).
4. NA RG 129, Bureau of Prisons, Central Administrative File 1937–67, Prisoners' Welfare, Box 41, File Segregation: Wardens' Conference, Leavenworth Kansas, 9 Dec. 1954, minutes and proceedings, 16.
5. Ibid.: letter from James Bennett Bureau Dir. to Jean Henry, Sec. Com. against Race Discrimination in the War Effort (5 Aug. 1943).
6. Ibid.: letter from Bennett to Warden Lowell Naeve (1 Sept. 1943), 1.
7. USBP, Archives Division, Proceedings of the Federal Prison Wardens' Conference 1947, 'Discipline, Morale and Problems of Racial Relations', 11.
8. McKelvey, *American Prisons*, 16. See also Lewis, *Development of American Prisons and Prison Customs 1776–1845*; Rothman, *Discovery of the Asylum*.
9. *American Prisons*, 172.
10. Ibid.
11. Ibid. 181.
12. Ibid.
13. Ibid. 183.
14. Ibid. 227–8.

15. *Congressional Record*, 70th Congress, 2nd sess., vol. lxx pt. 3 (31 Jan. 1929), 2579–82. The com. was titled 'Special Committee on Federal Penal and Reformatory Institutions', established under House Resolution 233, 70th Congress, 1st sess. The chairman was John Cooper of Ohio and the members were W. F. Kopp (Ia.), John Taber (NY), John J. Boylan (NY), and Thomas M. Bell (Ga.).
16. Ibid. 2580.
17. Ibid.
18. Ibid.
19. Ibid. 2582.
20. USBP, Archives Division, Proceedings of the Federal Prison Wardens' conference 1944, p. 5. 'Introductory Remarks' by Bureau Dir. James V. Bennett.
21. Ibid., Proceedings of the Federal Prison Wardens' Conference 1948, p. 32.
22. NA RG 129, Bureau of Prisons, Central Administrative File 1937–67, Prisoners' Welfare, Box 41, File Segregation: letter from Marshall to Director James Bennett (1 Sept. 1942).
23. Ibid.: letter from lawyer acting for Benjamin J. Davis, Jr. to Howard J. McGrath, US Attorney Gen. (15 Oct. 1951).
24. Ibid.: letter from Reed Cozart, Warden to James Bennett Dir. Bureau of Prisons (26 Nov. 1951), 1.
25. Ibid.: letter from J. V. Bennett, Dir. to George Harper, Nat. Conference of Methodist Youth (1 Aug. 1951); see also Harper's letter (24 July 1951).
26. Distributed symbolically in 1954, the year of the *Brown* decision.
27. NA RG 129, Bureau of Prisons, Central Administrative File 1937–67, Prisoners' Welfare, Box 41, File Segregation: Letter from Dir. to Norman Will, Commission on World Peace of the Methodist Church (10 Sept. 1951), 1.
28. Ibid.: Wardens' Conference, Leavenworth, Kan., 9 Dec. 1954, minutes and proceedings, 17.
29. USBP, Archives Division, Proceedings of the Federal Prison Wardens' Conference 1948, 'Racial Minorities and Frictions', 28.
30. Ibid. 28–9.
31. NA RG 129, Bureau of Prisons, Central Administrative File 1937–67, Prisoners' Welfare, Box 41, File Segregation: letter from Dir. Bennett to Hironimus (30 Nov. 1945), 1.
32. Ibid.
33. Ibid. 2.
34. Ibid.: letter from Dir. Bennett to Warden Lowell Naeve (1 Sept. 1943), 2.
35. D. Glaser, *The Effectiveness of a Prison and Parole System* (New York: Bobbs-Merrill Co., 1964), 152–4.
36. USBP, Archives Division, Proceedings of the Federal Prison Wardens' Conference 1948, 'Racial Minorities and Frictions', 30.
37. Ibid.
38. Ibid. 32.
39. Ibid.
40. NA RG 129, Bureau of Prisons, Central Administrative File 1937–67, Prisoners' Welfare, Box 41, File Segregation: Wardens' Conference, Leavenworth, Kan., 9 Dec. 1954, minutes and proceedings, 18.

41. Ibid.
42. Ibid. 22.
43. Ibid. 24.
44. Ibid. 22.
45. Ibid. 20: 'strangely enough in governmental zeal to avoid discrimination we do not know how many negro personnel we have in the Prison Service. In the classification and parole work the number has increased from none ten years ago to nine, or more than 10 per cent now.'
46. Ibid. 18–19.
47. Ibid.: letter from Bureau Dir. to Norman Will, Commission on World Peace of the Methodist Church (10 Sept. 1951), 1.
48. Ibid.: answers to questionnaire of 10 June 1954 re segregation, 11.
49. Glaser, *Effectiveness of a Prison and Parole System*, 128.
50. Ibid. 131.
51. USBP, Archives Division, Proceedings of the Federal Prison Wardens' Conference 1944, pp. 35–8.
52. NA RG 129, Bureau of Prisons, Central Administrative File 1937–67, Prisoners' Welfare, Box 41, File Segregation: letter from Warden R. P. Hagerman, Ashland, Ky. to Dir. Bennett (24 Mar. 1947), 1.
53. Ibid.
54. Ibid. 2.
55. Ibid.: memorandum from M. E. Alexander to Dir. Bennett 'Inter-racial Baseball Games' (19 Mar. 1947).
56. Ibid.: memorandum to the Dir. from Warden G. W. Humphrey 'Racial Tension' (2 Dec. 1946).
57. Ibid.: office memorandum by Asst. Dir., M. E. Alexander (26 Mar. 1947). The conflict had much to do with housing.
58. USBP, Archives Division, Proceedings of the Federal Prison Wardens' Conference 1947, 'Discipline, Morale and Problems of Racial Relations', 12.
59. Ibid. 13.
60. Ibid. 14.
61. Ibid. 15.
62. NA RG 129, Records of the Bureau of Prisons, Central Administrative Files 1937–67, Mill Point, Box 11, File General: letter to Kenneth Thieman Superintendent Mill Point from the Dir. (9 Oct. 1952), 1.
63. Ibid. 2.
64. For the established routine response to riots see ibid., Box 25, File Riot Procedure: 'General Procedure for Handling Riots' (7 May 1948).
65. Ibid.: memorandum to the files by Warden Frank Loveland (27 Aug. 1951).
66. Ibid.: memorandum from Superintendent K. E. Thieman to Dir. of Federal Prisons 'Recent Incident—Racial Tension' (29 Aug. 1951), 1.
67. Ibid.
68. Ibid.
69. Ibid. 3.
70. Ibid. 5–6.
71. Ibid., Prisoners' Welfare, Box 41, File Segregation: letter to Thurgood Marshall from Dir. James Bennett (7 Sept. 1942), 2.

72. Ibid.: Letter from James Bennett Bureau Dir. to Jean Henry, Sec. Com. against Race Discrimination in the War Effort (5 Aug. 1943).
73. Ibid.: Wardens' Conference, Leavenworth, Kan. 9 Dec. 1954, minutes and proceedings.
74. Ibid. 14–15.
75. Ibid. 15.
76. Ibid. 16.
77. USBP, Archives Division, Proceedings of Federal Prison Wardens' Conference 1950: Warden Hardwick of El Reno reporting, 137.
78. USBP, Archives Divisions, Proceedings of Federal Prison Wardens' Conference 1956: Director's Opening Statement, 5.
79. NA RG 129, Bureau of Prisons, Central Administrative File 1937–67, Box 41, File Segregation: see memorandum to the US Attorney Gen. from J. V. Bennett Dir. Bureau of Prisons 'Racial Tensions' (21 July 1964), 2–3, in which Bennett discussed incidents at Marion, Petersburg, Chillicothe, and New York prisons.
80. Ibid. 3. On Rustin's civil rights role see entries in T. Branch, *Parting the Waters: America in the King Years 1954–1963* (New York: Simon & Schuster, 1988).
81. NA RG 129, Bureau of Prisons, Central Administrative File 1937–67, Box 41, File Segregation: memorandum from Bureau Acting Dir. Fred T. Wilkinson to all institutions (7 Aug. 1964).
82. Ibid.: letter from Myrl Alexander to Laughlin McDonald (11 Oct. 1966); see also McDonald's letter of 5 Oct.
83. Ibid.: see e.g. Leavenworth's statement 2 Feb. 1966.
84. Ibid.: 'Integration' Policy Statement 1001.1, Bureau of Prisons, 7 Feb. 1966.
85. Ibid.
86. Ibid., File Segregation: see copies of correspondence.
87. Ibid.: memo from Warden J. T. Willingham to Alexander (18 Feb. 1966).
88. NA RG 129, Records of the Bureau of Prisons, Administrative Files, Correspondence Box 98: letter from Warden A. C. Aderhold to Dir. Bureau of Prisons (10 Feb. 1934), 1–2.
89. NA RG 129, Bureau of Prisons, Central Administrative File 1937–67, Box 41, File Segregation: memorandum to M. Alexander from Eugene N. Barkin (26 May 1966).
90. Ibid.: memorandum from O. G. Blackwell Warden Atlanta to Myrl Alexander Bureau Dir. (1 Mar. 1966).
91. Ibid. 1–2.
92. Ibid. 2.
93. Ibid. 3.
94. Ibid.
95. Ibid.: See memorandum to the US Attorney Gen. from J. V. Bennett Dir. Bureau of Prisons 'Racial Tensions', 21 July 1964 in which Bennett discussed incidents at Marion, Petersburg, Chillicothe, and New York prisons.
96. Ibid.: memorandum to M. Alexander from Eugene N. Barkin (26 May 1966).
97. Ibid.: letter from Dir. Myrl Alexander to Hubert L. Will US District Court, Chicago (26 May 1966).
98. Ibid., File Segregation. For another case see US District Court for the District of Court, Civil Action No. 1983–63 memorandum re Clarence R. Edwards and Richard James, plaintiffs v. Thomas T. Sard defendant by Justice Luther W. Youngdahl 25

Feb. 1966. On p. 4 the Judge notes: 'since the decision in Brown v. Board of Education, 347 U.S. 483 (1954), the course of history in civil rights cases and legislation has made it unmistakably clear that racial discrimination by governmental authorities cannot be tolerated. Therefore, the plaintiffs in this case will prevail in their suit if they convince the Court that a policy of racial discrimination has been followed in making dormitory assignements.'

99. NA RG 129, Bureau of Prisons, Central Administrative File 1937–67, Box 41, File Segregation: letter from Howard W. Rogerson US Commission on Civil Rights to Acting Dir. Bureau of Prisons (31 Aug. 1964).
100. Ibid.: letter to Howard W. Rogerson US Commission on Civil Rights from Myrl Alexander Dir. Bureau of Prisons (11 Sept. 1964).
101. Ibid. 2.
102. Ibid.: memorandum to Bureau Dir. from Eugene Barkin (30 July 1965) re Pulaski County Jail in Arkansas.
103. Ibid.: memorandum from Nicholas deB Katzenbach Attorney General to Alexander (27 Jan. 1966).
104. Ibid.: memorandum to the Attorney Gen. from Bureau Dir. Myrl Alexander, 'Racial Segregation in City and County Jails and in State Penitentiaries' (7 Feb. 1966).
105. Derived from US Dept. of Justice, Federal Bureau of Prisons *State of the Bureau 1992* (Washington: Federal Bureau of Prisons, 1992), 37.
106. Burleigh documents the differing perspectives of patients, visitors, workers, and doctors: M. Burleigh, *Death and Deliverance* (Cambridge: Cambridge University Press, 1994). See also Burleigh's earlier study of academics, *Germany Turns Eastward* (Cambridge: Cambridge University Press, 1988). Such detailed empirical analysis stands as a valuable and necessary counterbalance to the fashionable tendency to depersonalize bureaucratic institutions.
107. C. W. Eagles, *Outside Aggressor: Jon Daniels and the Civil Rights Movement in Alabama* (Chapel Hill, NC: Univ. of North Carolina Press, 1993). The study would have been strengthened by a richer portrait of the unsympathetic White Southerners in addition to the more easily comprehensible Northern liberal. A book without theoretical pretensions but no less acutely informed by the nature of social institutions is W. J. Cash, *The Mind of the South* (1941: New York: Vintage, 1991).

CHAPTER 6

1. NA RG 183, BES/USES, Papers of Lawrence A. Oxley [Negro U] Box 3, Folder Missouri SES: letter from Cochran to Persons (19 Mar. 1938), 2. He continued: 'it is my job, as Chairman of the Committee on Expenditures in the Executive Departments to see that money is properly spent and although I am just as good a Democrat as any one in Washington, and just as strong a supporter of the Administration, I am not going to sit idly by and see appropriations used for making speeches that result in the Administration being criticised without protest.'
2. NA RG 207, Records of the Dept. of Housing and Urban Development, HHFA, Subject Files 1947–60, Box 189, Folder Racial Relations: letter from Archibald Carey, chairman of the President's Com. on Govt. Employment Policy to Norman P. Mason, Administrator, HHFA 24 Sept. 1959. Carey noted that 'the regulations

of the President's Committee (Section I-B) provide that the maintenance of segregated units is in violation of Executive Order 10590'.

3. US Com. on Civil Rights, *Housing in Washington: Hearings before the US Commission on Civil Rights 12–13 Apr. 1962* (Washington: US Commission on Civil Rights, 1962), 4.
4. Ibid. The speaker was John Hannah.
5. These processes have been documented elsewhere. See esp. K. T. Jackson, *Crabgrass Frontier: The Suburbanization of the United States* (New York: Oxford University Press, 1985). For an analysis of the persistence of residential segregation see D. S. Massey and N. A. Denton, *American Apartheid: Segregation and the Making of the Underclass* (Cambridge Mass.: Harvard University Press, 1993).
6. NA RG 183, Records of the BES/USES, Papers of Lawrence A. Oxley [Negro U], Box 2, Folder Survey, Indiana SES: 'A Report on the Availability of the Services of the US Employment Offices to Negro Applicants in Indianapolis' (27 July 1936), 3–4.
7. L. A. Oxley, 'Employment Security and the Negro', *Employment Security Review* (7 July 1940), 13.
8. NA RG 183, Records of the BES/USES, Papers of Lawrence A. Oxley [Negro U], Box 2, Folder Survey Maryland SES: 'Report on the Availability of the Services to Negroes of the Maryland State Employment Service' (23 Dec. 1936), 8: 'the physical setup and equipment of the Baltimore Employment Center was the best observed in any of the state or city offices visited in twelve states.'
9. He wrote:

   > employment opportunities and working conditions for the Negro workers are almost identical in character in Georgia and the adjacent states. Seasonal cotton planting and picking afford job opportunities for thousands of Negro marginal workers. The Georgia State Employment Service must find jobs for large numbers of unskilled workers . . . Negro males and females continue to find employment in domestic and personal service despite the fact that they have been replaced in many instances with white workers. In Atlanta practically all the hotels have replaced Negro bell boys with white help. Negro maids in the hotels and other public places appear to be holding their own.

   Ibid., Folder: Survey—Georgia SES: 'A Report on the Availability of the Services of the US Employment Service to Negro Applicants in Georgia' (16 Dec. 1936), 6.
10. Just how precarious this position was is suggested in Oxley's study of Arkansas: 'a marshal of an Arkansas city was found guilty in November 1936 by a United States District Court jury of violating the anti-slavery statute. He was charged specifically with arresting eight Negro men on vagrancy charges and forcing them to clean lands during the cotton choppers' strike early last spring in Arkansas. This conviction should go a long way toward breaking up this forced labor practiced on Negroes in the South and toward changing materially the deplorable condition of the Southern sharecropper.' Ibid., Folder Survey—Arkansas State ES: 'Report on the availability of services to Negro applicants of the Arkansas State Employment Service Office' (16 Dec. 1936), 8. 'A higher percentage of Negroes than whites are found on the relief rolls of all the eight important cities in Tennessee, Arkansas, Texas, Alabama, Louisiana, and Georgia.' Ibid. 4.
11. Ibid., Folder Survey Illinois SES: 'A Report on the availability of the Services of the US Employment Office to Negro Applicants in Chicago and East St Louis, Illinois' (1 Aug. 1936), 3.

12. For details see D. S. King, *Actively Seeking Work? The Politics of Unemployment and Welfare Policy in the United States and Great Britain* (Chicago: University of Chicago Press, 1995), 2.
13. NA RG 183, Records of BES/USES, Papers of Lawrence A. Oxley [misc.], Box 6: Metropolitan Chicago Conference on Employment Problems of the Negro 23 May 1940, Peter Swanish Commissioner of Placement and Unemployment Compensation Illinois State Dept. of Labor, 1 (my emphasis).
14. Ibid., Box 2, Folder Kentucky SES, Survey: Report (30 Nov. 1937), 1. Some of the conditions had improved by the time of this visit, six months after the original one.
15. Ibid. 1–2.
16. Ibid., Folder: Survey Maryland SES: 'Report on the Availability of the Services to Negroes of the Maryland State Employment Service' (23 Dec. 1936), 7: 'the physical setup and equipment of the Baltimore Employment Center was the best observed in any of the state or city offices visited in twelve states.'
17. Ibid., Box 4, Folder NC—Surveys and Reports: memorandum from Oxley to USES Director Frank Persons, 'Special Report on North Carolina Services to Negro Applicants' (5 Nov. 1937), 2, 3.
18. Ibid. 1–2. The memorandum was prepared for the Dir. of the BES, of which the USES was a part. When the memorandum was forwarded to Burr (in Jan. 1938) a five-page memo prepared by Lyle S. Garlock was attached in which Garlock identified measures under way to rectify the problems Oxley analysed.
19. Ibid., Box 1, Folder Illinois SES: 'A Report on the availability of the Services of the US Employment Office to Negro Applicants in Chicago and East St Louis Illinois' (1 Aug. 1936), pt. II, p. 4. The Dir. was Dr. A. Attwood.
20. Ibid., Folder Survey—CA SES: 'Analysis of Employment Service Files', 1.
21. LC NAACP, II-A, Box A234, Folder Discrimination, Civil Service—Henry Alston 1940–3: letter to Glenn E. Brockway, Chief Employment Service Division, WMC from Roy Wilkins (26 Feb. 1943).
22. Ibid.
23. Ibid.: letter from Alston to FEPC (9 Feb. 1943), 1.
24. Ibid., Box A238, Folder Discrimination, NJ SES 1941: letter from NJSES Dir. Russell J. Eldridge to Mrs Lila B. Terhune, Executive Sec., Public Welfare Soc. of Long Branch & Deal Inc. (30 June 1941), 1.
25. NA RG 183, Records of the BES/USES, Papers of Lawrence A. Oxley [Negro U] Box 2, Folder: Michigan SES, Detroit: Report of conference (held 30 Nov. 1937), 1. Oxley urged appointing Black staff members. He concluded: 'your representative was very much impressed with the keen interest and earnestness of the Michigan State Employment Service administrative staff in an attempt to work out a constructive approach to a problem which at the present time has become the major problem in the larger urban centers of Michigan.' Ibid. 2.
26. Ibid., Box 1: Folder Georgia SES: memorandum from Oxley to Burr (14 Sept. 1938).
27. Ibid., Box 4, Folder NC—Surveys and Reports: memorandum from Garlock to Burr (22 Jan. 1938), 'Special Report on North Carolina Services to Negro Applicants', 2.
28. Ibid. 3.

29. Ibid., Box 1, Folder Illinois SES: 'A Report on the availability of the Services of the US Employment Office to Negro Applicants in Chicago and East St Louis Illinois' (1 Aug. 1936), pt. II, p. 3. The Dir. was Dr A. Attwood.
30. See e.g. ibid.: Folder DC ES, Complaints: letter from NAACP to the USES (7 May 1935).
31. Ibid., Box 3, Folder Missouri SES: memorandum from Oxley to Mr Rual (22 May 1936), 2.
32. Ibid.: minutes of special meeting with Mr Lawrence A. Oxley, Special Advisor on Negro problems to Sec. of Labor, Miss Frances Perkins and Field Rep. of Employment Service, US Dept. of Employment Service (14 Jan. 1938), 1.
33. Ibid., Box 1, Folder DC ES, Complaints: letter from NAACP to Mary LaDame Associate Dir. of USES in the Dept. of Labor (7 May 1935), 2. On problems within the DC office for Black staff see ibid., Folder Survey DC Employment Center: memoranda from Harry McAlpin, a Black officer, to the Dir. Lamson (6 Nov. 1937 and 10 Feb. 1938).
34. See e.g. ibid. Folder DC ES Complaints: letter from NAACP to Mary LaDame Associate Dir. USES (7 May 1935), 2.
35. LC NAACP, Group II, Box A653, Folder USES 1940–2 General: letter from Byron Mitchell to Addison Cutler (17 Apr. 1940), 1.
36. NA RG 183 Records of BES/USES, Papers of Lawrence A. Oxley [Negro U] Box 1, Folder Survey DC Employment Center (Aug. 1937), 1.
37. NA RG 174, Office of the Sec., Subject Files, Box 14, Folder ES 1946: letter from Schwellenbach to Congressman Gordon L. McDonough (12 Aug. 1946).
38. Ibid.: memorandum from Phillip Hannah and Robert C. Goodwin to Sec. of Labor, 'Meeting with AFL Representatives re Segregation in District Employment Office' (26 Aug. 1946), 1–2.
39. Ibid.: letter from L. B. Schwellenbach to Congressman Gordon L. McDonough (12 Aug. 1946).
40. Ibid.: memorandum from Fred Z. Hetzel USES Dir. for the DC to John F. Foy Regional Dir. Region IV (5 Aug. 1946), 'Meeting with AF of L Representatives Regarding Segregation Policies—Fifth and K Street Office', 1.
41. Ibid.: letter from Henry Beitscher to Schwellenbach (22 Aug. 1946).
42. NA RG 183, Records of BES/USES, Papers of Lawrence A. Oxley [Negro U] Box 3, Folder New York SES: Wilkinson, 'Suggestions for Improvement of Relations Between the Public Employment Services and Minority Groups in New York State', attached to memorandum from William H. E. Wilkinson to W. D. Holden (16 Jan. 1937), 1.
43. Ibid. 2–6.
44. LC NAACP, Group II-A, Box A665, Folder WMC, 1942: quoted in a letter from the California CIO to Walter White (11 Aug. 1942) (emphasis added).
45. Ibid.: letter from Federal Security Agency to Roy Wilkins NAACP (3 Sept. 1942), 1.
46. Ibid. 1–2.
47. See e.g. NA RG 174, Office of the Sec., Subject Files, Box 14, Folder USES 1946: memorandum from Robert Goodwin to the Sec. re 'Filling Anticipated Vacancy for Chief, Minority Groups Section, Standards and Methods Division' (3 Apr. 1946).

48. LC NAACP, Group III-A, Box A146, Folder Govt.—Nat. Dept. of Labor 1960–5: 'Implementation of Policy and Procedure With Respect to Serving Minority Groups' (12 Mar. 1964).
49. NA RG 228, Records of the FEPC, Office Files of the Chairman, Box 63, Folder D. Includes memorandum documenting USES #510 Reports from several states: memorandum from Eugene Davidson to Lawrence W. Cramer executive sec. FEPC 'USES #510 Reports' 15 May 1943; and Eugene Davidson 'The Processing of USES #510 Reports on Discriminatory Hiring Practices' 27 July 1943.
50. NA RG 174, Office of the Sec., Subject Files, Tobin, Box 43: Folder 1950 Employment Security—General: 'Current Information Regarding Minority Group Workers' (12 Sept. 1950), 3; memorandum from Dir. Robert Goodwin to Sec. of Labor Tobin (15 Sept. 1950).
51. LC NAACP, Group II-B, Box B95, Folder Labor—State Employment Services 1947–49: see letter from Clarence Mitchell to Oscar Ewing, Administrator Federal Security Agency (21 Mar. 1949).
52. Ibid.: see letter from Clarence Mitchell to Robert Carter Asst. Special Counsel NAACP (27 Apr. 1949), 1.
53. For the formulation of the Agency's position see NA RG 174, Office of the Sec., Subject Files, Box 14, Folder ES 1946: memorandum from Robert Goodwin to the Sec., 'USES Policy and Procedures for Handling Orders which Discriminate Against Minority Groups' (14 Aug. 1946). This included the draft which became the object of criticism by the NAACP and others.
54. LC NAACP, Group II-B, Box B95, Folder Labor—State Employment Services 1947–9: see letter from J. Donald Kingsley, Acting Administrator, to Mitchell (26 Apr. 1949).
55. The California State ES would make records available to the Dept. of Justice Civil Rights Division, as late as 1968, only on condition that any persons wanted for other changes were not pursued. NA RG 60, Records of the Dept. of Justice, Records of John Doar, Asst. Attorney Gen., Civil Rights Division 1960–7, Box 1, Folder Legal Memos—Employment: memorandum from John Rosenberg Acting Chief Western Section to David L. Rose Special Assistant on Title VI, Civil Rights Division, 'Problems of Confidentiality' (2 Feb. 1968).
56. NA RG 174, Office of the Sec., Subject Files, Box 14, Folder ES 1946: memorandum to all regional directors from Goodwin re 'USES Policy and Procedures for Handling Orders which Discriminate Against Minority Groups' (Aug. 1946).
57. Ibid.: memorandum from Robert Goodwin to Sec. of Labor 'Filling Anticipated Vacancy for Chief, Minority Groups Section, Standards and Methods Division' 3 Apr. 1946, 2–3.
58. Ibid., Tobin, Box 43, Folder 1950 Employment Security—General: 'Current Information Regarding Minority Group Workers' (12 Sept. 1950), 4, attached to memorandum from Goodwin to Sec. of Labor Tobin (15 Sept. 1950).
59. Ibid. 5.
60. The affiliate was the United Public Workers of America, Local 10. Ibid., Subject Files Schwellenbach, Box 31, Folder Discrimination: letter from Roy M. Patterson, Labor Dept. Research Local 10 UPW-CIO to Sec. Schwellenbach (16 Dec. 1947).
61. NA RG 146, Civil Service Agencies, FEB, Correspondence with Agencies 1948–54, Box 3, Folder Labor Dept.: report of Meeting with A. V. Motley, Asst. Dir.

Employment Service, and Mrs Norford, Minority Groups Consultant, Labor Dept. (18 Mar. 1953), 6.

62. Ibid. 4. The Executive Sec. posing the question was L. Lawhorn.
63. Ibid. 5.
64. Based on the report prepared by the Federal Advisory Council of the USES.
65. NA RG 146, Civil Service Agencies, FEB, Correspondence with Agencies 1948–54, Box 3, Folder Labor Dept.: press release (14 Nov. 1953), 1.
66. In 1947 the USES had decided against issuing a non-discrimination statement because 'such a policy is already a matter of government-wide policy expressed in executive orders'. NA RG 174, Records of the Dept. of Labor, Papers of Lewis B. Schwellenbach, Box 31, Folder Employment Service—General: memorandum to Sec. Schwellenbach from R. M. Barnett. USES (13 Feb. 1947).
67. Ibid.: memorandum from Goodwin to Sec. of Labor Lewis Schwellenbach (20 Sept. 1948), 1 (my emphasis).
68. NA RG 146, Civil Service Agencies, FEB, Correspondence with Agencies 1948–54, Box 3, Folder Labor Dept.: see minutes of meeting with A. V. Motley, Asst. Dir., Employment Service, and Mrs Norford, Minority Groups Consultant, Labor Dept. (18 Mar. 1953), 1.
69. Ibid.: see minutes of 186th Meeting of the Board (18 Mar. 1953), 1–2.
70. For the relevant papers see NA RG 220, President's Com. on Govt. Employment Policy, Agency Files 1955–61, Box 15, Folder Labor: correspondence between Ross Clinchy Executive Dir. of the President's Com. on Govt. Employment Policy and A. W. Motley Bureau of Employment Security Dept. of Labor (20 and 28 Feb.).
71. Ibid., USES BES 20—Employers' Benefits, Part 604—Policies of the USES, Amendment 29 Mar. 1957.
72. Ibid.: Summary Minutes of the 49th Meeting of the Committee (17 Apr. 1957), 1.
73. NA RG 174, Office of the Sec., Subject Files, Tobin, Box 43: Folder 1950 Employment Security—General: 'Current Information Regarding Minority Group Workers' (12 Sept. 1950), 3, memorandum from Dir. Robert Goodwin to Sec. of Labor Tobin (15 Sept. 1950).
74. Ibid.
75. NA RG 146, Civil Service Agencies, FEB, Correspondence with Agencies 1948–54, Box 3, Folder Labor Dept.: Report of Com. on Minority Policy, Federal Advisory Council USES (11 Mar. 1953), 2.
76. Ibid. 2.
77. NA RG 174, Office of the Sec., Subject Files, Tobin, Box 43: Folder 1950 Employment Security—General: 'Current Information Regarding Minority Group Workers' (12 Sept. 1950), 3, memorandum from Dir. Robert Goodwin to Sec. of Labor Tobin (15 Sept. 1950).
78. LC NAACP, Group II-A Box A 653, Folder USES 1940–2 General: from a memorandum of a conference between Ewan Clague Head of the USES and Walter White of the NAACP (17 Dec. 1940), 1.
79. Ibid., Group II-B, Box B95, Folder Labor—State ESs, 1947–9: Report on Missouri State ES (30 Apr. 1947), 1, 6.
80. Ibid.: letter from Clarence Mitchell, NAACP Labor Sec. to Robert Carter Asst. Special Counsel at the NAACP, commenting on a letter from J. Donald Kingsley Acting Admin. of the Federal Security Agency (27 Apr. 1949), 1.

81. Ibid., Box A 653, Folder USES Discrimination 1944–7: statement from NAACP to Sec. of Labor Lewis Schwellenbach on the return of the USES to the states (11 Sept. 1946); and Memo on meeting with Dept. of Labor on Transfer of USES to the states (17 Sept. 1947). The NAACP was one of ten organizations meeting with the Labor Sec.
82. Ibid., Folder USES Mitchell, Clarence 1946–7.
83. Ibid., Folder: USES Discrimination 1944–7: Nat. Citizens Political Action Com. 'Retention of Employment Service as National Agenda essential to Fair Employment in Reconversion Period' (10 Nov. 1945), 3.
84. Ibid.: NAACP press release (25 Apr. 1947), 1.
85. NA RG 146, Civil Service Agencies, FEB, Correspondence with Agencies 1948–54, Box 4, Folder VA: letter from White (17 May 1951) attached to Minutes of the 110th Meeting of the FEB (18 May 1951).
86. Ibid. 2.
87. NA RG 207, General Records of the Dept. of Housing and Urban Development, HHFA, General Subject Files 1947–60, Box 96, Folder Racial Relations: memorandum from Joseph R. Ray, Racial Relations Service to Albert M. Cole, Administrator 'Racial Policy to Govern Administration of HHFA Programs' (13 Aug. 1954), 1.
88. Ibid. 2.
89. Before the 1920s segregated residential housing was effected in northern and midwestern cities by zoning ordinances stipulating who could and could not live in designated areas. These were outlawed by the Supreme Court in 1917, a decision which did not terminate segregation however. *The Decision of the U.S. Supreme Court in the Louisville Segregation Case (Buchanan vs. Warley 245 U.S. 60)* (New York: NAACP, 1917). For the earlier period see e.g. *Segregation in Baltimore and Washington* (New York: NAACP, 1913), an address delivered before the Baltimore Branch of the NAACP by Oswald Garrison Villard 20 Oct. 1913 (copy in LC, Papers of Moorfield Storey, Box 11, Folder 1913).
90. See Jackson, *Crabgrass Frontier*, ch. 11: it was the 'case in every city [that] any Afro-American presence was a source of substantial concern to the HOLC', p. 201.
91. NA RG 195, Records of the Federal Home Loan Bank Board, Home Owners' Loan Corp., Records Relating to the City Survey File 1935–40, Box 1, Folder Greater Kansas City: Division of Research and Statistics Federal Home Loan Bank Board 'Security Area Map Folder: Greater Kansas City' (1 Apr. 1939), 1–2.
92. Ibid. 4.
93. Ibid., Box 109, Folder Metropolitan St Louis, MO & Ill.: #1 Resurvey Report vol. 1 (2), 'Confidential Report of a Re-survey of Metropolitan St Louis, Missouri and Illinois' for the Division of Research and Statistics, Home Owners' Loan Corporation (Nov. 1940), 85.
94. NA RG 207, Gen. Records of the Dept. of Housing and Urban Development, HHFA, Subject Files 1947–60, Box 96, Folder Racial Relations: 'Housing Problems of the Philadelphia Nonwhite Population' by I. Maximilian Martin (Philadelphia: Isadore Martin, 1953), 16.
95. Ibid.: memorandum from Joseph R. Ray, Racial Relations Service to Albert M. Cole, Administrator 'Racial Policy to Govern Administration of HHFA Programs' (13 Aug. 1954), 3.

96. Ibid.
97. The New York Alumni Chapter of the Atlanta University School of Social Work. Ibid., Box 134, Folder Racial Relations: letter to Administrator Albert Cole (29 Sept. 1956).
98. Ibid.: letter to Pres. Eisenhower from Algernon Black Vicechairman Council on Housing Policy (3 Aug. 1956), 1. The same organization had lobbied the FHA and White House for several years: see ibid., Box 59, Folder Racial Relations: letter from Robert Weaver, Nat. Com. against Discrimination in Housing to John Egan Commissioner Public Housing Authority (25 Sept. 1952) and letter to Raymond Foley Administrator HHFA from Weaver (6 Feb. 1951).
99. Ibid., Box 116, Folder Racial Relations: letter from Congressman Craig Hosmer, 18th District CA to Joseph Ray Asst. to the Administrator, HHFA (3 Nov. 1955).
100. NA RG 207, Gen. Records of the Dept. of Housing and Urban Development, Urban Renewal Administration, General Subject Files 1949–60, Box 330, Folder Racial Relations: 'Housing and Redevelopment: Dangers and Possibilities—The Viewpoint of Minority Groups' by Reginald A. Johnson, NUL, paper to the National Housing Conference (3 Apr. 1950).
101. NA RG 207, Gen. Records of the Dept. of Housing and Urban Development, HHFA, Subject Files 1947–60, Box 96, Folder Racial Relations: telegram to Eisenhower (21 Oct. 1954).
102. Ibid.: letter from Shad Polier, chairman (3 Aug. 1954), 1.
103. NA RG 207, Gen. Records of the Dept. of Housing and Urban Development, Urban Renewal Administration, General Subject Files 1949–60, Box 291, Folder Racial Relations: American Friends Service Committee 'Equal Opportunity in Housing' (Mar. 1955), 7.
104. Ibid. 8.
105. NA RG 207, Gen. Records of the Dept. of Housing and Urban Development, HHFA, Subject Files 1947–60, Box 96, Folder Racial Relations: 'Housing Problems of the Philadelphia Nonwhite Population' by I. Maximilian Martin (Philadelphia: Isadore Martin, 1953), 18. Martin identified also 'unwritten laws' as a barrier facing Black homebuyers and notes the collusion of real estate agents in their maintenance.
106. Ibid., Box 59, Folder Racial Relations: letter from Marshall to Commissioner John Egan (4 Feb. 1950).
107. He wrote:

> though many persons appear to assume its applicability, the Supreme Court of the United States has never applied the 'separate but equal' doctrine to the provisions of housing accommodations. As long ago as 1917 in Buchanan vs Warley the Supreme Court first held racial zoning ordinances unconstitutional, affirming the right of a Negro to occupy the particular premises he sought to purchase, despite the attempt of the city involved to make parcels available to whites in certain parts of the city and to Negroes in other sections. Moreover, as the Supreme Court pointed out in its racial restrictive covenant decision in 1948, Congress itself has made plain that the transfer of real property is a matter of same not equal rights.

NA RG 207, Gen. Records of the Dept. of Housing and Urban Development, Urban Renewal Administration, General Subject Files 1949–60, Box 330, Folder Racial Relations: memorandum by George B. Nesbitt to Nathaniel Keith Dir. Slum Clearance and Urban Redevelopment, 'Basic Approaches to Racial Considerations' (9 Mar. 1950), 9–10.

108. Ibid.: included in memorandum from Frank S. Horne, Racial Relations Service to FHA Administrator, Raymond Foley (13 July 1950) 'Racial Policy in Federally-Aided Housing Programs in Light of Recent Decisions of the U.S. Supreme Court'.
109. Ibid., Box 269, Folder Racial Relations: letter from Clarence Mitchell NAACP to Nathaniel S. Keith Dir. Division of Slum Clearance and Urban Redevelopment, HHFA (17 Dec. 1951), 3.
110. Ibid., Box 284, Folder Racial Relations: memorandum to J. W. Follin, Dir. Division of Slum Clearance and Urban Redevelopment from Joseph Guandolo, Associate Gen. Counsel 'An Approach to Racial Policy in HHFA' (24 Aug. 1954), 1.
111. Ibid.: Box 291, Folder Racial Relations: American Friends Service Committee 'Equal Opportunity in Housing' (Mar. 1955), 7.
112. Ibid. 24.
113. Ibid., Box 278, Folder Racial Relations: memorandum from Nesbitt, Special Asst. (Racial Relations) to N. S. Keith Dir. Division of Slum Clearance and Urban Redevelopment (22 June 1953) and attachment, 10. See also LC NAACP, Group II, Box A317, Folder Housing, Urban Renewal and Relocation 1952–3: 'The Changing Score of Anti-Slum Activity and Its Racial Minority Implications', statement by George B. Nesbitt, before the National Assocation of Intergroup Relations Officials (11 Nov. 1953).
114. NA RG 207, Gen. Records of the Dept. of Housing and Urban Development, HHFA, Subject Files 1947–60, Box 134, Folder Racial Relations: letter from Cole to Senator Bush (9 May 1956), 1.
115. Ibid. 2.
116. Ibid.
117. 'Procedures which have been developed in the carrying out (1) the Slum Clearance and Community Redevelopment Program, and (2) the Low-Rent Public Housing Program, to assure that such programs will not result in decreasing the total living space available in any community to Negro or other racial minority families.' LC NAACP Group II, Box A317, Folder Housing 1952–3: HHFA, Office of the Administrator (15 Jan. 1953). A copy was sent by Raymond Foley, Administrator of the HHFA to Walter White.
118. 'In the case of public housing projects, which are locally planned and controlled, a Federally imposed requirement for racial integration would certainly result in the rejection of this form of Federal aid by many communities where the need for low rent housing, especially for minority group families, is more pressing.' NA RG 207, Gen. Records of the Dept. of Housing and Urban Development, HHFA, Subject Files 1947–60, Box 134, Folder Racial Relations: letter from Cole to Sen. Bush (9 May 1956), 3.
119. Ibid. 4.
120. Ibid.: letter from Administrator Cole to Sen. Charles E. Potter (1956). Cole continued: 'I can assure you, however, that it is the desire of the President and the policy of this Agency and its constituent Administrations to exert every feasible effort within the limits of our authority in encouraging and assisting both private and public resources and endeavours to expand and improve the housing and home financing supplies available to all segments of need, with the objective of equalizing the opportunity for decent housing and economical home finance among all of our citizens.'

121. Ibid., Box 59, Folder Racial Relations: letter from John Egan, Commissioner FHA to Sen. M. M. Neely (10 June 1952). For background see ibid.: memorandum from Warren R. Cochrane to Anber Silverman 'Development Program WVA-1–3, Charleston, West Virginia—Racial Occupancy' (5 Feb. 1952), which documents the dubious calculation of racial equity employed in the scheme.
122. Ibid., Box 96, Folder Racial Relations: letter from Administrator Cole to Pres. NAACP, Albuquerque Branch (27 May 1954). See also the NAACP's letter (13 May).
123. Ibid., 'FHA-insured housing available to minority groups', memorandum from Cole to Jacob Seidenberg, Executive Dir., President's Com. on Government Contracts, (17 May 1954), 1.
124. NA RG 207, Gen. Records of the Dept. of Housing and Urban Development, Urban Renewal Administration, General Subject Files 1949–60, Box 309, Folder Racial Relations: letter from Cole to Val J. Washington, Dir. of Minorities, Republican Nat. Com. (30 July 1957).
125. NA RG 207, Gen. Records of the Dept. of Housing and Urban Development, HHFA, Subject Files 1947–60, Box 166, Folder Racial Relations: letter from Siciliana to Cole (4 Dec. 1958).
126. Ibid.: letter from Cole to Black (19 Dec. 1958).
127. Ibid., Box 96, Folder Racial Relations: HHFA, 'Observations Regarding Implications of Decisions of the U.S. Supreme Court for HHFA Programs and Policies' (1 July 1954), 3.
128. NA RG 207, Gen. Records of the Dept. of Housing and Urban Development, Urban Renewal Administration, General Subject Files 1949–60, Box 330, Folder Racial Relations: memorandum by George B. Nesbitt to Nathaniel Keith Dir. Slum Clearance and Urban Redevelopment 'Basic Approaches to Racial Considerations' (9 Mar. 1950), 2.
129. Ibid. 4.
130. Ibid., Box 269, Folder Racial Relations: speech of Clarence Mitchell, Dir. of the Washington Bureau NAACP (6 Dec. 1951), 2.
131. Ibid. 3, 5.
132. Ibid.: memorandum from Frank Horne to Raymond Foley FHA Director, 'Speech of Clarence Mitchell, Director, Washington Bureau NAACP December 6 1951', 1, 2.
133. LC NAACP, Group II-B Box B 95, Folder Labor: State Employment Services 1947–9, memorandum prepared for Pres. Marshall (20 June 1949), 1. The memo added: 'job orders received at the central-white employment service in which no specification of white or colored is made receive first attention from the white office with the result that white workers have a prior opportunity for the job . . . [T]he existence of a segregated office initiates the suggestion that an employer express a preference by calling one or the other of the agencies.' Ibid. 2.
134. DDEL, Papers of James P. Mitchell, Box 68, Folder 1959 DoL Misc.: confidential draft memo prepared for Mitchell by John W. Leslie 'Draft of a Position on Civil Rights' (5 June 1959), 3.
135. DDEL, Whitman File: Cabinet Series, Box 15: Cabinet Meeting (18 Dec. 1959), 4.
136. USES Task Force, *A Report to the Secretary of Labor from the Employment Service*

Task Force (1965), 10. This task force was chaired by George Schultz Dean of the Graduate Business School at the University of Chicago.

137. LC NAACP, Group-III, Box A-146, Folder Govt.—National DoL 1960–5: memo from BES to All State Employment Security Agencies (12 Mar. 1964): 'Implementation of Policy and Procedure With Respect to Serving Minority Groups'.
138. LBJL, memo for the Pres. from Willard Wirtz (20 Jan. 1964) WHCF FG Box 237, Folder 160–6 USES, 1.
139. Nat. Urban Coalition and the Lawyers' Com. for Civil Rights under Law, *Falling Down on the Job* (Washington: National Urban Coalition and the Lawyers' Com. for Civil Rights under Law, June 1971) p. 64.
140. The Com. made two proposals for presidential action: (1) State the constitutional objective of equal opportunity in housing and direct all Federal agencies to shape their policies and practices to make the maximum contribution to the achievement of this goal; and (2) Request the Com. on Civil Rights to continue to study and appraise the policies of Federal housing agencies with a view to preparing and proposing plans to bring about the end of discrimination in all federally assisted housing.
141. NA RG 207, Gen. Records of the Dept. of Housing and Urban Development, HHFA, Subject Files 1947–60, Box 166, Folder Racial Relations: Telegram from Algernon Black, chairman National Committee against Discrimination in Housing to Eisenhower (10 Nov. 1959). He received a very brief and vague reply from Rocco C. Siciliana, Special Asst. to the Pres. (1 Dec. 1958).
142. Ibid., Box 189, Folder Racial Relations: letter from Sen. Jacob Javits to HHFA Administrator Norman Mason (19 Jan. 1960), 1.
143. Ibid.: letter from Mason to Harold Tyler Asst. Attorney Gen., Civil Rights Division Dept. of Justice (4 Oct. 1960).
144. Ibid.: letter from Mason to Sen. Javits (23 Aug. 1960), 2.
145. Ibid., Box 134, Folder Racial Relations: letter from Cole to Sen. Bush (9 May 1956), 4.

CHAPTER 7

1. The passage of the Act was contorted and built upon previous efforts dating from Truman's presidency: Pres. Truman's decision to establish a Com. on Civil Rights in 1947, his introduction of anti-segregation legislation and permanent FEPC proposal into the Congress in Feb. 1948. Truman's stance was a direct challenge to Southern Democrats: in the House 74 Democrats opposed to civil rights legislation formed into a group to cooperate with Southern governors. In the so-called Dixiecrat revolt of 1948 a group of Southerners defected from the party convention, and Truman lost four Southern states in the presidential election. He did, however, win the election with a commitment to civil rights and desegregation—one strengthened by the inclusion of a convention floor amendment congratulating the Pres. on his stand. This commitment failed to be translated into congressional initiative: Southern Democrats and conservative Republican leaders proved an insurmountable barrier to the Pres. Truman's efforts signalled a powerful shift in the Democratic party

leadership's assessment of its electoral bases; and his creation of investigative committees, issuance of EOs desegregating the military, and outlawing discrimination in Federal agencies and in govt. contracts were significant markers. Whether for purely party political and pragmatic reasons or for personal conviction, these measures by a Democratic pres. were of profound importance. Truman's reaction, described in Chapter 1, to the Black army sergeant whose eyes were gouged out two hours after his discharge from the military, seems one of personal horror about the circumstances of Black Americans.

Truman's Republican successor, Dwight Eisenhower, was reluctant to maintain the legislative momentum toward civil rights. Eisenhower's statement, while a serving officer, reported in Chapter 4, suggests that he had serious reservations about imposing national legislation on Southern states to reform their race practices. The Republican party's 1953 platform made civil rights principally the responsibility of individual states. Eisenhower preferred persuasion to law. Furthermore, his decision to deploy Federal troops to enforce school desegregation in Arkansas was reached reluctantly. Subsequently, the Administration pushed through two civil rights bills, in 1957 and 1960 (PL 85–315 and PL 86–449). The 1957 Act created a Civil Rights Com. but lacked the enforcement powers sought by Black Americans. Its report in 1959 recommending Federal action in housing, education, and voting echoed those of Truman's Com. on Civil Rights in 1947. The force of the 1960 Act, already limited, was further diluted by the adroit organization and tactics of a Southern Democrat–Republican opposition group. Pres. Kennedy's 1962 Civil Rights bill was considerably weaker than that to which the Democrats had committed themselves in their 1960 party platform; it focused on anti-lynching and literacy tests for voting. The bill failed to pass.

Kennedy submitted a tougher and more comprehensive civil rights bill to Congress in 1963, a reaction in large part to the mounting civil rights movement; several other bills were introduced in both chambers, and committees held hearings. The House Judiciary Com. approved a bill, with bipartisan support, in Oct. 1963 which was stronger than the White House had wished. The bill provided Federal support for the desegregation of public facilities such as playgrounds, swimming pools, and parks and for the establishment of a Federal EEOC empowered to stop discrimination by employers and unions. Kennedy's death and Lyndon Johnson's unwavering commitment to civil rights ensured that the bill was passed by the House in Feb. 1964 with a substantial majority: 290–130 (R 138–34; D 152–96 (ND 141–4; SD 11–92)). The Senate filibustered for three months, before a cloture motion succeeded on 10 June (71–29: D 44–23, R 27–6) (the first successful such motion on civil rights in the Senate). The final bill passed in the Senate by 73–27 (21 Democrats and 6 Republicans opposing). This bill then received House support 289–126 (R 136–35; D 153–91 (ND 141–3; SD 12–88)). The 1964 Civil Rights Act (PL 88–352) was signed by Pres. Johnson on 2 July. In the subsequent presidential election, where Johnson achieved spectacular successes in most states, he lost—in common, and honourably, with Truman in 1948—several Southern states.

2. NA RG 60, Records of the Dept. of Justice, Records of Burke Marshall, Attorney, Civil Rights Division 1961–5, Box 3, File Public Accommodation: see memorandum from John Doar to David Rubin, 'Procedures to be Followed Under Titles II, III and IV of the Civil Rights Act of 1964' (20 July 1964).

3. US Com. on Civil Rights, *Equal Employment Rights for Federal Employees* (Washington: US Com. on Civil Rights, 1993). However, the new regulations remain the object of criticism. Public-sector unions and interest groups representing minorities (such as Blacks in Government and the Washington Lawyers' Com. for Civil Rights under Law) would like the new procedures strengthened further.
4. US House of Representatives, 95th Congress, 2nd sess., Com. on Education and Labor, Subcom. on Employment Opportunities, Staff Report Comparing Figures for Minority and Female Employment in the Federal Government, 1975 and 1977, and in Forty-four Selected Agencies (May 1978), 1.
5. Amongst a growing literature see the important study by D. S. Massey and N. A. Denton, *American Apartheid: Segregation and the Making of the Underclass* (Cambridge, Mass.: Harvard University Press, 1993); for historical perspective see K. Taeuber and A. Taeuber, *Negroes in Cities: Residential Segregation and Neighborhood Change* (Chicago: Aldine, 1965). See also R. Farley, 'Residential Segregation of Social and Economic Groups among Blacks, 1970–1980', in C. Jencks and P. Peterson (eds.), *The Urban Underclass* (Washington: Brookings Institution, 1991); M Gottdiener, *The New Urban Sociology* (New York: McGraw Hill, 1994); R. D. Bullard and J. R. Feagin, 'Racism and the City', in M. Gottdiener and C. G. Pickvance (eds.), *Urban Life in Transition* (Newbury Park, Calif.: Sage, 1991); and J. H. Mollenkopf, *A Phoenix in the Ashes* (Princeton: Princeton University Press, 1992).
6. See esp. the important studies: J Quadagno, *The Color of Welfare* (New York: Oxford University Press, 1994); and M. Weir, *Politics and Jobs* (Princeton: Princeton University Press, 1992). See also D. S. King, *Actively Seeking Work? The Politics of Unemployment and Welfare Policy in the United States and Great Britain* (Chicago: University of Chicago Press, 1995), and G. Lafer, 'The Politics of Job Training: Urban Poverty and the False Promise of JTPA', *Politics and Society*, 22 (1994), 349–88.
7. See Quadagno, *Color of Welfare*; id., 'From Old-Age Assistance to Supplemental Security Income: The Political Economy of Relief in the South, 1935–1972', in M. Weir *et al.* (eds.), *The Politics of Social Policy in the United States* (Princeton: Princeton University Press, 1988); D. S. King, 'Citizenship as Obligation in the United States: Title II of the Family Support Act 1988', in U. Vogel and M. Moran (eds.), *The Frontiers of Citizenship* (London: Macmillan, 1991); id. and J. Waldron, 'Citizenship, Social Citizenship and the Defence of Welfare Provision', *British Journal of Political Science*, 18 (1988), 415–45; and P. J. Conover, I. Crewe, and D. Searing, 'The Nature of Citizenship in the United States and Great Britain: Empirical Comments on Theoretical Themes', *Journal of Politics*, 53 (1991), 800–32.
8. See Weir, *Politics and Jobs*; and King, *Actively Seeking Work?*
9. P. M. Sniderman and T. Piazza, *The Scar of Race* (Cambridge, Mass.: Harvard University Press, 1993), 20.
10. Ibid. 30.
11. NA RG 129, Records of the Bureau of Prisons, Central Administrative Files 1937–47, Prisoners' Welfare, Box 41, Folder Segregation: letter from Thurgood Marshall to James Bennett (1 Sept. 1942), 2.
12. Again amongst a large literature see Sniderman and Piazza, *Scar of Race*. See also E. G. Carmines and J. A. Stimson, *Issue Evolution: Race and the Transformation of American Politics* (Princeton: Princeton University Press, 1989).

13. NA RG 220, President's Com. on Govt. Employment Policy 1955–61, Agency Files, Box 13, File Civil Service Com.: letter from Ross Clinchy, Com. Executive Dir., to John W. Macey, chairman US Civil Service Commission (1 Feb. 1961), 3.
14. See H. D. Graham, *The Civil Rights Era: Origins and Development of National Policy 1960–1972* (New York: Oxford University Press, 1990); and J. M. Kousser, 'The Voting Rights Act and the Two Reconstructions', in B. Grofman and C. Davidson (eds.), *Controversies in Minority Voting* (Washington: Brookings Institution, 1992).
15. See *inter alia* P. Evans, D. Rueschemeyer and T. Skocpol (eds.), *Bringing the State Back In* (New York: Cambridge University Press, 1985); S. Krasner, *Defending the National Interest* (Princeton: Princeton University Press, 1978); J. P. Nettl, 'The State as a Conceptual Variable', *World Politics*, 20 (1968), 559–92; and E. Nordlinger, *On the Autonomy of the Democratic State* (Cambridge, Mass.: Harvard University Press, 1981).
16. In his valuable essay on voting rights Kousser explains how the same political system, used by different political coalitions, at first restricted and later facilitated equality of voting rights: 'The Voting Rights Act and the Two Reconstructions'.

Bibliography

1. PRIMARY SOURCES

Unpublished and Archival

In the endnotes to the text I have provided extensive detail for each archival reference with the intention of making it possible for other researchers to consult any of the records I used germane to their own research. Here, I confine the listing to the main collections studied and do not provide detailed listings of the sets of papers consulted in each collection.

National Archives and Record Administration Washington DC and National Archives at College Park

Record Group (RG):

RG 12 Records of the Office of Education
- Papers of Ambrose Caliver
- Records of School Desegregation
- Division of Equal Educational Opportunity

RG 16 Records of the Department of Agriculture
- Office of the Secretary of Agriculture

RG 28 Records of the Post Office Department

RG 31 Records of the FHA

RG 40 Records of the Department of Commerce
- Office of the Secretary, Records of the Advisors on Negro Affairs

RG 46 Records of the US Senate
- Committee on the Civil Service
- Special Committee to Investigate Civil Service
- System, 77th Congress (Chairman: Senator Allen J. Ellender, La.)

RG 48 Records of the Department of the Interior
- Office of the Secretary, Central Classified Files

RG 60 Records of the Department of Justice
- Civil Rights Division

RG 86 Records of the Women's Bureau

RG 129 Bureau of Prisons
- Central Administrative Files

RG 146 Civil Service Agencies
- Records of the US Civil Service Commission
- Minutes of Proceedings, 1886–1929 (series ends)
- Records of the Personnel Classification Division
- FEB 1948–55

RG 174 Records of the Department of Labor
Papers of the Office of the Secretary Files
General Subject Files
RG 183 Records of the BES (previously USES)
Papers of Lawrence A. Oxley
RG 188 Records of the OPA
Records of Racial Relations Advisor
RG 195 Records of the Federal Home Loan Bank System
Home Owners' Loan System/Corporation
RG 196 Records of the Public Housing Authority
RG 207 Records of the Department of Housing and Urban Development
HHFA
Urban Renewal Administration 1949–60
RG 220 Records of the President's Committee on Government Employment Policy 1955–61:
Compliance Reports
Appeals
Records of the President's Committee on Equal Opportunity Policy 1961–4
RG 228 Records of the FEPC
Office Files of Malcolm Ross
Records of the Legal Division
Office Files of John A. Davis
Office Files of George M. Johnson
Office Files of the Chairman
RG 233 Records of the US House of Representatives
Committee on Reform in the Civil Service, 63rd Congress
Committee on the Civil Service, 76th Congress: Accompanying Papers, Committee on the Civil Service
RG 302 Records of the National Capital Housing Authority
RG 318 Records of the Bureau of Engraving and Printing
RG 325 Records of the CGCC
RG 453 Records of the Commission on Civil Rights

Library of Congress, Manuscript Division

Papers of the NAACP
Papers of the NUL
Papers of the Washington Urban League
Papers of A. Philip Randolph
Papers of Moorfield Storey
Papers of Albert S. Burleson
Papers of Josephus Daniels
Papers of William Gibbs McAdoo
Papers of Eleanor Roosevelt (University Publications of American—micro edn.)
Papers of Joseph Tumulty

Franklin D. Roosevelt Library

President's Secretary Files
President's Official File
Papers of Harry Hopkins
Papers of Harold Smith
Records of the President's Committee on Civil Service Improvement 1939–40
Papers of Frances Perkins
Papers of John Winant
Papers of I. Rubin
Papers of M. Dimock
Papers of W. Cohen

Harry S. Truman Library

Committee on Equality of Treatment and Opportunity in the Armed Services
  Minutes of proceedings
Committee on Civil Rights
  Minutes of proceedings
Papers of National Committee on Segregation in the Nation's Capital
Papers of Philleo Nash
Papers of David Niles
Papers of Robert Goodwin
Oral History of Robert Goodwin
Papers of John W. Gibson
White House Central File
President's Secretary Files
President's Official File
Papers of Gerhard Colm
Papers of Oscar Ewing

Dwight D. Eisenhower Library

Papers of James P. Mitchell
Whitman File: Cabinet Series
President's Official File
Office of the Special Assistant to President for Personnel Management

Lyndon B. Johnson Library

White House Central File

Public Record Office, Kew, UK

War Cabinet minutes 25 Jan. 1940, CAB 65/5, WM 23 (40) 3; 10 and 31 Aug. 1942, CAB 65/27, WM (42) 109/6 and 119/6
Cabinet Office papers, CAB 79/20 COS 126 (42) 11, 21 Apr. 1942, CAB 80/62 COS (42) 104 (0)

Home Office circular, 4 Sept. 1942, annexe to CAB 66/29 WP (42) 456 CAB 66/29 WP (42) 441

US Bureau of Prisons, Archives Division, Washington DC

Proceedings of the Conference of Wardens and Superintendents of the Federal Prison Service 1938–1958 (1938 was the first such conference though the Bureau was founded in 1930)
US Bureau of Prisons, Classification and Education Staff, *Progress Report* (bi-monthly 1947–)

US Department of Labor, Washington DC

Archive and Library

US Equal Employment Opportunity Commission Archives

EEOC, *Report to the President* (Washington: GPO, 1963)

Georgetown University Library

Robert F. Wagner Papers

The Tom Harrisson Mass-Observation Archive, University of Sussex Library, UK

File Report 1569, 22 Jan. 1943: Feelings about America and the Americans
File Report 1944, 11 Oct. 1943: The Colour Bar
Topic Collection: Town and District Survey (Portsmouth) 17/E, 14 Jan. 1944

Published

BRADLEY, O. N., *A Soldier's Story* (New York: Holt, 1951).
Congressional Record, 1883– .
FOSTER, W. Z., *et al.*, *The Communist Position on the Negro Question* (New York: New Century Publishers, 1947).
HASTIE, W., *On Clipped Wings* (Washington: NAACP, 1943).
National Committee on Segregation in the Nation's Capital, *Segregation in Washington* (report) (Chicago: National Committee on Segregation in the Nation's Capital, 1948).
National Urban Coalition and the Lawyers' Committee for Civil Rights under Law, *Falling Down on the Job* (Washington: National Urban Coalition and the Lawyers' Committee for Civil Rights under Law, June 1971).

National Association for the Advancement of Colored People

Crisis (monthly from 1908–).
Annual Reports (New York: NAACP, 1908–).
The Decision of the US Supreme Court in the Louisville Segregation Case (*Buchanan vs. Warley 245 US 60*) (New York: NAACP, 1917).

Fighting a Vicious Film: Protest Against 'The Birth of a Nation' (Boston: Boston Branch NAACP, 1915).

VILLARD, O. G., *Segregation in Baltimore and Washington* (New York: NAACP, 1913).

OXLEY, L. A., 'Employment Securtiy and the Negro', *Employment Security Review* (7 July 1940), 12–15.

President's Committee on Civil Rights, *Report: To Secure These Rights* (Washington: GPO, 1947).

President's EEOC, *Report to the President* (Washington: GPO, 1963).

ROOSEVELT, THEODORE, *The Letters of Theodore Roosevelt*, ed. E. E. Morison, J. M. Blum, and J. J. Buckley (Cambridge, Mass.: Harvard University Press, 1951–4).

US Civil Service Commission

Annual Reports (Washington: GPO, 1883–1978).

The Reorganization of the Civil Service Commission (Washington: GPO, 1953).

Organization and Activities of the United States Civil Service Commission (Washington: GPO, 1955).

Federal Civilian Workforce Statistics, *Equal Employment Opportunity Statistics* (1976–80).

Political Activity and Political Assessments of Federal Officeholders and Employees (Washington: GPO, 1936).

Study of Minority Group Employment in the Federal Government (1967, 1969–72, 1974).

US Commission on Civil Rights

Housing in Washington: Hearings before the US Commission on Civil Rights 12–13 April 1962 (Washington: US Commission on Civil Rights, 1962).

For All the People . . . By All the People (A report on equal opportunity in state and local government employment) (Washington: US Commission on Civil Rights, 1969).

Equal Opportunity in the Foreign Service (Washington: US Commission on Civil Rights, 1981).

Family Housing and the Negro Serviceman (Washington: US Commission on Civil Rights, 1963).

Civil Rights 63: 1963 Report of the Commission on Civil Rights: The Negro in the Armed Forces (Washington: US Commission on Civil Rights, 1963).

Equal Employment Rights for Federal Employees (Washington: US Commission on Civil Rights, 1993).

US Congress Committee hearings

US House of Representatives, 63rd Congress, 1st and 2nd sess. House Committee on Civil Service Reform. Segregation of Clerks and Employees in the Civil Service, hearings (on HR 5968 and HR 13772) (1914).

US House of Representatives, House Committee on District of Columbia, Report amending H 1718, 'to require transportation companies, firms, and persons within the District of Columbia to provide separate accommodations for White and Negro races, and to prescribe punishments and penalties for violating its provisions, and to provide for its enforcement'. H Rept. 1340 pt. 1 1915. Submitted by Mr Caraway (1 Feb. 1915).

US House of Representatives, 64th Congress, 1st sess., Hearings before the House Committee on the District of Columbia, on HR 12, HR 13, HR 274, HR 326, HR 618, HR 715, and HR 748 (11 Feb. 1916), 'Intermarriage of Whites and Negroes in the District of Columbia and Separate Accommodations in Street Cars for Whites and Negroes in the District of Columbia'.

US Congress House of Representatives, 72th Congress, 1st sess. on HR 8389, Departmental Reports to Committee on Expenditures in the Executive Departments, 'Consolidation of Civil-Service Activities'.

US Congress House of Representatives, 74th Congress, 1st sess. on HR 3980, Hearing before the Committee on the Civil Service, 'For Improvement of the Government Service' (18 Feb. 1935).

US Congress House of Representatives, 76th Congress, 1st sess. on HR 960, Hearing before the Committee on the Civil Service on 'Merit System and Classification' (1939).

US Congress House of Representatives, 78th Congress, 1st sess. on H Res 16, Hearing before the Committee on the Civil Service, 'A Resolution to Authorize the Committee on the Civil Service to Investigate Various Activities in the Departments and Agencies of the Government' parts 1, 2, and 3 (Mar. 1943).

US Senate, 80th Congress, 2nd sess., Hearings before the Subcommittee of the Committee on Post Office and Civil Service on Senate Resolutions 105 and 124, 'Efficiency Rating System for Federal Employees' (21 May and 1 June 1948).

US Senate, 81st Congress, 1st and 2nd sess., Hearings before the Committee on Post Office and Civil Service, Bills to Implement Recommendations of the Commission on Organization of the Executive Branch of the Government (The Hoover Commission) 20 June, 20 and 27 July 1949; 1, 14, and 21 Mar., 29 June, 18 and 27 July, and 7 Aug. 1950.

US Senate, 82nd Congress, 1st sess., Hearings before the Committee on Post Office and Civil Service, Bills to Implement Recommendations of the Commission on Organization of the Executive Branch of the Government (The Hoover Commission), 30 Aug., 5 and 12 Sept. 1951.

US Senate, 82nd Congress, 2nd sess., Committee on Labor and Public Welfare, Subcommittee on Labor and Labor Management Relations, 'Discrimination and Full Utilization of Manpower Resources', Hearings on S. 1732 and S. 551 (8 Apr. 1952).

US House of Representatives, 84th Congress, 2nd sess., *The Civil Service Commission* (House Report, 1844; Mar. 1956).

US Senate, 85th Congress, 1st sess., Report to the Committee on Post Office and Civil Service, 'Administration of the Civil Service System' (1957).

US House of Representatives, 88th Congress, 1st ses., Hearings before the Subcommittee on Manpower Utilization of the Commitee on Post Office and Civil Service, 'Use of Contractors: Equal Opportunities in the Military Services' (5 and 6 Nov. 1963).

US House of Representatives, 92th Congress, 2nd sess., Hearings before the Subcommittee on Investigations of the Committee on Post Office and Civil Service, 'Legislative Oversight Review of the Civil Service Commission' (26, 27, and 28 Sept., 3 and 4 Oct. 1972).

US Congress House of Representatives, 95th Congress, 2nd sess., Committee on Education and Labor, Subcommittee on Employment Opportunities. Staff Report Comparing Figures for Minority and Female Employment in the Federal Government, 1975 and 1977, and in Forty-four Selected Agencies (May 1978).

US House of Representatives, 102nd Congress, 1st sess., Hearing before House Subcommittee on the Civil Service of the Committee on Post Office and Civil Service and the Subcommittee on Employment Opportunities of the Committee on Education and Labor (20 Nov. 1991), Casualties of the Federal Equal Employment Opportunity Complaint Process.

US House of Representatives, 102nd Congress, 2nd sess., Hearing before the House Subcommittee on Employment Opportunities of the Committee on Education and Labor (9 Apr. 1992), Joint Legislative Hearing on HR 3613: The Federal Employees Fairness Act of 1991.

US Department of Justice, *Federal Prisons Annual Reports 1940–1959* (Washington).

USES Task Force, *A Report to the Secretary of Labor from the Employment Service Task Force* (1965).

US EEOC

Federal Sector Report on EEO Complaints and Appeals 1991 (Washington, 1991).

US EEOC Combined Annual Report FYs 1986, 1987, 1988 (Washington, 1988).

Annual Report on the Employment of Minorities, Women & Individuals with Handicaps in the Federal Government FY 1987 (Washington, 1988).

A Report on the Operation of the Office of General Counsel, 1992 (Washington, 1992).

US HHFA, Office of the Administrator, *Our Nonwhite Population and its Housing* (Washington: HHFA, 1963).

US GAO

State Department: Minorities and Women are Underrepresented in the Foreign Service (report to Congress) (Washington: GAO, 1989).

Affirmative Action: Assessing Progress of EEO Groups in Key Federal Jobs can be Improved (Report to the Chairman, Committee on Governmental Affairs, US Senate) (Washington: GAO, 1993).

US Office of Personnel Management (formerly US Civil Service Commission), *Federal Civilian Workforce Statistics; Affirmative Employment Statistics 1982, 1984, 1986, 1988, 1990* (Washington).

Urban Institute, *The Validity and Discriminatory Impact of the Federal Service Entrance Examination* (Washington: Urban Institute, 1971).

Vaughn, Robert, *The Spoiled System: A Call for Civil Service Reform* (Washington: Common Cause DC, 1972).

Wilson, Woodrow, *Papers of Woodrow Wilson*, ed. A. Link (Princeton: Princeton University Press), 50 vols.

2. SECONDARY SOURCES

ABRAHAM, H. J., *Freedom and the Courts* (New York: Oxford University Press, 5th edn. 1988).

BALDWIN, J., *The Fire Next Time* (Harmondsworth: Penguin Books, 1964).

BANTON, M., *Racial Theories* (Cambridge: Cambridge University Press, 1987).

BATES, B., *Bargaining for Life: A Social History of Tuberculosis, 1876–1938* (Philadelphia: University of Pennsylvania Press, 1992).

BELKNAP, M. E., *Civil Rights, the White House and the Justice Department 1945–1968*, iv. *Employment of Blacks by the Federal Government* (New York: Garland, 1991).

BENSEL, R. F., *Sectionalism and American Political Development 1880–1980* (Madison: University of Wisconsin Press, 1984).

—— *Yankee Leviathan: The Origins of Central State Authority in America, 1859–1877* (New York: Cambridge University Press, 1990).

BERMAN, W. C., *The Politics of Civil Rights in the Truman Administration* (Columbus, Oh.: Ohio State University Press, 1970).

BLUM, J. M., *The Republican Roosevelt* (Cambridge, Mass.: Harvard University Press, 1977).

BONADIO, F. A. (ed.), *Political Parties in American History*, ii. *1828–1890* (New York: G. P. Putnam's Sons, 1974).

BOWLES, N. P., *The Government and Politics of the United States* (Basingstoke: Macmillan, 1993).

BRADY, D. W., *Critical Elections and Congressional Policy-Making* (Stanford, Calif.: Stanford University Press, 1988).

BRANCH, T., *Parting the Waters: America in the King Years 1954–1963* (New York: Simon & Schuster, 1988).

BROGAN, H., *The Pelican History of the United States* (Harmondsworth: Penguin Books, 1985).

BULLARD, R. D., and FEAGIN, J. R., 'Racism and the City', in M. Gottdiener and C. G. Pickvance (eds.), *Urban Life in Transition* (Newbury Park, Calif.: Sage, 1991).

BUNCHE, R. J., *The Political Status of the Negro in the Age of FDR* (1940; Chicago: University of Chicago Press, 1973).

BURLEIGH, M., *Germany Turns Eastward* (Cambridge: Cambridge University Press, 1988).

—— *Death and Deliverance* (Cambridge: Cambridge University Press, 1994).

BUTTON, J. W., *Blacks and Social Change* (Princeton: Princeton University Press, 1989).

CARMINES, E. G., and STIMSON, J. A., *Issue Evolution: Race and the Transformation of American Politics* (Princeton: Princeton University Press, 1989).

CASH, W. J., *The Mind of the South* (1941; New York: Vintage, 1991).

CHONG, D., *Collective Action and the Civil Rights Movement* (Chicago: University of Chicago Press, 1991).

CLEMENTS, K. A., *The Presidency of Woodrow Wilson* (Lawrence, Kan.: University Press of Kansas, 1992).

CLEMMER, D., *The Prison Community* (New York: Holt, Rinehart and Winston, 1940).

COHEN, S., and SCULL, A. (eds.), *Social Control and the State* (Oxford: Basil Blackwell, 1983).

COLLIER, C., 'The American People as Christian White Men of Property: Suffrage and Elections in Colonial and Early National America', in D. W. Rogers (ed.), *Voting and the Spirit of American Democracy* (Urbana, Ill.: University of Illinois Press, 1990).

CONOVER, P. J., CREWE, I., and SEARING, D., 'The Nature of Citizenship in the United States and Great Britain: Empirical Comments on Theoretical Themes', *Journal of Politics* 53 (1991), 800–32.

DALFIUME, R. M., 'The "Forgotten Years" of the Negro Revolution', *Journal of American History*, 55 (1968), 90–106.

—— *Fighting on Two Fronts: Desegregation of the Armed Forces* (Columbia, Mo.: University of Missouri Press, 1969).

DODD, L. C., and SCHOTT, R. L., *Congress and the Administrative State* (New York: John Wiley and Sons, 1979).

DOUGLAS, M., *How Institutions Think* (London: Routledge and Kegan Paul, 1987).

EAGLES, C. W., *Outside Aggressor: Jon Daniels and the Civil Rights Movement in Alabama* (Chapel Hill, NC: University of North Carolina Press, 1993).

ESKRIDGE, W. N., Jr., 'Race and Sexual Orientation and the Military', *Reconstruction*, 2 (1993), 52–7.

EVANS, P. E., RUESCHEMEYER, D., and SKOCPOL, T. (eds.), *Bringing the State Back In* (New York: Cambridge University Press, 1985).

EWING, C. A. M., *Congressional Elections 1896–1944* (Norman, Okla.: University of Oklahoma Press, 1947).

FARLEY, R., 'Residential Segregation of Social and Economic Groups among Blacks 1970–1980', in Jencks and Peterson (eds.), *The Urban Underclass*.

—— and ALLEN, W. R., *The Color Line and the Quality of Life in America* (New York: Russell Sage Foundation, 1987).

FESLER, J. W., and KETTL, D. F., *The Politics of the Administrative Process* (Chatham, NJ: Chatham House Publishers, 1991).

FIELDS, B. J., 'Ideology and Race in American History', in J. M. Kousser and J. M. McPherson (eds.), *Region, Race and Reconstruction* (New York: Oxford University Press, 1982).

—— 'Slavery, Race and Ideology in the United States of America', *New Left Review*, 181 (1990), 95–118.

FISHER, L., *The Politics of Shared Power* (Washington: Congressional Quarterly Inc., 3rd edn. 1993).

FONER, E., *Free Soil, Free Labor, Free Men: The Ideology of the Republican Party before the Civil War* (New York: Oxford University Press, 1970).

—— *Reconstruction: America's Unfinished Revolution 1863–1877* (New York: Harper and Row, 1988).

—— 'Blacks and the US Constitution 1789–1989', *New Left Review*, 183 (1990), 63–74.

—— 'From Slavery to Citizenship: Blacks and the Right to Vote', in D. W. Rogers (ed.), *Voting and the Spirit of American Democracy* (Urbana, Ill.: University of Illinois Press).

FONER, J. D., *Blacks and the Military in American History* (New York: Praeger, 1974).

FONER, P. S., *Organized Labor and the Black Worker 1619–1981* (New York: International Publishers, 2nd edn. 1982).

FRANKLIN, J. H., *Racial Equality in America* (Columbia, Mo.: University of Missouri Press, 1976).

FREDERICKSON, G. M., *The Black Image in the White Mind* (New York: Harper and Row, 1971; repr. Hanover, NH: Wesleyan University Press, 1987).

—— *White Supremacy* (New York: Oxford University Press, 1981).

FREIDEL, F., *FDR and the South* (Baton Rouge, La.: Louisiana State University Press, 1965).

GARDINER, J., *'Over Here': The GIs in Wartime Britain* (London: Collins and Brown, 1992).

GARFINKEL, H., *When Negroes March: The March on Washington Movement in the Organizational Politics of the FEPC* (Glencoe, Ill.: Free Press, 1959).

GLASER, D., *The Effectiveness of a Prison and Parole System* (New York: Bobbs-Merrill Co., 1964).

GOFFMAN, E., *Asylums* (1961; Harmondsworth: Penguin Books, 1991).

—— 'On the Characteristics of Total Institutions: The Inmate World', in D. R. Cressey (ed.), *The Prison: Studies in Institutional Organization and Change* (New York: Holt, Rinehart and Winston, 1961).

—— 'On the Characteristics of Total Institutions: Staff–Inmate Relations', in Cressey (ed.), *The Prison.*

GOLDFIELD, D. (1990), *Black, White and Southern: Race Relations and Southern Culture 1940 to the Present* (Baton Rouge, La.: Louisiana State University Press, 1990).

GOODWIN, D. K., *No Ordinary Time: Franklin and Eleanor Roosevelt: The Home Front in World War II* (New York: Simon & Schuster, 1994).

GOODWIN, G., Jr., 'The Seniority System in Congress', *American Political Science Review*, 53 (1959), 412–36.

GOTTDIENER, M., *The New Urban Sociology* (New York: McGraw-Hill, 1994).

GRAHAM, H. D., *The Civil Rights Era: Origins and Development of National Policy 1960–1972* (New York: Oxford University Press, 1990).

GREENSTONE, J. D., *The Lincoln Persuasion* (Princeton: Princeton University Press, 1993).

GROFMAN, B., and DAVIDSON, C. (eds.), *Controversies in Minority Voting* (Washington: Brookings Institution, 1992).

HACHEY, T. E., 'Document: Jim Crow with a British Accent: Attitudes of London Government Officials toward American Negro Soldiers during World War II', *Journal of Negro History*, 59 (1974), 65–77.

HALLER, J. S., Jr., *Outcasts from Evolution: Scientific Attitudes of Racial Inferiority 1859–1900* (Urbana, Ill.: University of Illinois Press, 1971).

HARRIS, J. P., *Congressional Control of Administration* (Washington: Brookings Institution, 1964).

HARRIS, W. H., 'A. Philip Randolph as a Charismatic Leader 1925–1941', *Journal of Negro History*, 64 (1979), 301–15.

HARTGROVE, W. B., 'The Negro Soldier in the American Revolution', *Journal of Negro History*, 1 (1916), 110–31.

HARTZ, L., *The Liberal Tradition in America* (New York: Harcourt, Brace and World, 1955).

HATTAM, V. C., *Labor Visions and State Power* (Princeton: Princeton University Press, 1993).

HAYES, L. J. W., *The Negro Federal Government Worker* (Washington: Howard University, 1941).

HECLO, H., *A Government of Strangers* (Washington: Brookings Institution, 1977).

HENDERSON, A. B., 'FEPC and the Southern Railroad Case: An Investigation into the Discriminatory Practices of Railroads during World War II', *Journal of Negro History*, 61 (1976), 173–87.

HIRSCH, A. J., *The Rise of the Penitentiary* (New Haven: Yale University Press, 1992).

HOFSTADTER, R., *The Age of Reform: From Bryan to F. D. R.* (New York: Vintage, 1955).

HOOGENBOOM, A., 'The Pendleton Act and the Civil Service', *American Historical Review*, 64 (1959), 301–18.

JACKSON, K. T., *Crabgrass Frontier: The Suburbanization of the United States* (New York: Oxford University Press, 1985).

JACOBS, J., *Stateville: The Penitentiary in Mass Society* (Chicago: University of Chicago Press, 1977).

JANOSKI, T., *The Political Economy of Unemployment* (Berkeley and Los Angeles: University of California Press, 1990).

JAYNES, G. D., and WILLIAMS, R. M. (eds.), *A Common Destiny: Blacks and American Society* (Washington: National Academy Press for the Committee on the Status of Black Americans, National Research Council, 1989).

JENCKS, C., and PETERSON, P. (eds.), *The Urban Underclass* (Washington: Brookings Institution, 1991).

JENNINGS, J. (ed.), *Race, Politics and Economic Development* (London: Verso, 1992).

JOHNSON, C. S., *Patterns of Negro Segregation* (New York: Harper, 1943).

JOHNSON, D. M., and CAMPBELL, R. R., *Black Migration in America* (Durham, NC: Duke University Press, 1981).

KATZNELSON, I., GEIGER, K., and KRYDER, D., 'Limiting Liberalism: The Southern Veto in Congress 1933–1950', *Political Science Quarterly*, 108 (1993), 283–306.

—— and PIETRYKOWSKI, B., 'Rebuilding the American State: Evidence from the 1940s', *Studies in American Political Development*, 5 (1991), 301–39.

KESSELMAN, L. C., *The Social Politics of FEPC: A Study in Reform Pressure Movements* (Chapel Hill, NC: University of North Carolina Press, 1948).

KEY, V. O., Jr., *Southern Politics* (New York: Vintage, 1949).

—— *Politics, Parties and Pressure Groups* (New York: Thomas Y. Crowell Co., 3rd edn. 1952).

KING, D. S., 'Citizenship as Obligation in the United States: Title II of the Family Support Act 1988', in U. Vogel and M. Moran (eds.), *The Frontiers of Citizenship* (London: Macmillan, 1991).

—— ' "The Longest Road to Equality": The Politics of Institutional Desegregation under Truman', *Journal of Historical Sociology*, 6 (1993), 119–63.

—— *Actively Seeking Work? The Politics of Unemployment and Welfare Policy in the United States and Great Britain* (Chicago: University of Chicago Press, 1995).

—— 'The Segregated State: Black Americans and the Federal Government', *Democratization*, 2 (forthcoming).

—— and ROTHSTEIN, B., 'Institutional Choices and Labor Market Policy: A British–Swedish Comparison', *Comparative Political Studies*, 26 (1993), 147–77.

—— and WALDRON, J., 'Citizenship, Social Citizenship and the Defence of Welfare Provision', *British Journal of Political Science*, 18 (1988), 415–45.

KIRBY, J. B., *Black Americans in the Roosevelt Era* (Knoxville, Tenn.: University of Tennessee Press, 1980).

KIRSCHENMAN, J., and NECKERMAN, K. M. (1991), ' "We'd Love to Hire Them, But . . .": The Meaning of Race for Employers', in Jencks and Peterson (eds.), *Urban Underclass*.

KLARMAN, M. J., 'How *Brown* Changed Race Relations: The Backlash Thesis', *Journal of American History*, 81 (1994), 81–118.

KNIGHT, J., *Institutions and Social Conflict* (New York: Cambridge University Press, 1992).

KOUSSER, J. M., *The Shaping of Southern Politics: Suffrage Restriction and the Establishment of the One-Party South 1880–1910* (New Haven: Yale University Press, 1974).

—— 'The Voting Rights Act and the Two Reconstructions', in Grofman and Davidson (eds.), *Controversies in Minority Voting*.

KRASNER, S., *Defending the National Interest* (Princeton: Princeton University Press, 1978).

KRISLOU, S., *The Negro in Federal Employment: The Quest for Equal Opportunity* (Minneapolis: University of Minnesota Press, 1967).

KRYDER, D., 'The Fair Employment Practices Committee and Black Americans, 1941–1945', Paper presented to the annual meeting of the American Political Science Association, 1994.

LAFER, G., 'The Politics of Job Training: Urban Poverty and the False Promise of JTPA', *Politics and Society*, 22 (1994), 349–88.

LINK, A. S., 'The Negro as a Factor in the Campaign of 1912', *Journal of Negro History*, 32 (1947), 81–99.

LEWIS, O. F., *The Development of American Prisons and Prison Customs 1776–1848* (1922; Montclair, NJ: Patterson Smith, 1967).

LOFGREN, C. A., *The Plessy Case* (New York: Oxford University Press, 1987).

McCoy, D., and Ruetten, M., *Quest and Response* (Lawrence, Kan.: University Press of Kansas, 1973).

MacGregor, M. J., Jr. (1985), *Integration of the Armed Forces 1940–1965* (Washington: US Army, 1985).

McKelvey, B., *American Prisons* (Montclair, NJ: Patterson Smith, 1977).

Maclean, N., *Beyond the Mask of Chivalry: The Making of the Second Ku Klux Klan* (Oxford: Oxford University Press, 1994).

Mandelbaum, D. G., *Soldier Groups and Negro Soldiers* (Berkeley and Los Angeles: University of California Press, 1952).

March, J., and Olsen, J., 'The New Institutionalism: Organizational Factors in Political Life', *American Political Science Review*, 78 (1984), 734–49.

Massey, D. S., and Denton, N. A., *American Apartheid: Segregation and the Making of the Underclass* (Cambridge, Mass.: Harvard University Press, 1993).

Meier, A., 'The Negro and the Democratic Party, 1875–1915', *Phylon*, 17 (1956), 173–91.

—— and Rudwick, E., 'The Rise of Segregation in the Federal Bureaucracy 1900–1930', *Phylon*, 28 (1967), 178–84.

—— —— *Black History and the Historical Profession 1915–1980* (Urbana, Ill.: University of Illinois Press, 1986).

Miller, N., *Theodore Roosevelt: A Life* (New York: Quill William Morrow, 1992).

Mollenkopf, J. H., *A Phoenix in the Ashes* (Princeton: Princeton University Press, 1992).

Mullen, R. W., *Blacks in America's Wars* (New York: Monad Press, 1973).

Myrdal, G., *An American Dilemma: The Negro Problem and American Democracy*, 2 vols. (New York: Harper and Row, 1944).

Nettl, J. P., 'The State as a Conceptual Variable', *World Politics*, 20 (1968), 559–92.

Nordlinger, E., *On the Autonomy of the Democratic State* (Cambridge, Mass.: Harvard University Press, 1981).

Northrup, H. R., *Organized Labor and the Negro* (New York: Harper, 1944).

Orfield, G., and Ashkinaze, C., *The Closing Door: Conservative Policy and Black Opportunity* (Chicago: University of Chicago Press, 1991).

Overdyke, W. D., *The Know-Nothing Party in the South* (Baton Rouge, La.: Louisiana State University Press, 1950).

Patterson, J. T., *Congressional Conservatism and the New Deal* (Lexington, Ky.: University of Kentucky Press, 1967).

Parris, H., *Constitutional Bureaucracy: The Development of British Central Administration since the Eighteenth Century* (London: Allen & Unwin, 1969).

Pinkney, A., *The Myth of Black Progress* (Cambridge: Cambridge University Press, 1984).

Quadagno, J., 'From Old-Age Assistance to Supplemental Security Income: The Political Economy of Relief in the South, 1935–1972', in M. Weir *et al.* (eds.), *The Politics of Social Policy in the United States* (Princeton: Princeton University Press, 1988).

—— *The Color of Welfare* (New York: Oxford University Press, 1994).

Reddick, L. D., 'The Negro Policy of the United States Army 1775–1945', *Journal of Negro History*, 34 (1947), 9–29.

—— 'The Negro in the United States Navy during World War II', *Journal of Negro History*, 32 (1947), 201–19.

—— 'The Negro Policy of the American Army since World War Two', *Journal of Negro History*, 38 (1953), 196–215.

REYNOLDS, D., 'The Churchill Government and the Black American Troops in Britain during World War II', *Transactions of the Royal Historical Society*, 5th ser., 35 (1985), 113–33.

ROEDIGER, D. R., *The Wages of Whiteness* (London: Verso, 1991).

ROSENBERG, C., *The Care of Strangers: The Rise of America's Hospital System* (New York: Basic Books, 1987).

ROTHMAN, D. J., *The Discovery of the Ayslum* (Boston: Little Brown, 1971).

ROWAN, C. T., *Breaking Barriers* (London: Little Brown, 1991).

RUCHAMES, L., *Race, Jobs and Politics: The Story of FEPC* (New York: Harper, 1953).

RUESCHEMEYER, D., STEPHENS, E. H., and STEPHENS, J. D., *Capitalist Development and Democracy* (Chicago: University of Chicago Press, 1992).

SASNA, M., 'The South in the Saddle: Racial Politics during the Wilson Years', *Wisconsin Magazine of History*, 54 (1970).

SCHATTSCHNEIDER, E. E., *The Semi-Sovereign People* (New York: Holt, Rinehart and Winston, 1960).

SCHEINER, S. M., 'Theodore Roosevelt and the Negro, 1901–1908', *Journal of Negro History*, 47 (1962), 169–82.

SCHUMAN, H., STEEH, C., and BOBO, L., *Racial Attitudes in America* (Cambridge, Mass.: Harvard University Press, 1985).

SHANNON, F. A., 'The Federal Government and the Negro Soldier, 1861–1865', *Journal of Negro History*, 11 (1926), 563–83.

SILBERMAN, B. S., *Cages of Reason* (Chicago: University of Chicago Press, 1993).

SITKOFF, H., 'Racial Militancy and Interracial Violence in the Second World War', *Journal of American History*, 58 (1971), 661–81.

—— 'Harry Truman and the Election of 1948: The Coming of Age of Civil Rights in American Elections', *Journal of Southern History*, 37 (1971), 597–616.

—— *A New Deal for Blacks* (New York: Oxford University Press, 1978).

SKOCPOL, T., 'Bringing the State Back In', in Evans, Rueschemeyer, and Skocpol (eds.), *Bringing the State Back In*.

SKOWRONEK, S., *Building a New American State* (New York: Cambridge University Press, 1982).

SMEDLEY, A., *Race in North America: Origin and Evolution of a World View* Boulder, Colo.: Westview Press, 1993).

SMITH, D. H., *The United States Civil Service Commission* (Baltimore: Johns Hopkins University Press, 1928).

SMITH, G., *When Jim Crow Met John Bull: Black American Troops in World War II in Britain* (London: I. B. Taurus & Co, 1987).

SMITH, R. M., 'Beyond Tocqueville, Myrdal and Hartz: The Multiple Traditions in America', *American Political Science Review*, 87 (1993), 549–66.

SNIDERMAN, P. M., and PIAZZA, T., *The Scar of Race* (Cambridge, Mass.: Harvard University Press, 1993).

STEINMO, S., THELEN, K., and LONGSTRETH, F. (eds.), *Structuring Politics: Historical Institutionalism in Comparative Analysis* (New York: Cambridge University Press, 1992).

STEWART, F. M., *The National Civil Service Reform League* (Austin, Tex.: University of Texas Press, 1929).

STILLMAN II, R. J., *Integration of the Negro in the US Armed Forces* (New York: Praeger, 1968).

—— *The American Bureaucracy* (Chicago: Nelson-Hall, 1987).

TAEUBER, K., and TAEUBER, A., *Negroes in Cities: Residential Segregation and Neighborhood Change* (Chicago: Aldine, 1965).

URQUHART, B., *Ralph Bunche: An American Life* (New York: W. W. Norton, 1993).

VALELLY, R. M., 'Party, Coercion, and Inclusion: The Two Reconstructions of the South's Electoral Politics', *Politics and Society* (1993), 37–67.

VAN RIPER, P. P., *The History of the United States Civil Service* (Evanston, Ill.: Row, Peterson and Co., 1958).

WALTON, H., Jr., *When the Marching Stops* (Albany, NY: State University of New York Press, 1988).

WARE, A., *The Breakdown of Democratic Party Organization 1940–1980* (Oxford: Oxford University Press, 1985).

WEIL, F. E. G., 'The Negro in the Armed Forces', *Social Forces*, 26 (1947), 95–8.

WEISS, N. J., 'The Negro and the New Freedom: Fighting Wilsonian Segregation', *Political Science Quarterly*, 84 (1969), 61–79.

—— *Farewell to the Party of Lincoln: Black Politics in the Age of FDR* (Princeton: Princeton University Press, 1983).

WEIR, M., *Politics and Jobs* (Princeton: Princeton University Press, 1992).

WESLEY, C. H., 'The Concept of Negro Inferiority in American Thought', *Journal of Negro History*, 25 (1940), 540–60.

WHITE, L. D., *Trends in Public Administration* (New York: McGraw Hill, 1933).

—— (1958), *The Republican Era 1869–1901* (Chicago: University of Chicago Press, 1958).

WILLIAMS, L. F., 'The Constitution and the Civil Rights Movement: The Quest for a More Perfect Union', in D. W. Rogers (ed.), *Voting and the Spirit of American Democracy* (Urbana, Ill.: University of Illinois Press, 1990).

WILSON, W. J., *The Truly Disadvantaged: The Inner Ciy, the Underclass and Public Policy* (Chicago: University of Chicago Press, 1987).

WINANT, H., *Racial Conditions: Politics, Theory, Comparisons* (Minneapolis: University of Minnesota Press, 1994).

WOLGEMUTH, K. L., 'Woodrow Wilson's Appointment Policy and the Negro', *Journal of Southern History*, 24 (1958), 457–71.

WOLTERS, R., *Negroes and the Great Depression* (Westport, Conn.: Greenwood, 1970).

WOODWARD, C. V., *The Strange Career of Jim Crow* (New York : Oxford University Press, 3rd edn. 1974).

—— 'Seeds of Failure in Radical Race Policy', in F. A. Bonadio (ed.), *Political Parties in American History*, ii. *1828–1890* (New York: G. P. Putnam's Sons, 1974).

Index

Abraham, H. J. 256 n. 98
Acheson, Dean 33, 265 n. 203
Advisory Board of the Civil Service
  267 n. 16
affirmative action 209
  see also US Civil Service Commission
Aid to Dependent Children 207
  see also welfare policy
Aid to Families with Dependent
  Children 207
  see also welfare policy
Alexander, Myrl Director US Bureau of
  Prisons 166, 168, 171
  see also US Bureau of Prisons
Alexander, Dr Will 98
  see also US Office of Education
Alien Property Custodian 81
Allen, W. R. 262 n. 165
Alley Dwelling Authority, *see* National
  Capital Housing Authority
Alston, Mrs Demaris 176
Alston, Henry 55–6, 176, 272 n. 82,
  272 n. 83, 272 n. 84, 302 n. 21
Altmeyer, A. 74, 276 n. 3
American Battle Monuments
  Commission 81
American Civil Liberties Union 166
American Council on Race Relations
  282–3 n. 89
American Federation of Labor (AFL) 8,
  102
  and apprenticeships 102
  and Black Americans 8
  and USES 180–1, 261 n. 152,
    303 n. 38
American Friends Service Committee
  307 n. 103, 308 n. 111
American Jewish Congress 193
  see also US Federal Housing
    Authority
Anderson, Secretary of Agriculture
  Clinton P. 25, 260 n. 148
Anderson, Eugenie 265–6 n. 204
Andrews, W. T. 263 n. 180, 269 n. 47
Appleby, Secretary Paul 16
Apprenticeships, *see* Black Americans;
  NAACP; US Department of Labor
Armed Services, *see* US Armed Services
Aswell, Congressman James B. 21–3,
  258 n. 129
  and NAACP, 22–3
  racial doctrines 258 n. 129

Banton, M. 250–1 n. 51, 290 n. 63
Barkin, Eugene 300 n. 102
Bates, B. 246 n. 4
Beecher, John 99–100, 272 n. 90,
  272 n. 100, 283 n. 95
  see also FEPC
Beitscher, Henry, 303 n. 41
Belknap, M. E. 252 n. 63, 255 n. 92
Bell, Congressman Thomas M. 297 n. 15
Bennett, James Director US Bureau of
  Prisons 10–11, 143, 151, 152, 156,
  170–171
  see also US Bureau of Prisons
Bensel, R. F. 247 n. 14, 249 n. 27,
  249 n. 28, 252 n. 63, 260 n. 149,
  264 n. 185, 265 n. 189
Bergman, William D. 277–8 n. 19
Birth of a Nation 248 n. 25, 257 n. 119
  see also NAACP
Black, Algernon 197, 307 n. 98,
  310 n. 141
Black Americans:
  and AFL 8, 102, 180–1
  apprenticeships, 96–103, 207–8,
    285 n. 151, 285 n. 153
  attitudes to Second World War
    112–14, 118, 248 n. 22, 287 n. 9,
    287 n. 11, 288 n. 14, 288 n. 17,
    291 n. 73
  in Bureau of Engraving and Printing
    3, 10, 46, 47
  civil rights 254 n. 90
  and Congress 257 n. 120
  CIO, 181
  and Democratic Party 72–4
  and discrimination 83, 84, 209–10,
    272 n. 100; Federal government and

Black Americans: (*cont.*):
discrimination 209–10, 276 n. 7, 283 n. 95; non-discrimination compliance clauses 97
and FEB survey of discrimination 103–5
in Federal government 4–5, 10, 72–108, 280 n. 47, 281 n. 52; Black American employees in field offices 81–2, 84–7; occupational distribution 72–108, 205, 207, 246 n. 10; post-Civil Rights Act (1964) occupational distribution 207; temporary positions 76, 88–96
and Federal housing 4
and Federal penitentiaries 4
government contract compliance 96–103
Ku Klux Klan 28
labour market 173–4
March on Washington Movement 25, 77
migration from the South 28
NAACP report on apprenticeships 101–3
NAACP reports on segregation 29–31
and National Parks 4, 247 n. 15, 248 n. 19
and New Deal 31–2, 277 n. 19
numbers in civil service 46–7
Office of Price Administration 282 n. 86, 282 n. 87
and Pendleton Act (1883) 40–51
photograph requirement for civil service 48–50
Ramspeck Act (1940) 49
and President Franklin D. Roosevelt 31–3, 58, 72; and Black American government employees 74–5
and Commissioner Theodore Roosevelt 47
and President William Taft 262 n. 167, 269 n. 50
and President Harry S. Truman 33–5
and recruitment to civil service 39–71, 68–72
rule of three recruitment procedure 51–7
and Second World War 31–2, 33–4, 282–3 n. 89
and Social Security Act (1935) 207
and social rights of citizenship 207–8
and unemployment 79
and US Armed Services 4, 8, 11, 33, 111–41; Black American attitudes to segregation 111, 113–16; Navy 123–5
and US Civil Service Commission 9, 283 n. 9
and US Employment Service 4, 172–89, 199–201
and US Office of Education 8, 100–1; discrimination on training programmes 99–101
and US Government Printing Office 16
and Urban Renewal 200–1
and Washington DC 3–5, 9
and President Woodrow Wilson 12–13, 28–31, 262 n. 168, 263 n. 174
Blease, Senator Cole L. 8, 23, 259 n. 136
Bledsoe, Sam 287 n. 10
Blum, J. M. 249 n. 30, 268 n. 37
Board of Investigation and Research 81
Bobo, L. 248 n. 23
Bonadio, F. A. 249 n. 31
Borras, Chauncey 53, 271 n. 71
Bowles, Chester 87
see also Office of Price Administration
Boylan, Congressman John J. 297 n. 15
Bradley, General Omar 130, 132, 293 n. 125
Brady, D. W. 261 n. 154
Brockway, Glenn E. 302 n. 21
Brooks, Major General 128–9
Brophy, John 100, *see* FEPC
Brotherhood of Sleeping Car Porters, *see* A. Philip Randolph
Brown, Justice Henry Billings 256 n. 100
Brown v. *Board of Education Topeka, Kansas*, *see* Supreme Court
Buckley, J. J. 268 n. 37
Bullard, R. D. 312 n. 5
Bunche, R. J. 264 n. 185, 270 n. 59
Bureau of Apprenticeship, *see* US Department of Labor
Bureau of the Budget 81
Bureau of Employment Security (BES), *see* US Employment Service
Bureau of Engraving and Printing, *see* US Treasury

Bureau of Internal Revenue, *see* US Treasury
Bureau of Standards, *see* US Department of Commerce
Bureau of Statistics, *see* US Department of Labor
Burleigh, Michael 171, 300 n. 106
Burleson, US Postmaster General Albert 45, 268 n. 29
Burton, Senator Theodore E. 258 n. 124
Bush, Senator Prescott 195, 197, 308 n. 114, 308 n. 118, 310 n. 145

Calder, Senator William 54
Caliver, Dr Ambrose 292 n. 92
Campbell, Phil 277 n. 19
Campbell, R. R. 260 n. 146, 280 n. 37
Cannon, Congressman Clarence 279 n. 28
Carey, Archibald 281 n. 64, 300 n. 2
Carmines, E. G. 312 n. 12
Carr, Robert 60, 261 n. 161, 270 n. 65, 272 n. 97, 289 n. 43
Carter, President Jimmy 71
  and Civil Service Reform Act (1978), 71
Carter, Robert 304 n. 52, 306 n. 80
Cash, W. J. 300 n. 107
Chapital, Arthur J. 275 n. 150, 275 n. 152
Churchill, Prime Minister Winston 134
Civil Rights Act (1957) 310–11 n. 1
Civil Rights Act (1960) 310–11 n. 1
Civil Rights Act (1964) 4, 17, 19, 28, 35, 107, 205, 206–7, 246 n. 5
  enactment 206, 310–11 n. 1
  enforcement 311 n. 2, 312 n. 3
Civil Rights Act (1968) 257 n. 111
civil service committee, *see* Congress
civil service reform 40–5
  Civil Service Reform Act (1978) 71
  opposition to civil service reform 47–8
  Pendleton Act (1883) 40–51, 70
  Personnel Classification Act (1923) 50
  photograph requirement 48–50; abolition 57–9; Civil Service Commission opposition to abolition 54; introduction 48–50
  and Progressivism 40
  Ramspeck Act 43, 49, 54, 64
  and President Theodore Roosevelt 44
  spoils system 39–45
  see also US Civil Service Commission
Civil Service Reform Act (1978) 71
Civil Service Reform Association 269 n. 45, 283 n. 90
Clague, Ewan 305 n. 78
Clapp, Gordon R. 265 n. 194, 277–8 n. 19
Clark, Attorney-General Tom 34–5
Clemmer, D. 296 n. 3
Cleveland, President Grover 43
Clinchy, Ross 275 n. 147, 313 n. 13
Clinton, President Bill 207
  and apprenticeships 207–8
Cochran, Congressman John J. 24, 172, 259 n. 139
Cochrane, Warren R. 309 n. 121
Cole, Albert 195–8
  see also US Federal Housing Authority
Commission on Civil Rights, *see* US Commission on Civil Rights
Commission on World Peace of the Methodist Church 151
Committee on Equality of Treatment and Opportunity in the Armed Services, *see* President Harry Truman
Committee on Government Contract Compliance, *see* President Harry Truman
Committee against Race Discrimination in the War Effort 142, 296 n. 5, 299 n. 72
Congregationalist and Christian World 251 n. 57
Congress 7, 20–7, 47, 49, 60, 210, 269 n. 52
  bill to abolish photograph requirement for applicants to civil service 269 n. 52
  bills to exclude Black Americans from US Armed Services 111, 258 n. 121
  bills to segregate civil service 20–3, 257 n. 120, 258 n. 122
  Civil Rights Act (1964) 206; enactment 310–11 n. 1
  discrimination in housing 194, 196; Housing Act (1954) 194; Senator P. Bush 195
  failure to make FEPC permanent 60, 77–9

Congress (*cont.*):
 FEPC 279 n. 28
 Secretary of Commerce Hebert Hoover 259 n. 132
 House Appropriations committees 77, 180, 200, 261 n. 155
 House Rules committee 77
 opposition to civil service reform 47–8
 opposition to segregation 258 n. 124
 oversight of civil service 39, 54–5, 65–6; rule of three 54–5; segregation 74
 Pendleton Act (1883) 41–3, 70, 267 n. 9, 267 n. 12, 267 n. 16
 Post Office Department 103
 committee on Post Office and Civil Service report 270 n. 63, 271 n. 68
 Ramspeck Act (1940) 43, 49, 54, 64, 271 n. 68
 and racial doctrines 7–9, 27, 258 n. 129, 258 n. 131
 report on *US Civil Service Commission* 275 n. 138
 Senate Civil Service Committee report 51
 special committee on Federal penitentiaries 145–6, 297 n. 15
 support of segregation 20–7, 210, 259 n. 132, 259 n. 136, 260 n. 148
 and USES 26, 172, 180, 187–8, 261 n. 153, 261 n. 155, 274 n. 128; Congressman John J. Cochran 172, 259 n. 139, 300 n. 1; decentralization 261 n. 155, 261 n. 158; Congressman John Fogarty 200, 274 n. 128; Congressman Gordon McDonough, 180–1, 303 n. 37, 303 n. 39; Congressman Wilbur Mills 201; Secretary of Labor Lewis Schwellenbach 180; Task Force on USES 1965 199–200; weak congressional oversight, 187–8, 200–1, 261 n. 157
 and US Federal Housing Authority 192
 and Washington DC 26–7, 174, 179–80, 257 n. 120, 258 n. 123
 House Ways and Means committee 200–1
Congress of Industrial Organisation (CIO) 62, 78, 181, 184, 260 n. 146, 273 n. 118
 see also AFL and FEPC
Conover, P. J. 312 n. 7
Coolidge, President Calvin 7, 28, 263 n. 176
Cooper, Congressman John 297 n. 15
Cosey, Alfred B. 263 n. 174
Coxton, Fred 286 n. 167
Cramer, Lawrence 265 n. 195, 272–3 n. 101
Cressey, D. R. 296 n. 1
Crewe, I. 312 n. 7
Cunningham, James 54, 271 n. 78
Customs Service 69

Dahlquist, Major General 128–9
Dalfiume, R. M. 288 n. 16, 289 n. 48
Daniels, Jon 171, 259 n. 141, 265 n. 201
Davidson, C. 246 n. 5, 249 n. 27, 313 n. 14
Davis, Benjamin O. Sr 117
 see also US Armed Services
Davis, John A. 264 n. 187, 266 n. 208, 268 n. 31, 269 n. 51
 see also FEPC
deB Katzenbach, Nicholas 300 n. 103
de Tocqueville, Alexis 144
Democratic Fair Play Association 21
Democratic Party 7, 20, 23–4, 70, 108, 251 n. 54, 258 n. 124, 259 n. 136, 259 n. 138, 262 n. 166
 and Black Americans 7, 70, 72, 251 n. 54, 257 n. 136
 and Civil Rights Act (1964) 108
 in Congress 20–7, 108
 Dixiecrat revolt 25
 electoral strength 20, 23–4, 29, 70, 115, 122, 254 n. 54, 258 n. 124
 and FEPC 33, 77; 1944 party platform, 77
 opposition to permanent FEPC 77
 party platform 1948 115
 and post-Reconstruction 7–9
 Southern Governors' Conference, 115; Senator Richard B. Russell, 115
Denmark 34
Denton, N. A. 301 n. 5, 312 n. 5
Department of Housing and Urban Development 189

see also US Federal Housing Authority
Dickerson, Earl 56
Dirksen, Congressman Everett M. 26, 261 n. 155
discrimination, *see* segregation
District of Columbia, *see* Washington DC
Division of Slum Clearance and Urban Redevelopment 194
see also US Federal Housing Authority
Dixiecrat revolt, *see* Democratic Party
Dixon, Thomas 5–6, 248 n. 25
Doar, John 168, 256 n. 108, 280 n. 46, 304 n. 55, 311 n. 2
Dodd, L. C. 255 n. 96
Donahue, Alphonus 288 n. 33
Donovan, Daniel 265 n. 195
Dowling, Robert W. 257 n. 118
Du Bois, W. E. B. 287 n. 7

Eagles, Charles, 171, 300 n. 107
Eden, Anthony 134
Edwards, Lieutenant-General 128
Eisenhower, General Dwight D. 116, 289 n. 38, 294 n. 141
Eisenhower, President Dwight D. 19, 28, 79, 104, 140, 192, 199, 200, 201
civil rights legislation 310–11 n. 1
and desegregation 19, 28, 35, 140
Executive Order 10590 80
and Federal housing policy 20, 201, 307 n. 98
and National Committee Against Discrimination in Housing 192, 201, 310 n. 141
and National Urban League 192
President's Committee on Government Employment Policy 68, 79–80, 83, 104–5, 186, 208–9, 275 n. 146, 275 n. 154, 286 n. 174, 300 n. 2; coordination with US Employment Service 186; complaints received 286 n. 171; and discrimination 84, 209, 275 n. 154, 275 n. 155, 305 n. 70; establishment, 79–80; Executive Order 10590 80; redress for discrimination 209; Southern Regional Council 104; survey of Black American employment 83; surveys of discrimination 104
and US Employment Service 199, 200
Egan, John 307 n. 98, 309 n. 121
Eldridge, Russell J. 302 n. 24
Ellender, Senator Allen J. 278 n. 21
Employment Service, *see* US Employment Service
Equal Employment Opportunity Commission (EEOC) 80, 105–7, 206–7
Civil Rights Act (1964) 206
Equal Employment Opportunities Enforcement Act (1972) 206
regulations for nondiscrimination 207
survey of discrimination in Federal departments 206–7
Equal Employment Opportunities Enforcement Act (1972) 206
Eskridge, W. N. 296 n. 174
Ethridge, Mark 279 n. 35
Evans, P. 313 n. 15
Ewing, Oscar, 304 n. 51
Executive Office of the President 81
Export-Import Bank 81

Fahy, Charles 125, 128, 288 n. 33, 292 n. 92, 295 n. 160, 295 n. 166
Fahy Committee (President Truman's Committee on Equality of Treatment and Opportunity in the Armed Services)
see President Harry Truman
Fair Employment Board (FEB) 57, 61, 68, 79, 103–5, 184, 185–6, 188–9, 272 n. 92
anti-discrimination regulations 286 n. 161, 305 n. 75
criticisms of rule of three 57, 286 n. 168
criticisms of US Civil Service Commission 61
establishment 68, 79–80
Post Office Department 103, 286 n. 166
survey of departments' fair employment practices 103–5
US Department of the Interior 103
US Department of Labor 272 n. 91, 273 n. 109
US Employment Service 184, 185–6,

Fair Employment Board (*cont.*): 188–9, 273 n. 109; discrimination 188–9; placement in Federal civil service 185–6
VA, 286 n. 165
Fair Employment Practice Committee (FEPC) vii, 25, 31, 32, 59, 60, 61, 67, 69, 72, 74–5, 77–9, 80–3, 88–96, 107, 208, 247 n. 12, 260 n. 143, 260 n. 146, 264 n. 187, 265 n. 195, 271 n. 66, 276 n. 4, 283 n. 92
agreement with US Civil Service Commission to monitor discrimination 65, 274 n. 132
agreement with CIO 78, 280 n. 38
agreements with other agencies 279 n. 33, 304 n. 49
anti-discrimination policy 265 n. 199, 268 n. 31, 269 n. 51, 274 n. 130, 274 n. 134, 275 n. 140
apprenticeship and training 97–8; and US Office of Education 98–9
John Beecher 99–100, 272 n. 90
Black American employees 58–9
Black American employment in field offices 84–7
John Brophy 100
and Congress 25, 279 n. 28
coordination with USES 182–3
critics 279 n. 25
John A. Davis 245 n. 1, 264 n. 187, 266 n. 208, 268 n. 31, 269 n. 51
Earl Dickerson 56
and discrimination 83, 88–96, 265 n. 199, 272 n. 90, 272 n. 100, 274 n. 130, 283 n. 94; hearing on Personnel Classification Division 89–96, 284 n. 114, Miss Fox 89–96 Miss Landes 90, 93, Mrs Ellen Manchester 90, 92–3, Miss Miller 90, Clarence Mitchell 92–5, Miss Settle 90–3, Joseph Spilman 89–95, E. Trimble 89–95, US Civil Service Commission 284 n. 116, 284 n. 117
and discrimination on training programmes 98–9, 285 n. 144, 285 n. 145, 285 n. 147; Alabama 99 Florida 99; Georgia 100; Tennessee 100
establishment 25, 74–5, 77–9, 259 n. 142, 277 n. 9, 278 n. 21, 278 n. 24; March on Washington Movement 77, 259 n. 142
Executive Order 8802 77–8
Elmer Henderson 84–5, 272 n. 89
Department of Labor 54; case of George Nesbitt 54
membership of Committee 260 n. 143, 279–80 n. 35
Leslie Perry 276 n. 1, 276 n. 2, 277 n. 13, 277 n. 17, 283 n. 94
Personnel Classification Division 89–96
powers of investigation 77–8, 279 n. 31, 283 n. 93
public hearings 78, 285 n. 137
A. Philip Randolph 4, 32, 77, 112–13, 114, 116, 210, 259 n. 142
and FEPC 25, 210, 278 n. 23
March on Washington Movement 25, 77, 210, 259 n. 142
President Roosevelt 25
Malcolm Ross 61–2, 66, 78, 88, 265 n. 200, 265 n. 203, 279 n. 28
rule of three, 56–7, 281 n. 63
surveys of Black American employees 80–3, 246 n. 10, 271 n. 70, 272 n. 89, 277 n. 16, 281 n. 51, 281 n. 52, 282 n. 69, 282 n. 71, 282 n. 75, 282 n. 80; non-responses from agencies 280 n. 48; Second World War 271 n. 70, 277 n. 12, 277 n. 16, 281 n. 55, 281 n. 63, 282–3 n. 89
temporary status of Black American employees 77, 88–96
US Armed Services: transportation 291 n. 74
US Civil Service Commission 59, 61–2
US Office of Education 99–101
Farley, James A. 271 n. 72
Farley, R. 262 n. 165, 312 n. 5
Feagin, J. R. 312 n. 5
Federal Deposit Insurance Corporation 81
Federal Home Loan Bank Board 189
see also US Federal Housing Authority
Federal government 4–5, 10, 17
and Black Americans 72–108

Black American employees in field offices, 81–2, 84–7
distribution of Black American employees by job level 72, 80–4
nature of 210
President Woodrow Wilson and segregation 12–13
and segregation of Black Americans 10, 12–13
see also Black Americans; FEPC; segregation; US Civil Service Commission
Federal housing programmes, *see* US Federal Housing Authority
Federal Housing Administration 20, *see* US Federal Housing Authority
Federal penitentiaries 4, 10–11, *see also* US Bureau of Prisons
Federal Power Commission 81
Federal Security Agency 67, 74, 183, 188
Federal Trade Commission 81
Federal Works Agency 67, 86
Fesler, J. W. 255 n. 91
Fields, B. J. 250–1 n. 51, 290 n. 63, 290 n. 65, 290–1 n. 66
Fitzgerald Act (1937) 96, 284 n. 123
Fleming, G. James 272–3 n. 101
Fleming, John R. 287 n. 10
Flemming, Civil Service Commissioner Arthur 52, 54–5, 272 n. 95, 274 n. 129
Fogarty, Congressman John 200, 274 n. 128
Foley, Raymond 307 n. 98, 308 n. 117, 309 n. 132
Follin, J. W. 308 n. 110
Foner, Eric 5, 7, 249 n. 30, 249 n. 34, 249 n. 36, 290 n. 65
Foner, J. D. 289 n. 48
Foner, P. S. 273 n. 117
Foreman, Clark 264 n. 185, 277 n. 19
Forrestal, Secretary of Defense James 123, 289 n. 39, 291 n. 72, 295 n. 155, 295 n. 157
Foster, G. W. 256 n. 109
Foster, W. Z. 265 n. 202
Foulke, William Dudley 269 n. 45
Foy, John F. 303 n. 40
Franklin, Dr Harold 124–5, 291 n. 86
see also US Armed Services
Frederickson, George 7, 248 n. 23, 248 n. 25, 249–50 n. 36, 250 n. 42, 250 n. 51, 258–9 n. 131, 290 n. 65

Gaines, *see* Supreme Court
Gardiner, J. 293 n. 134
Garfinkel, H. 259 n. 142, 278 n. 23
Garlock, Lyle 177–8
Geiger, K. 247 n. 14, 259 n. 138
Gibson, Truman 117, 290 n. 54, 290 n. 56, 291 n. 75
see also US Armed Services
Giegengack, Augustus E. 254 n. 85
Gilhooley, John 260–1 n. 151
Gillem, Lieutenant-General Alvan C. 126–9
see also US Armed Services
Gillem Board, *see* US Armed Services
Glaser, D. 297 n. 35, 298 n. 49
Goffman, Erving 107, 142, 287 n. 183, 296 n. 1
Golder, Cecil E. 104
Goldfield, D. 249 n. 29
Goodwin, D. K. 278 n. 23
Goodwin, G. Jr 274 n. 135, 274 n. 135
Goodwin, Robert Director of USES 183–5, 261 n. 157, 303 n. 38
see also USES
Gottdiener, M. 312 n. 5
Government Administration Office 30, 107
Graham, H. D. 257 n. 110, 313 n. 14
Granger, Lester 11, 117, 120–1, 129, 131, 288 n. 33, 289 n. 39, 290 n. 64, 292 n. 95
see also NUL; US Armed Services
Grant, Colonel U. S. 264 n. 183
Gray, Assistant Secretary 132
Green, William 261 n. 152
Greenstone, J. D. 247–8 n. 18
Grigg, Secretary of State for War Sir James 134, 294 n. 144
Grofman, B. 246 n. 5, 249 n. 27, 313 n. 14
Guandolo, Joseph 308 n. 110

Haas, Mgr. Francis J. 279–80 n. 35
Hachey, T. E. 294 n. 137, 294 n. 144, 294 n. 149
Haller, J. S. 250–1 n. 51
Hannah, Phillip 303 n. 38

Harding, President Warren 7, 28
Harlan, Justice John Marshall 18
Harper, George 297 n. 25
Harris, J. P. 66, 274 n. 136, 274 n. 136
Harris, W. H. 259–60 n. 142
Harrison, President Benjamin 43
Hartgrove, W. B. 287 n. 4
Hartz, L. 247 n. 18
Harvard 250 n. 43
Hastie, William 117, 119, 290 n. 57, 290 n. 58
see also US Armed Services
Hayes, L. J. W. 269 n. 48
Heflin, Senator Thomas J. 23
Henderson, Elmer 84, 265 n. 195, 272 n. 89, 281 n. 51
see also FEPC
Henry, Jean 296 n. 5, 299 n. 72
Hetzel, Fred Z. 303 n. 40
Hewes, Laurence 282–3 n. 89
Hirsch, A. J. 296 n. 3
Home Owners' Loan Corporation (HOLC) 189, 191
see also US Federal Housing Authority
Hoogenboom, A. 256 n. 95, 266 n. 3, 267 n. 17, 268 n. 37
Hoover, Secretary of Commerce Herbert 23, 259 n. 132
and Department of Commerce 23
desegregation 259 n. 132
Hoover, President Herbert 28, 189
and origins of Federal housing policy, 189
Hopper, Edward 4
Horne, Frank 198
see also US Federal Housing Authority
Hosmer, Congressman Craig 307 n. 99
Houghteling, James 273 n. 109, 286 n. 163
see also FEB
housing, *see* US Federal Housing Authority
Housing Act (1949) 197, *see also* US Federal Housing Authority
Housing Act (1954) 194
see also US Federal Housing Authority
Housing and Home Finance Agency (HHFA) 194
see also US Federal Housing Authority
Houston, Charles H. 260 n. 143, 271 n. 71, 271 n. 72, 271 n. 73, 271 n. 74, 271 n. 75, 279–80 n. 35
Howard University 41, 48, 72
Howes, W. W. 271 n. 73, 271 n. 74, 271 n. 75
Humphrey, Mayor Hubert 25
Hunt, H. A. 277 n. 19
Hunton, W. A. 273 n. 108

Ickes, Secretary of the Interior Harold 264 n. 185, 265 n. 193
Indritz, Phineas 254 n. 83, 254 n. 84
see also US Department of the Interior
International Bank 67
Interstate Conference on Employment Security Agencies (ICESA), *see* US Employment Service

Jackson, K. T. 250 n. 49, 264 n. 185, 301 n. 5, 306 n. 90
Jacobs, J. 296 n. 3
Janoski, T. 260–1 n. 151
Javits, Senator Jacob 116, 201–2, 310 n. 142
Jaynes, G. D. 259 n. 140
Jencks, C. 312 n. 5
Jennings, E. H. 272 n. 84
Jim Crow, *see* segregation
Johnson, Congressman Ben 21
Johnson, C. S. 259 n. 140
Johnson, D. M. 260 n. 146, 280 n. 37
Johnson, George M. 266 n. 208
Johnson, Gilbert 125, 292 n. 95
Johnson, James 264 n. 183
Johnson, Louis 293 n. 112
Johnson, President Lyndon B. 27, 70, 108, 200
Civil Rights Act 1964 28, 35, 108, 310–11 n. 1
and discrimination in the civil service 70
Equal Employment Opportunity Commission 105
Executive Order 11246 80
US Employment Service 200, 310 n. 138
Johnson, Reginald A. 307 n. 100
Johnson, Mrs Thomasina W. 293 n. 113
Jones, Eugene Kinckle 277 n. 19

Katznelson, I. 247 n. 14, 259 n. 138, 260 n. 150, 261 n. 159
Keith, Nathaniel 257 n. 113, 307 n. 107, 308 n. 109, 308 n. 113, 309 n. 128
Kennedy, President John F. 35, 105, 108, 200
civil rights legislation 310–11 n. 1
Equal Employment Opportunity Commission 105–6
US Employment Service 200
Kessleman, L. C. 259 n. 142, 278 n. 23, 279–80 n. 35
Key, V. O. Jr 7, 17, 24, 33, 77, 247 n. 14, 248 n. 26, 249 n. 27, 255 n. 94, 259 n. 137, 265 n. 198, 279 n. 28, 288 n. 31
Kettl, D. F. 255 n. 91
King, D. S. 250 n. 46, n. 47, 260 n. 150, 285 n. 152, 302 n. 12, 312 n. 6, 312 n. 7, 312 n. 8
Kingsley, J. Donald 304 n. 54, 305 n. 80
Kinkead, Congressman E. F. 262–3 n. 170
Kirby, J. B. 259–60 n. 142, 278 n. 23
Klarman, M. J. 256–7 n. 109
Klein, Congressman Arthur G. 54–5, 65, 262 n. 163, 271–2 n. 80
Know-Nothing movement 79
Knox, Frank 290 n. 62
Kopp, Congressman W. F., 297 n. 15
Korean War 139
Kousser, J. M. 247 n. 14, 249 n. 27, 262 n. 164, 290 n. 63, 313 n. 14, 313 n. 16
Krasner, S. 313 n. 15
Krislou, S. 252 n. 63, 255 n. 92
Kryder, D. 247 n. 14, 259 n. 138
Ku Klux Klan 5, 28, 79, 168, 198, 262 n. 165

LaDame, Mary 303 n. 33, 303 n. 34
Lafer, G. 312 n. 6
Lankford, Congressman William 8, 27, 250 n. 43
Lawhorn, L. 305 n. 62
Leslie, John W. 309 n. 134
Lewis, O. F. 296 n. 3, 296 n. 8
Lewis, Vernon 276 n. 7
Lofgren, C. A. 256 n. 97
Long, C. R. 276 n. 7
Luckman, Charles 288 n. 33
Ludlow, Congressman Louis 276 n. 5
Lyons, Louis 69–70, 275 n. 150, 275 n. 152

McAdoo, Secretary William Gibbs 13–14, 252 n. 61, 253 n. 74, 253 n. 79, 254 n. 80, 263 n. 171
and segregation 13, 14–15, 29, 253 n. 79, 263 n. 171
McCloy, John J. 118, 132
McCoy, D. 266 n. 212, 295 n. 168
McCoy, W. Arthur 281 n. 64
McDonald, Laughlin 299 n. 82
McDonough, Congressman Gordon 180–1, 303 n. 37, n. 39
McEntee, J. J. 277 n. 19
McFarland, Senator E. W. 24
McGehee, Congressman Dan R. 25, 260 n. 148
McGrady, Edward F. 277–8 n. 19
MacGregor, M. J. 289 n. 48
McIntyre, Rear Admiral Ross T. 124
McKellar, Senator Kenneth 58
McKelvey, B. 144–5, 296 n. 3, 296 n. 8, 296 n. 9
McKittrick, Hugh 268 n. 37
MacLean, N. 262 n. 165
McPherson, J. M. 289 n. 63
McReynolds, W. H. 277–8 n. 19
Macey, John W. 275 n. 147, 276 n. 158, 313 n. 13
Mandelbaum, D. G. 287 n. 3, 289 n. 48
March on Washington Movement, *see* A. Philip Randolph
Maritime Commission 81, 97
Marshall, Thurgood 11, 208
Martin, I. Maximilian 306 n. 94, 307 n. 105
Maslow, Will 266 n. 208, 274 n. 133, 279 n. 25
Mason, Norman P. 202, 300 n. 2
see also US Federal Housing Authority
Massey, D. S. 301 n. 5, 312 n. 5
Mead, Senator J. 58, 272 n. 94
Meier, A. 252 n. 63, 255 n. 92, 255 n. 93
Mellon, Secretary of the Treasury Andrew 14, 15–16, 254 n. 81
Miller, Professor Kelly 269 n. 45
Miller, N. 267 n. 17
Mills, Congressman Wilbur 201

Mitchell, Clarence 183, 188–9, 198, 309 n. 130
see also NAACP
Mitchell, Civil Service Commission President Harry B. Mitchell 49–50, 51–2, 58, 270 n. 53, 270 n. 65, 271 n. 66, 271 n. 68, 271 n. 79, 272 n. 94
see also US Civil Service Commission
Mollenkopf, J. 312 n. 5
Moran, M. 312 n. 7
Morgenthau, Henry 276 n. 2
Morison, E. E. 268 n. 37
Mortgage Bankers' Association, 197
see also US Federal Housing Authority
Motley, A. V. 184
see also USES
Moyer, L. A. 284 n. 116, 284 n. 117
Mullen, R. W. 250 n. 38, 289 n. 48
Murtha, Joseph 67, 289 n. 43, 291–2 n. 90
Myrdal, G. 250 n. 51, 259 n. 140

Nash, Philleo 104, 259 n. 141, 265 n. 201, 266 n. 205, 272 n. 86
National Association for the Advancement of Colored People (NAACP) viii, 5, 9, 10, 11, 13, 15, 16–17, 22–3, 26, 30, 34, 59–61, 68, 70, 101–3, 111–13, 121–3, 133–6, 137, 150, 176, 181–2, 187–8, 193–4, 196, 198, 208, 253 n. 66, 257 n. 112, 263 n. 172, 263 n. 176, 264 n. 183, 272 n. 82, 272 n. 99, 287 n. 8
Birth of a Nation 248 n. 25
and civil service recruitment 58–9, 68, 69–72
and President Calvin Coolidge 263 n. 179
criticisms of US Civil Service Commission 59–61, 269 n. 41
desegregation of military 139–41
Division of Slum Clearance and Urban Redevelopment 194
and Gillem Board 127–8
Thurgood Marshall, Special Counsel 1, 121, 150, 193–4, 208, 272 n. 83; and Federal penitentiaries 150, 208, 298 n. 71, 312 n. 11; and Public Housing Administration, 193–4
and Secretary Andrew Mellon 15, 254 n. 81
Clarence Mitchell 183, 188–9, 198, 274 n. 128, 275 n. 155, 403 n. 51; US Employment Service 274 n. 128, 305 n. 80; Federal Housing Authority 198, 309 n. 130
NAACP report on apprenticeships 101–3, 285 n. 151, 285 n. 153
NAACP reports on segregation 29–31, 250 n. 50, 251 n. 53, 254 n. 88, 262 n. 169, 263 n. 172, 263 n. 175, 263 n. 180, 269 n. 47
New Orleans, 275 n. 150
photograph requirement for civil service, 48–50; abolition 57–9; Civil Service Commission support, 54; introduction, 48–50
Post Office Department 53–4, 69, 262 n. 167, 271 n. 72
President's Committee on Government Employment Policy 275 n. 154, 275 n. 155, 287 n. 181
and Eleanor Roosevelt 264 n. 185
and President Franklin D. Roosevelt 58, 273 n. 103
racial covenants 257 n. 114, 306 n. 89
and rule of three procedure 52–4, 55–6
and President William Taft 262 n. 167, 269 n. 50
and President Harry Truman 34–5, 60, 273 n. 106
and US Armed Services 111, 112, 121–3, 129–30, 288–9 n. 36, 291 n. 79; Black American soldiers abroad 133–6; Dr Harold Franklin, 291 n. 86; George Nesbitt 114; Bernard Randolph 111, 287 n. 1; segregation 291 n. 79; Tuskegee, 289 n. 51
and USES 26, 64, 176, 178–9, 181, 182, 187–8, 303 n. 44, 303 n. 45, 305 n. 78, 309 n. 133; and anti-discrimination policy, 182; failure to classify Black American jobseekers appropriately 176; opposition to states' control 26, 64, 188, 306 n. 81
Walter White 30, 60, 127–8, 135, 137, 187, 263 n. 181, 272 n. 99, 273 n. 103, 273 n. 106, 303 n. 44, 305 n. 78

Washington DC 251 n. 52
Roy Wilkins 123, 136, 140, 264 n. 185, 287 n. 2
and President Woodrow Wilson 5, 10, 248 n. 20, 262 n. 168, 263 n. 174, 269 n. 43
National Association of Home Builders 197
see also US Federal Housing Authority
National Capital Housing Authority 246 n. 8
Alley Dwelling Authority 246 n. 8
establishment 246 n. 8
National Citizens' Political Action Committee 188, 306 n. 83
National Civil Service Reform League 47
National Committee Against Discrimination in Housing 192, 195, 307 n. 98, 310 n. 141
see also US Federal Housing Authority
National Committee on Segregation in the Nation's Capital 61, 258 n. 125, 261 n. 159, 263 n. 182, 273 n. 110, 282 n. 82
see also Washington DC
National Council of the Churches of Christ 197
see also US Federal Housing Authority
National Mediation Board 81
National Parks 4, 247 n. 13, 247 n. 15, 248 n. 19
see also US Department of Interior
National Urban Coalition and the Lawyers' Committee for Civil Rights Under Law, 1971 study of the USES 199–201, *see* US Employment Service
National Urban League (NUL) viii, 11, 20, 67, 116, 125–6, 192–3, 257 n. 118
and Federal housing policy 192–3, 257 n. 118
and President Eisenhower 192
and segregation in the US Armed Services 116, 125
Washington Urban League 246 n. 6
National War Labor Board 85
Neely, Senator M. M. 309 n. 121
New Deal 24, 31–3, 96, 172, 201, 264 n. 185
Black Americans 31–2, 201, 264 n. 185
electoral coalition 27–8
see Black Americans; President Franklin D. Roosevelt
Nerney, May 29–30, 250 n. 50, 251 n. 51, 254 n. 88, 262 n. 169, 263 n. 175
see also NAACP
Nesbitt, George 54, 114, 195, 197, 257 n. 113, 307 n. 107, 308 n. 113, 309 n. 128
see also US Federal Housing Authority
Nettl, J. P. 313 n. 15
Niles, David 266 n. 205, 266 n. 206, 266 n. 212, 272 n. 86, 288 n. 29, 295 n. 159, 295 n. 161
Nordlinger, E. 313 n. 15
Norks, Senator John 119, 257 n. 119
Northrup, H. R. 250 n. 46
Nutt, Louis H. 10

O'Mahoney, Senator Joseph 24
Office of Censorship 81
Office of Civilian Defense 85
Office of Economic Warfare 81
Office of Personnel Management 71
Office of Price Administration (OPA) 59, 84, 87–8, 277 n. 8, 282 n. 83, 282 n. 86
Black Americans in field offices 84, 282 n. 84, 282 n. 86, 282 n. 87
Chester Bowles 87–8, 282 n. 83
Racial Relations Officer 277 n. 8
Office of Strategic Services 81
Ovington, M. White
Oxley, Lawrence 24, 172, 301 n. 7
see also US Employment Service

Palmer, Dwight 288 n. 33
Panama Canal 81
Panama Railroad Company 81
Parris, H. 266 n. 1
Patent Office 67
Patterson, Under-Secretary of War Robert P. 119–20, 276 n. 4, 289 n. 53
Patterson, Roy, 266 n. 209, 266 n. 210
Patterson, J. T. 259 n. 138, 264 n. 185

Pendleton Act (1883) 40–51, 70, 267 n. 9, 267 n. 12, 267 n. 16
Pendleton, Senator George 41–2, 266 n. 4, 267 n. 9, 267 n. 12, 267 n. 16
Perkins, Frances 271 n. 77, 303 n. 32
Perry, Leslie 72, 75, 276 n. 1, 276 n. 2, 277 n. 13, 277 n. 17, 283 n. 94
  see also FEPC
Personnel Classification Act (1923) 50
Personnel Classification Board, *see* US Civil Service Commission
Persons, Frank 259 n. 139, 300 n. 1
Peters, Congressman Andrew 258 n. 124
Peterson, P. 312 n. 5
Philadelphia Transportation Company 32
Piazza 208, 209, 312 n. 9, 312 n. 12
Pickvance, C. 312 n. 5
Pietrykowski, P. 260 n. 150, 261 n. 159
Plessy v. *Ferguson* (1896), *see* Supreme Court
Pohlhaus, J. Francis 287 n. 181
Poletti, Charles 290 n. 54, 290 n. 56
Potter, Senator Charles E. 308 n. 120
Powell, Congressman Adam 116
President's Advisory Committee on Housing Policies and Programs 192
  see also US Federal Housing Authority
President's Committee on Civil Service Improvement 273 n. 108
  see also President Franklin D. Roosevelt
President's Committee on Government Employment Policy, *see* President Dwight D. Eisenhower
prisons, *see* US Bureau of Prisons
Progressivism 20, 28, 40, 44, 46, 48, 249 n. 30, 257 n. 119
  and civil service reform 40, 44, 46
  and racial doctrines 257 n. 119
Public Health Service 67
Public Housing Authority, *see* US Federal Housing Authority

Quadagno, J. 250 n. 46, 250 n. 49, 312 n. 6, 312 n. 7

racial covenants 193–4, 257 n. 114, 306 n. 89
  see also US Federal Housing Authority
racial doctrines 7–8, 20–7, 249 n. 30, 250 n. 44, 257 n. 119, 258 n. 129, 258 n. 131, 290 n. 63, 290–1 n. 66
Racial Relations Advisers 197, 198, 245 n. 1
Railroad Retirement Board 86
Ramspeck, Congressman Robert 50, 66, 270 n. 53, 271 n. 68, 271 n. 79
Ramspeck Act (1940) 43, 49, 54, 58, 64
Randolph, A. Philip 4, 32, 77, 112–13, 114, 116, 210, 259 n. 142, 278 n. 23
  Brotherhood of Sleeping Car Porters 259 n. 142, 278 n. 23
  Committee against Jim Crow in Military Service and Training 116
  and FEPC 25, 210
  March on Washington Movement 25, 77, 210, 259 n. 142, 278 n. 23
  and Eleanor Roosevelt 259–60 n. 142
  segregation in the US Armed Services 112–13, 114
Randolph, Bernard 111, 287 n. 1
Rankin, J. Lee 284 n. 118, 285 n. 134
Ray, Joseph 190
  see also US Federal Housing Authority
Reconstruction (1865–76) vii, 4–9, 40, 46, 206
  collapse of 5–9
  and segregation of Black Americans 4–7
  and separate but equal 4–5
Reddick, L. D. 287 n. 6, 288 n. 35
Republican Party 20–1, 24, 49, 197, 258 n. 124, 309 n. 124
  and Black American voters 7, 49
  Director of Minorities 197
  and segregation 6–9, 21, 49, 258 n. 124, 309 n. 124
Reynolds, David 133–5, 294 n. 137, 294 n. 138, 294 n. 141, 294 n. 143, 294 n. 145
Richardson, Thomas 62–3, 260 n. 146, 273 n. 118, 280 n. 37
Riot in Cell Block 11 151
Rogerson, Howard W. 300 n. 99, 300 n. 100
Roos, Charles F. 277–8 n. 19
Roosevelt, Eleanor 31, 124, 259–60 n. 142, 264 n. 185

and Black Americans 31
Dr Harold Franklin 124
A. Philip Randolph 259–60 n. 142
Roy Wilkins 264 n. 185
Roosevelt, President Franklin D. 25, 27, 31–3, 40, 43, 52, 58, 66, 72, 74–5, 76–7, 78, 108, 115, 122, 144, 172, 210
and Black Americans 58, 273 n. 103
and Black American government employees 74–5
Executive Order 8802 77
Executive Order 9346 75
and FEPC creation 25, 77–9, 210
and Federal expansion 43, 50–1, 58
and March on Washington Movement 77, 210, 259 n. 142
New Deal 31–3, 40–5, 50–1, 58, 96, 172, 201, 264 n. 185, 277 n. 19
New Deal electoral coalition 27–8, 31, 115, 122
President's Committee on Civil Service Improvement 273 n. 108
and A. Philip Randolph 77, 259 n. 142
Second World War 31–2
Roosevelt, Commissioner Theodore 43, 47, 48, 268 n. 37
Bureau of Engraving and Printing 47
and patronage 44
and photograph requirement for civil service 48–9
Roosevelt, President Theodore 7, 28, 44, 249 n. 30
and Black Americans 7, 28, 249 n. 30
and civil service recruitment 44
Rosenberg, Mrs Anna 272 n. 90, 272 n. 100, 283 n. 95
Ross, Malcolm 61, 66, 78, 260 n. 143, 265 n. 203, 271 n. 67, 272 n. 95, 279–80 n. 35, 282–3 n. 89
see also FEPC
Rossell, Charles 58–9
Rothman, D. J. 296 n. 3, 296 n. 8
Rowan, Carl 114, 288 n. 23, 289 n. 52
see also US Armed Services
Royall, Kenneth C. 127, 132
Ruchames, L. 260 n. 143, 279–80 n. 35
Rudwick, E. 252 n. 63, 255 n. 91, 255 n. 93
Rueschemeyer, D. 249 n. 27, 313 n. 15
Ruetten, M. 266 n. 212, 295 n. 168
rule of three, *see* US Civil Service Commission
Russell, Senator Richard B. 77, 115, 279 n. 25
Rustin, Bayard 165–6

Sady, Rachel 261 n. 161
Sasna, M. 257–8 n. 120
Scheiner, S. M. 250 n. 37
Schott, R. L. 255 n. 96
Schuman, H. 248 n. 23
Schwellenbach, Secretary of Labor Lewis 180, 261 n. 152, 266 n. 209, 303 n. 37, 303 n. 39, 303 n. 41, 304 n. 60
Searing, D. 312 n. 7
Searle, W. D. 277–8 n. 19
Sectionalism 5–9
self-segregation 208
Sengstacke, John 288 n. 33
segregation 3
apprenticeships 96–103
bills to segregate civil service 20–3
Bureau of Engraving and Printing 3, 46, 47
Committee against Jim Crow in Military Service and Training 116
congressional oversight of civil service 65–6, 74
congressional support 20–7, 257 n. 120, 258 n. 123
defined 9–17, 205–6
and Democrats 251 n. 54
in Department of Commerce 23
desegregation of schools 19
and discrimination 83, 263 n. 176
FEB surveys of departments 104–5
in Federal government 10, 254 n. 84, 257 n. 120, 262 n. 166, 262 n. 168, 263 n. 174; early forms of 251 n. 53; introduction 262 n. 169, 262 n. 170
in Federal penitentiaries 150–60, 170, 208
in housing 19
in hospitals 246 n. 4
Jim Crow 3, 6–7, 8, 18–19, 30, 32, 33, 64, 78, 88, 113, 114, 137, 187, 245–6 n. 2, 249 n. 29
government contract compliance 96–103

segregation (*cont.*):
Government Printing Office 107
labour market 173–4
National Committee on Segregation in the Nation's Capital 61
NAACP reports on segregation 29–31
National Parks 4, 247 n. 13, 247 n. 15, 248 n. 19
New Deal 31–3, 50–1, 58, 264 n. 185, 277 n. 19
occupational distribution of Black American government employees 80–4
origins of 4–9
Pendleton Act (1883) 45–51
photograph requirement for civil service 48–50; abolition 57–9; Civil Service opposition to abolition 54; introduction 48–50
Post Office Department 29–30, 44, 53–4, 69
post-Second World War trends 62, 88, 113, 137–9
President's Committee on Government Employment Policy surveys 104–5
and presidential politics 27–35
Ramspeck Act (1940) 43, 49
Congressman Robert Ramspeck 271 n. 68
and recruitment to civil service 39–71; rule of three 51–7
Second World War 32, 88, 113–16, 248 n. 22, 271 n. 70, 277 n. 12
self-segregation 208
social ostracism 95
Supreme Court support 18–20
President William Taft 269 n. 50
US Armed Services 112–41
US Civil Service Commission 45–51, 205
US Department of the Interior 30
US Department of State 30
US Employment Service 63–4, 172–89, 199–201
US Treasury 29–30
US Government Printing Office 16
Washington DC 3–4, 26–7, 60–1, 257 n. 120, 258 n. 123
President Woodrow Wilson 28–31, 87, 107–8, 257 n. 119, 262 n. 168, 263 n. 174

Seidenberg, Jacob 309 n. 123
Selective Service Act (1940) 113, 144, 147
Sengstacke, John 131
separate but equal 4, 17, 19, 79, 150, 205
see also Supreme Court
Shannon, F. A. 287 n. 5
Sherman, Senator Lawrence Y. 258 n. 124
Shishkin, Boris 260 n. 143, 279 n. 35
Siciliano, Rocco 197, 310 n. 141
Silberman, B. 256 n. 95, 266 n. 2
Silverman, Anber 309 n. 121
Sitkoff, H. 250 n. 48, 260 n. 147, 265 n. 197, 265 n. 200, 266 n. 213, 288 n. 30, 289 n. 45
Skocpol, T. 313 n. 15
Skowronek, Stephen 43, 44, 48, 266 n. 4, 267 n. 18, 267 n. 21, 267 n. 22, 268 n. 27, 269 n. 39
Smaller War Plants Corporation 81
Smedley, A. 250–1 n. 51, 290 n. 63
Smith, D. H. 267 n. 21
Smith, G. 294 n. 137
Smith, Senator Hoke 21
Smith, R. M. 247–8 n. 18, 249 n. 30
Smith, Robert 271 n. 77
Smoot, Senator Reed 259 n. 136
Sniderman, Paul 208, 209, 312 n. 9, 312 n. 12
Social Security Act (1935) 207–8
see also welfare policy
Social Security Administration 69
Southall, Sara E. 260 n. 143, 279–80 n. 35
Southern Governors' Conference 115
Southern Regional Council 104–5, 286 n. 174, 287 n. 176
Spilman, Joseph 89–95
see also FEPC
spoils system, *see* civil service reform
State Park Citizens' Committee for Housing and Planning 197
see also US Federal Housing Authority
Steeh, C. 248 n. 23
Stephens, E. H. 249 n. 27
Stephens, Senator Hubert D. 23
Stephens, J. D. 249 n. 27
Stevenson, William 288 n. 33

Stewart, F. M. 269 n. 38
Stewart, Milton D. 67, 261 n. 161, 289 n. 43, 291–2 n. 90
Stillman II, Richard 117, 255 n. 91, 288 n. 22, 289 n. 40, 289 n. 48, 291 n. 70, 293 n. 128, 295 n. 168
Stimson, Secretary of War James 118, 135, 295 n. 153
Stimson, J. A. 312 n. 12
Storey, Moorfield 10, 30, 251 n. 55
  and President Calvin Coolidge 30
  and President Woodrow Wilson 10, 251 n. 55
Supreme Court 17, 18–20, 79, 140, 151, 164, 169, 171, 193, 194, 201, 246 n. 5, 255 n. 100, 257 n. 114, 257 n. 117, 309 n. 127
  Brown v. *Board of Education, Topeka Kansas* 347 US 483 (1954) 19–20, 35, 117, 131, 140, 142, 143, 146, 151, 158, 163, 164, 166, 194, 199, 246 n. 5, 256 n. 107, 256–7 n. 109, 257 n. 117, 299–300 n. 98
  Buchanan v. *Warley* 245 US 60 19, 193, 257 n. 112
  Henderson v. *United States* 339 US 816 (1950) 256 n. 105
  Missouri ex rel. Gaines v. *Canada* 305 US 337 (1938) 18, 256 n. 102
  McLaurin v. *Oklahoma State Regents for Higher Education* 339 US 637 (1950) 256 n. 104
  Morgan v. *Virginia* 328 US 373 (1946) 19, 256 n. 105
  Plessy v. *Ferguson* 163 US 537 (1896) 18–20, 143, 189–90, 194 256 n. 97, 256 n. 100; separate but equal 4, 17, 19, 79, 150, 194, 205
  and racial covenants 193
  Shelley v. *Kraemer* US 1 (1948) 257 n. 115
  Smith v. *Allwright* 321 US 649 (1944) 19, 256 n. 106
  Sweatt v. *Painter* 339 US 629 (1950) 18, 256 n. 103
Swanish, Peter 302 n. 13

Taber, Congressman John 297 n. 15
Tade, Irving P. 10
Taeuber, A. 312 n. 5
Taeuber, K. 312 n. 5
Taft, President William Howard 28, 44, 262 n. 167, 269 n. 50
Tariff Commission 81
Tarver, Congressman Malcolm C. 8, 74, 250 n. 44
Tennessee Valley Authority 32, 86, 265 n. 194
  and segregation 32
Thompson, Luella 60, 273 n. 105
Tillman, Senator Benjamin R. 21
Tobin, James 305 n. 73
Trent, W. J. Jr 247 n. 13, 247 n. 15, 248 n. 19
  see also US Department of the Interior
Trimble, E. 89–95
  see also FEPC
Trotter, William Monroe 10, 11–13, 16–17, 251 n. 54
  and President Woodrow Wilson 10, 11–12, 13, 16–17, 251 n. 54, 252 n. 64
Truman, President Harry viii, 3, 24, 27, 60, 108, 114, 115–16, 137, 139, 179, 265 n. 200, 266 n. 206
  civil rights commitment 24, 34–5, 266 n. 206, 266 n. 207, 266 n. 211
  civil rights legislation 310–11 n. 1
  Committee on Civil Rights 3–4, 33, 34–5, 58, 60, 61, 62, 66, 67, 115, 129, 179, 246 n. 7, 261 n. 161, 272 n. 97, 273 n. 106, 273 n. 110, 273 n. 118, 274 n. 125, 275 n. 140, 275 n. 142, 275 n. 144, 310–11 n. 1; Black Americans in the Armed Services 291–2 n. 90, 292 n. 96, 293 n. 111; subcommittees 273 n. 113, 289 n. 43; subcommittee on Federal employment 67
  Committee on Equality of Treatment and Opportunity in the Armed Services 11, 35, 115–16, 120–1, 131–2, 136, 137–9, 141, 151, 289 n. 48, 295 n. 158; establishment 288 n. 33; Charles Fahy 292 n. 92, 295 n. 160, 295 n. 166; influence in US Bureau of Prisons 151; racial categorization of recruits 120–1, 290 n. 64; racial conflicts 121–3; segregation in the Navy 123–5; support for segregation 131–2, 137–9; *To Secure These Rights* 116

Truman, President Harry (*cont.*):
  Committee on Government Contract Compliance 35, 96–9, 186, 196–7, 309 n. 123; anti-discrimination contract clauses 97; coordination with US Employment Service 186; and housing policy 196–7
  Democratic Party platform 115
  and decentralization of USES 26, 261 n. 153, 261 n. 155
  and Dixiecrat revolt 24, 25, 115
  and NAACP 60
Trumbull, Senator Lyman 6
Tumulty, Joseph 45, 263 n. 174, 268 n. 29

United Public Workers 63, 246 n. 7, 273 n. 118, 304 n. 60
US Armed Services 4, 8, 11, 33, 84, 87, 111–41, 247 n. 11
  attitude to Black Americans 11, 111
  Black American attitudes to the Navy 122
  Black American attitudes to segregation 111, 113–16
  Black American employment in field offices 84
  Black American soldiers in Britain and Europe 133–6, 294 n. 135, 294 n. 136; attitudes of British 294 n. 135, 294 n. 142, 294 n. 148
  Black American women 293 n. 113
  civil rights' counsellors 117; Truman Gibson (War) 117, 290 n. 54, 290 n. 56; Lester Granger (Navy) 117, 120–1, 129, 131; William Hastie (Army Air Corps) 117, 119, 127, 290 n. 57, 290 n. 58
  and Civil War 111–12
  Benjamin Davis 117
  Defense Department 114
  and discrimination 111; Bernard Randolph 111
  and EEOC 106; US Department of the Air Force 106; US Department of the Army 106; US Department of the Navy 106, 290 n. 62
  Gillem Board 126–9, 292 n. 97; and NAACP 127–8; recommendations 292 n. 106
  integration 137–41, 295 n. 167, 295–6 n. 169
  morale 291 n. 77, 291 n. 78, 293 n. 125
  George Nesbitt 114; Fort Stewart, Georgia 114, 288 n. 24
  opposition to desegregation 130–2, 137–9, 293 n. 116
  racial conflicts 33, 114, 118, 121–3, 250 n. 48, 293 n. 114; in Britain 135; Detroit 250 n. 48; Guam 122, 291 n. 71; southern training camps 121–3; transportation 122–3
  Racial Policy conference 291 n. 82, 292 n. 100
  Carl Rowan 114, 289 n. 52
  segregation 112, 116–21, 137–9, 247 n. 11, 290 n. 62; and morale of White recruits 131–2, 293 n. 125; War Department 291 n. 79
  Tuskegee Institute training base 119, 289 n. 51
  US Commission on Civil Rights report 140–1
  US Department of the Air Force 119–20, 128
  US Department of Navy 116–17, 130, 264 n. 184; discrimination 295 n. 155; Dr Harold Franklin 124–5, 291 n. 86; Marine Corps 125–6; stewards' branch 116–17, 120, 123–5
  and War of Independence 111
US Bureau of Prisons 10–11, 14, 142–71, 208
  Myrl Alexander 166, 168, 171, 298 n. 55, 298 n. 57
  James Bennett 10–11, 143, 151, 152, 156, 157, 161–2, 165, 170–1, 299 n. 79; and Warden H. Hironimus 152–6, 297 n. 31; and Warden L. Naeve 156, 296 n. 6, 297 n. 34
  and Black Americans 145
  Black American prison officers 145, 158
  Brown and desegregation of prisons 151–2, 153–9, 163–9, 297 n. 26, 299 n. 84, 299–300 n. 98; Atlanta, Ga 157, 166–7; Bureau policy 166; Chillicothe, Oh 165; Danbury,

US Bureau of Prisons (*cont.*):
Conn 166; El Reno, Okla 165, 166; Englewood, Colo 164–5; La Tuna, Tx 165, 166; Lewisburg, Pa 165, 166; McNeil Island, Wash 165, 166, 167–8; Milan, Mich 165, 166; National Training School of Boys, DC 165, 166; Petersburg, Va 165, 166; Seagoville, Tx 165, 166; Tallahassee, Fla 165, 166; Terre Haute, Indiana 165; Texarkana, Tx 165, 166
Warden Reed Cozart 152, 297 n. 24
development of Federal penal system 144–5; post-Reconstruction influence 145–6; southern influence 145
distribution of Black American inmates 146–9
early Federal prisons 145; Atlanta, Georgia 145; Leavenworth, Kansas 145; McNeil Island, Washington 145
establishment of Bureau of Prisons 142, 145–6
Warden R. P. Hagerman 159, 298 n. 52
Warden Helen Hironimus 152, 156
Warden G. W. Humphrey 298 n. 56
Warden Lowell Naeve 156
Conscientious Objectors 144, 163
prison officers 159, 165, 298 n. 45; attitudes to desegregation 159, 165–6
prisoners by race 147, 164–5, 169
racial conflict in prisons 152, 158–9, 161–3, 166–7, 297 n. 29, 297 n. 36, 298 n. 56, 299 n. 79, 299 n. 95; Atlanta, Ga 166–7; Chillicothe, Ohio 161, 162, 299 n. 79; El Reno, Okla 162; Milan, Mich 160; Mill Point, W Va 152, 162–3; Petersburg, Va 299 n. 79; riot procedure 298 n. 64
Riot in Cell Block 11 151
Bayard Rustin 165–6
segregation in prisons 150–60, 170, 296 n. 2, 299 n. 89; county penitentiaries 300 n. 104; prisons in the South and North 157; Seagoville, Texas 150–1; state penitentiaries 300 n. 104; Terre Haute, Indiana 150, 156
self-segregation 208
Superintendent Kenneth Thieman 162, 163, 298 n. 62, 298 n. 66
US Commission on Civil Rights 168
US Department of Justice 168–9; John Doar 168
Fred Wilkinson 299 n. 81
US Civil Service Commission 7, 9, 39–71, 88, 107, 184, 185, 205, 206, 209, 267 n. 20, 268 n. 24, 268 n. 28, 269 n. 40
affirmative action 209
agreement with FEPC to monitor discrimination 65
and Black Americans 45–51, 283 n. 91
and Bureau of Engraving and Printing 46–7
Civil Rights Act (1964) 206; nondiscrimination 206; EEOC 206
Civil Service Reform Act (1978) 71
CIO criticisms 62–3
desegregation 259 n. 132
and discrimination 70, 83, 84, 209, 263 n. 176, 270 n. 64; redress for discrimination 209, 270 n. 64
equal employment opportunity 70
EEOC 206
establishment 42–3
FEB criticisms 61
FEPC surveys 80–3, 271 n. 70
Commissioner Arthur Flemming 52, 54–5, 272 n. 95, 274 n. 129
first three decades 43–51
and President Lyndon Johnson 70
merit appointments 42–3, 45, 256 n. 95, 268 n. 28
Commission President Harry B. Mitchell 49–50, 51–2, 58, 270 n. 53, 270 n. 65, 271 n. 67, 271 n. 68, 271 n. 79, 272 n. 94, 272 n. 97
National Committee on Segregation in the Nation's Capital 61
and NAACP criticisms 59–61, 269 n. 41
New Deal 50–1
number of Black American civil service employees 46–7, 49
occupational distribution of Black American employees 80–4, 205,

US Civil Service Commission (*cont.*):
207, 246 n. 10, 277 n. 8, 277 n. 12; post-Civil Rights Act (1964) occupational distribution 207, 312 n. 4
oversight by Congress 65–6
patronage appointments 41–3, 45
Pendleton Act (1883) 40–51, 70, 256 n. 95, 267 n. 9, 267 n. 12, 267 n. 16
Personnel Classification Act (1923) 50, 270 n. 56
Personnel Classification Board 50, 89–96, 108; discrimination at the Personnel Classification Division 89–96, 284 n. 116, 284 n. 117
photograph requirement 48–50, 205, 269 n. 52; abolition 57–9, 205, 269 n. 52; introduction 48–50; opposition to abolition 54
President's Committee on Government Employment Policy 83
Ramspeck Act (1940) 43, 49, 54, 58, 64, 271 n. 68
Congressman Robert Ramspeck 50, 66, 270 n. 53, 271 n. 68, 271 n. 79
redress for discrimination 209, 270 n. 64; affirmative action 209
response to criticisms 64–5
and President Theodore Roosevelt 44
rule of three recruitment procedure 51–7, 281 n. 63; Henry Alston 55–6; CIO criticisms 62–3; FEB criticisms 57; FEPC criticisms 54–7; NAACP objections 52–4, 55–6; origins 52
temporary positions 76, 88–96
War Service Regulations 75–6
Washington DC 60–1
Welch Act (1928) 270 n. 58
US Commission on Civil Rights 140–1, 168, 173, 201, 296 n. 170, 296 n. 172, 300 n. 99, 312 n. 3
and housing 173, 201, 301 n. 3, 310 n. 140
and US Bureau of Prisons 168, 300 n. 99
US Department of Agriculture 12, 16, 25, 29, 59, 63, 74, 81, 106, 260 n. 148
distribution of Black American employees 74
and EEOC 106
failure to respond to FEPC survey 81
and NAACP 251 n. 56
and recruitment 59, 63
and segregation 16, 25, 29, 260 n. 148
US Department of Commerce 23, 28, 67, 72, 86, 259 n. 132
Bureau of Standards 67
Secretary of State Herbert Hoover 259 n. 132
and recruitment 72
US Department of the Interior 15, 16, 23, 32, 63, 103, 145, 247 n. 13, 254 n. 83, 254 n. 84, 264 n. 184, 264 n. 185, 277 n. 19
FEB 103
Clark Foreman 264 n. 185, 277 n. 19
Geological Survey unit 32
Phineas Indritz 254 n. 83, 254 n. 84
interdepartmental advisory group 264 n. 188, 277 n. 19
National Parks 4, 247 n. 13, 247 n. 15, 248 n. 19
and recruitment 63
and segregation 30, 32, 264 n. 184
W. J. Trent Jr, Adviser on Negro Affairs 247 n. 13, 247 n. 15, 248 n. 19
US Department of Justice 80, 81, 86, 97, 145, 168–9, 206, 256 n. 108, 286 n. 170
Civil Rights Act (1964) 206
contract regulations 280 n. 46
failure to respond to FEPC surveys 80, 81
and US Bureau of Prisons 168–9
and US Employment Service 304 n. 55
US Department of Labor 34, 54, 63, 67, 80, 81, 181, 266 n. 209, 271 n. 77
Apprenticeships 96–9, 284 n. 123; Bureau of Apprenticeship 96–7; Federal committee on apprenticeship training 96–7; Fitzgerald Act (1937) 96, 284 n. 123; NAACP report on apprenticeships 101–3
Bureau of Statistics 67
failure to respond to FEPC surveys 80, 81
and FEB 272 n. 91
and minority groups 304 n. 48
and recruitment 63
and segregation 34

US Department of the Navy 30, 32
Norfolk Navy Yard 32
US Department of State 30, 86
US Employment Service (USES) 8, 24, 26, 99, 172–89, 199–201, 206, 260 n. 144
AFL 180–1, 261 n. 152
and Black Americans 24, 174–89; classification of Black American jobseekers 176
budget 261 n. 159
Bureau of Employment Security 61, 200
CIO 181, 184
congressional support 24, 180–1, 261 n. 155, 274 n. 128, 300 n. 1; Task Force on USES 1965 199–200; weak congressional oversight 187–8, 261 n. 157
Consultant on Racial Relations 182
decentralization 26, 261 n. 153, 261 n. 155, 261 n. 157, 261 n. 158, 274 n. 128, 306 n. 81, 306 n. 83
desegregation 199, 200; Alabama 200; Louisiana 200; North Carolina 200
discrimination 179, 181–9, 260 n. 144; anti-discrimination policy 181–5, 285 n. 160, 304 n. 48, 304 n. 49, 304 n. 53, 304 n. 56, 305 n. 66, 310 n. 137; Birmingham, Ala 188–90, 274 n. 127; coordination with FEPC 182–3, 304 n. 49; coordination with President's Committee on Government Employment Policy 186; Denver, Colo 183; failure of anti-discrimination policy 186–9, absence of sanctions 187, autonomy of state offices 186–7; Congress 187–8
establishment 172; Wagner–Peyser Act (1933) 172
FEB 184, 185, 188, 273 n. 109
FEPC 182–3, 184
Federal Advisory Council 177, 184, 186–7
Lyle Garlock 177–8, 302 n. 18
Director Robert Goodwin 183–5, 261 n. 157, 273 n. 109, 303 n. 47
ICESA 260–1 n. 151, 274 n. 128
and President Lyndon Johnson 200
and President Kennedy 200
Assistant Director A. V. Motley 184, 304 n. 61, 304 n. 68, 305 n. 70
and NAACP, 176, 178–9, 187–8, 305 n. 78
National Urban Coalition and the Lawyers' Committee for Civil Rights Under Law, 1971 study of the USES 199–201, 310 n. 139
Lawrence Oxley 24, 172, 174, 175–6, 177–8, 245 n. 1, 274 n. 127, 300 n. 1, 301 n. 7, 303 n. 42; labour market studies 173–4, 206, 301 n. 6, 301 n. 9, Chicago 174, southern states 174, 301 n. 9, 301 n. 10
placements in Federal civil service 185–6; Baltimore 185
and President Eisenhower 199, 200
President's Committee on Government Contract Compliance 186
Racial Relations Unit 182, 260 n. 144
segregated facilities 63–4, 172–89, 199–201, 301 n. 8, 301 n. 11, 302 n. 16, 302 n. 17, 309 n. 133; Black offices 174–7, Charlotte, NC 175, Chicago 175–6, Fort Worth, Tx 176, Louisville, Kentucky 175, Michigan 177, Nashville, Ten 187, New Jersey 176–7, St Louis 187–8, 199; Black staff 177–81, 302 n. 25, Chicago 178, Georgia 177, Missouri 178, North Carolina 177–8, St Louis 178, Tennessee 179
Task Force on USES 1965 199–200, 309–10 n. 136
and training programmes 99
Wagner–Peyser Act (1933) 172
Washington DC 178–81, 303 n. 33, 303 n. 36, 303 n. 38, 303 n. 40
Secretary of Labor Willard Wirtz 200
US Employment Service Task Force of 1965 199–200
see also US Employment Service
US Engineers 69
US Federal Housing Authority 4, 20, 173, 189–99, 201–2
and American Jewish Congress 193
Atlanta 173
Buchanan v. *Warley* 245 US 60 19, 193, 307 n. 107
Black American homeowners' 193
Albert Cole 195–8, 306 n. 95, 308 n. 114, 308 n. 118, 308 n. 120

US Federal Housing Authority (*cont.*):
Department of Housing and Urban Development (1965) 189
and desegregation 195–9; Senator J. Javits 201–2; Senator P. Bush 195
and discrimination 194, 257 n. 117; anti-discrimination measures 195; criticisms by Republican National Committee 197; failure to include non-discrimination clause in grants 195; Housing Act (1949) 197, tenant selection requirements 197; Housing Act (1954) 194; George Nesbitt 195, 197; President's Committee on Government Contract Compliance 196–7
Division of Slum Clearance and Urban Redevelopment 194, 198, 257 n. 113; Baltimore 194; racial policy 309 n. 128
establishment 189–90; National Housing Act 189
Federal Home Loan Bank Board 189
Home Owners' Loan Corporation (HOLC) 189, 191
Frank Horne 198, 308 n. 108, 309 n. 132
Housing Act (1949) 197; tenant selection requirements 197
Housing Act (1954) 194
Housing and Home Finance Agency (HHFA) 194, 195, 196, 197, 201, 257 n. 117; racial policy 306 n. 87, 306 n. 95, 308 n. 110, 308 n. 117, 308 n. 118; Racial Relations Adviser 197, 198, 257 n. 117
Administrator Norman Mason 202, 300 n. 2
Mortgage Bankers' Association 197
and NAACP 193–4, 196, 198
National Association of Home Builders 197
and National Committee Against Discrimination in Housing 192, 195, 201
National Council of the Churches of Christ 197
and National Urban League 192, 257 n. 118
George Nesbitt 195, 197, 257 n. 113, 308 n. 113
Plessy doctrine 189–90, 194
President's Advisory Committee on Housing Policies and Programs 192
President's Committee on Government Contract Compliance 196–7
Public Housing Authority 192, 193
racial covenants 193–4, 257 n. 114, 306 n. 89
Joseph Ray 189, 306 n. 87, 306 n. 95
and segregation 19, 189–99, 201–2; and Black American homeowners' 193; Kansas City, Missouri 191; St Louis, Missouri 191, 306 n. 93; racial covenants 193–4; residential housing 207–8; underwriting policy 191–2, 202, 306 n. 91
State Park Citizens' Committee for Housing and Planning 197
Supreme Court decisions 193–4, 309 n. 127
Urban Renewal Administration 195, 197; racial policy 307 n. 107, 308 n. 113
US Commission on Civil Rights 301 n. 3
Veterans Administration 194
Voluntary Home Mortgage Credit Programme 192–3, 195
US Federal Trade Commission 63
US General Accounting Office 67, 264 n. 184, 286 n. 161
US Government Printing Office 16, 107
and segregation 16
and discrimination 107, 254 n. 85
US Office of Education 8, 98, 256 n. 109
Dr Will Alexander 98–9
and Black Americans 8
and discrimination on training programmes 98–9; Alabama 99; Florida 99; Georgia 100; Tennessee 100
Division of Equal Educational Opportunities 256 n. 109
US Post Office Department 29–30, 48, 53–4, 69, 85–6, 103, 106, 262 n. 167, 271 n. 72, 271 n. 73
and EEOC 106
and FEB 103, 286 n. 166
and patronage appointments 44
and recruitment 69
and rule of three 53–4
US Treasury 3, 11, 14, 23, 48, 67, 80, 86, 106, 276 n. 7
Black American employees 80, 253 n. 76, 276 n. 7
Bureau of Engraving and Printing 3,

10, 13–14, 29, 32, 46, 47, 245 n. 1, 246 n. 3, 251 n. 53, 253 n. 66, 262 n. 169, 262 n. 170, 276 n. 7, 277 n. 18, 278 n. 20; Miss Ellen E. Converse 246 n. 3; Director J. E. Ralph 245 n. 1, 251 n. 53, 252 n. 58, 252 n. 61, 253 n. 73, 253 n. 75, 253 n. 76, 263 n. 171
Bureau of Internal Revenue 63, 67, 69
and EEOC 106
and NAACP 253 n. 66
Register's office 14, 15–16
segregation of employees 29–30, 251 n. 53
Universal Negro Improvement Association 276 n. 7
Urban Renewal Administration 195, 197
see also US Federal Housing Authority

Van Riper, P. P. 49, 51, 58, 252 n. 63, 255 n. 91, 255 n. 92, 266 n. 4, 268 n. 26, 269 n. 38, 269 n. 44, 269 n. 48, 269 n. 49, 270 n. 56, 270 n. 58, 270 n. 60, 270 n. 62, 272 n. 96
Vann, Robert L. 277 n. 19
Vardaman, Senator James K. 21
Veterans Administration 69, 86, 106, 194, 286 n. 165
and EEOC 106
and housing 194
Villard, Oswald 13, 251 n. 52, 251 n. 54
and Congressman James B. Aswell 22–3
and President Woodrow Wilson 13, 263 n. 174, 263 n. 175
Vogel, U. 312 n. 7
Voting Rights Act, 1965 19
Voluntary Home Mortgage Credit Programme 192–3
see also US Federal Housing Authority

Wage Stabilization Board 63
Wagner–Peyser Act (1933) 172
Waldron, J. 312 n. 7
Walton, H. 285 n. 136
War Department 32, 133, 291 n. 79
War Manpower Commission 67, 79, 176, 183, 275 n. 141, 302 n. 21
War Production Board 81, 99
Negro Employment and Training Branch 99
War Service Regulations, *see* US Civil Service Commission
War Shipping Administration 81
Washington DC 3–5, 9, 60, 63, 75, 143, 173, 174, 178–80, 246 n. 6, 251 n. 52, 258 n. 123
and Black Americans 3–5, 9, 60–1, 179–80, 251 n. 52
and Congress 26–7, 180, 258 n. 123
housing 173
National Capital Park and Planning Commission 27, 81
National Committee on Segregation in the Nation's Capital 61, 258 n. 125, 261 n. 160, 263 n. 182, 273 n. 110, 282 n. 82
US Employment Service 63–4, 174, 178–9, 303 n. 33, 303 n. 36, 303 n. 38, 303 n. 40
Washington, Forrester B. 277 n. 19
Washington, President George 111
Washington, Val 309 n. 124
Washington Urban League, *see* National Urban League
Weaver, George 274 n. 125, 277–8 n. 19
Weaver, Robert 99, 245 n. 1, 307 n. 98
Webster, Milton P. 260 n. 143, 279–80 n. 35
Weir, M. 312 n. 6, 312 n. 7, 312 n. 8
Weiss, N. J. 249 n. 30, 250 n. 41, 252 n. 63, 255 n. 92
Welch Act (1928) 270 n. 58
see US Civil Service Commission
Welfare policy 207–8
Aid to Dependent Children 207
Aid to Families with Dependent Children 207
social rights of citizenship 207–8
Social Security Act (1935) 207–8
Wesley, C. H. 249 n. 30
White, L. D. 255 n. 91, 268 n. 25
White, Walter 30, 60, 122, 127–8, 135, 137, 187–8, 263 n. 180, 263 n. 181, 265 n. 194, 266 n. 212, 269 n. 47, 272 n. 103, 291 n. 72, 295 n. 153, 295 n. 157, 305 n. 78
see also NAACP
White House Office 81
Wilkins, J. Ernest 281 n. 64
Wilkins, Roy 123, 136, 140, 264 n. 185, 265 n. 192, 265 n. 193, 287 n. 2,

Wilkins (*cont.*):
290 n. 55, 291 n. 75, 302 n. 21, 303 n. 45
see also NAACP
Wilkinson, Fred T. 299 n. 81
Will, Norman 297 n. 27, 298 n. 47
Williams, James D. 276 n. 158
Williams, J. S. 3, 29, 245 n. 1
see US Treasury
Williams, R. M. 259 n. 140
Wilson, Senator Henry 6
Wilson, President Woodrow 3, 5, 17, 20, 27, 28, 43, 45, 47, 48, 50, 70, 87, 107–8, 111, 124, 130, 150, 158, 257 n. 119, 263 n. 174
and Black Americans 5, 12–13, 257 n. 119, 262 n. 168
and civil service 45
and Democratic Fair Play Association 21
and Thomas Dixon 5–6, 248 n. 24, 248 n. 25
election of 20, 251 n. 54
photograph requirement for civil service 48–50
and segregation 12–13, 28–31, 87, 107–8, 124, 130, 150, 248 n. 20, 249 n. 30, 257 n. 119
and Moorfield Storey 10
and William Monroe Trotter 10, 11–12, 13, 16–17, 251 n. 54, 252 n. 64, 253 n. 68
and Oswald Villard 13, 253 n. 69, 253 n. 69, 263 n. 174
and Robert Wood 254 n. 87
Wirtz, Secretary of Labor Willard 200, 310 n. 138
see also US Employment Service
Wolgemuth, K. L. 252 n. 63
Wolters, R. 264 n. 185
Wood, Robert 254 n. 87
Woodward, C. Vann 6–7, 245 n. 2, 249 n. 35, 265 n. 200
Work, Secretary Hubert 30

Yanks 133